THE PEOPLES OF LAS VEGAS

WILBUR S. SHEPPERSON SERIES IN NEVADA HISTORY

The Peoples of Las Vegas

One City, Many Faces

EDITED BY Jerry L. Simich AND Thomas C. Wright

UNIVERSITY OF NEVADA PRESS ▲▲ RENO / LAS VEGAS

Wilbur S. Shepperson Series in Nevada History
Series Editor: Michael Green

University of Nevada Press, Reno, Nevada 89557 USA
Copyright © 2005 by University of Nevada Press
All rights reserved
Manufactured in the United States of America
Design by Carrie House

Library of Congress Cataloging-in-Publication Data
The peoples of Las Vegas : one city, many faces / edited
by Jerry L. Simich and Thomas C. Wright.
p. cm. — (Wilbur S. Shepperson series in Nevada
history)
Includes index.
ISBN 0-87417-614-x (hardcover : alk. paper)
ISBN 0-87417-616-6 (pbk. : alk. paper)
1. Ethnology—Nevada—Las Vegas. 2. Las Vegas (Nev.)
—Population. 3. Pluralism (Social sciences)—Nevada—
Las Vegas. 4. Las Vegas (Nev.)—Ethnic relations.
I. Simich, Jerry L. II. Wright, Thomas C. III. Series.
F849.L35P46 2005
305.8'00973'135—dc22   2004017576

The paper used in this book meets the requirements
of American National Standard for Information
Sciences—Permanence of Paper for Printed Library
Materials, ANSI Z.48-1984. Binding materials were
selected for strength and durability.

FIRST PRINTING
14 13 12 11 10 09 08 07 06 05
5 4 3 2 1

Publication of this book was supported in part by a
grant from the Las Vegas Centennial Celebration.

CONTENTS

ILLUSTRATIONS

PREFACE

This is the first book to focus on ethnicity in Las Vegas—a city known for gambling, entertainment, hypergrowth, and extreme summer weather and for constantly reinventing itself, but not known for its ethnic diversity. The city is rarely cited in studies of ethnicity or immigration. Yet one need only scratch the surface to find peoples from around the world living and working in Las Vegas. While Las Vegas has been home to people of varied ethnic backgrounds since its founding in 1905, much of today's rich diversity is the product of changes in the past two decades. In the early 1980s, when we first entertained the idea of studying Las Vegas's ethnicity, the challenge would have been to discover what peoples called Las Vegas home. Today, the challenge is the opposite—to detect which of the world's peoples are *not* found in Las Vegas.

The literature on ethnicity in the United States is growing exponentially, and the 2000 census, which revealed dramatic changes in the country's makeup, will undoubtedly stimulate further research. This book is offered in the hope of contributing to a greater understanding of ethnic diversification and the processes that fuel it, thereby also providing a different perspective on Las Vegas history. Our intended audience includes specialists in ethnicity, general readers interested in Las Vegas and its culture, and the peoples who constitute ethnic Las Vegas.

This project is the outgrowth of our long-standing interest in Las Vegas's ethnicity. We attended the first International Food Festival (today's International Food and Folklife Festival of Southern Nevada) in 1976 and have observed the growing diversity of participating groups over the years. Our taste for ethnic foods, formerly indulged only by travel to Los Angeles, led us to discoveries of once-scarce restaurants and markets catering to new arrivals in Las Vegas. The growing visibility of new cultures in the Las Vegas Valley in the 1990s finally convinced us that the time was right to recruit authors and launch the project.

We are indebted to many people for their contributions to this volume. First, we wish to thank the authors of the individual chapters, without whom the book could not have been done. Some of the authors brought to the project established records of research and publication on the topics they address in the following pages. Others took time away from their usual academic and professional pursuits to undertake research on topics new to them. To all, our warmest thanks.

When we first noticed and began discussing the changing ethnicity of Las Vegas in the early 1980s, Andy Tuttle and Dina Titus encouraged us to pursue the inquiry; this book, belatedly, owes much to their support. We thank Trudy McMurrin, formerly of the University of Nevada Press, for approaching us to do the book. We are deeply indebted to University of Nevada Press Director and Editor in Chief Joanne O'Hare for her support and guidance as well as the dispatch with which she shepherded the book to completion. We also thank Sara Vélez Mallea and Michelle Filippini for their expert editing. The project owes much to the photographic expertise of Jeanne Sharp Howerton and to the editorial and technical assistance of Mary Wammack. Finally, we thank the very diverse peoples of Las Vegas for their contributions to the book and to our community.

The monumental *Harvard Encyclopedia of American Ethnic Groups* was published in 1980.[1] In the work's introduction, the editors referred to the Slovenian American immigrant Louis Adamic, a popular writer and journalist. During the Great Depression, Adamic proposed a project that, in his words, "would excite all America about herself." He conceived of a vast encyclopedia ranging "from the Indians down to the latest immigrant groups" that would reveal "of what sort of human stuff America is made." This pioneering work, he opined, "would appeal not only to New Americans and their immigrant parents . . . but to America as a whole."[2]

Adamic contemplated a vast project of between five and twenty-five volumes. Because he was unable to secure funding from the Federal Relief Administration, the project died. Working on his own, however, Adamic wrote several books portraying the ethnic experience in America, including *My America* (1938), *From Many Lands* (1940), and *What's Your Name?* (1942).

The *Harvard Encyclopedia* represented a partial fulfillment of Adamic's dream. A wonderful source book and an indispensable starting point for further research, the *Harvard Encyclopedia* contains 106 entries on ethnic groups, from Abkhazians to Zoroastrians. Since the work was published over two decades ago, readers readily see that, owing to recent immigration, it stands in need of revision and additions. To cite just a few cases, there is no entry for the Hmong (although they are mentioned in the entry on Indochinese); Ethiopians, Nigerians, and Sudanese are subsumed under "Africans"; and many (not all) groups from Latin America are covered collectively as "Central and South Americans." Reflecting the broadening of immigration and the advance of research, the 1997 *American Immigrant Cultures* covered 161 immigrant cultures in the United States, including such groups as Circassians, Igbo, Vlachs, and Punjabi Mexicans.[3]

Although most of the groups described in the *Harvard Encyclopedia* and *American Immigrant Cultures* are found in Las Vegas, there is little awareness of their presence. There are several explanations for the near invisibility of Las Vegas's demographic diversity. Many tourists still do not believe there is a Las

Vegas beyond the hotel casinos; for them, a Las Vegas ethnic experience may be a gondola ride at the Venetian, shopping at the Desert Passage in the Aladdin, or dining at the Paris. But if they were to venture beyond the resorts' casinos and showrooms to their kitchens and housekeeping facilities, they would encounter a veritable United Nations of people serving them.

Nor are Las Vegans themselves much more aware of the human variety of their own town. Lacking traditional ethnic neighborhoods, except for the black Westside and the Southern Paiute reservation, Las Vegas accommodates immigrants and migrants in older areas of small houses and inexpensive apartments or in new cookie-cutter suburban tracts that show little or no evidence of ethnicity. Two important manifestations of Las Vegas's diversity—ethnic restaurants and markets—are usually housed in the Valley's innumerable and indistinguishable strip malls, which one drives by with scant notice; thus, outside the Latino northeast and the Asian commercial district in the west, few locals are aware of the many manifestations of ethnicity tucked away throughout Las Vegas.

The 2000 U.S. Census focused the country's and Las Vegas's attention on diversity, but the broad categories that the census uses—and the media reproduce—tend to obscure the new realities. Embracing the census categories, people tend to think of the nearly one quarter of Las Vegans who are "Hispanic" as Mexicans or Mexican Americans, overlooking the growing presence of peoples from all the Latin American countries, most of which, in turn, are rich in ethnic diversity. Likewise, the "Asian" category tends, in the common sensibility, to homogenize peoples with profoundly different characteristics. Similarly, if we did not probe beyond the category "American Indian," we would not discover the great diversity of Las Vegas's tribal groups, just as the failure to distinguish among the new Las Vegans from Africa would obscure the variety of nationalities and ethnic groups from that continent that are represented here.

The present diversity of the peoples of Las Vegas is based on immigration, migration, and internal growth. The city has been more ethnically diverse from its inception than is commonly assumed, and the gradual growth of early populations of African Americans, Chinese, Mexicans, and various European Americans has contributed to today's mix. Migration from within the United States is responsible for much of Las Vegas's diversification. Offering jobs, entrepreneurial opportunities, reasonable costs of living, and retirement with sun and entertainment, Las Vegas has attracted "old" ethnics—Irish, Germans, Italians, and other Europeans—from eastern and northern cities and midwestern towns and farming communities; Mexican Americans from the Southwest; Hawaiians from the islands; and African Americans and Native Americans from around the country.

But without the impact of recent currents of immigration, Las Vegas would not have attained the ethnic diversity that characterizes it today. Immigration to the United States has increased in each decade since the 1950s, after largely disappearing during the Great Depression and World War II. In the 1990s, the greatest decade of immigration in American history, over thirteen million foreign born came to the United States. In 2000 over thirty-one million people, representing over 11 percent of the U.S. population, were born abroad.[4]

In contrast to the traditional immigration patterns, which primarily involved Europeans, small numbers of Mexicans, and Asians drawn from only a few countries, recent immigrants have come from around the world. Today the very European countries that supplied the bulk of the U.S. population are also receiving massive waves of immigration from the same poorer countries that are supplying the United States, although in different proportions. So too are wealthy countries such as Australia, New Zealand, Singapore, and Saudi Arabia, and Japan's traditional resistance to immigration is being tested.

The new immigration is driven by poverty, ethnic strife, war, repression that sometimes rises to the level of state terror, and genocide such as that seen in the 1980s in Guatemala and in Rwanda and Bosnia in the 1990s, as well as by displacement through globalization of the economy. The pull factors emanating from the developed world are a demand for cheap labor, consumerism, and the offer of economic opportunity and of democratic political systems that minimize repression. Today, instant mass communication brings home to even the remotest communities around the globe the yawning gap between life on the periphery and life at the center of the world economy, propelling millions of people onto the route toward a better life. The fortunate obtain legal papers and travel in comfort and safety. The others are the ones who make the news by perishing in sealed trailer trucks, drowning in leaky boats, being held in makeshift camps, or being repatriated. But these calamities cannot hold back the tide of worldwide migration.[5]

On the receiving end of international migration, cities that absorb immigrants from around the world become demographically globalized as immigrants arrive, establish their communities, and recreate as much of their homeland culture as possible. The largest cities—New York, Chicago, and Los Angeles—are the places where the new global ethnicity is most pervasive and visible in the United States. But Las Vegas is not far behind in the pace of ethnic diversification that is transforming America's cities.

The following chapters introduce readers to the peoples of Las Vegas. Of necessity, we have been selective. One may well wonder why Las Vegas's Irish, Germans, Arabs, Japanese, or Cubans are not represented in this volume. First, we did not intend to cover only the large and highly visible ethnic groups;

rather, we selected some small and/or newly arrived groups to illustrate more fully the diversity of today's Las Vegas. Hence the Chileans, South Asians, and Salvadorans occupy space that otherwise might have been allocated to larger, longer established groups. In addition to space limitations, we were constrained also by the availability of authors willing and able to contribute to this project. We regret the exclusion of the numerous groups we were unable to accommodate, but we are confident that if this book succeeds in stimulating interest in Las Vegas's ethnicity, future research and publication will round out the partial picture that we present here.

In the first two chapters, we set the historical context for understanding the ethnic kaleidoscope that helps to define Las Vegas today. The remaining chapters cover individual ethnic groups and, in one case, several groups from the same region. Where appropriate, the chapters cover the groups' migration from their countries of origin to Las Vegas, analyzing motivations and processes. They then examine the groups' economic pursuits and status; their institutions and other means of preserving and transmitting their cultures; their involvement with the broader Las Vegas and U.S. communities and their transnational ties with their homelands; and recent trends affecting the groups. The chapters feature peoples with roots in five continents—Europe, Asia, Africa, and North and South America—and cover groups large and small, long established and newly arrived, well known and barely visible.

The contributors to this volume are also diverse. Most are members of the groups they write about. They come from a broad array of disciplines: anthropology, history, political science, ethnic studies, sociology, English, social work, and law. While the case studies naturally reflect their authors' methodologies, emphases, and perspectives, they all contribute to our common goal of elucidating Las Vegas's ethnicity.

Now, a few words about definitions are in order. First, the concept of ethnicity, write the editors of the *Harvard Encyclopedia,* "is an immensely complex phenomenon."[6] Rather than adopt a strict definition, they list a series of components of ethnicity, some or all of which may describe any particular ethnic group. These are: common geographic origin; migratory status; race; language or dialect; religious faith or faiths; ties that transcend kinship, neighborhood, and community boundaries; shared traditions, values, and symbols; literature, folklore, and music; food preferences; settlement and employment patterns; special interests in regard to politics in the homeland and in the United States; institutions that serve specifically to maintain the group; an internal sense of distinctiveness; and an external perception of distinctiveness. The weight given to any of these characteristics depends, of course, on a cluster of factors, such as the size of the group, the length of its time in the United States, and its degree of assimilation.[7]

Second, how do we define Las Vegas? For most people who consider them-selves Las Vegans, it is the Las Vegas Valley, which includes the cities of Las Vegas, North Las Vegas, and Henderson and the contiguous urban core of un-incorporated Clark County. The census defines Las Vegas as the city of Las Vegas, which includes only a portion of the urban area and excludes the Strip. Therefore, the statistics offered throughout the book refer either to Clark County or to the Las Vegas, Nevada–Arizona Metropolitan Statistical Area (MSA).

The urban core of the Las Vegas Valley constitutes 96.4 percent of Clark County's population; it comprises 84.9 percent of the MSA, which adds Nye County, Nevada, and Mohave County, Arizona, to Clark County. In several places the authors cite the MSA rather than Clark County statistics because demographers, including those at the Lewis Mumford Center for Compara-tive Urban and Regional Research, State University of New York, Albany, have refined census data for the MSA, and not for the county, to provide more detailed information on minority groups. Given the concentration of most non-European ethnic groups in the core urban area, the figures for Clark County, and even more for the MSA, underreport the percentage of Las Vegas Valley residents who belong to Latin American, Asian, and African groups.[8] Ethnic diversity in the Las Vegas Valley, then, is even more pronounced than our statistics suggest.

In closing this introduction, we invite the reader to go beyond Las Vegas's best-known features, the hotel casinos of the Strip and Downtown, to visit the other Las Vegas. This is the city of the new barrio, the traditional black Westside, the commercial Chinatown, the Southern Paiute reservation, hun-dreds of ethnic restaurants and markets, and a cycle of international festivals celebrating ethnic diversity. This is the Las Vegas where Assyrians, Seychel-loises, and Oneidas mingle with African Americans, Mexicans, Chinese, and the entire range of European Americans.[9] This is ethnic Las Vegas.

Notes

1. Stephan Thernstrom, Ann Orlov, and Oscar Handlin, eds., *Harvard Encyclope-dia of American Ethnic Groups* (Cambridge, Mass., and London: Belknap Press of Har-vard University Press, 1980).

2. The *Harvard Encyclopedia*, v, quoting Adamic's *My America, 1928–1938* (New York: Harper and Brothers, 1938).

3. David Levinson and Melvin Ember, eds., *American Immigrant Cultures: Builders of a Nation*, 2 vols. (New York: Simon and Schuster Macmillan, 1997).

4. U.S. Census 2000, American Factfinder, at http://factfinder.census.gov/bf_lang =en_vt_name=DEC_2000_SF3_U_DP2_geo_id=01000US.html; Alejandro Portes and Rubén G. Rumbaut, *Immigrant America: A Portrait,* 2d ed. (Berkeley: University of California Press, 1996); David W. Haines and Carol A. Mortland, eds., *Manifest Destinies: Americanizing Immigrants and Internationalizing Americans* (Westport, Conn.: Praeger, 2001).

5. A scholar of globalization argues that "global restructuring generates or amplifies migration and, in turn, the movement of people across borders is an indication of the globalization of societies and of the obsolescence of national boundaries." Helene Pellerin, "Global Restructuring and International Migration," in *Globalization: Theory and Practice,* ed. Eleonore Kofman and Gillian Youngs (New York: Pinter, 1996), 81. See also Malcolm Waters, *Globalization,* 2d ed. (London and New York: Routledge, 2001); Elizabeth Mudimbe-boyi, ed., *Beyond Dichotomies: Histories, Identities, Cultures, and the Challenge of Globalization* (Albany: State University of New York Press, 2002); Emek M. Ucarer and Donald J. Puchala, eds., *Immigration into Western Societies: Problems and Policies* (London and Washington, D.C.: Pinter, 1997); Charles Hirschman, Philip Kasinitz, and Josh DeWind, eds., *The Handbook of International Migration: The American Experience* (New York: Russell Sage Foundation, 1999); M. A. B. Siddique, ed., *International Migration into the 21st Century: Essays in Honour of Reginald Appleyard* (Cheltenham, England, and Northampton, Mass.: Edward Elgar, 2001); Peter C. Meilaender, *Toward a Theory of Immigration* (New York: Palgrave, 2001).

6. *Harvard Encyclopedia,* iv.

7. For an excellent elucidation of ethnicity, see William Petersen, "Concepts of Ethnicity," in the *Harvard Encyclopedia,* 234–42.

8. The Clark County figure is from Clark County Department of Comprehensive Planning, "Clark County Demographics Summary," March 2003; we assume little change in the core-periphery relationship between 2000 and 2003. The Lewis Mumford Center is easily accessed at www.albany.edu.mumford. Exceptions are found for Hispanics in the casino centers of Mesquite and Stateline (now Primm) and farming areas of the Moapa and Virgin Valleys, where their percentage of the local population exceeds their percentage of the Clark County population. Their total numbers in these outlying areas are so small that these exceptions do not skew the generalization about minorities being concentrated in the urban core. Also, American Indians constitute higher percentages of outlying Clark County as well as Nye and Mohave Counties than of the urban core. U.S. Census 2000, table DP-1. Profile of General Demographic Characteristics: 2000, for Clark County. For Mohave, Clark, and Nye Counties respectively, see Am Factfinder (Mohave) at http://factfinder.census.gov/ servlet/QTTable?_ts=78324215546; (Clark) at http://factfinder.census.gov/servlet/ QTTable?_ts=78324316390; (Nye) at http://factfinder.census.gov/servlet/QTTable?_ ts=78324357078.

9. *Las Vegas Sun,* April 23, 2003; Hazel Wong, interview by Thomas C. Wright, May 4, 2001; Richard Arnold, director, Las Vegas Indian Center, interview by Thomas C. Wright, July 27, 2003.

CHAPTER 1

Immigration, Ethnicity, and the Rise of Las Vegas

EUGENE P. MOEHRING

Paris, Luxor, Bellagio, the Rio, the Sahara, and the Imperial Palace are more than familiar Las Vegas icons. Together, they comprise an architectural montage of foreign lands on four continents from which the United States has drawn millions of its citizens, and Las Vegas thousands of its tourists and residents. Throughout American history, the presence of foreign cultures has influenced national development. Beginning with the original British beachheads at Jamestown and Plymouth, ethnicity has played a continuing role in forging America into the multinational society it is today.

The ethnic composition of cities such as New York, San Francisco, and Las Vegas has been shaped by the patterns of immigration to America over the past two centuries. The first great influx of people occurred after Napoleon's defeat cleared the oceans of hostile navies. This movement, the 1820–60 flood celebrated in every American schoolchild's history book, consisted primarily of northern and western Europeans. The push factors dominated, as the great potato famine teamed with religious oppression and poverty to drive millions of Irish out of their homeland. In addition the failed liberal revolutions of 1848 banished thousands of political refugees from France and Germany, while poverty, primogeniture, lack of space, and other factors forced many Scandinavians and other western Europeans across the Atlantic. People from the British Isles dominated these antebellum waves. But after the Civil War and for the rest of the century, eastern and southern Europeans began to comprise a significant portion of this torrent, until Congress imposed quotas in the 1920s to stem the tide of non–Anglo-Saxon peoples. The port of entry for many of these groups was New York City, except in the West, where—in addition to Mexicans crossing the border—thousands of Chinese (and in later decades, Japanese, Filipinos, and others) entered the country through San Francisco and other coastal cities.[1]

The antebellum newcomers flocked primarily to Boston, Philadelphia, and New York, where commerce and industry created many unskilled jobs. But after 1870, as Russia, Italy, and other governments in eastern and southern Europe began to ease their traditional restraints on emigration, millions of Italians, Greeks, and Slavs embarked for the United States. As America's industrial center gradually shifted westward after 1860, many of these newcomers found work in Chicago, Cincinnati, Milwaukee, and other manufacturing cities, which also served as portals to the region's farms for those preferring a rural life. For most of the nineteenth century, however, immigrants avoided the South because of its relative lack of cities and factories, its hostile climate, and its reliance upon African American slaves and free blacks for cheap labor.

The twentieth century brought major changes. Both World War I and II encouraged black migrations to northern cities for better paying jobs in guns-and-butter industries. In addition, the Great Depression combined with pestilence, drought, and mechanization to drive thousands of Dust Bowl Joads westward, creating a labor shortage that followed the attack on Pearl Harbor. But the century's major trend was the shift in sources of immigrants from Europe to Latin America, Asia, and the Pacific Rim. The quota acts of 1921 and 1924, hastily passed by an anti-Socialist Congress following the Red Scare, sharply cut back on southern and eastern European nationalities and instead filled business's spiraling need for cheap labor by allowing more Mexican and Caribbean peoples into the country.

After World War II and especially during the McCarthy Era, Congress began to reform many of the immigration laws that had favored northern and western Europeans. Nevertheless, between 1951 and 1965 53 percent of new arrivals to the United States were still European; only 6.6 percent were Asian. But the Immigration and Nationality Act of 1965, part of Lyndon Johnson's Great Society, dramatically altered the historic flow of peoples. Between 1966 and 1980 less than 25 percent of all newcomers came from Europe, a major drop from traditional levels. North (Canada and Mexico) and Central America contributed 35 percent, and Asia, the Pacific Islands, and Middle East accounted for 30 percent. By the 1980s the trend was even more pronounced. Between 1981 and 1985 the European share plummeted to only 11.2 percent, barely above South America's 6.6 percent. The Caribbean share, which had risen from 7 percent before 1965 to 18 percent in the 1970s, also fell a bit to 13 percent in the early 1980s. Even the North and Central American figure dropped to 18 percent, primarily because Asians constituted almost half (48 percent) of the total amount.[2]

A variety of events—including civil wars, revolutions, drought, pestilence, poverty, tribal conflict, political oppression, and religious persecution—pushed thousands of Asians, Hispanics, Africans, and other groups out of their countries. Many of these migrants settled in the Sunbelt states because of the South and West's proximity to their homelands, the familiar warm climate, and the "presence of existing colonies of the same or related ethnic groups." According to historian Elliott Barkan, the chain of towns stretching along the U.S. border from Florida to Southern California and over to Hawaii gradually formed "a regional axis for entry and settlement." He argued that the "rippling effect" of the civil wars, revolutions, and droughts in the Third World "created many new opportunities along the Miami-Honolulu Axis."[3]

Statistics indicate that cities such as Phoenix, Albuquerque, and Los Angeles became significant ports of entry after 1965. A comparison of the average annual number of immigrants processed in selected ports of entry shows that between 1955 and 1965 New York processed 122,000, while the Miami-Honolulu Axis (comprising Miami, New Orleans, other Gulf Coast ports such as Biloxi and Mexican border points such as El Paso, Nogales, and El Centro as well as San Diego, Los Angeles, and Honolulu) processed 94,000. But in 1966–79, the totals were 130,000 and 163,000 respectively and in 1982–85, 128,000 and 237,000. At the same time, figures for the Pacific Coast (encompassing ports from Monterey to Alaska) during those years were also impressive at 24,000, 88,000, and 166,000.[4]

Since 1970 the composition of the Southwest's city populations has reflected these demographic trends, supplemented by interregional and especially intraregional migration and high Hispanic and Asian birthrates within the United States. In El Paso, Albuquerque, Phoenix, Tucson, and San Diego, African American communities have grown substantially since 1960, but they have been outpaced by their Hispanic counterparts. In Phoenix, for example, the number of blacks rose from 25,000 in 1960 to over 48,000 in 1980, but their percentage of the total population in the Standard Metropolitan Statistical Area (SMSA) actually fell from 3.8 percent to 3.2 percent, partially because the Hispanic portion rose from 13.2 percent (193,000 people) in 1980 to 26.5 percent ten years later. The same was true of Tucson, where the absolute number of blacks rose from 8,000 to 15,000 between 1960 and 1980, but their percentage fell (from 3.0 to 2.8 percent), partially because the Hispanics' figure surged to 21 percent of the metropolitan population.[5]

The San Diego experience was similar. Once again, the black population soared from 39,000 (3.8 percent) to 104,000 (5.8 percent) during the same period, but by 1980 the Hispanic figure had already passed 275,000, or 14.8 percent of the metropolitan population. Farther east in Albuquerque, blacks were only 2.2 percent of the local population in 1980 compared with 36.1 percent for residents of Spanish origin (Hispanics). In El Paso the disparity was even greater (3.8 to 61 percent), with Hispanics representing a majority of the SMSA's population. And the gap has been widening across the urban Southwest. In 1996 blacks still totaled only 3.7 percent of Tucson's (Pima

County's) population, while the Hispanics approached 28 percent. Although the number of Asians and Pacific Islanders has not been as impressive in Tucson (2.3 percent) or Phoenix (where, for example, Chinese account for less than 1 percent), their totals in San Diego and other California cities more accurately reflect their recently high immigration rates. In the sprawling Los Angeles SMSA (which includes Orange County), between 1980 and 1997, the black share of the total population fell (from 17 to 8.3 percent) while figures for Hispanics (27.5 to 38.5 percent) and Asian Americans (6.6 to 11.1 percent) rose, and the same pattern held for San Diego.[6]

Since 1960 the changing composition of Las Vegas's population has reflected these southwestern trends, because thousands of immigrants entering through the Miami-Honolulu Axis eventually made their way to the resort center in search of employment. Still, Las Vegas's diversity is not a recent phenomenon; its roots lie deep in the city's past.

When Las Vegas began its life in 1905, a transportation-based economy dominated the scene. Unlike the typical mining camp, railroad towns, with their forwarding merchants, warehouses, and freight yards, tended to attract more married men and women but fewer Chinese and a different mix of ethnic groups. A survey of Las Vegas's first census in 1910 indicates that whites of European ancestry dominated a population that also included a native band of Southern Paiute Indians. But early Las Vegas was a town evenly split by first- and second-generation Americans. Although the vast majority of residents were American born, only 50.4 percent of adults claimed American-born parents.

In terms of ancestry, early Las Vegas reflected the nation's European bias. As in many mining towns, the Irish were the largest group, with the Germans, Scots, and Scandinavians following in that order. The Welsh accounted for only four adults—in stark contrast to their significant numbers in milling communities across the region. To be sure, western Europeans topped the figures; there were only a few residents of Romanian, Austrian (mainly Croatians and Serbians from the Austro-Hungarian empire), and Polish ancestry. Even the Italians, who were plentiful in Nevada milling communities such as Eureka, claimed only nine countrymen in Las Vegas.[7]

The early railroad town attracted a relatively small Asian population. Despite their reputation as railroad builders, the Chinese were not drawn in large numbers to the construction of the San Pedro, Los Angeles and Salt Lake Railroad or to the Las Vegas and Tonopah line in 1907. As a result, there were only four Chinese in town, and they engaged in laundry and culinary work. Nor was there a large Japanese contingent (only fourteen relatively young males), although this group did live near and work for the railroad. The town's black population was also small and clustered on North Second Street in the saloon district. In 1910 Hispanics represented the largest minority in Las Vegas, just as they do today. Fifty-six Mexicans (no other Latin American nationals were present) comprised roughly .06 percent of the population. In contrast to Asians and blacks, Mexicans did not cluster residentially but lived all over town. In addition they ranged through all ages, tended to live in families, and engaged in a variety of occupations beyond railroad work.[8]

Like many railroad-division towns without valuable agricultural or mining hinterlands, Las Vegas grew slowly, hosting only 2,300 people in 1920. A bitter strike against the Union Pacific in 1922 (which resulted in the company's moving its yards and repair facilities to Caliente) cost the city dozens of lucrative jobs as well as population. But the passage of the Boulder Canyon Act in 1928 and the start of dam construction helped boost the 1930 population to 5,100. Still, Americans of western European ancestry continued to dominate. Even though some blacks, Hispanics, and Asians came to town in response to the boom, by 1934 they held less than 1 percent of the more than 5,000 jobs on the project. Not surprisingly, the census taker counted only 150 African Americans in town in 1930, and just 28 more a decade later.[9]

Even after Nevada relegalized casino gambling in 1931, Las Vegas was still primarily a railroad town, servicing trains and transshipping cargoes. Only a few clubs catered to visitors and locals along Fremont Street and the Los Angeles Highway. The Meadows and Railroad Pass casinos served dam builders along the Boulder Highway, but following the end of construction in 1936 and the resulting exodus of workers, The Meadows club closed for lack of business.

It was World War II that enthroned gambling as the town's major industry. Between 1941 and 1945, 55,000 military men attended classes at the Army Gunnery School (today Nellis Air Force Base) northeast of town, while thousands more soldiers and marines guarded Hoover Dam or trained for the invasion of Africa at the Desert Warfare Center south of today's Laughlin. It was these weekend visitors, along with busloads of defense workers from Southern California and Basic Magnesium in Henderson, who thronged the city's growing number of casinos.

The early 1940s also witnessed the birth of the Strip. The opening of Thomas Hull's El Rancho Vegas in 1941 signaled a new era in which gambling migrated from its traditional confines in the small Downtown clubs serving the railroad station to the empty desert lands bordering the highway, where the green-felt world of poker and dice thrived in the glamorous atmosphere of a resort hotel. By 1948 the El Rancho, Last Frontier, Fabulous Flamingo, and Thunderbird casinos lured thousands of Angelenos to the budding Strip, where cheap desert lands provided the space required for parking, pools, showrooms, retail arcades, gourmet restaurants, luxurious hotels, and substantial casinos. By the end of the 1950s, the trend had only intensified with the Desert Inn, Sands, Sahara, Riviera, Dunes, Stardust, and other properties.

The rise of the Strip gradually altered the emerging metropolitan area's demographics. While many local whites had hoped the war's end would encourage African American defense workers to abandon the Valley, the development of a vibrant resort sector convinced them to stay. To curry favor with the growing swarm of white tourists in the late 1940s and early 1950s, resorts on the Strip and Downtown informally banned minorities from casinos, restaurants, and hotel rooms, while at the same time eagerly hiring them as custodians, room maids, and porters. The same was true of the city's motels, which handled tourist overflow and the low-end market. Although most of these positions were unskilled, the pay was better than that of comparable jobs in the South. As a result, black residents increased from 3,174 in 1950 (6.6 percent of the total population) to 11,005 (8.7 percent) a decade later.[10]

The trend continued into the 1960s and early 1970s, as the construction of larger resorts created more jobs. The opening of Caesars Palace (1966), the Aladdin (1966), the International–Las Vegas Hilton (1969), and the first MGM Grand (1973), created over 10,000 new jobs. By 1970 the number of African Americans had risen to 24,760, or 9.1 percent of the SMSA's total population—a modest percentage gain over the previous decade. Hispanic figures for this same period, however, were a harbinger of things to come. Although residents of Latin American origin had enjoyed a respectable presence in the city since its earliest days, as late as 1950 there were still only 236 Hispanics in the Las Vegas city proper, with another 342 scattered across North Las Vegas, Henderson, and unincorporated portions of Clark County. As historian Corinne Escobar has noted, Mexicans traditionally had avoided Nevada, which lay between the two great immigrant pathways out of Mexico: through Southern California to the Pacific Northwest and through Texas into Colorado and the Rocky Mountain states.[11]

Even though nineteenth-century Nevada had consistently led the nation in the number of aliens per capita, European Americans and Chinese had accounted for most of them. Hispanics had never migrated to the state in great numbers, and neither Hispanics nor Asians came to Las Vegas in significant waves until the 1960s. Between 1960 and 1970, the number of Hispanics in Clark County rose from 578 to 9,937 (3.6 percent of the total population), and in 1980 it reached almost 35,000 (7.2 percent). Although the number of African Americans in the 1970s nearly doubled to 46,000 (9.5 percent), the Hispanics, just as they did in other southwestern cities, were rapidly closing the gap. In contrast, the increased number of Asians and Pacific Islander residents in the 1950s and 1960s was as insignificant as it was in Phoenix, Tucson, and Albuquerque. The overall trend was clear. Even though Euramericans still dominated the Las Vegas population, as they do today, by 1970 it was obvious that their share of the SMSA population would only decrease.[12]

The town's rapid urbanization was crucial to this movement. But even the most optimistic of visionaries could not have foreseen the dramatic transformation of the Strip. In many ways the last two decades of the twentieth century changed the face of Las Vegas's skyline as well as its people. Following a downturn in business occasioned by Atlantic City's debut and the national recession of the late 1970s, Las Vegas emerged tough and plural in the early 1980s. Despite the recession several new hotels opened on or near the Strip, including Harrahs (1974), the Marina (1974), the Maxim (1977), the Imperial Palace (1979), and the Barbary Coast (1979). Moreover, the trend toward suburban resorts began to intensify with the arrival of the Bingo Palace (today the Palace Station) in 1976 and Sam's Town three years later. These new resorts, together with the dramatic increase in residential and commercial construction hastened by the arrival of many white middle- and upper-income residents, created thousands of jobs in the building industry.

Reinforcing the boom was the momentous decision in the mid-1980s by executives at the Del Webb and Howard Hughes Corporations to sell their casino properties and develop Hughes's lands west of Las Vegas with a new Sun City (later broadened to Summerlin). This project, along with new communities in Green and Spring Valleys, spawned a significant in-migration of mostly white, affluent retirees. But over the next fifteen years, developers attracted hundreds of thousands of younger buyers by superimposing gated and even master-planned communities across the metropolis.[13] These events only accelerated Las Vegas's ethnic diversification. As Clark County's population skyrocketed from 463,000 in 1980 to 741,000 in 1990 to more than 1.3 million in 2000, the number of construction, gardening, culinary, and other semiskilled and unskilled positions soared. Even with the influx of thousands of Euramerican migrants as well as thousands of nonwhites and Hispanics, Las Vegas's unemployment rate consistently hovered at record low levels (below 4 percent), an accurate barometer of the economy's vibrancy.[14]

Although the SMSA's African American population between 1980 and 1990 rose from 46,000 to 69,000, it dropped as a percentage of the total population from 9.5 to 9.3 percent. The same was true in 2000, when the number of African Americans hit nearly 125,000 in Clark County but their share of the total population dipped to 9 percent. This occurred partly because of the unprecedented growth of the Hispanic and Asian Pacific Islander groups. From 1980 to 1990, for instance, the number of Hispanics in the Las Vegas SMSA rose from 35,000 to almost 83,000 (7.2 to 11.2 percent), making Spanish-speaking Las Vegans the largest minority in town. At the same time Asians and Pacific Islanders, who had accounted for less than 2 percent of residents in 1980 (with 9,207 people), climbed to 3.4 percent (25,153) just a decade later.[15]

The explosive growth of Las Vegas's Asian and particularly its Hispanic populations continued into the 1990s. The 2000 census put the Hispanic (Mexican, Central and South American, and Caribbean) population in Clark County at 302,000, a whopping 264 percent increase over the 1990 figure. Residents of Latin American origin now constituted 21.9 percent of Las Vegas's total population. The Asian–Pacific Islander increase was also considerable. In terms of percentage, between 1980 and 1990 this figure exceeded both Hispanic and African American growth rates (169 percent to 130 percent to 54 percent). In 2000 there were 78,959 Asian and Pacific Islander Americans in Clark County (5.7 percent of the total population), with Filipinos comprising the largest portion (40 percent) of the group. If the trend continues, Las Vegas's Asian American population will also surpass the African American number by 2010. In fact the chair of the Las Vegas Philippine Chamber of Commerce predicts that there will be 300,000 Asian residents in the metropolitan area by the next decennial census.[16]

At the same time, many of the same growth-promoting forces that induced these demographic shifts have also widened the range of nationalities within the so-called white groups. In 1910 and for several decades thereafter, Las Vegas had few, if any, Latvians, Bulgarians, Egyptians, Iranians, or people from numerous other countries. But, as the following chapters will demonstrate, this generalization is no longer true. Today, Las Vegas is home to communities of people representing virtually every nation, a striking manifestation of global migration.[17]

What factors account for the general growth rate? And, more specifically, what have been the pull factors luring so many Hispanics and Asians to Las Vegas? Aside from the retirement industry and the overall increase in residential construction, the Strip boom of the 1990s and early twenty-first century is a major factor. When Steve Wynn opened The Mirage, with its flaming volcano and white tigers, in 1989, he triggered a revolution that changed Las Vegas forever. Recognizing the threats posed by riverboats, tribal casinos, Atlantic City, and legalized gambling in other states, Wynn raised the ante for all his competitors and forced them to reinvent the Strip. And, one by one, Kirk Kerkorian, William Bennett, Sheldon Adelson, and others complied, employing the alchemy of capital to transmute the empty lots and aging casinos of the Rat Pack era into glittering new mega-resorts boasting special attractions, toney retail shops, celebrity-chef restaurants, spectacular stage shows, and other features that boosted the annual Las Vegas visitor count from 14 million in 1985 to 34 million by century's end. Resort growth fueled metropolitan population growth even as the SMSA's defense sector declined with the Cold War's end.[18] Indeed, President George Bush's closing of the nuclear test site in 1991 and spending cuts at Nellis Air Force Base depressed Las Vegas's traditionally buoyant defense sector, a factor that should have exerted a noticeable drag on population, but it did not.

What accounts for the distinct increase in the Hispanic and Asian populations? Was it unique, or was it a regional phenomenon? A variety of pull factors have operated in the city's recent past to encourage these substantial in-migrations. For example, a 1996 survey of why people move to Las Vegas found that while 21.9 percent came because of a job transfer and 13 percent were retirees, 17.8 percent arrived looking for a better job and 11.6 percent sought a residence closer to relatives. Studies show that for many immigrants, the presence of friends, family, and even groups of fellow nationals can act as a powerful magnet. This is significant because, as the twenty-first century dawned, virtually all of the world's countries claimed at least small communities of expatriates in America's gaming capital.[19]

The growing number of Mexicans in Las Vegas was not only due to the global pull factors attracting most immigrants but also to unique factors such as the recent Border Patrol crackdown in Texas and California, which has, in effect, squeezed the flow of illegal aliens into a central pathway between the two states. This shift in policy has funneled thousands of Mexicans into Albuquerque, Tucson, and Phoenix. Along the Arizona portion of the corridor, the flow of aliens, legal and illegal, has been so great that despite the healthy industrial, commercial, agricultural, and service sectors of their economies, Phoenix, Tucson, and the state's smaller cities have been unable to absorb all of the laborers.[20]

So while some Mexicans headed west to the Golden State, many continued north to southern Nevada, where large numbers of their countrymen already lived. By late 1999 U.S. Census Bureau estimates put Nevada's overall immigrant population at 274,000, of whom 55,000 were undocumented. Not surprisingly, by the late 1990s Las Vegas was home to "the fastest-growing

Hispanic population of any metropolitan area in the country." Encouraging this movement were the historic absence of a U.S. Border Patrol office in Clark County and only a small Immigration and Naturalization Service (INS) operation. While INS agents in Las Vegas apprehended 2,913 illegal aliens in 1999 (a 49 percent increase over the previous year), their office has seen virtually no increase in staff since 1990.[21]

Along with the relative lack of an INS presence, there are numerous other incentives attracting immigrants and second-generation ethnics to Las Vegas. The cost of living is an obvious draw. As one local waitress, a Guatemalan national with an Employment Authorization Card, explained, "a two bedroom apartment in a good neighborhood in Thousand Oaks costs $1,500; in Las Vegas the same place rents for $530." She also credited the establishment of dependable bus service in the early 1990s with allowing immigrant families, many of whom bear the burden of rearing three or more children, to escape the expense of having to buy, maintain, and insure a vehicle.

This is a crucial point. Many immigrants and other ethnic poor have to work two or three jobs and even crowd other family members into the apartment to pay the rent, because many Las Vegas jobs pay little. The same waitress actually discourages her friends from applying for bus-person jobs even at the biggest resorts because of her own experience. While working at a restaurant in the MGM Grand in the mid-1990s, she earned only the minimum wage and averaged less than $30 a night in tips. According to her, it was common for customers, including some of the biggest names in show business and professional sports, to "stiff" servers out of their tips. She also added that many hotels now lease their restaurants and clubs to outside parties who are often antiunion, a trend that tends to depress wages and working conditions.[22] Moreover, a growing number of major resorts, such as the Venetian and the Aladdin, are discouraging union job applicants—a move that will only increase the demand for immigrant labor.

Lack of education is also a factor. One assistant restaurant manager credited the willingness of many Las Vegas employers (especially in the resort, fast-food, fine restaurant, and retail sectors) to waive the requirement for a high-school diploma with contributing to the town's appeal to Latinos and other ethnic and racial groups, who often lack advanced education. He emphasized the advantages of tapping a large immigrant and minority community, where substantial networks of friends and relations create surrogate employment agencies for fast-food chains and other small businesses. He noted, for instance, that the Mexican manager in his own restaurant could make one phone call for a dishwasher, a cook, or a waitress and, even before the people-calling-people process was over, have twenty applicants by morning ready to work in each position.[23]

What is creating this seemingly inexhaustible supply of low-cost labor? Why are Hispanics and other groups still coming to town in such numbers? As the same waitress explained, Las Vegas not only has a lower cost of living than California, it also boasts a decent school district and a low-cost community college and university system, in addition to a clean, resortlike atmosphere where even low-income apartments offer pools, palm trees, central air and heat, cable TV, and all the modern conveniences. Then there is the excitement of Las Vegas—not only the casinos, bars, and stores where many poor people (who often cannot afford it) love to gamble but also a vibrant club scene featuring Latin, Asian, and Middle Eastern dancing, music, and food, including homeland brands of beer and spirits. In short, just like U.S. citizens, many immigrants are enticed by the glitter, excitement, and all-night, party atmosphere of Las Vegas, conveniently filtered through the medium of their own culture—an experience they cannot get at home or even elsewhere in the United States.

For many West Coast emigrants, Las Vegas has become an extension of Los Angeles—a freeway suburb of Southern California with many of the same ethnic markets, churches, restaurants, and subcultures found in Southern California. Indeed, the surge in not only the Mexican, but the Salvadoran, Korean, Arab, Armenian, and other populations has created a substantial home market and an outlet for their country's exports, which nationals can retail to their own people and to the city as a whole. The growth of this subculture commerce has, in turn, created still more jobs and has contributed to the development of a merchant class, which—together with other business people and professionals—comprise each nationality's middle- and upper-income groups.

Another pull factor is the resort industry itself. Over the past ten years, white Americans have found it harder to obtain traditional employment in Las Vegas's hotel industry. On any shift today's tourists will encounter waiters and waitresses from Thailand, Iran, Bolivia, and Pakistan sharing trays and aisles with European American and African American workers from California, New Jersey, and Mississippi. By the late 1990s the increased number of non-native American employees in resorts had become evident. One experienced food server, an Indiana woman with seven years as a waitress Downtown and ten more in Florida, spent three months trying to find a job on the Strip before settling for a part-time position in a hotel coffee shop. She believes that many resorts no longer want employees over forty. As one restaurant manager noted, many hotels discourage the hiring of veteran waitresses because they are "set in their ways" and it often takes too long to retrain them. But there may be other reasons. During the 1990s many Las Vegas resorts have seemed reluctant to hire older workers, convinced perhaps that their customers prefer younger employees.[24]

Any youth movement would tend to favor hyphenated Americans and immigrants, in part because of the resort industry's insistence on frequent drug testing of all personnel. As one Desert Inn waiter observed, "many young whites today cannot pass a drug test, but most immigrants can, and the hotels know it." Added to this is the relatively low pay. As a veteran food server at the Desert Inn on a regular shift, he made $36,000 in wages and tips in 1999. With an increasingly vigilant IRS, this was hardly enough to support a wife and three children in a middle-class neighborhood. For these reasons, he believes, many white job seekers are not flocking to the hotel industry as they once did. In expectation of the Desert Inn's closing, this waiter decided to enroll in dealing school to qualify for a better-paying job.[25]

Of course one of the crucial prerequisites for pulling large numbers of Hispanics, Asians, Middle Easterners, and other minorities into Las Vegas has been the success of the local civil-rights movement. As one African American restaurant manager from Florida recently noted, "in general, blacks perceive the West as more tolerant than the South." At the same time average wages in Nevada and the Golden State, at least since the 1930s, have exceeded those of many southern states, and, most importantly, Nevada's cost of living is lower than California's. In addition, as several black room maids and waitresses have recently pointed out, the powerful Culinary Union has functioned historically as an effective instrument of reform within the resort industry, fighting to ensure the promotion, job security, and civil rights of both male and female minority workers.[26]

In the mid-1950s and 1960s, black Las Vegans were the driving force behind the civil-rights movement that eventually pressured the once "lily-white," male-dominated resort industry to open its doors and higher-paying jobs to African Americans, a breakthrough that ultimately made Las Vegas an attractive option for Cuban dealers, Mexican maids, Vietnamese cocktail waitresses, and thousands of workers from other ethnic and racial groups.

Led by Dr. James McMillan and a small group of activists, the local chapter of the NAACP in spring 1960 organized protests and threatened massive demonstrations in a successful effort to make hotel accommodations and casino play available to all customers. Despite this agreement, white employers continued to practice job discrimination (even after the enactment of a state civil-rights act in 1965) until 1971, when U.S. District Court Judge Roger D.

Foley finally pressured the Nevada Resort Association to sign a consent decree making minority applicants eligible for all hotel and casino positions. School desegregation and a fair housing act in that same year swept away most of the city's Jim Crow institutions. These events played a key role in promoting the movement of not only blacks but also Latinos, Asians, Arabs, and Africans into Las Vegas, because the new atmosphere of tolerance made the tourist mecca a friendlier place than many communities in California, Arizona, New Mexico, and Dixie.[27]

Despite these major advances in the 1960s and 1970s, European Americans continued to maintain their political control of the town and its region. Even as Las Vegas and other Sunbelt cities lowered their historic barriers to freedom and equality, minorities struggled to acquire political power and influence. Historian Carl Abbott has argued that in some states during the 1970s, African Americans and Mexican Americans "gained substantial direct representation on city councils and other policy-making bodies." In Texas and the Southwest particularly, these victories "followed roughly sixty years in which white minorities had gerrymandered local election systems to dilute the effect of minority votes." In Dallas and Houston, for example, business leaders began supporting black candidates for office in return for minority voters' joining the developers' growth coalition.[28]

But minorities did not necessarily make these deals everywhere. In Santa Ana, California, minority voters joined with middle-class whites and other antigrowth factions to block development plans in that city and Orange County. In Phoenix, on the other hand, Hispanics found a friend in mayoral hopeful Terry Goddard, who, for the most part, opposed conservative developers and other businessmen determined to preserve the at-large city-council system as a bulwark of their power. Goddard won substantial support from Hispanics, Asians, and other minorities by endorsing the 1982 ballot initiative mandating the creation of districts, which immediately empowered minority neighborhoods. In general, historians of the urban Southwest agree that Hispanics, Asians, and other minorities have made great strides in flexing their political muscle and gaining office over the last three decades of the twentieth century.[29]

In Las Vegas, however, ethnic advances have been more modest, lagging far behind the growth in minority population and income. Until the mid-1990s there had been only one black on the Las Vegas City Council, one on the North Las Vegas City Council, and two on the Clark County Commission. In 1994 North Las Vegas, with the highest Hispanic population of any municipality in the metropolitan area (21.7 percent), still operated with an at-large system for electing its city council twelve years after conservative Phoenix had rejected it. On a broader front, the absence of Hispanic office holders extends across the Silver State. Despite the presence in 2000 of 302,000 Hispanics in Clark County and 394,000 in Nevada (a 217 percent increase over 1990), a study found that less than 2 percent of the state's municipal leaders and none of its twenty-two city managers were Hispanic, and virtually the same figure (3 percent) held true for county officials.[30]

As in California's Orange and Arizona's Maricopa Counties, Clark County activists have been attempting to mobilize Hispanic power through voter registration drives. But the advocacy group Hispanics in Politics and the Latin Chamber of Commerce have struggled in this regard; as late as summer 2000, only 7 percent of registered Clark County voters had Spanish surnames. The scattered location of Hispanic residents (partially attributable to Las Vegas's historic lack of a central Latin community), political divisions within the Hispanic community (e.g. Puerto Ricans tend to be liberal Democrats, while Cubans tend to be conservative Republicans), and the homeland traditions of many new citizens where democracy was discouraged have tended to dilute Hispanic power by promoting voter apathy. And similar factors have slowed political activism among Asians, Middle Easterners, Africans, African Americans, native Southern Paiutes as well as thousands of migrant Indians, and other groups in town. While Hispanics can claim a mayor of Boulder City in the 1970s (Cruz Olague), an assemblyman and one-term county commissioner (Dario Herrera), a powerful county commissioner and president of the Convention and Visitors Authority (Manny Cortez), and a state attorney general (Brian Sandoval), their victories have been relatively few and far between.[31]

In short, these residents are in the midst of a transition. They finally enjoy a significant presence, thanks to their success in exploiting the opportunities provided by the town's burgeoning economy. The question now is to what extent can local ethnics replicate the success of their Jewish, Irish, and German predecessors in America's larger cities and use these newly won positions in Las Vegas's resort, building, and other industries as "mobility launchers" to raise their own standard of living and claim a rightful share of political power. But, as some recent observers have noted, interethnic tension may disrupt a minority political coalition, as Hispanics and eventually Asians pass blacks in population. Over the past few years, some black leaders have referred to the "creeping Miamization" of Las Vegas, as casino operators increasingly seem to be hiring more Hispanics than blacks.[32]

Ethnic rivalry, however, is nothing new to American cities; New York, Boston, Chicago, and San Francisco have experienced it for many decades. Its presence in Las Vegas, along with the growing diversity and spiraling number of minority residents, is just further evidence that the former whistle-stop has finally realized its century-long dream of becoming a metropolis.

Notes

1. The classic work on American immigration is Oscar Handlin, *The Uprooted: The Epic Story of the Great Immigrations That Made the American People* (Boston: Little, Brown, 1951), which emphasizes the view that many immigrants were alienated individuals after they arrived in America. A more recent interpretation is John Bodnar, *The Transplanted: A History of Immigration in Urban America* (Bloomington: Indiana University Press, 1985), which stresses the influences of culturally bound enclaves such as New York's "Little Italy." A model of particular value for the Las Vegas experience is Walter Kamphoefner, *The Westfalians: From Germany to Missouri* (Princeton: Princeton University Press, 1987), which highlights the importance of ethnic friends and families.

2. Elliott Barkan, "New Origins, New Homeland, New Region: American Immigration and the Emergence of the Sunbelt, 1955–1985," in *Searching for the Sunbelt: Historical Perspectives on a Region,* ed. Raymond A. Mohl (Knoxville: University of Tennessee Press, 1990), 127.

3. Ibid., 126.

4. Ibid., 133. For an overview of immigration statistics from 1950 to 1978, see the U.S. Department of Justice, *Annual Report of the Immigration and Naturalization Service* (Washington, D.C.: Government Printing Office, 1950–78).

5. For El Paso, see U.S. Department of Commerce, Bureau of the Census, *State and Metropolitan Area Data Book, 1979: A Statistical Abstract Supplement* (Washington, D.C.: Government Printing Office, 1979), 90–92; for Albuquerque, see ibid., 2–4; for Phoenix, see *State and Metropolitan Area Data Book, 1982: A Statistical Abstract* (Washington, D.C., Government Printing Office, 1982), 350, 222–24, 355; for Tucson, see ibid., 288–91, 439.

6. *State and Metropolitan Area Data Book, 1982,* 378, 266–68, 383; *State and Metropolitan Area Data Book, 1979,* 2–4. Figures for Tucson for 1996 can be found on line at http://www.census.gov.statab/usa98/04/019txt for Pima County (which is Tucson's SMSA). For Phoenix's Chinese population, see Bradford Luckingham, *Minorities in Phoenix: A Profile of Mexican American, Chinese American, and African American Communities, 1860–1992* (Tucson and London: University of Arizona Press, 1994), 2. See U.S. Department of Commerce, Bureau of the Census, *County and City Data Book, 1988* (Washington, D.C.: Government Printing Office, 1988), 610 for Los Angeles and 618 for San Diego; U.S. Census Bureau, *Statistical Abstract of the United States, 1999* (Washington, D.C.: Government Printing Office, 1999), 44.

7. U.S. Department of Commerce, Bureau of the Census, *Population Schedules of the Thirteenth Census of the United States, Nevada* (manuscript census) lists 937 people in the Clark County, Las Vegas precinct.

8. Eugene P. Moehring, "Profile of a Nevada Railroad Town: Las Vegas in 1910," *Nevada Historical Society Quarterly* 34 (Winter 1991): 466–87.

9. Roosevelt Fitzgerald, "The Impact of the Hoover Dam Project on Race Relations in Southern Nevada," paper, Special Collections, Lied Library, University of Nevada, Las Vegas.

10. U.S. Census Bureau, *County and City Data Book, 1962* (Washington, D.C.: Government Printing Office, 1962), 596; U.S. Census Bureau, *County and City Data Book, 1977* (Washington, D.C.: Government Printing Office, 1978), 696; U.S. Census Bureau, *County and City Data Book, 1983* (Washington, D.C.: Government Printing Office, 1983), 740.

11. Corinne Escobar, "Here to Stay: The Mexican Identity of Moapa Valley, Nevada," *Nevada Historical Society Quarterly* 36 (Summer 1993): 75.

12. Wilbur S. Shepperson, *Restless Strangers: Nevada's Immigrants and Their Interpreters* (Reno: University of Nevada Press, 1970), 14; *County and City Data Book, 1960–70*; see also Las Vegas Planning Department, *Population Profiles: Populations, Income, Housing, Occupation, Education, Analysis of the 1970 Census, Las Vegas SMSA* (Las Vegas: City of Las Vegas, n.d.), table 5, 16; R. Keith Schwer, comp., *Demographic and Economic Profile for Southern Nevada* (Las Vegas: UNLV Center of Business and Economic Research, 1995), 5.

13. An informative source for the development of Green Valley, Spring Valley, and Summerlin is M. Gottdiener, Claudia C. Collins, and David R. Dickens, *Las Vegas: The Social Production of an All-American City* (Oxford, England: Blackwell, 1999), 128–53.

14. In the 1980 census the Las Vegas SMSA consisted of Clark County. In 1990 the same was true for the Las Vegas Metropolitan Statistica Area (MSA). In the 2000 census the MSA consisted of Clark, Nye, and Mohave Counties, so for the 2000 census I will only use Clark County figures in order to provide the most accurate numbers for Las Vegas's metropolitan population. For the 2000 population of Clark County, see *Las Vegas Review-Journal,* March 14, 2001, 19A. For more on the census, see www.census.gov.

15. Schwer, *Demographic and Economic Profile,* 5; *Las Vegas Review-Journal,* March 14, 2001, 19A.

16. *Las Vegas Review-Journal,* March 14, 2001, 19A, December 5, 1999, 1E, 5E; *Las Vegas Review-Journal-Sun,* April 18, 1999, 1E, 4E.

17. See Las Vegas Planning Department, *Population Profiles,* table 7, 12–13, which details the increase in population from 1960 to 1970 in the Las Vegas SMSA, including a breakdown by city and nationality, for residents from twenty-nine (mostly European) countries.

18. *Las Vegas Perspective: The Magic of Southern Nevada* (Las Vegas: First Interstate Bank, Nevada Development Authority, *Las Vegas Review-Journal,* 1995), 72. For the 1999 tourist count of 33.8 million visitors, see *Las Vegas Review-Journal,* April 1, 2000, 2D.

19. *Las Vegas Perspective: Southern Nevada Comes of Age* (Las Vegas: Metropolitan Research Association, 1996), 10; Barkan, "New Origins," 126.

20. *Las Vegas Review-Journal,* December 5, 1999, 1E, 5E.

21. Ibid.

22. Saida Maldonado, conversation with author, July 14, 2000.

23. Kerwin Brown, conversation with author, July 14, July 15, 2000.

24. Diane Creeden, conversation with author, July 20, 2000.

25. Robert Garrison, conversation with author, July 17, 2000.

26. Kerwin Brown, conversation with author, July 15, 2000. For the remarks of blacks and other hotel workers regarding Culinary Union Local 226 as an agent of reform, see relevant sections of: *An Interview with Alma Whitney: An Oral History Conducted by Claytee D. White* (Las Vegas: University of Nevada, 1997); *An Interview with Essie Shelton Jacobs: An Oral History Conducted by Claytee D. White* (Las Vegas: University of Nevada, 1997); *An Interview with Lucille Bryant: An Oral History Conducted by Claytee D. White* (Las Vegas: University of Nevada, 1997); *An Interview with Viola Johnson: An Oral History Conducted by Claytee D. White* (Las Vegas: University of Nevada, 1997); Claytee D. White, "The Roles of African American Women in the Las Vegas Gaming Industry, 1940–1980" (master's thesis, University of Nevada, Las Vegas, 1997).

27. For an overview of the local civil-rights movement, see Eugene P. Moehring, *Resort City in the Sunbelt: Las Vegas, 1930–2000* (Reno and Las Vegas: University of Nevada Press, 2000), 173–202; see also U.S. District Court, District of Nevada, "Civil LV No. 1645, Complaint," then consult "Civil Action LV No. 1645 Consent Decree" in the court clerk's office, Roger D. Foley Federal Building, Las Vegas.

28. Carl Abbott, *The Metropolitan Frontier: Cities in the Modern American West* (Tucson and London: University of Arizona Press, 1993), 102–7.

29. Lisbeth Haas, "Grass-Roots Protest and the Politics of Planning: Santa Ana, 1976–88," in *Postsuburban California: The Transformation of Orange County Since World War II,* ed. Rob Kling, Spencer Olin, and Mark Poster (Berkeley and Los Angeles: University of California Press, 1991): 254–80; Bradford Luckingham, *Phoenix: The History of a Southwestern Metropolis* (Tucson: University of Arizona Press, 1989), 223–26.

30. See Earnest Norton Bracey, "The Political Participation of Blacks in an Open Society: The Changing Political Climate in Nevada," *Nevada Historical Society Quarterly* 42 (Fall 1999): 145; *Las Vegas Review-Journal-Sun,* October 3, 1999, 1E, 5E. The study was conducted in late 1996, so the figures are accurate for the period before the 1998 elections when the census estimate was made (see *Las Vegas Review-Journal,* March 14, 2001, 1A, 19A). North Las Vegas went to a ward-based city-council election system after the 1997 election.

31. *Las Vegas Review-Journal,* March 16, 2000, 2B; see also *Las Vegas Review-Journal-Sun,* September 15, 1999, 1 , 16A.

32. For the city, and especially the ethnic ghetto community, as a "mobility launcher," see Thomas Kessner, *The Golden Door: Italian and Jewish Immigrant Mobility in New York City, 1880–1915* (New York: Oxford University Press, 1977), 175–76; Mike Davis, "House of Cards," *Sierra Magazine* (November–December 1995): 41.

CHAPTER 2

The Ethnic Diversification of Las Vegas

DINA TITUS & THOMAS C. WRIGHT

On a hot August night in 2000, at a dinner party we attended, a young couple newly transplanted from Chicago contemplated the challenges of ad-justing to Las Vegas: "What we'll miss most about Chicago is the ethnicity," they lamented.[1] Indeed, their appreciation of Chicago's rich and dynamic ethnic scene is easily understood. Visiting the Windy City only a month ear-lier, we had dined on ethnic food at each meal and toured some of the tradi-tional ethnic neighborhoods, including the sprawling Polish and small Swed-ish districts, by bus and on foot. We experienced the impact of the "new" immigrants from Latin America, the Caribbean, and Asia on the older North Side immigrant neighborhoods, many of whose former residents had left for the suburbs. Our fellow bus riders were a mix of old and new immigrants, predominantly the latter, and English was rarely heard. Signs advertised goods and services in as many as a half dozen languages in a single block, and the numerous signs in Spanish announced products from virtually every Latin American country.[2]

Las Vegas is clearly very different from Chicago. The traditional European ethnic neighborhoods that characterize Chicago and other northern and east-ern cities never developed in Las Vegas, and the polyglot signage that trum-pets the presence of Chicago's new immigrants is subdued by comparison. Ethnic culture in Las Vegas is less visible than it is in many American cities. Understandably, it would take the newcomers awhile to discover that Las Vegas, like Chicago, is host to peoples from around the world who pursue the American dream while struggling to preserve their ethnic culture and iden-tity. But with a little effort, they should soon begin to appreciate ethnic diver-sity, Las Vegas style.

Observations of Ethnic Diversity

Census data are not completely reliable, particularly in relation to immi-grants, and the categories of ethnicity employed in censuses are too broad to provide a fine-tuned picture of Las Vegas's evolution since 1980. Thus, in addition to statistical information this chapter will present the observations of long-term Las Vegans, some key indicators of diversification, analysis of migration and immigration patterns, and snapshots of a few of Las Vegas's ethnic groups.

A drive around the Valley reveals a sprouting of ethnicity that sharply differentiates today's Las Vegas from that of a quarter century ago. While an embryonic Mexican barrio was visible in the northeastern Las Vegas Valley before 1980, today Mexicans and other Latinos are deeply entrenched in a large district surrounding Downtown Las Vegas, the most heavily Hispanic of which is the area around the North Las Vegas city hall. Areas of Asian markets and restaurants have also sprung up, culminating in the pan-Asian commercial Chinatown on West Spring Mountain.[3] While African Americans are found throughout the Valley, the historic Westside and large sectors of North Las Vegas are still largely black.

On the drive one might see new sights on the streets: the *paletero* pushing his cart of popsicles; informal, unlicensed vending on street corners; heads adorned with turbans, Islamic veils, and Mexican *norteño* cowboy hats. Commercial signs in Spanish and several Asian languages are found throughout the Valley; businesses proclaim "se habla español," and many post information for shoppers in Spanish and English. New on the scene are the numerous businesses for wiring immigrants' money to support families at home. Stopping at a restaurant or shopping at a mall, one hears a multitude of accents of immigrant food servers and sales clerks who have moved from the backs of these establishments to the fronts. Among the thousands of bumper stickers and flags affixed to automobiles to identify the national origins of the Valley's drivers, one occasionally sees an uncommon one such as "got injera?" (Ethiopian flat bread)—a play on the television commercial for milk. Sipping an espresso on the far west side reveals another, less visible aspect of Las Vegas's diversification: a small Italian restaurant run by recent immigrants from Rome where the staff and patrons speak Italian and read newspapers and view satellite TV from the old country—a new infusion of "old" immigrants. If driving on Sunday, one might observe uniformed soccer teams, composed primarily of immigrants, competing on the Valley's increasingly common soccer fields.[4]

Our drive around the Valley, the telephone directory, and the Internet reveal that Las Vegas cuisine has evolved beyond the $.99 shrimp cocktail and $5.95 prime rib familiar to yesterday's tourists and residents. Ethiopian, Lebanese, German, Salvadoran, soul-food, Bulgarian, Filipino, Armenian, Argentine, Kosher, Hungarian, Peruvian, Romanian, Persian, Hawaiian, Guatemalan, Swiss, Caribbean, Moroccan, Spanish, Polish, Brazilian, Russian, Colombian, Irish, Glatt Kosher, Honduran, Greek, French, Cuban, Cajun,

Puerto Rican, British, and pan–Middle Eastern restaurants compete with the much more common Thai, Korean, Indian, Chinese, Japanese, Mexican, Vietnamese, and Italian establishments. The food sections of the local newspapers periodically cover the newer ethnic restaurants in the Valley. There are also Indian, Cuban, Iranian, German, African, Brazilian, Thai, Kosher, Armenian, French, Salvadoran, Italian, Japanese, Mexican, Bosnian, Chinese, Argentine, Ethiopian, British, Korean, Russian, and Vietnamese as well as general Latino, Asian, and Middle Eastern markets, some housed with restaurants. A single strip mall in southeastern Las Vegas has Mexican, Indian, and Armenian-Russian markets, Mexican and Korean restaurants, a Spanish-language church, and a Spanish-language medical clinic. It is no longer impossible to find Inka Cola, Marmite, or seasoned cod gill in Las Vegas. And whatever food products from home one cannot obtain in these usually small stores will likely be available in the warehouse-sized International Marketplace on South Decatur Boulevard.[5]

The same sources reveal that religious practice in the Valley has been enriched by immigrants and domestic migrants alike. Besides the usual American mix of Protestant, Roman Catholic, Jewish, and scientific denominations, one finds a heavy presence of Mormons; numerous African American churches; five Korean Presbyterian churches; Latin rite and Byzantine Catholic churches; Greek, Serbian, Armenian, Romanian, and Ethiopian Orthodox congregations; four Buddhist temples; a Baháí center; three Muslim mosques; two Hindu temples; numerous Hispanic Protestant denominations; and splinter groups of all kinds. In addition, many Catholic churches advertise services for their faithful in Spanish, and one in Vietnamese.

The observer will also readily note that Las Vegas is home to several Spanish- and Asian-language newspapers, Spanish radio and television stations, Urban (black), Latin, Asian, Chinese, and Filipino Chambers of Commerce, and Spanish- and Asian-language yellow pages. Cable-television offerings include nine Spanish-language channels as well as channels in Chinese, Japanese, and Tagalog. Local radio offers limited programming in Arabic, Greek, and languages from the Philippines and Ethiopia as well as Saturday morning programs of pan-African and Hawaiian music. In any given week, individual ethnic clubs are likely to be holding celebrations involving their food, dance, and folklore, and a number of international festivals are held throughout the year. Clearly, Las Vegas has diversified since 1980 at a rapid pace.

Indices of Las Vegas's Diversification

Chicago, New York, and, closer to home, Los Angeles and San Francisco are not the only benchmarks for assessing the ethnicity of Las Vegas; the city's history offers another gauge by which to measure its ethnic diversity today. Las Vegas was too young, small, and remote from primary ports of entry to have been a major recipient of the "old" European immigration of the late nineteenth and early twentieth centuries. From its founding in 1905 through the 1970s, Las Vegas was a community of diverse European Americans; blacks; smaller minorities of Mexicans, Chinese, and Japanese; a small number of Southern Paiutes; and a sprinkling of other peoples. The most notable demographic change was the beginning of the rapid growth of the Hispanic, primarily Mexican, population in the 1960s.[6]

Then in the 1980s and 1990s, the sustained local economic boom that created an almost insatiable demand for labor and opportunities for managers and entrepreneurs, the dramatic increase in immigration to the United States, and the rise of Las Vegas as a retirement community profoundly altered the composition and look of the city. Both immigration and internal migration have fueled the diversification of Las Vegas's population. Some immigrants have come directly to Las Vegas from their homelands around the globe. Others have reached it after initially settling elsewhere in the United States, drawn to southern Nevada by the lure of better jobs, cheaper living costs, or the opportunity for family reunification. The internal migration of "old" immigrant stock from northern and eastern states—Irish, Italians, Swedes—as well as Hispanics from the Southwest and a large number of Hawaiians has also had a major impact on the Valley. The migration of Native Americans has been a key factor in ethnic diversification as well. The greatest number of these migrants are Navajos; the majority are from west of the Mississippi, but virtually every tribe from the United States and Canada is represented in Las Vegas's population.[7] Between the migrants and the immigrants, Las Vegas has been transformed into a multiethnic, multicultural, polyglot metropolis.

Nevada experienced the greatest percentage growth among the states in its Asian population during the 1990s and the second highest in Hispanics, with the greatest numerical gains occurring in Clark County. To deal with the burgeoning Latino population, Clark County provides free Spanish classes to its employees and offers bonus pay to bilingual staff. An article in the July/August 2003 edition of *Hispanic Magazine* suggests a further acceleration in the Latino population; citing good jobs, affordable housing, and low taxes, the magazine ranked Las Vegas as the tenth best U.S. city for Hispanics.[8]

In 1980 Las Vegas's population was approximately 82.5 percent white, 9.8 percent black, and 7.4 percent Hispanic, and a few thousand Asians and American Indians rounded out the local demography. The ethnic diversification that became noticeable in the 1980s exploded in the 1990s. Las Vegas grew by 83.5 percent between 1990 and 2000—to 1,563,282 persons—led by increases of 260.6 percent among Asians and 262.0 percent among Hispanics. In 2000 Las Vegas was approximately 63.1 percent white, 20.6 percent Hispanic, 8.4 percent non-Hispanic black, 6.2 percent Asian, 0.7 percent American Indian, 0.2 percent North African, and 0.2 percent black African.[9]

Clark County School District statistics on ethnicity reveal a deeper change in the school-age population than in the community at large, due to higher birth rates among minorities, including immigrants, as well as the impact of the migration of whites without school-age children, particularly the huge influx of retirees. Other Clark County School District data confirm the fact that the pace of ethnic change in Las Vegas is increasing, most dramatically in the 1990s. In the 1970–71 school year, the district's student population was 82.6 percent white, 12.6 percent black, 3.4 percent Hispanic, 0.5 percent Asian, and 0.4 percent American Indian. A decade later, all minorities had grown slightly. By 1990–91 Hispanics still trailed blacks, 12.1 percent versus 14.0 percent, while Asians had reached 3.9 percent. In 2000–2001 whites had become a minority, at 49.9 percent; Hispanics had reached 28.8 percent, while blacks accounted for 13.8 percent, Asians 6.6 percent, and American Indians 0.9 percent. Between the 1993–94 and the 2000–2001 school years, the number of students enrolled in the English Language Learners program increased 245 percent, to 35,296, while total district enrollment grew 59 percent. In the 1999–2000 school year, of the 1,200 new students entering the district monthly, 700 did not speak English; the same year, Clark County drew students from 110 foreign countries. The following year, minorities became the majority of students enrolled, reaching 50.1 percent.[10]

A further indication of this trend can be found in the records of the Clark County Court Interpreter's Office, which reveal that a modern Tower of Babel has sprung up in Las Vegas.[11] Prior to the office's establishment in 1975, the hiring of interpreters was an informal practice, but as Las Vegas was beginning to diversify, Judge John Mendoza took the initiative to put court interpreting on a formal footing. Records are fragmentary for the years prior to computerization in 1994, but surviving handwritten records for the year between September 1981 and August 1982 permit some comparisons. A total of 1,655 court cases (138 per month) required interpreters during 1981–82, and 25 languages were used, including Spanish and Portuguese, ten other European languages, and thirteen Asian languages.

By the mid-1990s things were very different. In 1994, 12,317 cases (1,026 per month) required interpreters; by 2000 the number had grown to 26,773 (2,231 per month), a 1,617 percent increase over the 1981–82 workload, and the office drew from a pool of 320 certified interpreters. By 2002 the monthly figure had risen to 2,953, a 33 percent increase in just two years. The office is currently charged with providing interpreters for 82 languages; in the seven years between 1994 and 2000, interpreters were used for seventy-nine of those languages, including four spoken in Ethiopia, four from the Philippines, Hawaiian, Goshute, and Afghani. By comparison, Los Angeles County—one of the country's largest and most ethnically diverse counties—employed 580 court interpreters of 104 languages.[12]

As a measure of diversity, even these impressive numbers do not adequately portray the extent of change in Las Vegas's population. While Spanish is by far the most common non-English language used in the courts, the proliferation of Spanish-language cases does nothing to reveal the influx of people from every Latin American country. And, of course, court cases heard in English tell us nothing about the presence of peoples from Great Britain, Canada, Africa, South Asia, the Caribbean, and other corners of the former British Empire, nor about Hawaiians and the many groups of Native Americans who make Las Vegas their home, nor about immigrants and ethnic migrants who choose to use English in court.

Statistics on immigration offer another window into Las Vegas's diversification. Of Clark County's census-counted population in 2000, 18.0 percent was foreign born, compared to 11.1 percent of the total U.S. population. Among the city's foreign born, 61.1 percent were from Latin America, 23.6 percent from Asia, 9.9 percent from Europe, 1.7 percent from Africa, 3.1 percent from "Northern America," and 0.4 percent from Oceania. Reflecting the impact of immigration, 25.5 percent of Las Vegas's population of over five years of age spoke a language other than English at home. In 2000 the Las Vegas MSA ranked twenty-sixth among the 331 U.S. metropolitan regions for its number of "new" immigrants—those who arrived in the last decade; in 1990, Las Vegas ranked forty-fourth.[13]

Naturalization, or the conferring of U.S. citizenship on immigrants, provides further insights. There were 3,578 immigrants naturalized in Nevada in the 1970s and 24,736 in the 1990s, a large majority of them in Las Vegas. While the number of naturalizations in the United States tripled during this period, Nevada experienced a sevenfold increase.[14] A look at two recent periods of naturalizations, 1985–87 and 1999–2000, reveals the increasing pace of diversification of Las Vegas's new citizens. In 1985–87 persons naturalized in Las Vegas came from 79 countries; in 1999–2000, from 131 countries. This change in provenance parallels the national trend away from western Europeans and toward Latin Americans, Asians, Africans, and eastern Europeans. After representing a major share of naturalized citizens in the 1960s and 1970s, western Europeans represented only 8.9 percent of those naturalized in Las Vegas in the mid-1980s and only 2.9 percent in 1999–2000. Indeed, the leading western European supplier of new citizens, the United Kingdom, ranked fourteenth in 1999–2000, and only three other European countries—Germany, Italy, and France—ranked in the top forty. The greatest number of Las Vegas's new citizens in 1999–2000 came, in order, from Mexico, the Philippines, El Salvador, China, and Cuba.[15]

The rising presence of immigrants in the Las Vegas population is reflected in the growth of specialized services. When immigration attorney Vicenta Montoya opened her practice in 1985, she was Las Vegas's only full-time specialist in immigration law. In 2003 Las Vegas had thirty-five members of the American Immigration Lawyers Association, half of whom were dedicated exclusively or primarily to immigration law. Meanwhile the number of notary services catering to immigrants had also proliferated. In 1987 Las Vegas was served one week per month by a single immigration judge based in Phoenix; in 1996 Las Vegas got its own immigration court with one full-time position, increased the following year to three judges. After serving since its inception as a dependency of the Phoenix office, the Las Vegas office of the U.S. Immigration and Naturalization Service (ins) was upgraded in 2001 to a district office, one of thirty-four in the country.[16]

Ethnic Institutions

Although traditional Little Italys and Chinatowns did not develop in Las Vegas, the Valley has a rich variety of ethnic institutions. Ethnic restaurants offer food, drink, music, and sometimes videos from home that affirm the national or ethnic culture. Some also serve as settings for important events such as weddings and baptisms. Ethnic markets provide sociability, foods, household items, and important elements of popular culture such as imported music on cassette or compact disc, films for rent or sale, popular literature, and newspapers and magazines from the "old country" and from the larger ethnic enclaves in U.S. cities. Some offer money wiring as well as check cashing, utility payment, and other services for people without bank accounts.[17]

Religion plays an important role in the culture of many new Las Vegans, both immigrants and migrants. In the case of peoples whose identity is bound up with a nationally based religion, such as Greek or Ethiopian Orthodox or the majority of Indians who are Hindus, the religious tie is particularly important in affirming ethnicity. Soccer is another institution that reinforces ethnic identities. Of the approximately three hundred teams comprising six leagues in the Valley, some 90 percent are Latino—primarily Mexican, but included within the Hispanic majority are several teams representing other

Latin American countries. Non-Latinos play as individuals, and a few teams are identified with other nationalities, including British, Yugoslav, and Japanese.[18]

Ethnic and national clubs are another index of Las Vegas's diversity. When groups attain a critical mass, they tend to form an organization to preserve and promote the culture of their country of origin. Some groups, including Germans, Italians, Filipinos, Poles, and Mexicans, have two or more clubs. Some clubs develop auxiliary musical, dance, and craft groups. Some of these clubs have a long history; many others were formed in the 1990s and early 2000s. A few own their own buildings, while others struggle to maintain even a minimal calendar of meetings.

Las Vegas's ethnic clubs have been in the public eye since 1976, when thirteen groups participated in the first International Food Festival, organized as part of the U.S. bicentennial celebration.[19] In the ensuing quarter century, the ethnic festival scene has expanded as festivals have become more frequent and better publicized and local government entities have lent their support to the events. The number of participating groups has grown over the years, although not proportionately to the formation of new ethnic associations. Several groups have participated sporadically, while many others hold their celebrations individually, without notice in local media.

At the largest annual event, the International Food and Folklife Festival of Southern Nevada, food, music, dance, and crafts from around the world are on display. Participating in the festivals between 2000 and 2003 were Southern Paiutes, African Americans, and Hawaiians (two groups); Asians from Thailand, the Philippines (two groups), China, Korea, Japan, Iran, and India; Latin Americans from Chile, Mexico, Argentina, Venezuela, Colombia, Peru, Puerto Rico, and Trinidad and Tobago; Europeans from Norway, Italy, Greece, Italy, Ireland, Germany, the Basque country (Spain and France), Sweden, Romania, Armenia, Scotland, the Ukraine, Poland, Russia, and Spain; and pan-African, pan-Native American, pan-Arabic, and pan-Latin American groups.[20] In addition to this annual festival, events and displays marking the nationally designated Hispanic, African American, Asian, and Native American months showcase the Valley's growing diversity.

Despite their visibility and their importance in cultural preservation, ethnic clubs attract only a fraction of Las Vegas's Colombians, Koreans, or Swedes. In part this reflects the waning of voluntary associations in the United States. Las Vegas's culture also appears to militate against high rates of participation in such organizations. Several members of ethnic clubs cite the city's twenty-four/seven schedule as a major impediment to attending meetings or functions. They also note that it is difficult for their elaborate ethnic dinners, usually the highlights of their social calendar, to compete with a $7.95 buffet. Las Vegas's sprawl discourages many from attending meetings, while for the poorer immigrant groups, working two or more jobs leaves little time or energy for gatherings. Moreover, some immigrants and ethnic migrants from other parts of the country come to the city precisely to escape the strictures of family and community; to them, Las Vegas's around-the-clock entertainment and atomized lifestyle appeal much more than participation in an ethnic club. And since the aforementioned Chicago couple's perception of a lack of ethnic presence is a common one, new residents simply may not know of the existence of a local organization representing their people.[21]

Ethnic clubs also compete for one's time, dues, and identity with hundreds of organizations in the Las Vegas Valley. The full range of national service clubs, the Sierra Club, the Nonsmoking Pinochle Group, the Tall Club of Las Vegas, Paradise Democratic Club, Overeaters Anonymous, Fossil Finders of Southern Nevada, Poets Circle, the Kingdom of Vega Empire of Chivalry and Steel (a Middle Ages club), Wyse Womyn (a social group for mature lesbians), and scores of other organizations advertise their meetings in the local press and welcome new members. Moreover, ethnics retiring to Las Vegas from northern and eastern cities may join the Chicago West Side Club, the New Pittsburgh Club, or the Michigan Social Club—for folks from Farmington Hills, Bloomfield, Novi, and Southfield—rather than the local Polish, Croatian, or Romanian clubs. And among the fans who congregate at designated bars during the National Football League season to cheer their teams from "back home" are many ethnic transplants manifesting their identities as supporters of the Buffalo Bills, the New England Patriots, or the Chicago Bears rather than their Italian, Irish, or Polish roots.[22]

Despite the constraints on membership and the competition of other types of organizations, clubs are the primary means of ethnic/national affirmation for European Americans, for whom ethnic identification is voluntary. Clubs are particularly important to those groups whose identity is not linked to a particular religion and who lack restaurants and markets in Las Vegas. Among these is the St. Andrews Society of Southern Nevada, which claims over 200 member families. Founded in 1995, it is one of dozens of loosely affiliated Scottish organizations of the same name throughout the United States. While most members are among the 22,000 Las Vegans who claim Scottish descent, the love of things Scottish, from Robert Burns to bagpipe music to the film *Braveheart,* attracts members such as Rick Pawlowski and Chris Sgambati who claim no Scottish ancestry at all. Members receive the newsletter *Desert Thistle* and the opportunity to participate in monthly meetings and a busy annual calendar of events, including Scottish Heritage Month activities, Tartan Day, the Kirkin (blessing of the tartan), the Ceilidh (a party highlighting Scottish food, drink, and entertainment), and the Burns Night Supper (featuring haggis). The society offers Scottish country-dance classes and tartan bowling, participates in international festivals, and sponsors the Silver Thistle Scottish Country Dancers. It has a scholarship fund for members' children.[23]

Southern Nevada hosts several other Scottish-inspired organizations, including the Desert Skye Pipes and Drums, the Las Vegas Highlander Pipe Band, and the Gaelic Arts and Education League (GAEL), which supports instruction in and preservation of Scots Gaelic. St. Andrews members commonly also belong to international clans, such as Clan Cunningham, Clan Donald, Clan Ross, and Clan Wallace. In 2001 the Nevada Legislature enacted Senate Bill 347, which made Nevada the thirteenth state to have an official tartan. Designed by Rick Pawlowski, the newly created tartan is woven in the traditional fashion incorporating Nevada colors and symbols.[24] The first-ever Highland games held in Las Vegas in April 2002, and the second in 2003, attest to the Scottish community's maturation and enthusiasm.

Another active European American club is the Sons of Norway, Vegas Viking Lodge 6-152, founded in 1992 as an affiliate of the International Sons of Norway. In common with several of the "old" immigrant organizations, the International Sons of Norway, established in Minneapolis in 1895, is a mutual insurance association as well as a fraternal and cultural organization that publishes a monthly magazine, *The Viking*, and sponsors heritage camps, cultural seminars, and charities. A perusal of *The Viking* gives insights into contemporary means of preserving old-country cultures in an era when many immigrants and their descendants are no longer concentrated in eastern cities or, as in the case of Norwegians, in farming communities in the upper Midwest. The magazine is full of advertisements for travel agents specializing in Norway and for Norwegian books, arts and crafts, and foods, all available over the Internet.[25]

Lodge 6-152 has approximately 130 members, mostly drawn from the 21,000 Las Vegans who claim Norwegian ancestry, along with a few immigrants. The lodge publishes a newsletter; holds monthly meetings, social gatherings, and annual events such as the lutefisk, *lapskaus,* and Leif Erikson dinners; and participates actively in Las Vegas international festivals. Vegas Viking also offers language, cooking, and craft classes; supports charities; raises funds for scholarships; and maintains two Web sites. Since Las Vegas lacks Norwegian restaurants and markets and the predominantly Lutheran

Norwegians do not claim one of the area's Lutheran churches as their own, the lodge plays the major institutional role in the Las Vegas Norwegian community; it is the most visible of the local Scandinavian organizations. Some active members profess to have learned more about Norway and its culture through participation in the Sons of Norway than they did growing up in ethnic Norwegian communities.[26]

Refugee Resettlement

Refugee resettlement has played a major role in the diversification of Las Vegas's population. Following World War II, the United States opened its doors to hundreds of thousands of European refugees, the displaced persons, or "DPS." As the Cold War intensified in the 1950s and 1960s, refugees from communist regimes received preferential treatment in the United States. Refugees from beyond Europe began arriving in large numbers following the Cuban Revolution of 1959, and the end of the Vietnam War in 1975 brought a large wave of Southeast Asian refugees. Refugee resettlement in the last quarter century has increasingly reflected the world's burgeoning refugee population, which surpassed 25 million in the mid-1990s. The spread of war and persecution around the globe brought new groups such as Afghans, Ethiopians, Iranians, Poles, Russian Jews, and Central Americans in the 1980s and Africans from several countries, Iraqis, Bosnians, and Kosovars in the 1990s. Since enactment of the 1980 Refugee Act, between 50,000 and 112,000 refugees per year had been accommodated until 2002, when—in reaction to the September 11, 2001, terrorist attacks on New York and Washington, D.C.—the U.S. government cut the number to 27,100. Alongside the formal refugees, defined by the United Nations as individuals who cannot return to their countries because of legitimate fear of persecution, many more people escaping famine and conflicts around the globe have entered the United States without benefit of official refugee status.[27]

Formal refugee resettlement began in Las Vegas in the 1970s.[28] Refugees have arrived under the auspices of Catholic Charities of Southern Nevada, the primary sponsor; the Franciscan Center, which closed in the 1980s; Episcopal Migration Services; and the Jewish Family Services Agency (JFSA). These groups' parent organizations at the national level contract with the U.S. Department of Health and Human Services to distribute the refugees throughout the country. Many of these refugees have been able to bring their families shortly after being settled. Other refugees, of course, arrive in Las Vegas from other points of entry in the United States, attracted by job opportunities. After a year refugees may apply for permanent resident status.

By the 1990s Las Vegas had become one of the country's most attractive destinations for refugees thanks to the booming local economy and the large number of service jobs in the city requiring low levels of skills, formal education, and knowledge of English. Numerous refugees have benefited from the Culinary Union Training Center, sponsored by Culinary Workers Union Local 226 and major hotel casinos, where, along with the native born and other immigrants, they can learn a skill, find a job in a resort hotel, and achieve a good income with health benefits in a very short time. Since its founding in 1993, the Culinary Union Training Center has graduated some 2,500 people per year.[29]

Between 1995 and 2001, Catholic Charities of Southern Nevada served 5,168 refugees from thirty-two countries. Over half were from Cuba, reflecting the continuation of Cold War–era policy that automatically grants Cubans refugee status upon reaching the United States. Other sizable contingents came from Bosnia (1,192), Iran (209), Vietnam (164), Sudan (127), Serbia (95), and Somalia (75). Among the countries supplying the smallest numbers were Angola, the Czech Republic, Rwanda, Togo, Uzbekistan, and Zaire (two persons each) and Armenia, Kazakhstan, and Tunisia (a single person each).[30]

Although refugee resettlement accounted for less than one percent of Las Vegas's population growth between 1995 and 2001, its impact on the Valley's diversification is much greater than that figure might suggest. Since the 1970s and increasingly in the 1980s and 1990s, resettled refugees from several countries undoubtedly became the first Las Vegans from their homelands; since immigrants tend to settle in locales where they have family, acquaintances, countrymen, or coethnics, the original Kosovars, Uzbeks, and Burundians launched migration streams—however small—of family members, refugees initially resettled elsewhere in the United States, and undocumented compatriots. Moreover, given the multiethnic composition of many refugee-sending countries, particularly in Africa and Asia, the impact of refugee resettlement on Las Vegas's diversification is considerably greater than the total number of refugees' countries of origin would suggest.

Refugee resettlement and the secondary migration that it fuels are responsible for the establishment and/or growth of several sizable groups found in Las Vegas, among the earliest of which are Cubans and Vietnamese. The Cuban community originated in the 1960s with flight from Fidel Castro's revolution. Over a thousand Cubans, initially attracted by the opportunity to work in casino jobs similar to those they held in Cuba, had made Las Vegas home by 1970. After sustained growth in the 1970s and 1980s, their numbers doubled during the 1990s, reaching some 12,000 in 2000. Cuban restaurants, markets, and organizations attest to the presence of an active Cuban community.[31]

The Vietnamese community is a product of refugee settlement following the end of the Vietnam War in 1975. Significant numbers of Vietnamese were settled in Las Vegas during the postwar exodus, but many of them left after short stays to join the burgeoning Vietnamese communities in Orange County and the San Jose area, both in California. Then in the 1990s, primarily as a result of the recession in California and the opportunities across the state line, the Vietnamese population of Las Vegas more than tripled to 4,341. A small minority of the new Las Vegas Vietnamese continued to arrive directly from Vietnam through a variety of resettlement programs. Vietnamese restaurants, markets, and organizations, and a Vietnamese priest assigned to St. Anne's Church, manifest the presence of a significant national/ethnic presence in Las Vegas. In October 2003 the Vietnamese community dedicated a shrine in southeast Las Vegas to Our Lady of La Vang.[32]

Numerous other groups established through refugee resettlement have contributed to Las Vegas's ethnic explosion of the last two decades. Among these are the Ethiopians from the 1980s and the Bosnians from the 1990s. Since the overthrow of Emperor Haile Selassie in 1974, Ethiopia has experienced a lengthy Marxist dictatorship, prolonged civil strife, and bitter warfare against the breakaway region of Eritrea, which since 1993 has been an independent state. Recurring famine has also taken a huge toll since the mid-1980s. The result of this turbulent quarter century has been the diaspora of millions of Ethiopians to neighboring African countries, Europe, and the United States. The U.S. Ethiopian population of approximately one million is concentrated in Washington, D.C., Atlanta, Dallas, Los Angeles, and Seattle.[33]

With its abundant work opportunities in the service sector, Las Vegas has drawn a steady stream of Ethiopians directly from Africa and from other U.S. cities, particularly Los Angeles. From its inception in the early 1980s, the Las Vegas Ethiopian community has grown to between 3,000 and 5,000.[34] The majority of Las Vegas Ethiopians work as taxi drivers and service employees in hotel casinos. They belong to a dynamic community that features some half-dozen restaurants, where music and videos from home complement the distinctive cuisine; additionally, two markets provide essential spices and grains for home cooking along with a range of cultural artifacts. The Ethiopian Mutual Association of Nevada, which is linked loosely with a national organization, sponsors cultural activities and raises money for relief in the homeland. Periodic performances by touring musicians from Ethiopia and U.S. Ethiopian communities provide another means of cultural affirmation. Las Vegas sends a soccer team to the annual North American Ethiopian tournament, a large-scale event that involves cultural activities and networking in addition to sport. Routine social interaction and celebrations of births and baptisms help to preserve Ethiopian identity in the alien setting of Las Vegas.

Reflecting the religious division of the homeland, Las Vegas Ethiopians are approximately half Christian and half Moslem. Moslems attend the Valley's mosques, while the Ethiopian Orthodox, or Coptic Christians, opened their own St. Michael's Ethiopian Orthodox Church in 2003. Citing Ethiopia's long tradition of religious tolerance, followers of both creeds deny that any friction exists between them but do admit a certain distance between themselves and the much smaller Eritrean community in Las Vegas, a natural but—in their view—unfortunate result of unnecessary, politically manipulated wars between groups that constitute a single people.

Las Vegas's Bosnian community likewise owes its existence to refugee resettlement. The post-1990 breakup of Yugoslavia reached a violent crescendo in Bosnia-Herzegovina, where between 1992 and 1995 fighting among Serbs, Croats, and Moslems led to massacres and ethnic cleansing. Hundreds of thousands of refugees made their way to neighboring countries, particularly Germany, and from there, beginning in 1993, many Bosnians came to the United States. From 1995 through 2001, 1,192 Bosnians were resettled in Las Vegas by Catholic Charities, and Episcopal Migration Services brought an additional 440. Community members estimate Las Vegas's Bosnian population at around 5,000; census figures are not available. The estimate includes those directly resettled, family members, secondary migrants from other U.S. cities (particularly Chicago and St. Louis), and some lacking papers.[35]

Bosnians work primarily in hotel casinos, above all in kitchens and housekeeping departments. Others work in construction, while some avail themselves of training opportunities in card dealing, sales, and other lines of work. Many have attained financial stability within a couple of years, allowing them to purchase homes and automobiles. The local Bosnian population is estimated to be approximately 50 percent Serbian, 40 percent Moslem, and 10 percent Croat. Against the backdrop of conflict at home, it is not surprising that the Bosnians appear not to have formed a close interethnic community in exile. Apart from a Bosnian-owned market that serves nationals of all three religions, the groups tend to go their own ways: Bosnian Serbs find a ready-made community in the Serbian Orthodox Church, some Bosnian Croats attend meetings of the Croatian American Club, and Bosnian Moslems with religious inclinations attend the local mosques. These fissures, combined with its newness, make the burgeoning Bosnian community in Las Vegas largely invisible.

Conclusion

While tripling in size, Las Vegas's population has experienced profound ethnic diversification since 1980. Both internal migration and immigration have expanded established ethnic groups, some of them present since Las Vegas's founding in 1905 or before. Even more impressive is the number of new ethnic groups, with little or no presence before 1980, that are found in the Valley today. Some have come from within the United States seeking better jobs, a reasonable cost of living, a warm climate, or a good place to retire. Others have come from around the world, many of them driven out of their countries by poverty, famine, war, or repression. For these people, Las Vegas is an irresistible magnet. Because of its booming economy and the explosion of jobs that require no English, formal education, or preexisting skills, Las Vegas since 1980 has attracted a disproportionately large share of the new immigrants to the United States from Latin America, Asia, and Africa. Together with the internal migrants, these new Las Vegans have created, almost overnight, a vibrant ethnic city in the desert.

Notes

1. This and the other observations on contemporary Las Vegas are based on the authors' experiences between 1999 and 2003.

2. Studies of the "old" immigration include Oscar Handlin, *The Uprooted: The Epic Story of the Great Immigration That Made the American People* (Boston: Little, Brown, 1951); John Bodnar, *The Transplanted: A History of Immigration in Urban America* (Bloomington: Indiana University Press, 1985). Roger Daniels, *Coming to America: A History of Immigration and Ethnicity in American Life* (New York: HarperCollins, 1990), covers both the traditional European and the beginnings of the "new" immigration. Studies of the "new" immigration include Alejandro Portes and Rubén G. Rumbaut, *Immigrant America: A Portrait*, 2d ed. (Berkeley: University of California Press, 1996); Sanford J. Ungar, *Fresh Blood: The New American Immigrants* (New York: Simon and Schuster, 1995); James P. Smith and Barry Edmonston, eds., *The New Americans: Economic, Demographic, and Fiscal Effects of Immigration* (Washington, D.C.: National Academy Press, 1997); David W. Haines and Carol A. Mortland, eds., *Manifest Destinies: Americanizing Immigrants and Internationalizing Americans* (Westport, Conn.: Praeger, 2001). Juan F. Perea, ed., *Immigrants Out! The New Nativism and the Anti-Immigrant Impulse in the United States* (New York: New York University Press, 1997) chronicles the negative response to the new immigration. Pat Buchanan, *The Death of the West: How Dying Populations and Immigrant Invasions Imperil Our Country and Civilization* (New York: St. Martin's Press, 2002) argues the case against immigration. For a broader look at international migrations, see Stephen Castles and Mark J. Miller, *The Age of Migration: International Population Movements*

in the Modern World, 2d ed. (Houndmills, Basingstoke, Hampshire, England: Macmillan Press, 1998); Robin Cohen, ed., *The Cambridge Survey of World Migration* (Cambridge, England: Cambridge University Press, 1995); Wayne A. Cornelius, Philip L. Martin, and James F. Hollifield, eds., *Controlling Immigration: A Global Perspective* (Stanford, Calif.: Stanford University Press, 1994).

3. *Las Vegas Sun,* July 22, 2001, points out that, while less defined than Hispanic and black districts, there is a significant concentration of Asians in the Spring Valley area in western Las Vegas.

4. Many public and private entities in the Valley have telephone menus in Spanish, and some have Web sites in Spanish. In 2001 Clark County began offering its employees free Spanish lessons and announced the inception of bilingual voting in efforts to accommodate Hispanics. *Las Vegas Sun,* August 24 and December 17, 2001. We spotted the "got injera?" bumper sticker on August 30, 2002.

5. This list includes only restaurants outside of resort hotels and whose clientele is primarily local. Some of these restaurants as well as markets discussed below may have closed and others may have opened since mid-2003. For overviews of ethnic markets, see *Las Vegas Review-Journal,* September 15, 1999; February 6, 2000; April 17, 2002.

6. See chapter 1. The Las Vegas metropolitan area experienced the highest economic growth rate in the United States during the 1990s: *Las Vegas Sun,* July 10, 2001. See also M. Gottdiener, Claudia C. Collins, and David R. Dickens, *Las Vegas: The Social Production of the All-American City* (Malden, Mass.: Blackwell, 1999), 30–67, 101–15.

7. On Native Americans, see *Las Vegas Review-Journal,* July 28, 2002; Richard Arnold, director, Las Vegas Indian Center, interview by Thomas C. Wright, July 27, 2003.

8. *Las Vegas Review-Journal,* August 30, 2000, March 20, 2000; *Las Vegas Sun,* September 10, 2000; August 24, 2001; http://hispaniconline.com/magazine/2003/july-aug/Features/top10-3.html.

9. U.S. Department of Commerce, Bureau of the Census, *1980 Census of Population and Housing, Las Vegas, Nev. Standard Metropolitan Statistical Area* (Washington, D.C.: Government Printing Office, 1983), P-28; http://factfinder.census.gov/servlet/DDTable?ts=77728578655; http://factfinder.census.gov/servlet/QTTable?tx=77724691468; http://mumford1dyndns.org/cen2000/BlackWhite/DiversityBWDataPages/412msaBWCt.htm.

10. Clark County School District statistics are courtesy of Tom Rodriguez, Executive Manager, Diversity and Affirmative Action Programs. Note that in some years the category "other" is used; the percentage of "other" ethnicities never exceeds 0.5 percent. These Clark County School District statistics do not take into account Las Vegas's entire school-age population, since a growing number of whites attend private schools. But given the preponderance of the public-school district in total enrollment, the distortion is minimal. *Las Vegas Sun,* April 18, 2001; June 10, 2001.

11. The official title of the office is Eighth Judicial District Court Interpreter Services, but it provides interpreters for all Clark County offices that need them as well as

Clark County courts. Mariteresa Rivera-Rogers, Program Administrator, interviews by Thomas C. Wright, June 19, 2000, February 26, 2001, September 9, 2003. Rivera-Rogers graciously provided the records alluded to. While tourists are responsible for some of the interpreter needs, Rivera-Rogers and her staff estimate that at least 90 and probably 95 percent of the users of interpreters are Las Vegas residents.

12. Rivera-Rogers interviews; *Los Angeles Times,* May 25, 2001.

13. http://factfinder.census.gov/servletQTTable?_ts=78316446843. See also http://mumforddidyndns.org/cen2000/NewAmericans/NewAmerData/4120msaNuAmer.htm.

14. The majority of immigrants, in Las Vegas and throughout the country, do not become citizens. For the United States in 2000, 40.3 percent of the foreign born had acquired citizenship; for Las Vegas, the figure is 36.7 percent. Noncitizen immigrants may hold permanent resident status or temporary, usually renewable work permits, or they are undocumented. For Las Vegas, see http://factfinder.census.gov/servlet QQTable?_ts=7497521926; for the United States, see http://factfinder.census.govbfl_lang=en_vt_name=Dec_2000_SF3_U_DP2_geo_id=01000US.html; U.S. Immigration and Naturalization Service, Statistics Branch, Operational Statistics Section, fax, November 28, 2001, courtesy of the office of U.S. Senator Harry Reid, Jerry Reynoldson, director in Las Vegas. Based on comparisons in selected years, Las Vegas was the site of at least two thirds of the naturalizations performed in Nevada.

15. This increase is greater than the increase in the number of new countries created during the 1990s primarily by the disintegration of the former Soviet Union and of Yugoslavia. Figures are from November 1985 through February 1987 and calendar years 1999–2000. These statistics come from the Las Vegas office of the U.S. Immigration and Naturalization Service, courtesy of U.S. District Court Judge Philip M. Pro. The Immigrant Workers Citizenship Project, founded in 2001 by the Culinary Workers Union Local 226, is a new tool for smoothing the path toward citizenship. See *Las Vegas Review-Journal,* February 23, 2002.

16. Vicenta Montoya, interview by Thomas C. Wright, August 17, 2001; Peter Ashman, interview by Thomas C. Wright, September 16, 2003; Thomas E. Walter, interview by Thomas C. Wright, September 23, 2003; *Las Vegas Review-Journal,* July 20, 2001.

17. Of necessity, these markets are unable to carry products reflective of the regional and, in some cases, ethnic diversity of their clients' countries. The growth of ethnic markets catering to wealthier, more educated groups may be limited by the competition of Internet marketing of ethnic foods, crafts, music, and literature.

18. Efraín Martínez, sports director of Univisión channel 15 television, interview by Thomas C. Wright and Jesse Dino Moody, June 21, 2001; Abel Cuevas, director, Liga Centroamericana de Fútbol, interview by Thomas C. Wright and Jesse Dino Moody, July 12, 2001. See chapters 4 and 13 for more information on soccer.

19. Dona Brown, president of the International Festival Association, interview by Thomas C. Wright, May 30, 2001.

20. Programs courtesy of Dorothy Wright, Cultural Program Administrator, Clark County Department of Parks and Recreation.

21. These observations about Las Vegas's ethnic clubs are derived from members of various clubs, including Redda Mehari, Ethiopian Mutual Association, interview by Thomas C. Wright, June 29, 2000; Manuel Abeyta, Las Vegas Basque Club, interview by Thomas C. Wright and Jerry L. Simich, July 24, 2001; Jon Cepoi, "Doina" Romanian-American Society of Las Vegas, interview by Thomas C. Wright and Jerry L. Simich, July 26, 2001; Francisco (Frank) Canales, Salvadoran Foundation, interview by Thomas C. Wright and Jesse Dino Moody, June 21, 2001; Gwen Knighton, Diane Seidlinger, and Lollo Sievert, Sons of Norway Vegas Viking Lodge 6-152, interview by Thomas C. Wright, July 25, 2001; Rick Pawlowski and Mike Steele, St. Andrews Society of Southern Nevada, interview by Dina Titus and Thomas C. Wright, March 1, 2001; Deborah Sgambati, St. Andrews Society of Southern Nevada, interview by Dina Titus and Thomas C. Wright, July 29, 2001.

22. All groups cited were announced in the "Around the Valley" section of the *Las Vegas Review Journal* during 2000 and 2001. The bars and their affiliations are published annually at the beginning of the NFL season, for example, in the *Las Vegas Review-Journal,* August 27, 2000.

23. Information in this and the following paragraph comes from various publications of the St. Andrews Society of Southern Nevada and from Rick Pawlowski and Mike Steele, interview by Dina Titus and Thomas C. Wright, March 1, 2001; Deborah Sgambati, interview by Dina Titus and Thomas C. Wright, July 29, 2001; http://factfinder.census.gov/servlet/QTTable?_ts=7497579273.

24. Jerry Lester, president of the St. Andrews Society, is credited with promoting the idea of a Nevada tartan. Senate Bill 347 was authored by Senator Dina Titus.

25. Information in this and the following paragraph comes from national and local Sons of Norway publications and from Gwen Knighton, Diane Seidlinger, and Lollo Sievert, interviews by Thomas C. Wright, July 25, 2001.

26. The population statistic is from http://factfinder.census.gov/servlet/QTTable?_ts=7497579273.

27. On refugees and resettlement see David W. Haines, ed., *Refugees in America in the 1990s: A Reference Handbook* (Westport, Conn.: Greenwood Press, 1996). The estimate of the number of refugees is from Castles and Miller, *The Age of Migration,* 87. See also Haines, *Refugees in America; Las Vegas Review-Journal,* May 30, 2003.

28. Information on refugee resettlement in Las Vegas comes primarily from Redda Mehari, director, Catholic Charities of Southern Nevada, Migration and Refugee Service, interview by Thomas C. Wright, June 29, 2000; Father Phil Carolin, Episcopal Migration Services, interview by Thomas C. Wright, June 1, 2001; Sister Klaryta Antoszewska, independent worker with refugees, interview by Thomas C. Wright, February 25, 2001; immigration attorney Vicenta Montoya, interview by Thomas C. Wright, August 17, 2001. Refugee resettlement gets little local press coverage; an exception is a *Las Vegas Sun* story on the arrival of 11 young Sudanese men in 2001, the

first part of a group of 40 being resettled in Las Vegas. They form part of the 3,600 so-called "Lost Boys" being resettled in the United States. See *Las Vegas Review-Journal,* June 17, 2001.

29. D Taylor, interview by Dina Titus and Thomas C. Wright, May 2, 2001; Culinary Union Training Center pamphlet.

30. These statistics are courtesy of Redda Mehari, Director, Catholic Charities of Southern Nevada, Migration and Refugee Service. These numbers represent a majority, but not all, of the refugees resettled in Las Vegas between 1995 and 2001.

31. William Clayson, "Cubans in Las Vegas: Ethnic Identity, Success, and Urban Life Late in the Twentieth Century," *Nevada Historical Society Quarterly* 38, no. 1 (Spring 1995): 1–18; Joseph Coleman, "Cubans," in Haines, ed., *Refugees in America,* 102–20; http://mumford1.dyndns.orgcen2000HispanicPopHspPopData4120msa.htm.

32. Nguyen Manh Hung and David W. Haines, "Vietnamese," in Haines, ed., *Refugees in America,* 305–30; Kim Le, interview by Thomas C. Wright, February 20, 2002; Redda Mehari, interview by Thomas C. Wright, June 29, 2000. The population estimate is from http://mumford1.dyndns.org/cen2000/AsianPop/AsianPopData/4120msa.htm; Le estimates the Vietnamese population at between 6,000 and 8,000. *Las Vegas Review-Journal,* October 19, 2003.

33. Information in this and the following paragraphs on Ethiopians is from Harold G. Marcus, *A History of Ethiopia,* rev. ed. (Berkeley: University of California Press, 2002); Tekle M. Woldemikael, "Ethiopians and Eritreans," in Haines, ed., *Refugees in America,* 147–69; Redda Mehari, interview by Thomas C. Wright, June 29, 2000; Gebrekristos Yimer, interview by Thomas C. Wright, February 11, 2002; Abas Mohammad, interview by Thomas C. Wright, February 11, 2002; *The Europa World Year Book 2001* (London: Europa Publications, 2001), 1:1473–83, 1503–22.

34. The 3,000–5,000 figure is the commonly held estimate of local Ethiopians. The census found 1,764 persons of Ethiopian ancestry, at http://factfinder.census .gov/servlet/QTTable?_ts=7497579273. The existence of some six Ethiopian restaurants and two markets suggests the census count is extremely low; *Las Vegas Sun,* June 23, 2000.

35. Information on Bosnians in this and the following paragraph comes David Rieff, *Slaughterhouse: Bosnia and the Failure of the West* (New York: Simon and Schuster, 1995); Father Phil Carolin, interview by Thomas C. Wright, June 1, 2001; Ana Puljic, interview by Thomas C. Wright and Jerry L. Simich, February 6, 2002; *The Europa World Year Book 2001,* 1:756–76.

CHAPTER 3

Southern Paiutes, the Native Americans

MARTHA C. KNACK

The first European Americans to arrive in southern Nevada in the 1820s found native Southern Paiutes already living there. The Las Vegas band of Paiutes were part of a widespread group long established throughout the arid lands of the southern half of what is now Utah, Nevada south of Pioche and Pahrump, the eastern half of the Mohave Desert of California, and Arizona north of the Grand Canyon. They all acknowledged fundamental similarities of language and culture which underlay minor band variations and called each other *nuwuvi,* "people," fellow Paiutes. Their language resembled the other Uto-Aztecan languages of adjacent Shoshones and others in the Great Basin, but Cahuillas in the western Mohave Desert and Mohaves to the east across the Colorado spoke other languages, had different cultures, were essentially strangers, and were not *nuwuvi.*[1]

Roughly 150 people lived in the Las Vegas Valley itself, with smaller affiliated groups based at the various outlying springs, such as Potosi, Indian Springs, and Pahrump. Together these 300 to 400 people of the Las Vegas band shared use of a territory that stretched from Indian Springs west to Death Valley, south to the Providence Mountains, up the western bank of the Colorado River to Las Vegas Wash, and around to the Sheep Mountain range.[2]

Paiutes lived in small camp groups primarily by hunting and gathering the natural produce of the desert and by farming a bit in favorable spots. The limited amount of plants and animals produced in this desert region assured that Southern Paiutes had few harvests exceeding their immediate needs and had to renew their food supplies nearly constantly. Most of that food came from more than a hundred kinds of plants harvested systematically—everything from tule and Joshua-tree roots and yucca flowers in the spring, to wild rhubarb and squaw-cabbage leaves later, prickly-pear cactus fruits in summer, and hearts of the agave plant to pit roast. Major staples were Indian rice grass, mesquite, and piñon. Each of these produced a surplus that could be sun dried and stored for later use. Ground to flour on a stone metate with a round mano stone, these were boiled into porridge or baked into breads.

When one of these foods grew enough in one place to support more people, several groups would collect temporarily. Although not uniformly productive from year to year, groves of piñons were one such source. Groups from Indian Springs and Potosi and Pahrump would convene on Mount Charleston not only to harvest food but also to visit, catch up on news, tell stories into the night, dance, sing, and enjoy one another's company, before breaking up again into smaller groups for the winter.[3]

Although deer and mountain sheep from the nearby uplands were preferred, Paiutes probably ate rabbits more often and did not eschew cold-blooded rattlesnakes, chuckwalla lizards, and desert tortoises. If Paiutes had been able to save any corn, beans, or gourds from last year, they planted an acre or two near the major springs in Downtown Las Vegas and those three miles west, sometimes adding the wild seeds of sunflower, amaranth, and devil's claw.

Wild plants grew at different seasons and in different ecological zones as well as fluctuating with annual rainfall, so Paiutes had to move from time to time to locate a steady food supply. The summer staple, rice grass, ripened on the Valley floor in April, as did the midsummer crop of mesquite seedpods. In autumn, however, after quickly harvesting their small gardens, Las Vegas Paiutes had to hurry to Mount Charleston to collect the all-important nuts of the piñon pine before returning to sheltered lowland campsites for the winter. In addition to foods, people harvested wild tobacco for ceremonial use, a wide range of leaves and roots for medicines, and raw materials for making tools, clothing, and shelter. While women gathered and processed plants, men hunted game nearby. The Paiutes' activities were diverse, complex, and constant.[4]

Paiute women made most of the tools they needed for their work, usually from narrow-leaf willow harvested in the fall. Over the cold winter days they scraped it into flat threads and painstakingly wove it into into the myriad baskets they used every day—gathering trays, pack baskets, seed beaters, winnowing trays, tightly woven eating bowls, water jugs sealed with pine pitch inside and out, caps, and cradles to carry their babies in. Sometimes they wove in patterns of dark devil's-claw fiber. They made pottery to cook in but often preferred not to carry these heavy, fragile objects. Then they cooked soups and stews in tightly woven baskets by waiting until the liquids had swelled the interstices shut and then dropping in fire-heated rocks. They sealed woven water jugs with piñon pitch. And they twisted the coarse fiber of yucca leaves into tough sandals to protect feet from the scorching desert sands, which, along with aprons of pounded cliff-rose bark and basketry caps, were the only clothing needed in the scorching summers. In the fall a twisted yarn of rabbit fur was finger woven into a four-foot square for a daytime cape that served as a nighttime blanket. Women beat the fiber out of dried milk-weed and twisted it into cordage to knot into rabbit nets, carrying nets, string belts, trap nooses, or just a handy piece of string. Tule became mats for house walls or floors. Men sought out rare, straight sections of serviceberry wood for bows. They also took shorter pieces of this, or squaw bush or greasewood, for arrow foreshafts and set these into longer sections of more readily available reed that were then feathered. And, of course, both men and women con-stantly gathered firewood. For what they could not produce from the re-sources of their own valley, Las Vegas Paiutes traded with neighboring bands and surrounding tribes. They traded yucca-fiber cordage with Chemehuevi Paiutes from the Colorado River near Needles for knives carved of the iron-wood that grew there. They exported finished rabbit nets and buckskins, soft red iron-ore face paint mined on Sunrise Mountain, and wild tobacco to Cahuillas in California for seashells to make beads and to Mohaves on the lower Colorado River for extra corn and beans.[5]

Throughout much of the year Paiutes traveled to these food sources and materials in small groups of families linked to each other through a variety of bilateral kinship ties. A man, his wife or wives, and their children, with per-haps a grandparent or two, a widowed uncle, or a married daughter, lived with a few other families.[6] A young, newly married couple was expected to live near the bride's family for awhile, but later they could live with his parents or any of her or his more distant relatives as they were invited, as they chose, or as there were resources available. This tied not only the couple but all of their relatives to each another in clearly expected ways. At minimum relatives by blood and by marriage were supposed to be pleasant and convivial in the tiny social groups so constantly in each another's company. A man shared any game too big for his family to eat by itself. When a relative was sick, others shared food or hunted for him. In times of drought relatives pooled their scant resources so that, although all might be hungry, none starved. The worst criticism one Paiute could level against another was that he or she was stingy—not acting as a relative should and violating both kinship and human ethics. The kinship system, by defining the rights and duties each expected from the others, was the primary glue that held families together and made them into a community.

Of course people could not always maintain such ideal, harmonious rela-tionships. After months spent with the same few families, Paiutes quarreled. When relationships became too strained or young people simply grew too restless, a family or even an individual moved away. Because kin ties were traced bilaterally and group size was small, to avoid incest people often had had to marry into other camp groups, so their descendants had relatives they could visit in any number of places. Camp groups were not fixed membership units but were flexible.

The camp leader was a headman, a still-active senior man who, in pursuit of a long life, had learned where flash floods would roll or springs still flow after prolonged drought. He shared his knowledge and experience tactfully without infringing on other people's autonomy. Often senior kinsman to other camp-group members, he was expected to be generous rather than authoritarian. His job was to suggest where the community might move next for the best food, to mediate quarrels that threatened the internal cohesion of the group, and to voice group decisions to outsiders.[7] At times a group of men joined the headman in a hunt or agreed to his proffered compromise in a dispute, while at other times they listened to someone else who had alternative ideas. If they did so too frequently, then de facto the headman's influence was usurped and the group had a different leader. People's individual autonomy, considered the unalienable right of every adult man and woman, was the ultimate check on the power of the headman. Without title, rank, ceremonial installation, salary, or special privileges, the headman was simply the one people chose, of their own volition, to follow. Paiutes were severely democratic.

The Paiute system was sufficiently flexible that virtually all unique personal talents were recognized and used for the public good in one or another particular situation without competing with the headman in any way. Knowledgeable senior women, for instance, led the women's work parties in daily plant harvesting.[8] Some men and a few women were believed to have obtained special concessions from supernatural beings to give them power over game animals, such as rabbits or antelope, or the power to cure certain types of illnesses. These people were shamans.

Southern Paiutes believed that the land in which they lived was permeated with beings having power far beyond that of humans to understand or control. These powerful, invisible beings sought out particular men and women for friendships through repeated, intense dreams in childhood or later in life. Although some people intentionally exposed themselves to supernaturals by frequenting places where they were thought to live, overt pursuit of supernatural sponsorship was considered inappropriately aggressive. The relationship between a shaman and a spirit being was seen as similar to reciprocal relations between humans, although the fundamental incomprehensibility of the nonhuman member made such partnerships both unpredictable and risky. Paiutes were drawn by supernatural offers to cure the numerous illnesses that struck them and their relatives without warning or apparent reason and were beyond the strength of routine domestic herbal cures.[9]

In the years before the arrival of non-Indian people, Southern Paiutes traveled their desert on foot, gathered seasonal wild-plant foods with lightweight basketry, and made small gardens when they could. They hunted wherever they were and saved whatever possible for winter. Each year was different, without a fixed sequence of resources to harvest or campsites to occupy. Camp groups aggregated when rabbit populations or piñon productivity allowed and then redivided into smaller groups. When resources failed, Paiutes visited their relatives elsewhere, perhaps staying a season or perhaps years. They socialized with their relatives, married nonkinsmen, and extended the privileges and obligations of kinship to these new affines. Without fixed rules of residence or rigid group membership, they found intergroup reciprocity and social openness to insure greater security than private ownership of property would have provided. They traveled lightly, avoiding personal possessions and distinctions of rank based on wealth. Individuals, male and female, were valued for the skills they had to share, whether to hunt, cure, mediate a dispute, or tell a good story on a winter evening.

Frugal, hard-working, provident, and knowledgeable about the resources of their environment, Paiutes used what they had with great creativity and flexibility, adjusting when they had to do so. Paiutes firmly believed that their land was nurturant and productive; they were secure in the knowledge that they could always make a living on their desert if they worked hard with imagination and persistence. They did not look at their land as a harsh and barren place, as did some other people who came later.

First European Explorations

The first of these strangers were Spaniards who significantly impacted Paiute society long before they actually laid eyes on Paiute territory. The traditional homeland of the Utes was more lushly pastured than Paiute country, and they could afford to keep the horses the Spaniards had imported. Mounted Utes quickly formed large, highly mobile bands under centralized leadership that crossed Paiute lands to Santa Fe and California to trade for manufactured goods. They had learned early on that the expanding European colonies would pay well for labor and had turned their military advantages of speed, mobility, and band size against the smaller, pedestrian Paiute camps through which they traveled; they seized Paiutes to sell as slaves in the European towns. This trade became so entrenched that by 1850 there were standard values for Paiute slaves, from $50 to $200 depending on their sex, age, and state of health.[10] This slave trade flourished throughout the Spanish Colonial period and into subsequent Mexican and American ones as well.

The first Euramerican to actually come to Las Vegas was probably Antonio Armijo, in 1829, who was trying to find a wagon road from the old Spanish trade center at Santa Fe to the missions in California. Although he did not report meeting any of the residents of the Las Vegas Valley, he said of Paiutes elsewhere that they were "a docile and timid nation" and offered no hostility.[11] His route became known as the Old Spanish Trail, along which came wagon trains that used the springs at "Los Vegas," the meadows, where Paiutes had long camped and farmed, to water draft animals that then grazed the surrounding grasslands. The impact of this transient grazing was so intense that the first official U.S. exploring party in 1844 said of the nearby Mohave River Valley, "We were now careful to take the old camping places of the annual Santa Fe caravans, which, luckily for us, had not yet made their yearly passage. A drove of several thousand horses and mules would entirely have swept away the scanty grass at the watering places, and we should have been obliged to leave the road to obtain subsistence for our animals."[12] Not only would travelers be driven away from the trail, but so too were the native people, whose campsites at springs were being usurped and whose own food sources were being fed to horses and oxen. Loss of the grasses that constituted an important summer food staple forced Paiute transhumance patterns away from the trails during prime harvest seasons.

By 1849 gold had been discovered in California, and the Old Spanish Trail became a major thoroughfare for immigrants headed for the West Coast. Las Vegas was an oasis on the desert trail where they could rest their draft animals. Immigrants preempted the campsites near the springs, often hiring Paiutes to guard grazing livestock overnight in return for breakfast or a small gift. The Paiutes also gleaned any useful objects immigrants abandoned as they attempted to lighten their loads before heading out across the Mohave Desert.

Euramerican Settlement

In 1855 the first non-Indians established residence in Las Vegas. Members of the Mormon Church, who had been settling the Utah area systematically for the last six years, were sent to establish a mission. They were charged with building a defensive fort; starting a farm and exploring the resources of the area; making friends with the Indians; and mediating any potential hostilities between traveling coreligionists and natives. They were to learn the native language so they could present church dogma and persuade the Paiutes to convert, if possible. Paiutes were as open to novel ideas as they were to new material goods brought by the Euramericans, and one of the missionaries soon reported, "I preached a little to the Indians after which they went into the water + we baptized 54 of them into the church of Latter Day Saints."[13] Because of political developments in Utah, the mission was abandoned in 1857.

Octavius Gass soon took over the old Mormon Fort property, and as a member of the Arizona state legislature he managed to get six soldiers assigned from Fort Mohave to guard him against Indian attack. For the next two years the troopers provided a market for his farm produce, but their only contact with Paiutes took place when they hired a native man to track one of the army's own deserters. Within a few years Gass, his successors the Stewarts, and other ranchers who moved onto the springs at the foot of Mount Charleston began paying Indian workers between $.50 and $1 a day to build fences, pull sagebrush, cut and haul firewood, track wandering cattle, and assist in all the various seasonal chores of general ranch life. Paiute women were hired to wash clothes and assist ranch wives with their housework.[14]

A federal explorer described the Las Vegas Paiutes' economy in 1872: "They have small farms or gardens, and besides the corn, pumpkins, melons, &c., raised by themselves, obtain scanty supplies from the Vegas ranches for what little work they do."[15] Most had learned some English from their employers and dressed like other ranch hands but also continued to do limited hunting and gathering throughout the nineteenth century, constructing a mixed economy that combined traditional foods with new ones. What proportion of their diet came from traditional sources and how much was acquired as wages or through trade from farmers cannot be determined, but the proportion undoubtedly shifted toward purchased foods as the number of non-Indians increased, taking over more and more of the countryside as their private property.[16]

Origins of the Las Vegas Indian Reservation

In contrast to the experience of many tribes elsewhere, the federal government had very little to do with Las Vegas Paiute affairs during the nineteenth century. The military never marched against them, treaties were not negotiated, and reservations were not established until nearly World War I. In 1869 the first Indian agent for Paiutes was assigned to Pioche, the leading town in Clark County.[17] In looking for sites for reservations four years later, his successor suggested that "the only suitable place in this country for a Reservation—what is called the Los [sic] Vegas Ranch."[18] Even after a small reservation was established at Moapa, fifty miles east, Las Vegas Paiutes were not interested enough to relocate and only occasionally visited kinsmen there. Oddly enough, much of the resistance to reservationization of Indians in southern Nevada came not from the native people themselves but from their employers: "The argument is frequently heard, locally, that the government should let these Indians alone—that they are good workers and can get along very well by their own efforts."[19]

In 1905 the San Pedro, Los Angeles, and Salt Lake Railroad was completed and built a watering station and repair yard about a quarter mile from the old Gass ranch. The town of Las Vegas grew up around the yards, and new jobs lured Paiutes from the depressed outlying mining towns of Goodsprings, El Dorado, and Searchlight and from Cottonwood Island, Indian Springs, Pahrump, Manse, and other places throughout southern Nevada and the Mohave Desert. When the Las Vegas Paiute community executed a shaman accused of murder by witchcraft in 1910 and sought revenge for a girl shot by a white miner, non-Indians suddenly became worried about the autonomous actions of native people who had "been let alone to come and go as they pleased, hold their own courts of justice and mete out justice according to the crime."[20] The federal Bureau of Indian Affairs (BIA) authorized its Moapa agent to advertise for "land (large or small tracts) suitable for a reservation for the Las Vegas Indians."[21]

Cost was a problem, as land near the town was already selling for between $40 and $1,000 per acre, but there was also the question of the type of land. The BIA's standard argument for founding reservations was that it was done to permit the Indians to become independent small farmers, but the harsh reality was that "there are no white men making a living from farming, and there is little land suitable for farming purposes in the Las Vegas Valley," the few isolated springs having been long since expropriated by non-Indian ranchers. The local agent suggested instead that "the reservation should be as near town as possible to enable the government employees in charge to keep a watch on the Indians and their squaws, their work, and the white bootleggers, and be in touch with the white [law] officers" specifically to monitor the relationship between the two ethnic groups.[22]

In response to its advertisement, the BIA was offered three plots that were infertile, heavily covered with black alkali and caliche. The fourth was a portion of Helen Stewart's ranch, including a small spring that lay within easy walking distance of employment in the town center. The several Paiute families who lived there showed the federal inspector the old springs where they had farmed before the arrival of settlers and up to the time when Stewart had sold it to the railroad. They asked for their old farm site back and for a school, because their children were barred from public education. The inspector knew the railroad would never yield its ownership of the well-watered section that had given the town its name, so he recommended the nearby portion that Stewart offered. The Nevada congressional delegation supported this purchase, and after a few technical delays Stewart sold the BIA ten acres off Main Street in Downtown Las Vegas for $500 on December 31, 1911.[23]

Clearly, the one hundred Paiutes who called Las Vegas home, or even the half who lived on Stewart's land, could not support themselves by farming those few acres. From the beginning, the small size of the purchase indicated that the Las Vegas Paiute Reservation was never intended to be a self-supporting unit but rather a homesite for wage earners reliant on the town for employment.

The Las Vegas Indian community was added to the jurisdiction of the Moapa agency, and the headquarters was moved into town. A day school for Paiutes was opened in the spring of 1912. Attendance averaged four students a day, fluctuating to as high as eight but also down to none as parents found work on distant ranches or left the Valley to gather desert foods. The student population never expanded, and the school closed permanently at the end of the first fall term.[24] Still barred from public schools, Las Vegas Paiutes went without elementary education for another generation.

By 1918 agency administration had moved back to Moapa, and the Las Vegas community was rarely visited thereafter by a federal agent. The town-dwelling Paiutes continued to live transiently in tents and brush dwellings. Their health was poor, with high rates of gonorrhea, tuberculosis, and infant mortality. In the rough railroad town it was reported that "girls of immature age are corrupted," and incidents of spouse abuse and intracommunity violence were not rare.[25]

Even water, such a basic requirement for life in the desert, was inadequate for the Las Vegas Paiutes. The original reservation purchase had included a small spring, the sole source of water, but pumping by the surrounding, rapidly growing city was already lowering the water table. In 1932 the BIA drilled a drinking-water well, deepening that and adding two more later and impounding any surplus behind a small dam; together, this produced culinary supplies and enough to irrigate two to four acres of gardens. Nevertheless, by the early 1950s the Indian drinking well frequently dried up in late summer. For another decade the reservation's federal jurisdiction legally prevented the city from connecting Paiutes to the urban water system that flowed within feet of their doorways.[26]

Las Vegas Paiutes in the Twentieth Century

The Great Depression affected Las Vegas Paiutes deeply. "Labor conditions have been so desperate in the region," the agent wrote, "that it has been necessary to give aid to practically all of the Indians in this settlement. This is unusual as in normal times only the old and ill required any help, and this only occasionally."[27] As ranches in the Valley faced financial difficulties and cut back operations, Paiutes faced loss of their accustomed source of employment, upon which they now depended. Further, Paiutes quite suddenly discovered that they no longer held the regional monopoly on unskilled labor that they had so long enjoyed. In the 1930s the federal government built Hoover Dam across the Colorado River just outside Las Vegas, drawing non-Indians from all over the country who were desperate for jobs. A federal observer saw that the Paiutes' "chance for employment has grown increasingly *less* with the great influx of people from all over the country seeking jobs at Boulder City and Hoover Dam."[28] When the gypsum mines opened at nearby Apex, Paiutes sought the $5-a-day wage, better than the usual $3-a-day ranch pay, despite the exhausting, dusty, choking labor in the hot desert sun.[29]

In 1952 conservative federal policy attempted to minimize governmental expenses, and the BIA was ordered to survey all services it was providing to every tribe in order to shift administration onto state, local, and tribal governments. This survey found that none of the twenty-six families of Las Vegas Paiutes was supported by the ten acres of reservation land; they all worked for wages, garnering family incomes of about $2,400 per year. The city had grown around them, and huge casino hotels nearby pumped ever more water from the aquifers, so that the original well, with its single hand-pump spigot, was the only functioning source for drinking and bathing water, and it went dry every summer. The Paiute population lived in two trailers, twenty-seven self-constructed houses, or in the open; all housing was described as "extremely substandard"[30] and "from a public health point of view none . . . [was] inhabitable."[31] Nine outhouses constituted the sanitation system; several lacked doors, and all drained into the ground. Health conditions were summarized as "loathsome."[32] In the midst of a city known worldwide for neon displays, there was no household electricity; in the midst of a desert with 115-degree summer heat, there was no air-conditioning. Garbage, old car parts, and trash were thrown into the dry wash alongside the railroad tracks, because the city garbage service would not collect on the reservation. Roadways were unpaved.

The Nevada agent felt unable to make a proposal for shifting administration of the Las Vegas Paiutes to other government bodies, because their condition was so underdeveloped that equalizing their quality of life with that of the surrounding non-Indians would be prohibitively difficult. The Paiute community was also gaining an unsavory reputation for poverty, drunkenness, violence, and unsanitary conditions, and the city did not want to take on the responsibility for native welfare. So the agency recommended acquiring right-of-way access to city streets for the landlocked property and then immediate sale.[33]

Relations between the Paiutes and other ethnic groups were becoming more complicated. Not only did they have to deal with Euramerican employers and government institutions, but just across the railroad tracks was an increasingly segregated African American district, the Westside, with which there were escalating racial tensions. In addition, over the last generation the "little reservation at Las Vegas [had] becom[e] of more importance as the town grows," wrote the agent, "as many Indians come there and live, making it their headquarters most of the time."[34] These "strange Indians" were not enrolled with the local reservation and were non-Paiutes, coming to Las Vegas for work. They gravitated to the Paiute community, where they found temporary shelter until they could locate a job and housing; there were often as many of these multitribal, transient, "urban" Indians living at the reservation as there were Paiutes.

The BIA, with no resident agent and with law-enforcement personnel no closer than Carson City, gratefully tolerated the extrajurisdictional intrusion of Las Vegas city police, until federal Public Law 280 transferred law enforcement openly to the state of Nevada, and hence the city, in 1955. Those police reported alcohol-related brawls, assaults, and spouse abuse averaging twice a week, a huge amount for so small a population; juvenile and solicitation arrests were constant. Policemen's complaints drew the attention of social workers, who were appalled by conditions in this pocket of poverty only blocks from the major tourist attractions on which the city's income depended. The mayor called the Paiute area a threat to public health and investigated dispersing the Paiutes into low-income housing facilities around town.[35] Paiutes were a federal matter, the BIA proclaimed defensively, and the city could not cavalierly sell the property and move the Indians; then the federal government had better do something about the conditions there, the mayor snapped back.

The BIA's own investigator then reported that "Las Vegas Colony is a hobo jungle, and a menace to the whole community." He thought it "futile to pursue the fiction that the continuation of Bureau activities offers any prospect for Indian betterment."[36] The Commissioner of Indian Affairs accepted that "the encroaching industrial developments and adjoining railroad and highway make unrealistic the development of the existing colony lands for residential purposes."[37] He supported sale of the property and relocation of the people to federal low-income housing. The necessary bill was defeated twice in Congress, because the Nevada state legislature refused to accept responsibility for Paiute welfare. The Las Vegas Paiute Reservation was not separated from federal administration.

Reversing the dismal conditions that those Paiutes faced on their reservation was a long and uneven process. In the 1960s the Las Vegas Paiutes joined with other Southern Paiutes throughout Utah, Arizona, and California in a lawsuit against the federal government, claiming illegal seizure and sale of tribal land to non-Indians without either treaty or due process of law. The Southern Paiutes won a negotiated settlement of $8.25 million in 1968.[38] The Las Vegas group insisted that their portion be distributed completely in per capita payments, setting aside none for community development or tribal economic projects. The $7,500 each person received was immediately spent on housing repairs, clothing, food, and other consumer goods, without altering the fundamental economic situation of the group.

Physical conditions improved slowly. In 1965 electricity and telephone lines were strung into the reservation for the first time. Federal programs added sewers and improved drinking water. In 1970 the Las Vegas Paiutes adopted a written constitution, establishing an elected tribal council that was legally recognized as a governing body with some administrative control over the reservation land and other specified powers, including the ability to pass ordinances, operate a police force and court to enforce those laws, hire lawyers to protect tribal interests, manage incomes from tribal enterprises, and set criteria for tribal membership.[39]

In 1975 the Las Vegas Paiutes converted the reservation's legal exclusion from state jurisdiction, which had so long denied them public schooling and police protection, into a benefit. In the early 1970s a tribe in Washington state had won a case in the U.S. Supreme Court that allowed them to sell cigarettes without charging state tobacco taxes, thus undercutting the price of off-reservation competitors. In 1975 a non-Indian proposed renting an abandoned building on the Las Vegas urban reserve for such cigarette sales, offering to share the profits. The dollar per carton savings attracted consumers and, despite legal protests from non-Indian competitors, more than three quarters of a million cartons were sold the first year. The tribe refused to renew the lease but instead bought a trailer, improved road access for customers, and went into business for themselves. Cigarette profits bought 2 ½ acres of land that gave Las Vegas Paiutes direct street access for the first time. The tribe then incorporated a construction company that built a community center and tribal headquarters on that land in 1981.[40]

With nearly 150 enrolled members and a little over 12 acres, Las Vegas Paiutes easily justified a request for more land. With their record of recent financial success, they won support from local, county, and state officials for 3,800 acres of surplus federal land straddling U.S. 95 at the foot of Mount Charleston. Congress added the parcel to the reservation in 1983.[41]

Tribal development of this land proceeded slowly. Some members who had been squeezed out of the tiny Downtown reservation brought in house trailers. The tribal council considered leases for light industry, but as always water supply was a problem. Nearly ten years later, after hiring a professional business planner, the Las Vegas Paiutes announced ambitious plans to build a resort complex on the property. This would require 150 times more water than had come with the land, and known water sources in the Valley were already overcommitted. The tribe announced that it would simply overpump its water right, and the Clark County Water District and the state of Nevada immediately filed suit. The tribe counterattacked with accusations of racism. Acrimonious negotiations won major concessions from the city, county, state, and water district, after which the tribal business manager calmly announced that this was only the first of five projected golf courses, several casino resorts, a theme park, and an artificial lake that they planned to construct on the property.[42]

The Las Vegas Paiutes had clearly learned the benefits that large-scale corporate investment could bring to confrontation politics. The tribe took out $13 million in bank loans, began construction, and opened the initial two golf courses for business in 1995. Then in the summer of 2000 they announced a $170 million expansion for the third and fourth golf courses and a casino/hotel/shopping complex.[43] Such expansion placed them into direct and, no doubt, continuing competition with established casino corporations and suburban developments for political influence and resources, particularly water. They had become players in the urban scene on a scale exponentially greater than had their parents only a generation before.

Profits from these successful enterprises were used partially for per capita distributions to tribal members. Reportedly amounting by 1990 to $40,000 annually per person, this had more than doubled ten years later.[44] Suddenly tribal membership was worth a great deal more than simply the right to live on reservation land and have access to Bureau of Indian Affairs programs. While disputes over tribal enrollment had occurred in the past, they escalated dramatically over the decade. In 1990 there was a move to alter the tribal constitution to tighten membership criteria from one-fourth Paiute ancestry to specifically one-fourth Las Vegas Paiute ancestry. Since the population of the band had always been small and traditional cultural definitions of incestuous marriage include a much wider range of relatives than did Nevada state law, this has meant that Las Vegas Paiute people had nearly always had to marry outside the band. With the passing of generations, a 25 percent band-specific ancestry requirement would have meant fewer and fewer qualified members and the eventual extinction of the group. It would also immediately disqualify a number of enrolled members and their descendants. There were challenges to the membership of a number of people on other grounds as well, including that of one young man whose father had been tribal chairman. He and others challenged the tribal court ruling and even appealed to the federal courts, which disclaimed jurisdiction, before negotiating an out-of-court settlement. Nevertheless, membership was whittled down to fifty-two adult members. Nine years later, just as the second wave of resort development was announced, this same young man, then tribal chairman, oversaw another purge of the membership rolls, further reducing membership to a mere forty adults. After more than three years and two cycles through the tribal court and appeals process, the Las Vegas Paiute Court of Appeals found that the disenrolled members had been denied due process of law. The court ordered that the lower tribal court itself should evaluate the evidence that the tribal council had used as the basis for its disenrollment decision and should determine whether the tribe's own procedures and constitutional provisions had been followed.[45] Many Paiutes saw this long squabble over membership as evidence that the tribe's financial success was threatening the very ethical and cultural foundations of the native community.

Conclusion

In the 150 years since California-bound non-Indians rolled into their territory, the lives of native Southern Paiutes have changed dramatically.[46] Quickly restricted in their free use of the land and its resources, Paiutes adapted to the new opportunities of material goods and wage employment brought by the newcomers. The establishment of a small federal reservation in the early twentieth century did not improve their physical conditions much and complicated their already complex relationships with non-Indian neighbors. When the city of Las Vegas grew up around them, flourishing on railroad traffic, federal dam construction, legalized gambling, and massive tourism, Paiutes were left out of the developing economy. Over the last 25 years, the Las Vegas Paiutes have striven to maintain their cultural identity with powwows, dance groups, and public displays of crafts, but more dramatically, they have established a recognized tribal government and used the legal benefits of their tribal status to advantage in a number of commercial projects. With their entry into the prevalent tourist-oriented economy of the city, they have met a degree of success that will change their ethnic community dramatically in years to come.

Paiutes are not the only Native American population in Las Vegas. During the second half of the twentieth century an increasing number of individual Indian families immigrated to the growing city. These included Mohaves and Hualapais from across the Colorado River, Navajos from Arizona, Ottos from the high plains, and even Mohawks from New York state. They came for jobs and stayed. Some sought out the local Paiutes, who could offer them only welcome. Not members of the Las Vegas Paiute tribe, they could not live on their reservation or participate in tribal government or enterprises. Rather, they settled in neighborhoods throughout the city. In the early 1970s these Indians organized the Las Vegas Indian Center, which has since then sponsored job-training programs, channeled information on housing and health facilities, sponsored workshops on education and money and alcohol management, and offered other practical services to Native American newcomers. These urban Indians formed a number of short-lived pan-tribal "clubs" for social contact, which put on potlucks, powwows, and dance exhibitions. Ironically, as indigenous Paiutes progressively reduced their enrollment numbers, the loosely organized, multitribal, urban Indians continued to expand, reaching a population of 10,600 by the year 2000.[47]

Notes

1. Inter-Tribal Council of Nevada, *Nuwuvi: A Southern Paiute History* (Provo: University of Utah Printing Service, 1976), 11; Robert H. Lowie, "Notes on Shoshonean Ethnology," American Museum of Natural History *Anthropological Papers* 20 (1924): 193.

2. Isabel T. Kelly, "Southern Paiute Bands," *American Anthropologist* 36 (1934): 555–56; John Wesley Powell and George W. Ingalls, *Report on the Condition and Wants of the Ute Indians of Utah, the Pai-Utes of Utah, Northern Arizona, Southern Nevada, and Southeastern California,* U.S. Congress, House of Representatives, Executive Document no. 157, 43rd Congress, 1st session, (Washington, D.C.: U.S. Government Printing Office, 1874), 10–11; Julian H. Steward, "Basin-Plateau Aboriginal Sociopolitical Groups," Smithsonian Institution, Bureau of American Ethnology *Bulletin* no. 120 (1938): 181–85.

3. Steward, "Basin-Plateau Aboriginal Sociopolitical Groups," 184–85.

4. Isabel T. Kelly and Catherine S. Fowler, "Southern Paiute," in *Great Basin,* ed. Warren d'Azevedo, *Handbook of North American Indians,* gen. ed. Willian Sturtevant (Washington, D.C.: Smithsonian Institution Press, 1986), 11:370–71; Lowie, "Notes on Shoshonean Ethnology," 195–201; Steward, "Basin-Plateau Aboriginal Sociopolitical Groups," 182–83.

5. Kelly and Fowler, "Southern Paiute," 375–77; Lowie, "Notes on Shoshonean Ethnology," 237–41, 245; Isabel T. Kelly, unpublished ethnographic fieldnotes from Southern Paiutes and Chemehuevis, section 18 Las Vegas, 1932–33, manuscript in University Archives, Bancroft Library, University of California, Berkeley, 54–57.

6. Isabel T. Kelly, "Southern Paiute Ethnography," University of Utah *Anthropological Papers* no. 69 (1964): 24–26, 121–30; Kelly and Fowler, "Southern Paiute," 380; Lowie, "Notes on Shoshonean Ethnology," 275, 283–88.

7. Kelly, "Southern Paiute Ethnography," 26–30; Kelly and Fowler, "Southern Paiute," 380.

8. Kelly, "Southern Paiute Ethnography," 29.

9. Isabel T. Kelly, "Southern Paiute Shamanism," University of California *Anthropological Records* 2 (1939): 151–67.

10. Thomas J. Farnham, *Life and Adventures in California and Scenes of the Pacific* (New York: Graham, 1846), 377.

11. Elizabeth V. Warren, *Armijo's Trace Revisited: A New Interpretation,* Master's thesis, University of Nevada, Las Vegas, 1974, 28.

12. John C. Frémont, *A Report of the Exploring Expedition to Oregon and North Callifornia, in the Years 1843–'44* (New York: A. Appleton, 1846), 160.

13. George Washington Bean, Diary, 1854–56, typescript copy, Ms. no. A-68, Utah State Historical Society, Salt Lake City, 16.

14. Dennis Casebier, "Camp El Dorado, Arizona Territory: Soldiers, Steamboats, and Miners on the Upper Colorado River," Arizona Historical Foundation, *Arizona Monographs* no. 2 (1970): 27, 33, 51, 52, 61–62; Martha C. Knack, "Nineteenth Century Great Basin Wage Labor," in *Native Americans and Wage Labor: Ethnohistorical Perspectives,* ed. Alice B. Littlefield and Martha C. Knack (Norman: University of Oklahoma Press, 1996), 153–55.

15. Daniel Lockwood to George Wheeler, February 28, 1872, in George Wheeler, *Preliminary Report Concerning Explorations and Surveys Principally in Nevada and Arizona,* U.S. Congress, Senate, 42d Congress, 2d Session, Executive Document no. 6 (Washington, D.C.: U.S. Government Printing Office, 1872), 75.

16. Martha C. Knack, "Role of Credit in Native American Adaptation to the Great Basin Ranching Economy," *American Indian Culture and Research Journal* 11 (1987): 43–65.

17. H. G. Parker to Commissioner of Indian Affairs, June 15, 1867, U.S. National Archives Microfilm M837, Records of the Nevada Superintendency, 1869–79, roll 1.

18. R. N. Fenton to H. Douglas, April 28, 1870, U.S. National Archives Microfilm M837, Records of the Nevada Superintendency, 1869–70, roll 1.

19. Edward Murtaugh to Commissioner of Indian Affairs, November 16, 1912, U.S. National Archives, Washington, D.C., RG 75, BIA Central Classified Files, 1907–39, 2.

20. Mary E. Cox to Commissioner of Indian Affairs, June 20, 1910, U.S. National Archives, Washington, D.C., RG 75, BIA Central Classified Files, 1907–39.

21. James Cox, advertisement, *Las Vegas Age,* June 17, 1911, 4.

22. Francis Swayne to Commissioner of Indian Affairs, November 6, 1911, U.S. National Archives, Washington, D.C., RG 75, BIA Central Classified Files, 1907–39, 3–4.

23. Francis Swayne to Commissioner of Indian Affairs, September 7, 1911, U.S. National Archives, Washington, D.C., RG 75, BIA Central Classified Files, 1907–39; Samuel Adams to Francis Swayne, November 27, 1911, U.S. National Archives, Washington, D.C., RG 48, Secretary of Interior Records, Indian Division.

24. F. M. Abbott to Edward Murtaugh, December 12, 1912, U.S. National Archives, Washington, D.C., RG 75, BIA Central Classified Files, 1907–39.

25. For relocation of agency, see E. G. Murtaugh to Commissioner of Indian Affairs, February 20, 1918, U.S. National Archives, Washington, D.C., RG 75, BIA Central Classified Files, 1907–39. For agency visitation, see John Alley, *Las Vegas Paiutes: A Short History* (Salt Lake City: University of Utah Printing Service, 1977), 11. For health and community violence, see Edward Murtaugh to Commissioner of Indian Affairs, August 28, 1913, U.S. National Archives, Washington, D.C., RG 75, BIA Central Classified Files, 1907–39.

26. For BIA water-development activities, see E. A. Farrow, Superintendent's Annual Narrative Report, 1932, U.S. National Archives Microfilm M1011, *Superintendents' Annual Narrative and Statistical Reports, 1907–1938,* Roll 98, 3; E. G. Murtaugh to Commissioner of Indian Affairs, December 15, 1915, U.S. National Archives, Washington, D.C., RG 75, BIA Central Classified Files, 1907–39. For water-supply failures, see Inter-Tribal Council, *Nuwuvi: A Southern Paiute History,* 126.

27. E. A. Farrow, Superintendent's Annual Narrative Report, 1933, U.S. National Archives Microfilm M1011, *Superintendents' Annual Narrative and Statistical Reports, 1907–1938,* roll 98, 6.

28. G. E. Lindquist, Report on the Paiute Indian Agency, Utah, 1933, U.S. National Archives, Washington, D.C., RG 75, Records of the Board of Indian Commissioners, Special Reports, 20.

29. L. B. Sandall, Superintendent's Annual Narrative Report, 1924, U.S. National Archives Microfilm M1011, *Superintendents' Annual Narrative and Statistical Reports, 1907–1938,* roll 88, 5.

30. A. R. Trelease to A. H. Kennedy, City Manager, September 1, 1955, U.S. National Archives, Washington, D.C., RG 75, BIA Central Classified Files, 1953–54, Accession 59A-643.

31. D. D. Carr to Mayor C. D. Baker, September 6, 1955, U.S. National Archives, Washington, D.C., RG 75, BIA Central Classified Files, 1953–54, Accession 59A-643.

32. F. Rittenhouse to Deputy U.S. Attorney General Joseph Lesh, February 3, 1956, U.S. National Archives, Washington, D.C., RG 75, BIA Central Classified Files, 1953–54, Accession 59A-643.

33. Nevada Indian Agency, Listing and Description of Tasks Remaining to be Done to Effect Complete Withdrawal of Bureau Services—Las Vegas, September 5, 1952, U.S. National Archives, Washington, D.C., RG 75, BIA Central Classified Accreted Files, 1940–56, Accession 68A-4937, Sect. c-5.

34. L. B. Sandall to Commissioner of Indian Affairs, June 5, 1923, U.S. National Archives, Washington, D.C., RG 75, BIA Central Classified Files, 1907–39.

35. 67 Stat. 588; 1955 Nev. Stat. 297; R. K. Sheffer, Chief of Police, to City Manager A. H. Kennedy, September 2, 1955, U.S. National Archives, Washington, D.C., RG 75, BIA Central Classified Files, 1953–54, Accession 59A-643; A. H. Kennedy to U.S. District Attorney Franklin Rittenhouse, January 10, 1956, U.S. National Archives, Washington, D.C., RG 75, BIA Central Classified Files, 1953–54, Accession 59A-643.

36. Homer Jenkins to Commissioner of Indian Affairs, March 8, 1956, U.S. National Archives, Washington, D.C., RG 75, BIA Central Classified Files, 1953–54, Accession 59A-643, 2.

37. Glenn L. Emmons to Joseph Lesh, April 13, 1956, U.S. National Archives, Washington, D.C., RG 75, BIA Central Classified Files, 1953–54, Accession 59A-643, 2.

38. 82 Stat. 1147.

39. Kenneth Anderson and Daisy Mike, "History of the Las Vegas Indian Colony," in Inter-Tribal Council of Nevada, *Personal Reflections of Shoshone, Paiute, and Washo* (Provo: University of Utah Printing Service, 1974), 20–21; Inter-Tribal Council of Nevada, *Nuwuvi: A Southern Paiute History,* 127; Las Vegas Paiute Tribe, Constitution and By-Laws, July 27, 1970.

40. *Washington* v. *Colville,* 447 U.S. 134; "Cigarette Tax Starts State 'Indian War,'" *Las Vegas Review-Journal,* December 13, 1977, 1; "State Taxes Indian Cigarette Sales," *Las Vegas Review-Journal,* July 3, 1980, 4A; "Access Road Planned to LV Paiute Colony," *Las Vegas Review-Journal,* August 27, 1981, 2B; "Paiute Center Readied," *Las Vegas Review-Journal,* September 2, 1981, 14B.

41. 97 Stat. 1383.

42. Phil Pattee, "Paiutes Plan Development of Newly Acquired Lands," *Las Vegas Review-Journal,* December 8, 1983, 4B; Mary Hynes, "Paiutes Seek Ground Water for Project," *Las Vegas Review-Journal,* May 18, 1994, 1A, 3A; Mary Hynes, "Paiutes Charge Racism in Water Denial," *Las Vegas Review-Journal,* August 25, 1995, 1B, 2B; Shaun McKinnon, "Water Settlement Reached with Las Vegas Paiutes," *Las Vegas Review-Journal,* April 13, 1996, 1A, 2A.

43. Dave Berns, "Tribe Set to Build New Resort," *Las Vegas Review-Journal,* June 29, 2000.

44. Alan Tobin, "Judge Alleges Pressure in Indian Case," *Las Vegas Review-Journal,* July 11, 1990, 1B, 2B; Greg Tuttle, "Blood Fight Splits Tribe," *Las Vegas Sun,* September 3, 2000, 1J, 5J.

45. Jeff Burbank, "NLV Judge Presides Over Paiutes," *Las Vegas Review-Journal,* February 24, 1991, 5B; Tuttle, "Blood Fight Splits Tribe"; Robert N. Clinton, Acting Chief Justice of Las Vegas Paiute Court of Appeals, Consolidated Opinion and Order no. CA-02-01, *Krishna Terry-Carpenter et al.* v. *Las Vegas Paiute Tribal Council,* and *Sheila Shearer and Darla Hatcher* v. *Las Vegas Tribe of Paiute Indians, Las Vegas Paiute Tribal Council, and Tonya Carter Means,* June 6, 2003.

46. Martha C. Knack, *Boundaries Between: The Southern Paiutes 1775–1995* (Lincoln: University of Nebraska Press, 2001).

47. Martha C. Knack, unpublished field notes, Las Vegas Urban Indian Populations, 1978–79; U.S. Department of Commerce, Economics and Statistics Administration, Bureau of the Census, 2000 U.S. Census, at http://www.factfinder.census .gov.

CHAPTER 4

The Mexicans

M. L. (TONY) MIRANDA

One in every nine people in this country was born beyond its borders. That amounts to 31.1 million people, the largest number of foreign born in the nation's history. For the last thirty years, over half of all the immigrants to this country have come from Latin America—most from Mexico.[1] The reasons for immigration to this country vary; however, the reasons Mexicans immigrate remain the same: to find prosperity and a better future for their children.

In Nevada, Mexican-descent peoples have a wide range of labels. Those who come to Las Vegas from New Mexico call themselves *Hispanos.* Those who migrate from Texas are *Tejanos.* Many from those states, as well as from California, identify themselves as *Chicanos* or Mexican Americans. Recent arrivals from Mexico call themselves *Mexicanos.* The term Mexican American or simply Mexican will be used here to describe the above-mentioned populations. The broader term Hispanic will be used to refer to all the ethnic and national groups originating in Latin America and Spain. Mexican-descent peoples constitute the vast majority of Hispanics in the Las Vegas Metropolitan Statistical Area, or MSA (77.8 percent) and in Nevada (78.7 percent) and a lower proportion of Hispanics in the United States (65.4 percent).[2]

A Brief Early History

With the end of the Mexican-American War in 1848, the United States annexed what had been the northwestern states of Mexico. Into the newly confiscated territory flowed thousands of non-Mexican immigrants from the eastern United States. From 1848 until 1900 Mexicans also migrated to the American Southwest in a continuous and legal, but small-scale, stream. It was not until the beginning of the twentieth century that migration from Mexico significantly increased, as Mexican migrant labor came to be relied upon in mining, in agriculture, and on the railroads throughout the Southwest.[3]

Although there were Mexican miners and mule skinners in Nevada prior to the Mexican-American War, it was not until the building of the railway system in the West that Mexican migration increased. Upon completion, the railroad connected the Mexican worker to the areas where his labor was needed. And in southern Nevada it was the railroad itself that employed hundreds of Mexican workers at the beginning of the twentieth century.[4]

Many Mexicans migrated north in the 1910s and 1920s to escape the turmoil of the Mexican Revolution, among them former Las Vegas judge John Mendoza's grandfather. He followed available work on the railroad to the hot, dusty desert town of Las Vegas, where a rail center between Salt Lake City and Los Angeles was developing. He worked at the roundhouse, which was eventually moved to Caliente, Nevada, and then at the mines around Sloan, Nevada.[5]

Mexican immigration fell off during the Great Depression of the 1930s, when thousands of Mexicans were forcibly repatriated. However, this flow was reversed during World War II, when labor shortages resulted in the recruitment of Mexican workers. The Bracero Program, implemented in 1942, was an agreement whereby Mexico would provide labor for American farms and railroads through a program that guaranteed Mexican workers a minimum wage, housing, transportation, meals, and medical care. The Bracero Program helped create an enormous migrant network throughout the west that introduced Mexican workers to farming and ranching regions. In Nevada these included the areas around Elko, Winnemucca, Reno, Carson City, Pioche, Caliente, Moapa, and Las Vegas. The Southern Pacific and Union Pacific Railroads contracted large numbers of Mexican nationals to work their lines in northern and southern Nevada, respectively.[6]

Whether arriving in Nevada through the Bracero Program or on their own, Mexicans usually found temporary, low-wage positions. Thus few were able to save enough to buy a home or attain the stability needed to organize politically. Prior to the 1960s the Mexican population was not large, nor had it been in Nevada long enough to establish Spanish-language media, Mexican restaurants, or other Mexican-owned enterprises.[7] This would change dramatically after the 1960s, when the Mexican population of Nevada, and particularly Las Vegas, soared.

The Boom in the Las Vegas Mexican Population

After growing significantly in the 1970s, the Mexican population in Las Vegas increased dramatically in the 1980s and 1990s. While reflecting national and statewide trends, the growth of the Mexican population in Las Vegas was much more pronounced than either. Nationally, the population of Mexican origin grew by 54.5 percent in the 1980s and 70 percent in the 1990s, reaching 23.1 million in 2000 and representing 8.2 percent of the national population and 65.4 percent of the U.S. Hispanic population. In Nevada the same periods witnessed growth of 52 and 270 percent, respectively, in the Mexican population. In 2000 the state's 309,013 Mexicans accounted for 15.5 percent of Nevada's population and 78.4 percent of its Hispanics. In the Las Vegas MSA the Hispanic population expanded rapidly in the 1980s and grew by 260.0 percent in the 1990s, reaching 322,038. After growing a phenomenal 333.7 percent in the 1990s, the Mexican population of the Las Vegas MSA reached 250,574, accounting for 77.8 percent of local Hispanics and 16.0 percent of total residents.[8]

A partial explanation of the rapid growth of Las Vegas's Mexican population is the high fertility rates among Mexican women. Precise information on Mexican fertility is not easy to obtain because of the undocumented status of many Mexican mothers, but data suggest that Mexican birthrates are at least 50 percent higher than those of Euramericans. Hispanics as a group were responsible for 45 percent of all births in the state in 1999.[9]

While the high birthrate accounts for part of the rise in Mexican population, migration to Las Vegas accounts for most of this growth. Economic opportunity is the lure for the vast majority of these new residents. Between 1980 and 2000, as earlier in the twentieth century, Mexicans came to Las Vegas from other points in the United States as well as directly from Mexico. The Southwest is the main domestic source of Mexican migrants to Las Vegas. Whether originally from Mexico or born in the United States, Mexicans from Texas, New Mexico, Arizona, and California have contributed significantly to Las Vegas's population boom. Twenty-two percent of the Hispanic population of the United States, predominantly Mexican, resides in the Los Angeles area, and Nevada Department of Motor Vehicles records reflect that most Hispanics registering vehicles and obtaining driver's licenses in Las Vegas are from California.[10]

Nonetheless, the majority of Mexican migrants to Las Vegas since 1980 have come directly from Mexico. Exact numbers are difficult to obtain, because undocumented workers constitute a significant proportion of these immigrants. What is clear is that, regardless of one's legal status in the United States, the push factor causing millions of Mexicans to abandon their country is the state of the Mexican economy. After four decades the "Mexican Miracle," a period of sustained economic growth that provided increased opportunity and improved standards of living for the majority of Mexico's rapidly growing population, ended abruptly in 1982 with the precipitous fall in international oil prices. During the remainder of the 1980s, unemployment rose dramatically while average wages fell by nearly half. This economic crisis propelled unprecedented numbers of Mexicans northward in search of a living. Despite a partial economic recovery in the 1990s, millions of Mexicans remained jobless and unable to secure a reasonable standard of living, and both documented and undocumented immigrants in massive numbers continued to seek work in the United States. Nevada's thriving economy, and especially the booming Las Vegas economy, are important pull factors for Mexican workers. The city was rated one of the top ten cities for Hispanics by *Hispanic Magazine* in 2003.[11]

Prompted by the unusually rapid growth of the Mexican community in Nevada, the Mexican government opened a consulate in Downtown Las Vegas in February 2002. Previously, Mexican nationals had to travel to San Bernardino, California, for the nearest Mexican consulate. The Mexican consul in Las Vegas, Berenice Rendon-Talavera, stated that the goals of her office are to serve the Mexican community living in Las Vegas and to foster closer relations between Mexico and the state of Nevada.[12]

According to a recent study conducted by the University of Nevada, Las Vegas (UNLV) Center for Business and Economic Research, industries that are particularly sustained by Hispanics/Mexicans in the local economy are services ($5.3 billion), construction ($4.7 billion) and retail and wholesale trade ($3 billion). Nevada's almost recession-proof boom economy, with its numerous service-industry jobs that offer relatively high wages for unskilled labor with minimal English-speaking ability, draws Mexican workers. Many of the people pouring the concrete foundations, framing, painting, and landscaping the new homes that sprawl across the Las Vegas Valley are Mexican. Moreover, Nevada's gaming industry and hotels offer jobs to Mexican American workers of all levels of education. Entry-level positions such as those of porters and maids are good stepping-stones in the state's hotel industry.[13]

In the Mexican American family it is common for several family members to work and contribute to the family's maintenance. One family member can earn $8.50 per hour, two members from the same family can earn $17 per hour, and so on. And like anyone else fortunate enough to have a university education, a Mexican American with a college degree can compete for managerial jobs in the tourism and gaming industry. Since many Spanish-speaking tourists from Latin America and Latinos from other parts of the United States vacation in Nevada, the Mexican American's bilingualism gives him/her an edge in hiring. It is projected that by 2004, Mexican Americans will be the largest workforce in Las Vegas. Another often overlooked reason why people of Mexican descent settle in Nevada is the lower cost of living compared to that found in other areas. Unlike California, Nevada offers housing that is relatively inexpensive, and there is no state income tax. In addition, particularly in comparison with California, commutes to work can be relatively short.[14]

Documented and Undocumented Immigrants

Two fundamental changes in U.S. immigration policy have facilitated the legal migration of Mexicans to the United States and given legal status to many who had arrived illegally. First, the abolition of the historic national origin quota system in 1965 and its replacement with a hemispheric allocations system caused a shift from predominantly European to Latin American and Asian immigration. This allowed for an increase in legal immigration from Mexico. Second, the Immigration Reform and Control Act (IRCA) of 1986 afforded legal residence to persons who could prove they had been in the United States since 1982. The bill granted citizenship to more than a million undocumented Mexican workers, while simultaneously making it illegal for employers to knowingly hire undocumented workers. Moreover, the bill had a family reunification clause that allowed entire Mexican families to live legally in the United States as long as one member of a household was a legalized resident.[15]

Despite these reforms, the impetus of potent push and pull factors continued to swell the ranks of undocumented workers in Las Vegas. Nevada is now home to at least 55,000 undocumented immigrants, or approximately 20 percent of the state's Mexican population. In addition to the availability of jobs that it offers, Las Vegas attracts undocumented workers because the Immigration and Naturalization Service (INS) is comparatively weaker than it is in other southwestern urban areas such as Los Angeles or Phoenix. The number of INS agents in Clark County did not grow appreciably between 1990 and 2000; understaffed and underequipped, the INS cannot cope with the crush of undocumented workers flocking to southern Nevada. Although the greatly enhanced presence of undocumented workers made it possible for the INS to apprehend 49 percent more illegal immigrants in 2000 than in 1995, the number of agents is still small enough that, after reaching Las Vegas, an undocumented worker has a good chance of staying.[16]

Since undocumented Mexican workers respond to U.S. Border Patrol tactics, recent changes in Border Patrol strategy may have resulted in an increase in the number of undocumented Mexican immigrants reaching Las Vegas. When U.S. authorities tightened border-crossing points in California and Texas in 1999 through mid-2000, undocumented workers headed for Las Vegas in growing numbers. The Border Patrol's increased presence in El Centro and San Diego, California, where the number of agents more than doubled, as well as in the El Paso, Texas, sector, forced undocumented workers into the blisteringly hot Arizona desert, then up and into Nevada's equally sweltering landscape.[17]

Once undocumented workers successfully cross the border, they become difficult to apprehend for repatriation to Mexico. There is no Border Patrol office in Nevada to stem the flow. If the local police or the Nevada Highway Patrol stops a van full of undocumented workers, the INS questions them. However, whether the Border Patrol apprehends them or not depends on the availability of agents in Blythe, California, or Yuma, Arizona. If they are unable to send an agent to pick up the undocumented workers, they are set free.[18]

Many undocumented workers have no higher than a sixth-grade education and thus seek the many Las Vegas jobs that require little education or skill: construction, landscaping, hotels and motels, and restaurants. The living conditions in Las Vegas are relatively less difficult than in Downtown Los Angeles, and at the same time rent is relatively inexpensive and transportation around the Valley is readily available. But despite Nevada's appeal to undocumented workers, all is not rosy. Employers often exploit undocumented workers. In construction, for example, U.S. citizens usually earn $15 an hour in addition to benefits, while an undocumented Mexican construction worker receives no benefits and is lucky if he or she earns $6 an hour. Some are paid according to the number of houses or units they complete in a given time period, forcing them to work on weekends and holidays without overtime. Undocumented workers commonly accept these exploitive conditions because they are able to make more in an hour than they would make in a day working in Mexico. To them, $6 an hour is a vast improvement over $6 a day. Many workers who might complain do not, fearful that their employer would call the INS and have them deported.[19]

Undocumented Mexican workers continue to flock to Nevada because businesses there, as well as in other areas of the country, need a cheap source of labor that they can exploit by withholding benefits and paying low wages. To Nevada's commercial and industrial enterprises, such workers are a convenient necessity. Indeed, they are ideal because they keep a low profile and do not complain, organize, or strike. When they are no longer convenient, they have historically been discarded; the undocumented worker has been likened to the disposable diaper "Pampers," in that after they have been used they are thrown away. It has been said that unless the government is willing to confront some very powerful business, commercial, agricultural, and industrial interests, undocumented workers from Mexico will continue to come to this country to earn a decent living. Moreover, immigration historically is driven by the local economy, and immigrants are more mobile and responsive to economic conditions than are homegrown workers.[20]

Mexico's president, Vicente Fox (elected in 2000), has made the question of Mexican migration to the United States a major issue. He has made it clear by word and deed that he considers people of Mexican origin, whether long-standing U.S. citizens or recent illegal immigrants, to be part of a greater Mexican nation. In concrete terms, he envisions broadening the North American Free Trade Agreement (NAFTA) to something akin to the European Union, in which citizens of all member countries are free to seek employment in any other member country. Through special development funds, he believes, enough well-paying jobs could be created to reduce the wage differential between Mexico and the United States, and thus the flow of job-driven immigration, at which point the border could be opened. As one might expect, the ideal of an open border with Mexico is objectionable to some in the United States. Opponents claim that if the border were opened, a quarter of Mexico's population, or approximately 25 million people, would migrate north to the Sunbelt states, including Nevada. However, after the September 11, 2001, terrorist attacks on the World Trade Center and the Pentagon, U.S. authorities have shown little disposition to liberalize immigration policy.[21]

Patterns of Migration

The creation of migration streams between specific source areas in Mexico and specific receiving areas in the United States depends upon the presence of established workers from previous waves of immigration, or migration networks. These networks are based on ties of kinship and friendship and on regional links; like gatekeepers, the established immigrants assist a recent arrival in the quest for work, housing, transportation, food, and social opportunities. The evolution of migration networks occurs gradually, when a few workers returning to Mexico with cash and material goods describe the economy and the job opportunities they have found. Thus begins the process that Richard C. Jones has labeled "migration channelization." As the links between the sending and the receiving areas increase, what he calls "migration facilitation" occurs.[22]

This migratory pattern is well established in Nevada. With every new Mexican worker links are formed in the migrant chain, and the chain expands quickly with links forming in specific areas. After initially taking entry-level jobs in construction, restaurants, hotels, and other low-paying occupations, immigrants become aware of their position at the bottom of the state's social and economic scale. This awareness motivates them to improve their status, and they begin to search for better paying and more secure positions. When a better paying job is found, the worker usually decides to settle permanently. It is at this point that he brings his family to live in Nevada. Usually, the worker passes his old job on to a relative or a friend.[23]

In addition to swelling the ranks of immigrants, Mexico's economic crisis of the 1980s also broadened the sources of immigration beyond the traditional labor-exporting states of Jalisco and Michoacán. For the first time large numbers of immigrants began to arrive from throughout Mexico, including central and southern states and the Federal District. The observer needs only to read the bumper stickers and window decals on vehicles driven by Mexicans in Las Vegas to recognize that important migration streams have been established from Zacatecas, Chihuahua, Morelos, Hidalgo, and numerous other states. Still, it is easier to immigrate from one of the traditional states, because earlier immigrant waves from them have established kinship and social networks in Nevada. Increasingly, Mexican immigrants are bypassing traditional entry points in Texas and California and heading straight for Nevada. In fact Clark County has become a major hub for Hispanic immigration in general and Mexican immigration in particular.[24]

Emergence of a Middle Class

In his review of the 1980 Census, Thomas Rodriguez found that Mexicans in Nevada were underrepresented in managerial, professional, technical, and administrative support positions and overrepresented in service, farming, production, and laborer occupations. Prior to the 1980s, Mexicans were occupationally disadvantaged because they were specifically hired for minimum wage, unskilled jobs. Since then, there has been substantial occupational diversification, with many Mexicans having moved on to better paying, more secure professional, managerial, and administrative positions. Occupational diversification leads to home ownership and establishing roots in the community. As I will discuss, a more stable Mexican population begins to create an organizational infrastructure and a Mexican cultural impact. As Mexican Americans gain positions of authority, their self-perception improves; simultaneously, the Euramerican perception of them is modified. As the social status of Mexican Americans improves, there is a concomitant decline in incidences of discrimination. An expanding and occupationally diverse Mexican American population eventually generates a Mexican American middle class, which becomes politically, socially, and economically organized. With occupational diversification come additional income and educational opportunities. Over time, the more affluent and better educated Mexican becomes middle class. A thriving Mexican American middle class emerged in Nevada in the 1990s.[25]

An indicator of the middle-class status of many Hispanics is their growing economic power in Clark County. Hispanics comprise 43 percent of the

eighteen-year-old to thirty-four-year-old demographic, and most of that number is Mexican American, making this population a very young market.
Since Hispanics in general, and Mexican Americans in particular, have larger
families—an average of 4.1 people compared to 2.9 people in non–Mexican
American households—it follows that they will be great consumers of goods
and services. They are having children and buying diapers, baby food, stroll-
ers, clothing; they are buying homes and furniture, paying mortgages and
utility bills. In fact, Las Vegas Hispanics alone have over $3.17 billion in an-
nual purchasing power. Of that amount they spend $2.55 billion a year on
retail sales and over $8.68 million daily on goods and services in Las Vegas.
Another important indicator of a developing middle class is the increasing
number of Mexican American entrepreneurs who have established small businesses in Nevada. In southern Nevada alone there are two thousand Mexican
American business enterprises.[26]

Mexican American Impact on the Clark County School District

The impact of the Mexican American population on the Las Vegas Valley is
blatantly evident in the nation's eighth largest and fastest growing school district, the Clark County School District. Of an approximate enrollment of
231,000 students in 2000, 57,750 students, or 25 percent, were Hispanic and
about 39,559 of those students were of Mexican descent. In other words, more
than one in four students in the Clark County School District is Hispanic,
while more than one in five and eight-tenths is of Mexican descent. Most of
the Mexican American children in the school district are enrolled in elementary or middle school and come from first-generation Mexican immigrant
families. Nearly all the schools in the district have a Hispanic enrollment of at
least 20 percent, with some schools reaching 70 percent. In 1990 there were
only about 150 Hispanic teachers in the district; by 2000 their number approached 600, and most were Mexican American.[27]

The growth of Clark County School District's English Language Learners
program in the 1990s reflects the explosion of immigration in the Las Vegas
area, including the burgeoning presence of Mexican immigrants, both legal
and undocumented. While the district's total enrollment has increased 50
percent since the 1992–93 school year, the number of students enrolled in its
program for non-English speakers skyrocketed 241 percent during the same
period. At the close of 1999, 14 percent of the district's students were enrolled
in the English program. By the academic year 2002–3 the number enrolled in
the English Language Learners program had tripled the 1992–93 figure, and
the school district spent $11.3 million on the program.[28]

The Mexican American Cultural Impact

After years of inequality, Nevada's Mexican Americans have begun to legiti-mize their language and culture. Mexican food has been incorporated into the mainstream diet. The Mexican dialect of Spanish is accepted by other Hispanics. In addition some Mexican and Mexican American music, like other Latin music, has crossed over to the general public. The presence of the Spanish language is so great that bilingual signs are commonplace and Spanish-language training is provided for police, social workers, and others whose professions place them in contact with Hispanics. Increasingly, Spanish-English bilingualism is a ticket to a good job.

Spanish-language television and publications are the primary media sources for Las Vegas's Mexican Americans. Eighty-eight percent of the Mexi-can Americans living in the Las Vegas area watch and read Spanish-language materials on a daily basis. Most Mexican American households in Las Vegas are predominantly Spanish speaking: 62 percent speak only Spanish at home. Twelve percent of Mexican American households are fully bilingual and speak equal amounts of Spanish and English at home, while 12 percent are fully bilingual and speak equal amounts of Spanish and English at home, revealing a high degree of acculturation.[29]

Local Spanish-language media also help build a sense of community. The growth of the Mexican American population in Las Vegas, combined with a failure of local mainstream newspapers to meet Mexican Americans' need for in-depth news and event coverage of their community, has resulted in the creation of Spanish-language newspapers. Four weekly newspapers are cur-rently in publication. The oldest is *El Mundo*, founded by Eddie Escobedo in 1980. *El Mundo*'s circulation has gone from five thousand in 1980 to thirty thousand today. The other newspapers are *El Heraldo, Latin American Press Spanish News*, and *El Tiempo Libre*, which plans to present the news in Span-ish on the Internet. In addition a section of a newspaper for Clark County's high-school students is printed in Spanish.[30]

Spanish-language radio and television generally appear after newspapers as a community's Hispanic population grows. Initially, only a few hours of Spanish-language radio are aired on stations owned by non-Mexicans. As the Mexican American population grows, a few radio stations convert to an all-Spanish-language format or new stations emerge to serve the rapidly increas-ing Mexican market. Spanish-language radio stations have proliferated in both northern and southern Nevada. Las Vegas has two AM radio stations broadcasting in Spanish—KLSQ 870 and KDOL 1280—and two FM stations, La Nueva at 103.5 FM and Super Estrella at 105.1 FM, which plays mostly contemporary Latin American music. There are three twenty-four-hour all-Spanish language television stations: Univisión's Spanish-language station KINC Channel 15, Telefutura's Channel 27, and Telemundo's Channel 39 KBLR. In addition each of the major network television stations in Clark County (Channels 3, 5, 8, and 13) employs Hispanic anchors, weather people, and reporters.[31]

Another important component of the increasing Mexican cultural impact is gastronomic. Nearly a hundred Mexican restaurants are listed in the local phone directory's yellow pages, and many others are neighborhood cafes that do not advertise. In addition most of the major hotel/casinos have their own Mexican restaurants. Mexican markets, bakeries (*panaderías*), and butcher shops (*carnicerías*) are found around the Valley where there is a significant Hispanic population. Among these are three market chains: the Supermercado del Pueblo, Carnicería Sonora, and Carnicería Mexicana.

Changes in the major supermarket chains, including Vons, Smiths, and Albertsons, indicate that the grocery business is reacting to a rapidly growing ethnic community and its dietary needs. Only a few years ago, one found canned chiles, bottled salsas, tortilla chips, and little more in the "Mexican foods" section of the neighborhood supermarket. Today, in addition to an expanded Mexican specialty aisle, Mexican foods are intermingled with "Anglo" foods throughout the store: tortillas and *pan dulce* with the breads, imported fruit juices and soft drinks in their respective aisles, tripe for the Mexican soup *menudo* at the meat counter, and a variety of fresh chiles—*serrano, chipotle, habanero, poblano, jalapeño,* and more—along with *tomatillos, cilantro,* and *jícama* coexist with the traditional staples of the vegetable section. This integration in the food realm reflects the process of syncretism in the cultural realm.

The Mexican cultural impact also includes the annual Cinco de Mayo and Mexican Independence Day (September 16) celebrations. These fiestas work at two levels. On the September 16 holiday, the Strip is transformed into a showcase of Mexican popular culture. Wealthy tourists from Mexico and Mexican Americans from around the United States are attracted to shows featuring Mexican and other Hispanic headliners such as singers Julio Iglesias (a Spaniard) and Linda Ronstadt and comedians such as Paul Rodríguez, Alex Reymundo, and George López. Championship boxing matches are also scheduled for the Independence holiday. In 1999, for example, the Mexican American welterweight champion, Oscar de la Hoya, unsuccessfully defended his title against Puerto Rican challenger Felix Trinidad at a major strip hotel. On the local level, the music and folkloric shows presented on these holidays have a social and psychological impact on Las Vegas's Mexican

American community. Traditional mariachi and *conjunto* bands play at Cinco de Mayo and Mexican Independence Day celebrations. These events allow Mexican working families to unwind, exchange information, and commiserate with each other. By reinforcing Mexican culture, fiestas to celebrate Mexican holidays act to ward off assimilation as well as generating money to support various Mexican religious, political, and social organizations.[32]

A number of cultural groups promote Mexican culture year-round. Ballet Folklórico Mexicano was founded by Martha Luevanos over twenty years ago. Today, Luevanos continues her work of promoting Mexican culture with the help of her children. México Vivo Dance Company, founded by the dynamic director and choreographer Icela Gutiérrez in 1995, has become the most recognized group in Las Vegas. This dance company not only promotes Mexican culture but the cultures of other Latin American countries as well. Tepuchalli, a folklore group founded by José Fajardo in 1996, consists mainly of teenagers and children. Espíritu Mexicano, founded in 2000 and directed by Juana María Quiñones, promotes Mexican folklore among children at the Cambridge Community Center. Priscilla Rocha and her organization HABLE (Hispanic Association for Bilingual Literacy and Education) founded the newest group, Herencia Mexicana. Another important cultural organization in Las Vegas is La Asociación de Autores y Compositores de Las Vegas. This group, founded by Jesús Amezquita in 1999, is made up of writers of traditional Mexican *corrido* and *balada* music. They meet every Friday night at Rafael Rivera Community Center. And finally, Roy Martin Middle School has implemented a program that promotes mariachi music, featuring its own mariachi band directed by Miguel Curiel.[33]

An important social institution for Mexicans is the Catholic Church. In the Roman Catholic Diocese of Las Vegas there are seventeen churches, five of which have services in Spanish. To many Las Vegas Mexicans the Virgin of Guadalupe is more than a cultural icon or religious symbol. Since they pray and converse with her daily, she is part of their everyday life. Some Mexican worshipers stand throughout the service facing an altar display of the Virgin surrounded by hundreds of bright red roses. They bow their heads in prayer and clutch their own wooden-framed paintings of the Virgin, which they bring as testaments of their faith. As the Mexican population grows and eventually settles, the church takes on a bigger role in Las Vegas. In addition to religious rituals, church functions include nonreligious activities such as assisting migrants through the bureaucratic maze to establish residency, registering them to vote, and helping them apply for amnesty through the IRCA.[34]

Other Christian denominations are competing with Las Vegas's Catholic churches for Mexican/Hispanic worshipers. There are over thirty non-Catholic churches in the Las Vegas/Henderson area offering worship in Spanish, including the Church of Jesus Christ of Latter-day Saints, Seventh-day Adventists, Evangélicos, Asamblea de Dios, Iglesia de Dios, and Southern Baptists. The Southern Baptists began making inroads into the Mexican/Hispanic community when they established the Iglesia Primera Bautista Hispana in 1968. In addition to Spanish-language services, these congregations offer Bible study, Sunday school, youth fellowships, brotherhood groups, and English classes.[35]

The local popularity of soccer in recent years also makes a Mexican cultural impact. Liga Azteca, one of several local leagues, is a Las Vegas soccer league consisting primarily of Mexican athletes. Founded in 1997 by Juan Araiza, the league has twenty to thirty teams, with six hundred players distributed among them. It is divided into an adult and a children's division, the latter consisting of players between the ages of six and sixteen. Generally, adults and children play every Saturday year-round on six fields at Orr Middle School behind the Boulevard Mall, within walking distance of many of the players' residences. Teams are sponsored by Mexican-related businesses such as La Barca, a Mexican seafood restaurant, and the newspaper *El Mundo* sponsors soccer tournaments each year. When the soccer season is in full swing in the spring, the local Spanish-speaking television station Univisión broadcasts game scores, highlights, and current information on all Latino-related soccer activities.[36]

Developing Political Power

The civil-rights movement of the 1960s caused changes throughout American society. Politically, in the Mexican American community, there were two extremes. At one end there was César Chávez and his nonviolent United Farmworkers movement, while at the other end were the activist Chicanos, at the time considered radical Mexicans, using a strategy of confrontation to fight for programs to benefit their communities. César Chávez, among other things, can be credited with improving working conditions for Mexican American migrant farmworkers throughout the Southwest. At the other extreme activist Chicano organizations focused their efforts upon a better, more meaningful education for Mexican American children in urban and rural areas. After many contentious battles with Euramerican opposition, federal funding became available for the implementation of bilingual/bicultural programs and Spanish-speaking teachers were recruited to teach them. The Teacher Corps was formed, in part, to train college students for teaching children of migrant farmworkers and for teaching in schools with large Mexican American enrollments.[37]

Mexican Americans coming to Nevada in the 1960s from other southwestern states described the Chicano movement in the state as being "way behind the times." While other universities in the West already had well-established Chicano studies programs, UNLV lacked such a program. It was not until 1971–72 that UNLV's Chicano students pressured the university administration to hire Chicano faculty and implement classes in Chicano studies. Though they were unable to achieve a freestanding Chicano studies program, the university did implement an ethnic studies program that included three Chicano studies classes and several African American classes.[38]

By the early 1970s broker organizations emerged and began operating in the political mainstream, taking the place of confrontational activism. A broker organization works within the system, negotiates or assists others to negotiate for funds and policies. By providing information and skills needed to successfully compete in the political arena, the activities of the broker organizations can be catalysts for economic, social, and political change.[39]

In Nevada, Mexican Americans—sometimes in cooperation with other Hispanics—have formed a variety of broker organizations. Two national organizations whose membership is mostly middle class and Mexican American have had sketchy histories in Las Vegas. The League of Latin American Citizens (LULAC), founded in 1929 in Texas, has been formed locally at least three times; in 2004 a chapter was functioning at the Community College of Southern Nevada. The American G.I. Forum, founded in 1948, grew out of a specific incident of discrimination against a Mexican American veteran of World War II who was refused burial by a funeral home in Three Rivers, Texas. Angered by this and other acts of discrimination against Mexican American veterans, Héctor García, a medical doctor, organized a veterans' group dedicated to fighting discrimination and improving the status of Mexican Americans. This organization functioned in Las Vegas in the 1970s but appears to be defunct today.[40] Two local organizations, the Nevada Association of Latin Americans (NALA) and the Latin Chamber of Commerce, have memberships more representative of the broader Las Vegas Hispanic community and have functioned since 1968 and 1976 respectively. In addition there is HABLE, an organization formed to help Hispanic parents who want to become involved in their children's education. Today the Latin Chamber of Commerce, whose president is Mexican American Tony Sánchez and whose secretary is Cuban American Otto Mérida, is probably the most influential Hispanic broker organization in Nevada.[41]

Another route to political power is the ballot box. Since voter registration data do not include ethnicity, determining the actual number of Mexican American registered voters is difficult. In Nevada, counting the number of

Spanish surnames on the voter rolls today would reveal about 54,000 registered Hispanic voters in the state. Using the figure of 78.7 percent as the proportion of Mexicans among Nevada's Hispanics, it could be estimated that Nevada has approximately 42,500 registered Mexican American voters, the majority of them in Clark County. Of course this method of calculating the Hispanic/Mexican American votes leaves out those who do not have Spanish surnames, such as state senator Bob Coffin, who claims Mexican descent through his mother.[42]

Historically, Mexican Americans in Las Vegas have had a very low voter registration rate. A number of factors explain this phenomenon. Many are undocumented or have resident status but not the citizenship required for voting; others have problems with English, face discrimination, or are primarily concerned with daily survival. The apathy that characterizes the general population affects Mexican Americans as well. Las Vegas mirrors the national scene: of the nearly 13 million Hispanics eligible to vote, only half are registered.[43]

The Alianza Latina and Hispanics in Politics (HIP) have conducted voter registration drives, supported by a broad coalition of organizations representing Las Vegas–area Hispanics, prior to recent elections. Representatives of these organizations appear at naturalization ceremonies to register as many newly minted citizens as possible. An effort backed by Spanish-language media resulted in the registration of 3,000 Mexican American voters in Clark County in 1998. Voter registration efforts by the Mexican American community and other Hispanic groups have become ongoing endeavors. Locally, volunteers with the Project 2000 Voter Registration Campaign worked feverishly from March to September 2000, going door-to-door to register Hispanic voters for the November election, using the slogan "su voto es su voz"—your vote is your voice. In 2002 Mexican American and other Hispanic activists across the country moved aggressively to register nearly a million Hispanic voters in time for the November presidential election.[44]

Mexican Americans in California and other western states have made visible strides in the political arena as a result of these kinds of efforts. In California, where Mexican Americans comprise 30 percent of the population, Cruz Bustamante was elected lieutenant governor in 1998, Ron Gonzales was elected mayor of the state's third largest city, San Jose, and Lee Baca was chosen sheriff of Los Angeles County, which has the largest sheriff's department in the United States. Most telling was Democratic U.S. Representative Loretta Sánchez's lopsided victory over conservative Republican "B-1" Bob Dornan in heavily Republican Orange County. In Colorado that same year (1998), Denver lawyer Ken Salazar was elected attorney general, while in New Mexico, Mexican Americans were elected to four statewide posts: attorney general, auditor, secretary of state, and treasurer. Mexican American political gains have snowballed since 1998, with the most visible victory being the election of Bill Richardson as governor of New Mexico in 2002.[45]

By contrast, despite the work of Hispanic organizations and unions, including the continuing efforts to register Mexican Americans and get them to the polls, Nevada Hispanics can claim no similar successes. In the history of Nevada one can count the number of Mexican Americans who have been elected to the state legislature on one hand. Today, fewer than 2 percent of Nevada's municipal elected officials and less than 3 percent of country commissioners are Mexican American. Until 2002, when Brian Sandoval was elected attorney general, no Mexican American had ever won statewide office in Nevada.

Of the various factors that account for Hispanics' inability to elect members of their own community to office, perhaps none is more important than Las Vegas's residential geography. In contrast to more traditional cities, Las Vegas, with the exception of the historically black Westside, did not develop ethnic neighborhoods until recently. While there are strong concentrations of Mexican Americans in North Las Vegas and northeastern Las Vegas, these have not yet jelled into cohesive, self-conscious communities with clearly defined political leadership.

Thus, despite the creation of a "Hispanic" district in the 1991 legislative redistricting, a non-Hispanic, Vonne Chowning, represented that district through the 1990s. In the 2001 redistricting, the legislature created several districts with strong Hispanic minorities. A number of Hispanic candidates contested these seats, but none succeeded. Under mandate from the state legislature, in 1999 the Las Vegas City Council expanded its membership from five to seven councillors in order to be more responsive to the city's ethnic minorities. However, in appointing their two new colleagues the sitting councillors named an African American and a Euramerican but no Hispanic. The response of the Hispanic community was more disappointment than outrage.[46]

On the other hand many southern Nevada office holders have Mexican Americans or other Hispanics working for them in visible positions to serve the Spanish-speaking community as well as harvest its votes. Some of the same politicians have Spanish-language Web sites and target Hispanics during elections. Nevada's senior U.S. senator, Harry Reid, has long employed Hispanics in key positions; his slim victory in the 1998 election can be credited to increased Hispanic voter turnout.[47] Yet, despite increasing their electoral clout, Mexican Americans are still represented overwhelmingly by non-Hispanics.

Mexican American Successes in Las Vegas

Only forty years ago, Las Vegas's relatively few Mexican Americans were thought of primarily as construction laborers, maids, and janitors. They were thought to be incapable of holding management positions or political office. Today the Mexican American population is a large, contributing part of Las Vegas society. Mexican Americans work in every profession, as physicians, dentists, lawyers, scientists, engineers, professors, university and college administrators, judges, businessmen/women, politicians, police officers, firefighters, and more.

Although there have been successes in every field, recent developments in education are most notable. In 1995, Larry Mason was elected the first Mexican American president of the Clark County Board of Education. In 2000 the Clark County School District hired its first Mexican American superintendent of schools, Carlos García, who in turn appointed Mexican American Agustín Orci as his new assistant for elementary education. Tony Flores was appointed vice president for finance at UNLV, and Ann Casados-Mueller was named assistant vice president for diversity at that institution. These are but a few examples of professional mobility among Mexican Americans.[48]

Conclusion

Nevada, especially the southern part of the state, is experiencing a demographic upheaval. The tide of Mexican immigrants and the rapid growth of Mexican American families are injecting new energy into the state. From Elko to Henderson, Mexican Americans are working at all levels of the economic system, in the traditional occupations of construction and kitchen workers and as professionals. At the same time they maintain their ethnic heritage by celebrating their traditional Cinco de Mayo and September 16 as well as by continuing traditional dietary, religious, and linguistic practices.

Some Mexicans took part in the mining of silver in the 1860s, others helped build the railroads throughout Nevada at the end of the nineteenth and beginning of the twentieth centuries, while at the beginning of the twenty-first century some (80 percent recent immigrants) are only just arriving in southern Nevada to work in all phases of construction, landscaping, the retail and wholesale trades, and the service industry.[49]

Today many Mexican Americans of the baby-boom generation are middle class, speaking mostly English, intermarrying, and spending a mountain of money on goods and services. Many of the younger generations perform a cultural balancing act, living in two worlds at the same time without losing anything in the translation. Some of the later generations are truly bicultural. They are entering their twenties and thirties with bilingual abilities, educational skills, and the beginnings of a demographic clout. While the newest arrivals have just crossed a geographic border, they are crossing or have crossed economic, political, social, and cultural borders.[50]

Nevada's Hispanic population in general, and the Mexican American population in particular, is young and getting younger, while the state's European American population is old and getting older. Nevada's past generations of Mexican Americans were forced to assimilate to the point of giving up their language, their foods, even their patriotic celebrations. Today's generation seems to be more assertively Mexican, more intent upon being bicultural. By holding onto the best of their Mexican cultural heritage, and being proud of it, they are not allowing themselves to become fully assimilated.[51]

Notes

1. See http://factfinder.census.gov/bf/_lang=en_vt_name=DEC_2002_SF3_U_DP2_geo_id=01000US.html; Associated Press, "Immigration Tide Continues with Changed Faces," *Las Vegas Review-Journal,* June 18, 2000, 1D; Michael Weissenstein, "Racial Picture Changes: Clark County Attracts Bulk of State's Soaring Population," *Las Vegas Review-Journal,* March 14, 2001, 1A, 19A. For a classic ethnographic study of Mexican immigration to the United States, see Manuel Gamio, *Mexican Immigration to the United States: A Study of Human Migration and Adjustment* (New York: Dover, 1971); for a more recent look at Mexican immigration, see Jorge Durand et al., "Mexican Immigration to the United States: Continuities and Change," *Latin American Research Review* 36, no. 1 (2001): 107–27.

2. For Nevada, see Latin Chamber of Commerce, *Year 2000 Business Directory,* (Las Vegas: Hispanic Publishing Group, 2000); http://mumford1.dyndns.org/cen2000/Hispanic Pop/HspPopData32st.htm; http://mumford1dyndns.org/cen2000/HispanicPop/Hsp Report/MumfordReport.doc. For the West and United States, see Linda Robinson, "Hispanics Don't Exist," *Special Report for U.S. News Report,* May 11, 1998; Terrence W. Haverluk, *Of Hispanics in the American West: A Descriptive Model for Understanding the Wider Distribution and Increasing Influence of Hispanics in the American West,* at http://hreweb.utsa.edu/. . /test/publication/04//04wpwebpub.htm, August 1994, 2–42.

3. M. L. Miranda, *A History of Hispanics in Southern Nevada* (Reno: University of Nevada Press, 1997), 30–49. For general histories of the Mexican experience in the United States, see Rodolfo Acuña, *Occupied America: A History of Chicanos* (New York: Harper and Row, 1988); James Diego Vigil, *From Indians to Chicanos: The Dynamics of Mexican-American Culture* (Prospect Heights, Ill.: Waveland Press, 1998); Manuel G. Gonzáles, *Mexicanos: A History of Mexicans in the United States* (Bloomington: Indiana University Press, 1999).

4. Miranda, *A History of Hispanics,* 74–87; Haverluk, *Of Hispanics,* 2–42.

5. Haverluk, *Of Hispanics,* 7; Miranda, *A History of Hispanics,* 74–86.

6. Haverluk, *Of Hispanics,* 8; Miranda, *A History of Hispanics,* 95–99, 74–86. For more about Mexican workers see John Mason Hart, *Border Crossings: Mexican and Mexican-American Workers* (Wilmington, Del.: Scholarly Resources, 1998).

7. Miranda, *A History of Hispanics,* 74–86.

8. Ibid., 101; Latin Chamber of Commerce, *Year 2000,* 7–8; http://mumford1 .dyndns.org/cen2000/HispanicPop/HspPopData32st.htm; http://mumford1dyndns .org/cen2000/HispanicPop/HspPopData/4120msa.htm/; U.S. Census Bureau's Public Information Office, *Census Bureau News: Hispanic Data,* at http:/www.census .gov/ Press-Release/www/1999/cb99-253.html, September 11, 2000, 3 of 5; Jeff Hard castle, *Nevada Age Sex Race and Hispanic Origin Estimates and Projections 1990 to 2010* (Reno: Nevada State Demographer's Office, University of Nevada) June 2000, 4; Weissenstein, "Racial Picture Changes," 19A. For case studies of Mexicans in other cities and states, see James B. Lane and Edward J. Escobar, *Forging a Community: The Latino Experience in Northwest Indiana, 1919–1975* (Chicago: Cattails Press, 1987); Shirley Achor, *Mexican Americans in a Dallas Barrio* (Tucson: University of Arizona Press, 1978); Ricardo Romo, *History of a Barrio: East Los Angeles* (Austin: University of Texas Press, 1988); Dennis Nodin Valdes, *Al Norte: Agricultural Workers in the Great Lakes Region, 1917–1970* (Austin: University of Texas Press, 1991); Douglas E. Foley et al., *From Peones to Politicos: Class and Ethnicity in a South Texas Town, 1900–1987* (Austin: University of Texas Press, 1988); Latin Chamber of Commerce, *Year 2000,* 4, 6; Michael Weissenstein, "First Census Results Released: State Gains Seat in House," *Las Vegas Review-Journal,* December 29, 2000, 1A.

9. Haverluk, *Of Hispanics,* 2–42; Ken Ward, "C'mon Down to Our School," *Las Vegas Review-Journal,* August 30, 2000, 9B; http://factfinder.census.gov/servlet/QTTable ?_ts=77724463811.

10. Latin Chamber of Commerce, *Year 2000,* 6; Launce Rake, "Hispanics Fight Political Exclusion: Rapidly Growing Community Seeks Fair Share of Power," *Las Vegas Sun,* October 3, 1999, 1E, 5e; Ed Vogel, *Las Vegas Review-Journal,* "Hispanic Population Growth Has Yet to Hit Legislature," September 1, 2000, 1A–4A.

11. Soledad Loaeza, ed., *Mexico 1982–1988: Los tiempos del cambio* (Mexico City: Fondo de Cultura Económico, 1992); Christine Granados, "Top 10 Cities for Hispanics, 10: Las Vegas, Nevada," *Hispanic Magazine,* at www.hisp.com/may96/lasvegas .html., on-line magazine.

12. Sean Whaley, "Mexico Announces Plan to Establish Las Vegas Consulate: Downtown Office to Open in Early December," *Las Vegas Review-Journal,* October 6, 2001, 2B; Juliet V. Casey, "Senators Announce Name of New Consul of Mexico in LV," *Las Vegas Review-Journal,* November 9, 2001, 7B; Juliet V. Casey, "Consult to Help Community," *Las Vegas Review-Journal,* January 29, 2002, 2B; Juliet Casey, "New Mexican Consulate Busy on Opening Day," *Las Vegas Review-Journal,* February 5, 2002, 4B.

13. Hubble Smith, "Hispanic Impact Noted: UNLV Report Cites Effect on Jobs, Output, Revenue," *Las Vegas Review-Journal,* July 8, 2003, 1D, 5D; Michael Weissen-

stein, "State's Growth Spurt Tops for 14th Year," *Las Vegas Review-Journal,* December 29, 1999, 5B; Granados, at www.hisp.com/may96/lasvegas.html; Jace Radke, "Hispanics Flocking to Valley: Clark County Population Boom Fastest in Nation," *Las Vegas Review-Journal,* September 15, 1999, 1A, 8A; Genaro Armas, "Nevada Grew Fastest in '90s," *Las Vegas Review Journal,* August 30, 2000, 1A.

14. Granados, at www.hisp.com/may96/lasvegas.html; Latin Chamber of Commerce, *Year 2000,* 6; Steve Kanigher, "Census Charts Changes in LV," *Las Vegas Sun,* September 10, 1998, 1–3, at www.lasvegassun.com/sunb . . . 9010.html?census+charts +changes.

15. Haverluk, *Of Hispanics,* 10; Miranda, *A History of Hispanics,* 132–34.

16. Kim Smith, "Border Squeeze Funnels Aliens to Vegas," *Las Vegas Review-Journal,* December 5, 1999, 1E, 5E. Pauline Arrillaga, "Border of Fear," *Las Vegas Review-Journal,* August 20, 2000, 23A, 24A; Megan Stack, "Agents, Immigrants Locked in Conflict on Nation's Edge," *Las Vegas Review-Journal,* August 20, 2000, 25A.

17. Smith, "Border Squeeze", 1E, 5E.

18. Ibid.

19. Ibid.

20. Ibid.

21. Associated Press, "Leader Calling for Open Border," *Las Vegas Review-Journal,* August 18, 2000, 24A; Mary Jordan, "Mexico's President-Elect Shares Visions in the U.S.," *Las Vegas Review-Journal,* August 25, 2000, 5A; Associated Press, "Bush Touts Free Trade in Latin America, with One Exception," *Las Vegas Review-Journal,* August 26, 2000, 4A; Letta Tayler, "Anti-Terrorism Tactics Take Toll South of the Border," *Las Vegas Review-Journal,* October 4, 2001, 7A.

22. Haverluk, *Of Hispanics,* 11, 42; Armas, "Nevada Grew Fastest," 1A and 5a; Richard C. Jones, "Channelization of Undocumented Mexican Migrants to the U.S.," *Economic Geography* 58 (1982): 88–98. Haverluk's theory is timeless; he is referenced throughout this chapter for his theory, not for data.

23. Haverluk, *Of Hispanics,* 12; Associated Press, "Census Figures Reveal Growing Ethnic Diversity in United States," *Las Vegas Review Journal,* September 15, 1999, 13A; Douglas Massey, Rafael Alarcon et al., *Return to Aztlan: The Social Process of International Migration from Western Mexico* (Berkeley: University of California Press, 1987), 161.

24. Haverluk, *Of Hispanics,* 11; Smith, "Border Squeeze," 1E, 5E.

25. Thomas Rodriguez, *A Profile of Hispanics in Nevada: An Agenda for Action* (Las Vegas: Latin Chamber of Commerce Publications, 1982), 23; Haverluk, *Of Hispanics,* 16, 17, 26.

26. Latin Chamber of Commerce, *Year 2000,* 6; Radke, "Hispanics Flocking to Valley," 8A.

27. Radke, "Hispanics Flocking to Valley," 8A; Latin Chamber of Commerce, *Year 2000,* 6; Genera Armas, "Nevada Grew Fastest in '90s," *Las Vegas Review Journal,* August 30, 2000, 1A, 5A.

28. Latin Chamber of Commerce, *Year 2000,* 6; Ken Ward, "Getting Bigger, Not

Better," *Las Vegas Review Journal,* May 15, 2002, Review Journal Internet Archive; Juliet V. Casey, "Study Reveals Hispanics' Contributions," *Las Vegas Review-Journal,* April 17, 2003, 2B.

29. Latin Chamber of Commerce, *Year 2000, 6.*

30. Haverluk, *Of Hispanics,* 19; Debra D. Bass, "Spanish Spreads Across Valley," *Las Vegas Review-Journal,* September 5, 1999; Weissenstein, "Hispanics Flocking to Valley," 19A. Haverluk's data comes from the period 1999–2003.

31. Miranda, *A History of Hispanics,* 175; Haverluk, *Of Hispanics,* 19; Bass, "Spanish Spreads Across Valley," 19A; Irma Varela-Wynants, Clark County Department of Parks and Recreation, personal communication to author, February 12, 2002.

32. Haverluk, *Of Hispanics,* 25; Michael Squires, "Growing Hispanic Population Finds Niche," *Las Vegas Review Journal,* March 14, 2001, 1A, 18A; Ken White, "Universal Message: Mexico Vivo Keeps Folklore Alive with Children's Shows," *Las Vegas Review-Journal Neon: Guide to Entertainment,* July 7, 2000, 48J; Haverluk, *Of Hispanics,* 18; Laurie K. Sommers, "Inventing Latinismo: The Creation of 'Hispanic' Panethnicity in the United States," *Journal of American Folklore* 104, no. 61 (1991): 32–53.

33. Mike Weatherford, "Fighting for Attention: Latin Comics, Musicians Hope to Attract More Than Boxing Fans," *Las Vegas Review-Journal Neon: Guide to Entertainment,* September 17, 1999, 3J, 27J; Haverluk, *Of Hispanics,* 25; Irma Varela-Wynants, personal communication to author, February 12, 2002.

34. Advertisement in *Las Vegas Review-Journal,* April 17, 2003, 16A; Leticia Huerta, "Faithful Fill Churches for Virgin's Feast Day," *Las Vegas Review-Journal,* December 13, 2002, 1B, 10B; Haverluk, *Of Hispanics,* 25.

35. Patricia Morgan, "Ethnic Churches' Foreign-born Congregate for Services," *Las Vegas Review-Journal,* October 18, 1988, 1AAA, 4AAA; *Frontier Telephone Book, Paginas Amarillas,* 2002–3, 36–42.

36. Salvador Avila, "Community Institutions: Mexican American Soccer Leagues," August 15, 2000, e-mail communication to author; Haverluk, *Of Hispanics,* 18.

37. Foley, *From Peones to Politicos,* 96; David Montejano, *Anglos and Mexicans in the Making of Texas, 1836–1986* (Austin: University of Texas Press, 1987), 278; F. Chris García and Rudolph O. de la Garza, *The Chicano Political Experience: Three Perspectives* (North Scituate, Mass.: Duxbury Press, 1977), 163; Mike O'Callaghan, "Work of Farm Labor Organizer Cesar Chavez Still with Us," *Las Vegas Sun,* March 16, 2002, 12B; Haverluk, *Of Hispanics,* 25.

38. Haverluk, *Of Hispanics,* 2–42.

39. Miranda, *A History of Hispanics,* 414; Acuña, *Occupied America,* 379.

40. Irma Wynants, personal communication to author, February 5, 2001; Ivet Albaba, personal communication to author, May 4, 2004.

41. Acuña, *Occupied America,* 147–48; Miranda, *A History of Hispanics,* 142; John G. Edwards, "Lawyer Works as Advocate for Burgeoning Hispanic Community," *Las Vegas Review-Journal,* July 6, 2003, 1F.

42. Miranda, *A History of Hispanics,* 148–51, 184.

43. Ibid., 148–51; Rake, "Hispanics Fight Political Exclusion," IE, 5E.

44. Rake, "Hispanics Fight Political Exclusion"; "Voter Registration Drive Shifts into High Gear," *Latin Chamber News* II, no. 1 (Spring 2000): 1; Vogel, "Population Growth," 4A.

45. Associated Press, "Sanchez Symbol of Democrats' Hope," *Las Vegas Review-Journal,* September 28, 1998, 4B; Nedra Pickler, "Record Number of Hispanics, Women in House," *Las Vegas Review-Journal,* January 7, 2003, 7A.

46. Jon Ralston, "Hispanic Vote Is Suddenly Desirable," *Las Vegas Sun,* August 27, 2000, 2D. A coalition of Mexican and Cuban American voters, with a large mainstream constituency, was able to help elect a young Hispanic of Cuban descent, Dario Herrera, to the Clark County Commission in 1998. Prior to that he had been in the state legislature. He lost a bid for Congress in 2002. LaRed Latina of the Intermountain Southwest, *Community Leaders and Organizations,* n.d., at http://www.inconnect.com/~rvasquez/Vorgans.htm, 2; Al Gibes, "Senator, Family History Highlight Another Net Notes," *Las Vegas Review-Journal,* June 11, 2000, 1L.

47. Associated Press, "Study: Immigration Affects Congressional Seats," *Las Vegas Review-Journal,* October 7, 1998, 9A; Ed Vogel, "Ensign Gains 11 Votes After All Counties but One Finish Recount," *Las Vegas Review-Journal,* December 9, 1998, 1B, 5; Associated Press, "Bush Aggressively Courts Hispanic Support," *Las Vegas Review-Journal,* June 29, 1999, 3A.

48. Dario Herrera, "Impact of Hispanics on Southern Nevada's Growth—Social, Economical, and Political," *Latin Chamber News* (Spring 2000): 4; Vogel, "Hispanic Population," 4A; Ed Vogel, "Nevada Ready to Draw Lines on Lack of Hispanic Legislators," *Las Vegas Review-Journal,* April 9, 2001, 1A, 5A; Miranda, *A History of Hispanics,* 202; Ralston, "Hispanic Vote," 2D; Lisa Kim Bach, "Garcia Appoints Assistant," *Las Vegas Review-Journal,* August 2, 2000, 1B, 2B; "Assistant Vice President for Diversity at UNLV Named," *Las Vegas Review-Journal,* November 10, 2001, 6B.

49. M. L. Miranda, "Exploration, Development, and Discrimination: The Hispanic Experience in the Great Basin of Nevada from 1540 to 1905," *National Social Science Journal* 1, no. 5 (Spring 1990): 54–66; Smith, "Hispanic Impact Noted," July 8, 2003, 5D.

50. John Leland and Veronica Chambers, "Generation N," *Newsweek,* July 12, 1999.

51. Ibid.

CHAPTER 5

The African Americans

EARNEST N. BRACEY

Early on May 29, 2003, an arson fire burned down the Moulin Rouge casino on Bonanza Road at the edge of historically black West Las Vegas. The event was of symbolic importance to Las Vegas's African American community for many reasons. The Moulin Rouge had opened in 1955 in a legally and culturally segregated part of town. It became the first integrated hotel-casino and later the site of a historic meeting at which business and political leaders agreed to end segregation in Las Vegas hotel-casinos. It went through a variety of owners, white and black, most lacking the capital to redevelop the once-proud resort. It also suffered from being surrounded by the kinds of lower-income homes and businesses to be expected in a segregated area, and from time and opportunity depriving West Las Vegas of some of its leaders. Thus, the Moulin Rouge's story involves hope and promise, national factors and local changes—it is a microcosm of the past and present.[1]

Black Migration and the Establishment of a Black Community

The black migration to Las Vegas must be understood as a microcosm of black history itself. As historian Darlene Clark Hine wrote, "Central to all of this black movement was the compelling quest for that ever so elusive, but distinctly American property: freedom and equality of opportunity." Indeed, the great migration to the West, and to Las Vegas, was caused by push and pull factors: an effort to escape racism, poor educational facilities, disfranchisement, and physical threats, to seek opportunities and more freedom. Blacks had looked west at the height of the fur trade, and other blacks followed during the gold rush and the building of the transcontinental railroad during the 1860s. The end of the Civil War meant not only the end of slavery but troubled times in the South; with the economy shattered and whites out to reimpose a form of slavery, blacks who could do so went west. Only a few hundred blacks lived in nineteenth-century Nevada, especially after the Comstock mining boom went bust in the early 1880s and a twenty-year depression began. But until 1900, Las Vegas remained no more than a few ranches with white owners and, occasionally, Paiute workers—and the tiny town would prove to be anything but an oasis for African Americans.[2]

The auction that began Las Vegas on May 15, 1905, marked the true beginning of the city's African American population. The first black residents arrived to help build the San Pedro, Los Angeles and Salt Lake Railroad, which prompted the creation of the Las Vegas townsite; these workers lived first in camps and later, when they were part of the maintenance crew, in railroad dormitories near the depot at Main and Fremont. Since the population was still less than one thousand by the time of the first official Las Vegas census in 1910, African Americans obviously were few in number—only sixteen, including the Lowes, who were believed to be the first black family to settle in town. But from the beginning, they faced racism and segregation. The railroad, which owned the original townsite, had set aside two blocks at the northern end of town as the only places where liquor could be sold. Block 16 eventually was filled with bars that had second-story rooms for prostitutes, but Las Vegas proved too small to attract more businesses to sell alcohol in Block 17, Second Street (now Casino Center), between Ogden and Stewart. Instead, railroad agent Walter Bracken and other executives redlined minorities, making the block Las Vegas's first segregated area. While the process was not systematic, blacks and other minorities allowed to live within the boundaries of the townsite had to go to the far end or perhaps the other side of the tracks.[3]

That area west of the tracks was called Oldtown, Ragtown, or McWilliams Townsite. Surveyor John T. McWilliams laid out his townsite, which extends from A to H Streets and from Washington to Bonanza, to compete with the town across the track. This became the historic West Las Vegas or Westside. It burned late in 1905, not only because its buildings were almost entirely canvas or wood, but because it had no running water; the main reason for the site's failure is that the railroad had sewn up the water rights. But as far as the local white power structure was concerned, that made the less desirable land the perfect place to segregate ethnic minorities.[4]

Minorities remained few in number until the building of Boulder—later Hoover—Dam. To be sure, some fared better than others: A. B. "Pop" Mitchell arrived in the early 1910s, owned a ranch and resort, and cofounded churches and civic groups, and he and his wife, Minnie, were the parents of the first black child born in Las Vegas. But the white community evinced little interest in its black neighbors, and a Ku Klux Klan chapter's formation in the 1920s did nothing to make blacks feel welcome in Las Vegas. By 1930 Las Vegas's black populace had reached 143 out of 5,165 in the city—enough to support housing and small businesses in West Las Vegas and to prompt the formation of a Las Vegas chapter of the National Association for the Advancement of Colored People (NAACP) in 1926, with Mitchell as its first president. Some of these residents, and others who came west to seek employment when Six Companies began building the dam in 1931, were disappointed that the federal contractors refused to hire them and trade unions excluded them from membership. Blacks responded by forming the Colored Citizens Labor and Protective Association of Las Vegas on May 5, 1931, less than two months after dam construction began. By September membership reached 247, demonstrating the increasing black population. In the months to come, national and regional NAACP representatives visited the dam and neighboring Las Vegas several times, meeting with politicians and local NAACP leader Arthur McCants. Finally, federal officials pressured Six Companies into hiring the first ten black workers on the dam in July 1932. One Las Vegas historian called it "a token response": by the time of the dam's completion in 1936, more than twenty thousand different whites had worked on it but only forty-four blacks, only a few of them several different times.[5]

As the dam became barely integrated, Las Vegans reacted with more stringent segregation. With gaming legalized in 1931 and small casinos proliferating on Fremont Street, operators apparently reasoned that tourists and recent migrants from the South preferred not to mingle in Las Vegas with those segregated back home. And while Mayor Ernie Cragin joined in pushing Six Companies to hire blacks, he also joined in redlining West Las Vegas and segregating black customers in his Fremont Street theatre, the El Portal. In 1939 these developments prompted local black leaders to support a legislative measure to integrate public accommodations, but the bill died in committee. That year, too, white west Las Vegans even tried to segregate their area into white and black sections; the city commission said no, thanks in part to the work of R. L. Christensen, president of the Las Vegas Colored Progressive Club.[6]

The next federal project to speed local growth greatly affected local blacks—but less positively than they had hoped. In 1941, with federal help, Basic Magnesium opened a plant southeast of town, complete with a townsite. The news inspired a black migration from the South, especially two depressed towns—Tallulah, Louisiana, and Fordyce, Arkansas. In three years, according to population estimates, while the white populace also expanded rapidly, well over three thousand African Americans lived in Las Vegas and the surrounding area. As with its predecessors on the damsite, the operators of Basic Magnesium had no desire to accede to worker demands—whether it was whites trying to unionize or blacks simply requesting employment. Again, an assortment of public and private pressures compelled the federal job site to hire blacks—again, mainly for menial or dangerous, low-paid labor. Basic also provided a segregated housing tract for its black workers: Carver Park, with about 324 units varying from dormitories to three-bedroom bungalows.[7]

This combination of Basic's discrimination and the huge influx of blacks profoundly changed West Las Vegas. As the magnesium plant opened, a new army air corps gunnery school began north of Las Vegas and the El Rancho Vegas's construction marked the beginning of the Strip. Just as Highway 91 and Fremont Street attracted white visitors, black soldiers barred from white establishments frequented West Las Vegas—until problems with local police and a 1944 riot prompted a city crackdown. Nor did all black migrants seek work at Basic; they fanned out through Las Vegas. Accordingly, West Las Vegas increasingly developed its own business community and cultural life. It also developed its own casino district along Jackson Street, thanks in part to Las Vegas city commissioners' blocking a proposed interracial hotel-casino at Main and Bonanza, just east of the segregated community. Consequently, even blacks working at Basic often preferred to move west of the railroad tracks, despite the lack of paved streets and amenities. In the 1940s and 1950s the New Town and Tavern, the Cotton Club, the Brown Derby, the El Morocco, and the Ebony Club, among others, attracted a black clientele—and black entertainers who finished their shows on the Strip but had to stay in West Las Vegas motels and boardinghouses.[8]

With the war's end and Las Vegas's growth, the fissures between black and white deepened. Under Cragin's leadership, city officials destroyed 375 West Las Vegas houses because they failed to meet building standards. The city declined to pave the main artery (E Street) or install public works, but in 1947 it built a swimming pool—which freed Las Vegas leaders to ban blacks from pools east of the tracks. But this discrimination served a unifying purpose. During the war, a police commissioner forced a West Las Vegas tavern to close for "catering to an interracial clientele." This kind of segregation had the obviously unintended—and, for the sake of social organization, highly beneficial—effect of bringing the black community closer and concentrating the population. The result would change Las Vegas.[9]

The Black Civil-Rights Struggle and Protest Organizations

As Las Vegas boomed after World War II, the public became aware of the glittering hotel-casinos and the role of organized crime—and the town's reputation as "the Mississippi of the West." In 1954 *Ebony* magazine scathingly described Las Vegas as like "some place in Mississippi—downright prejudiced" and "rigidly Jim Crow by custom." Many black Las Vegans lived in crowded and often crumbling houses without indoor toilets, running water, or air-conditioning. But change was in the air—from both outside and inside.[10]

As they did in the wake of new federal policies and U.S. Supreme Court decisions at the national level, whites showed signs of gradual change while blacks became increasingly activist. The federal Fair Housing Act of 1949—and a survey that year that showed 80 percent of West Las Vegas housing to be below building standards—led to the building of Marble Manor, consisting of 100 rental units. In defeating Cragin for a fourth term as mayor in 1951, engineer and former state senator C. D. Baker promised to pave Westside streets—and did. He also sought to direct the construction of Interstate 15 through West Las Vegas, which would lead to more federal funding for urban renewal—and 160 single-family homes were built as a result. In 1953 Las Vegas attorney George Rudiak introduced the third state legislative bill ever to protect civil rights. Its failure, despite the efforts of Rudiak and the NAACP's Las Vegas and Reno chapters, helped inspire further activism.[11]

What one journalist called "a thriving night-life and the beginnings of economic self-sufficiency" also helped. When Las Vegas city commissioners denied a permit for an interracial hotel-casino in the Downtown area in 1942, blacks went on to protest that and other indignities and redoubled efforts to build their own parallel community. In the end, west Las Vegans proved the great black scholar and activist W. E. B. DuBois correct: It would take separate success and power for blacks, and the accompanying development of a group of leaders in business and politics, to make whites sit up and take notice.[12]

What also aided the growth of Las Vegas's civil-rights movement was the growth of the white community, and with them enlightened leaders. The elections of Governor Grant Sawyer in 1958 and Mayor Oran Gragson in 1959 put in place officials who believed in equality—and, ironically, Las Vegas blacks had supported Gragson's opponent. Businessmen like Lloyd Katz (and his wife Edythe), who ran several theaters, newspaper publisher Hank Greenspun, attorneys such as Rudiak, Dean Breeze, and Ralph Denton, and others did much to boost the efforts of the group developing in West Las Vegas.[13]

During the 1950s West Las Vegas already boasted strong leaders ready to organize and protest. They included educator Mabel Hoggard and her husband David, a policeman and truant officer; Lubertha Johnson, Nevada's first black nurse, grocer, and social worker; Woodrow Wilson, cofounder of Westside Federal Credit Union and Las Vegas's first black scoutmaster; casino official Clarence Ray; and such ministers as Donald Clark, Prentiss Walker,

Leo Johnson, John Simmons, and Bill Stevens. Joining them in the middle of the decade were three figures whose influence would long be felt inside and outside the black community: Charles West, Las Vegas's first black doctor; James McMillan, an old friend of West's and the first black dentist in Las Vegas; and William "Bob" Bailey, an entertainer who went on to be a disc jockey, television host, and, like the others, a shrewd political activist.[14]

Bailey's arrival was linked to a key event in the history of West Las Vegas, the opening of the Moulin Rouge. The $3.5 million hotel opened on May 24, 1955, as southern Nevada's first major interracial resort. Its owners were white—Joe Louis, the legendary heavyweight boxing champion, served as a host and held a 2 percent share—and its goal was not social justice, but profits. That proved to be a sticking point: several hotel-casinos opened at the same time, glutting the Las Vegas market; the Moulin Rouge was not only off the beaten path, but even at the edge of West Las Vegas, which already had several established clubs for residents to patronize; and, as Roosevelt Fitzgerald pointed out, many blacks "refused to travel, even from Southern California, merely to participate in what they viewed as a 'Jim Crow' operation." But the Moulin Rouge attracted black performers who finally had a place to stay in West Las Vegas and white entertainers who joined their friends in its lounge after they finished performing on the Strip and Downtown; better to stay there than to be denied the right to walk through the casino or swim in the hotel pool. It became known as the town's best late-night entertainment spot. It brought Bailey to Las Vegas as an emcee, and he remained to fight for civil rights. Its eventual owner, Sarann Knight-Preddy, a veteran of the casino business and the civil-rights movement in northern Nevada, later became the first black to hold a gaming license for a Las Vegas casino. And its occasional profits and greater possibilities helped awaken white casino owners to the money to be made from black customers.[15]

While the Moulin Rouge waxed and waned through the late 1950s, patrons stepped up efforts to win civil rights. McMillan and David Hoggard started a newspaper that West took over and turned into the *Voice*—a strong advocate for the black community that continues to publish today as the *Sentinel-Voice*. Because the NAACP legally could not participate in partisan politics, West and McMillan formed the Nevada Voters League and started running campaigns, backing candidates, and organizing voters. They engineered a battle for a senior housing complex and used a boycott to force a dairy to hire black drivers.[16]

However, the most significant step was the end of segregation in hotel-casinos. In March 1960 McMillan watched reports on sit-ins and thought, "What can we do to really start a movement here to eliminate segregation?"

Perhaps defying the less-militant NAACP executive board's wishes, McMillan and Hoggard wrote to Gragson, demanding action against segregation within thirty days or the NAACP would organize protests. When a national radio program reported on the letter, McMillan said, "all hell broke loose." While white business and political leaders tried to negotiate with McMillan, black leaders and friends patrolled outside his house when he received numerous death threats. Finally, with West Las Vegas casino owner Oscar Crozier as an intermediary, almost all Strip and Downtown operators agreed to allow blacks to frequent their casinos. "Politicians played almost no role in it. The hotels had settled because it was good business to settle," McMillan said. Officials of the NAACP, local white political leaders, and several casino operators met at the Moulin Rouge to announce the agreement. "Years later the Moulin Rouge was named a historic site because that's where we supposedly met to sign the agreement. . . . But there was nothing signed . . . ," McMillan said.[17]

Nor was the fight over—far from it. Their pressure and Sawyer's efforts created the Nevada Equal Rights Commission, with Bailey eventually chairing it, but state legislators gutted it by limiting its budget and subpoena powers. McMillan, Knight-Preddy, and Jimmy Gay pushed, with little success, for the powerful Culinary Union to promote blacks through the ranks. When NAACP president Jim Anderson proposed a demonstration at a heavyweight fight in 1963, casino owners agreed to start hiring black workers. And when Charles Kellar became Nevada's first black attorney, the Las Vegas black community increasingly turned to the courts, winning a consent decree for casinos to train black workers, taking the Culinary Union before the National Labor Relations Board, and suing the Clark County School District to integrate. The result was a compromise: the creation of sixth-grade centers, meaning that for one year, white children took a bus to predominantly black schools and black children attended schools in mostly white neighborhoods. Changes in federal laws meant that discrimination became illegal, but the struggle continued to change the hearts and minds of Las Vegans.[18]

Just as it did nationally, the local civil-rights movement changed. While there had been individual and sporadic cases of violence, two sets of riots broke out in 1969, leading to school closures, looting, and fires; it would be the largest-scale racial violence in Las Vegas until 1992, when riots near Downtown followed the acquittal of four white Los Angeles police officers for beating Rodney King. More crucially to the effort to secure equality, the black community divided. This was due in part to the movement's success: West Las Vegas remained the heart and soul of the area's black social and cultural life, but with banks no longer redlining blacks, the freedom to live where they could afford to live made organizing and unity harder.[19]

Another economic factor was the problems faced by poorer blacks. The movement needed a professional or business class to succeed—and ground troops, many of whom felt left out of decision making and the fruits of the movement's victories. The main leader of this group was Ruby Duncan, a onetime welfare mother who came to Las Vegas to work as a maid. In 1972 she began Operation Life, a self-help poverty program for West Las Vegans. She organized protests, including one at the governor's mansion in Carson City, another at the Stardust Hotel, and one along the Strip that drew Jane Fonda, the Reverend Ralph Abernathy, and Sammy Davis Jr. as participants. These activities won Duncan threats and derision at the time—and later, a Distinguished Nevadan Award and an honorary degree from the University and Community College System of Nevada.[20]

Yet West Las Vegas remains a predominantly low-income area. A significant number of the 124,885 blacks counted in the 2000 census live in that historic section of town. But at 9.1 percent, blacks now are the second-largest ethnic group in Las Vegas and the largest, Latinos, who account for more than 20 percent, are beginning to move into the old Westside in greater numbers. In his later years McMillan observed, "You can have all the civil rights you want, you know . . . but if you don't have capital in your community. . . . I hate to say this, but in Las Vegas, through the success of the civil rights movement and our NAACP actions, we actually hurt the black population. When blacks were confined to the Westside, that's where their money stayed. . . . I'm saying that black businesses went under when we got our civil rights." Yet many African Americans also have prospered and thrived in Las Vegas.[21]

Black Politicians and Participation

One of the areas in which black Las Vegans made substantial progress is elective politics. In the late 1950s and early 1960s, the newly formed Nevada Voters League made its presence felt in several races, most notably in Sawyer's gubernatorial campaigns; Sawyer, in turn, strongly backed civil rights. The group ran several candidates for office, with mixed success. In 1960 Helen Lamb Crozier was elected to the state board of education—but may have benefited from voters' thinking she was part of the politically powerful (and white) Lamb family; she lost her reelection bid. The group's leaders were less fortunate: West lost a Las Vegas city commission race and McMillan lost the 1964 Democratic U.S. Senate primary.[22]

Several black Las Vegans have been elected to the state legislature. Nevada's first black legislator was Wilson, elected in 1966 after reapportionment created newer districts balanced more by race and population. "My election gave courage to the black community that they could have one of their own in the legislature," Wilson said. "I was a Republican, and only a few blacks were Republicans; therefore, I had to be elected by the majority community, and that in itself was an important factor." Wilson served four terms, and his greatest achievement—with support from a veteran civil-rights advocate, Democratic governor Mike O'Callaghan—was the Fair Housing Act of 1971.[23]

Wilson's success encouraged other black politicians, especially after the 1971 decennial redistricting created minority districts. In 1972, in the newly created State Senate District 4, Wilson tried to move up from the assembly in a largely Democratic district and lost to Joe Neal, a longtime Nevada Test Site employee and West Las Vegas activist who became Nevada's first black state senator. During a lengthy senate career, Neal chaired the Human Resources and Natural Resources committees and served as president pro tem, which meant that he twice held the post of acting governor. In 1998 and 2002 he sought the Democratic nomination for governor, and on his second try became the first black ever to win a statewide primary before losing in the general. He chose not to seek reelection in 2004.[24]

Las Vegas blacks have enjoyed greater representation in the assembly. The Rev. Marion Bennett won the first of five terms in 1972, followed by Gene Collins, who won two terms as a Democrat before losing a reelection bid as a Republican. Cranford Crawford also won a term in 1972 before Lonie Chaney won five terms in that district. In 1984 businessman Morse Arberry won Bennett's old spot, and he has remained ever since, with several sessions as chair of the powerful Ways and Means Committee. In 1986, after switching to the Republicans, Collins lost to Democrat Wendell Williams, a longtime City of Las Vegas employee who became Education Committee chair and speaker pro tem, the highest-ranking assembly position ever held by a black. The 2002 election brought their first black colleagues from Las Vegas, fellow Democrats Kelvin Atkinson and William Horne. Although Horne's district was more diverse, both represented areas with significant minority populations.[25]

The same characteristic has been true of another office in which blacks have made inroads, the board of regents. Blacks have won a seat in a largely black district beginning in 1979, when June Whitley was appointed to complete a term on the board. She was reelected until retiring in 1994, having also served a two-year term as chair. Her successor, elected in 1994, was attorney Dave Phillips, Ruby Duncan's son. In turn Phillips lost his reelection campaign in 2000 to the second black woman to serve on the board, Linda Howard, whom he had defeated in 1994 and who fought during the ensuing debate over redistricting to keep her mostly black district intact. As Howard was winning, the minority district on the state board of education elected Marcia Washington, a veteran of the school district whose husband, David, became Las Vegas's first black fire chief in 2001.[26]

Black members of the county commission have also represented minority areas. Aaron Williams became the first black member of the North Las Vegas City Council and later the first black elected to county-wide office as a member of the Clark County Commission. He lost his bid for reelection and observed "that he was too light to be black and to represent black folks," McMillan said. Woodrow Wilson returned to the political fray in 1980, defeating a white incumbent in a mostly white district, albeit with a large minority population. Unfortunately, Wilson had to resign when a federal sting operation caught him accepting a bribe. His successor was William Pearson, a dentist, the first black Las Vegas city councilman and the husband of a longtime local teacher and counselor. Pearson served two terms before losing in the Democratic primary to a political protégé, Yvonne Atkinson Gates, who was completing her third term on the commission in 2004.[27]

Given the premium that civil-rights leaders have placed on public education, the important role of Las Vegas black leaders on the county school board should be no surprise. The first, teacher Bernice Moten, beat the Rev. Leo Johnson for the seat in 1972, resigned shortly before her term ended to pursue graduate education, and later returned to Las Vegas as an administrative assistant to then-governor Richard Bryan. Moten's successor, Virginia Brewster, won three terms on the board before resigning. Atkinson Gates began her elective career by winning two terms before running for the county commission. McMillan then won the office and dedicated himself to building better schools in West Las Vegas and gaining them better equipment and teachers before his defeat by longtime schoolteacher and administrator Shirley Barber, who won the first of two terms in 1996.[28]

Blacks have been prominent in one office elected by all the residents of Clark County: district court judge. In 1975, when the legislature created an eleventh district judgeship for the county, O'Callaghan named Addeliar "Dell" Guy to the bench. Another judge called Guy "the Jackie Robinson of the judiciary," with good reason: he became Las Vegas's first black prosecutor in 1964, then the first black chief deputy district attorney. He won several terms as judge before retiring from the bench for health reasons in 1996, a year before his death; a veterans affairs center in West Las Vegas was named for the decorated veteran of World War II and the Korean War. In 1985 the second black to join him on the bench, Earle White, was also appointed, then elected to a term, but defeated for reelection; he has since held numerous community posts, including chair of the City of Las Vegas Ethics Review Board. Shortly after White's defeat came the appointment of former public defender and private practitioner Lee Gates, who since has won several terms. In 1996 Michael Douglas was appointed, went on to win two elections, and then was appointed to the Nevada Supreme Court, becoming its first black member—but not the first judge in Las Vegas above the district court level. That distinction belongs to Johnnie Rawlinson, a onetime prosecutor in the district attorney's office who rose in the late 1990s to become Nevada's first black and female U.S. district judge and Ninth Circuit Court of Appeals judge. But at least as significant as the possibility of Douglas's statewide election is the fact that the judges have been elected to countywide offices not in minority districts.[29]

Indeed, the trend of blacks winning in mostly black areas has been the case at the municipal level. In North Las Vegas—which has long had a significant black population—after Williams moved to the commission, veteran community college administrator Thomas Brown won office when a recall removed three City Council members, but he lost his bid for another term. Theron Goynes spent seventeen years as a councilman but lost his bid to move up to the mayor's post, while William Robinson has been in office since 1983. John Rhodes, previously appointed to a school-board position for which McMillan defeated him in the election, won a North Las Vegas City Council seat and later lost his reelection bid. In Las Vegas Pearson became the first black councilman when he received the appointment to fill a vacancy in ethnically diverse Ward 3. Later, former professional football player and West Las Vegas businessman Frank Hawkins won election to the Ward 1 seat, which also encompassed part of the traditional black community. Hawkins then helped engineer the appointment of banker Ken Brass to a vacancy in Pearson's old ward. But both men lost election bids in 1995 to white candidates. When the Las Vegas City Council expanded from five to seven seats in 2000, the appointee for newly created Ward 5 was Lawrence Weekly, a city employee who since has been elected to a full term in his own right.[30]

Unique among this group of politicians is Lynette Boggs McDonald. Since moving to Las Vegas she has worked mainly in marketing, but she entered politics as a Democratic candidate for the assembly in 1998—the same year in which Neal lost the Democratic gubernatorial primary and Rose McKinney-James, a businesswoman, lost the general election for lieutenant governor. Boggs McDonald, too, was defeated. She subsequently switched to the Republican party, later running for the U.S. House of Representatives in 2002 and losing to two-term Democrat Shelley Berkley. But Boggs McDonald also made political history when she received the city council appointment to represent Summerlin, a mostly white and Republican planned community in northwestern Las Vegas, and went on to handily win a term of her own. In 2004 the governor appointed her to a vacancy on the more powerful county commission.[31]

These politicians face a burden, in Las Vegas and elsewhere: following in large footsteps. Many of the early fighters for civil rights have died; Bailey remains as a kind of local gray eminence and living link to an illustrious past. Just as they faced criticism as being overly activist and allegations of connections to left-wing groups, current black politicians face special scrutiny. The recent elections of Atkinson and Horne, Douglas's quest for higher judicial office, and the unsuccessful but strong recent candidacies of young black lawyers Uri Clinton for the state senate and Denise McCurry for municipal judge suggest that the future is in good hands.

Black Culture and Consciousness

The Las Vegas black community is at something of a cultural crossroads. On the one hand West Las Vegas and nearby Downtown Las Vegas remain the center of its population and its business and cultural life. And, like most of the black diaspora, Las Vegas blacks tend to be on the lower end of their income class. On the other hand legal segregation is long past, and blacks can and do live in the newer master-planned communities of Summerlin and Green Valley, as well as other upscale areas. Thus, the presence of black doctors, lawyers, dentists, and other trained and educated professionals is less unusual than it used to be. At the same time, however, numerous civic, religious, and business organizations exist, many of them centered in West Las Vegas, to serve the black community.[32]

Two decades ago, a Las Vegas newspaper reporter called the black church "still the heart and soul of black life, the brick and mortar of black hope." Historically, that has been true from the days of slavery, when religious services offered what little hope might exist in bleak lives. It remains true today in Las Vegas, with church attendance remaining high on Sundays and politicians visiting before elections to meet with ministers and visit with congregants. While not all churches even have buildings, much less official locations, an estimated sixty churches of various Protestant denominations—Methodists, Lutherans, Jehovah's Witnesses, Seventh-day Adventists, Baptists, and Presbyterians—reportedly can be found throughout West Las Vegas, from the A. M. E. Zion Church and the Church of Christ to the Zion Union Methodist Church and the St. James the Apostle Catholic Church. As early as 1916, Las Vegas's white Methodist church discouraged black members, prompting them to form their own "home mission." One of the oldest black churches, the Second Baptist Church, opened in a twenty-by-forty-foot canvas tent on February 22, 1942, and now numbers well over one thousand congregants in its large structure at 500 West Madison in the heart of West Las Vegas. Some of these churches are crucial to the Witness Project, a national health program for African American women to promote awareness of breast and cervical cancer. The Black Muslim community has also grown with the expansion of the local black population and holds observances. And just as they did at the height of the civil-rights movement, today's ministers—such as Bennett, Willie Davis, Robert Fowler, James Rogers, and Sylvester Rogers—continue to wield great influence on the lives of their congregants.[33]

Of course black churches are hardly the only local outlet for celebrating black culture. Kwanzaa, created by Dr. Maulana Karenga in 1966, is the seven-day holiday of African heritage between Christmas and New Year's Day, and in Las Vegas events at family homes and local community centers focus on family values, faith, and togetherness mixed with feasts, stories, and reunions. The annual Rev. Dr. Martin Luther King Jr. birthday holiday includes a Downtown parade each January. And each February, Black History Month events include various heritage festivals, programming, and scholarship fund-raisers at local libraries, the Community College of Southern Nevada, and the University of Nevada, Las Vegas, as well as programs in local schools and the West Las Vegas Arts Center. Travel companies offer tours of local black historic sites, from West Las Vegas churches and casinos to the Downtown wedding chapel where Michael Jordan was married. The West Las Vegas Library features numerous arts and cultural events, with an emphasis on African American subjects and a special collections department for them. The Las Vegas–Westside African American Society is involved in genealogical research. The Walker African American History Museum and the Westside Academy of Performing Arts also provide means of connecting today's black residents with their historic culture. Programs on black culture range from the Olabisi African Dance Troupe to the Austin Savoy Dancers.[34]

Black businesspeople have several places to turn for help and community. The Urban Chamber of Commerce started in 1980 as the Black Chamber of Commerce, founded by a group that included McMillan, Bailey, and Knight-Preddy. In 1996 its name changed to the Urban Chamber of Commerce to help reflect its inclusiveness beyond the black community. Under the leadership of Louis Overstreet, an engineer and a longtime businessman, it continues to serve as a clearinghouse of information, a promoter of diversity, and a mechanism for networking. Organizations assisting blacks also include the Black Business Council, the National Association of Minority Contractors, the Southern Nevada Coalition of Concerned Black Women, and the Nevada Minority Purchasing Council. The Las Vegas Black Expo also provides networking opportunities, as do such groups as the Southern Nevada Black Nurses Association, local African American fraternity chapters, and the Professional Black Women's Alliance. A Black Business Directory keeps Las Vegans informed about black-owned businesses while the National Bar Association brings together black attorneys.[35]

The number of black professionals has mushroomed with the city's population. Teachers no longer face their own form of segregation: assignment to West Las Vegas schools simply on the basis of their color. Dr. Claude Perkins became the first black school superintendent in 1978. In 1983 Dr. Paul Meacham began more than a decade as the first black president of what was then Clark County Community College; he retired in 1994 to a chair in the UNLV College of Education. And the legal community has grown well beyond the days when Dell Guy in the district attorney's office and Charles Kellar in private practice were unique.[36]

Blacks have been important to the broadcast media—which, in turn, have been important to them. For many years Lee Winston headed news and community programming at KLVX Channel 10, the local Public Broadcasting affailiate, and he now runs KCEP 88.1 FM, owned and operated by the Clark County Economic Opportunity Board and based in West Las Vegas, which features a mix of national and local programming, including broadcasts of some local church services on Sunday. The local major network affiliates and newspapers have employed numerous black journalists, many of whom have pursued other careers—including longtime *Sun* courts reporter Bill Gang, who became the spokesman for the Nevada Supreme Court; Paul Dawkins, who reported and anchored for Channel 8 for many years before moving into community relations and station operations; Lillian McMorris, who hosted *A.M. Southern Nevada,* the city's longest running public-affairs television show, before moving into consulting; Ray Willis, a newscaster who became the public affairs officer for the Clark County School District; and Deborah Campbell, a television reporter before becoming an executive for the local United Way and then St. Rose hospitals.[37]

Meanwhile, the *Sentinel-Voice* remains both the sentinel and the voice of the black community. Published from an office at 900 West Charleston in Downtown Las Vegas, it appears weekly with local news stories about everything from the Rev. Al Sharpton's National Action Network holding its "Women Changing America Awards Banquet" in Las Vegas at the Mandalay Bay, to progress in diversity in the gaming industries. Local contributors include Urban Chamber director Louis Overstreet, while the *Sentinel-Voice* prints national columns by National Urban League president Marc Morial and scholars such as Manning Marable and Ronald Walters. Proclaiming "the truth shall set you free" on its masthead, "Nevada's Only African-American Community Newspaper" reported more than thirty thousand readers in 2003.[38]

Nor has the black community stopped its efforts at political organization—although those efforts have often been controversial. In December 1997 the NAACP's landlord—Operation Life, Duncan's organization—evicted the organization from its offices for failing to pay fees, and later the national suspended the local's charter for failing to file required reports. Las Vegas NAACP president Gene Collins, the former assemblyman, then became head of the local branch of the National Action Network. Uri Clinton, who challenged Neal for the state senate in 2000 and barely lost, became chair of the Democratic Caucus for Urban Development, a recently created group bringing together younger black activists to mobilize voters and discuss issues of concern. Whatever their differences, these groups continue the struggle for better economic, educational, and cultural opportunities for blacks in Las Vegas.[39]

One controversy that was tied to the local NAACP chapter's suspension was reminiscent of the action that led to the Moulin Rouge Agreement. Collins discovered that casino giant MGM Mirage failed to employ minority contractors and went public. In turn, MGM instituted a diversity program, created a position related to diversity, hosted a conference, and subsequently donated $500,000 to the William F. Harrah College of Hotel Administration at UNLV for minority scholarships and diversity. But after Collins demanded that MGM Mirage pour $100 million into West Las Vegas redevelopment, the national NAACP suspended the charter, arguing that a local chapter has no authority to deal with a national or multinational corporation, while Collins accused the national of succumbing to financial pressure from MGM Mirage, a donor. Yet it was also true that others applied pressure to MGM Mirage and other casino companies, most notably Bobby Siller, a longtime FBI agent who retired as Las Vegas agent-in-charge to accept an appointment to the Nevada Gaming Control Board—the first black member of that body, which helps to regulate the industry.[40]

Most black gaming executives have been involved in human resources and diversity, but the industry has moved forward in ownership and executive positions. Former judge and Mississippi gaming regulator Lorenzo Creighton held several executive positions with Park Place Entertainment before becoming president of the Flamingo. Robert Johnson, who owned Black Entertainment Television, became the first black licensed in Nevada as director of a casino corporation when the Gaming Commission approved him for the board of Hilton Hotels in 1997. In 1999 he became the first black licensed as an owner of a Strip hotel restaurant when he was approved for Tres Jazz in the Paris. An even bigger step in 2001 was Don Barden's acquisition of the Downtown Fitzgeralds and sister properties in Colorado and Mississippi. Barden, a Detroit construction and real-estate investor who had that city's first cable-television franchise, planned to market the property in conjunction with his other holdings.[41]

Conclusion

Barden's purchase of the Downtown Fitzgeralds was ironic. The property was originally the Sundance, and landlord Moe Dalitz was one of the Strip operators who contributed to the segregation of that part of Las Vegas, then was instrumental in the agreement to desegregate it. Indeed, the past is prologue. Clearly, African Americans have made great progress in Las Vegas; no longer is it "the Mississippi of the West." They have come a long way but still have a long way to go—there are still no predominantly black banking or gaming establishments, but many small businesses and isolated large enterprises represent the gains in black ownership and executive positions. More blacks hold office than at any time in the history of Las Vegas, yet a predominantly white media and power structure continue to bring up issues of black ethics and corruption—as they do, to be sure, with regard to white politicians. From early black community leaders to those in the civil-rights movement and the leaders of today, in various forms and venues, Las Vegas African Americans continue to battle for racial and economic justice—for real power. Until they acquire their own major businesses and powerful political offices, and perhaps even then, the battle is far from over.

Notes

1. *Las Vegas Review-Journal,* May 30, 2003; *Las Vegas Sun,* May 24, 30, 2003.
2. Darlene Clark Hine, "Black Migration to the Urban Midwest: The Gender Dimension, 1915–1945," in *The Great Migration in Historical Perspective: New Dimensions of Race, Class, and Gender,* ed. Joe William Trotter (Bloomington: Indiana University Press, 1991), 127; Elmer R. Rusco, *Good Time Coming?: Black Nevadans in the Nineteenth Century* (Westport, Conn.: Greenwood Press, 1975). See also Milton C. Sernett, *Bound for the Promised Land: African American Religion and the Great Migration* (Durham, N.C.: Duke University Press, 1997), 2. While many fine works have been written about the black experience in the West, an excellent general history is

Quintard Taylor, *In Search of the Racial Frontier: African Americans in the American West, 1528–1990* (New York: Norton, 1998).

3. Roosevelt Fitzgerald, "The Evolution of a Black Community in Las Vegas, 1905–1940," *Nevada Public Affairs Review* 2 (1987): 23; correspondence relating to this appears in the Union Pacific Railroad Collection, Department of Special Collections, Lied Library, UNLV; *Las Vegas Sun*, March 2, 1998, March 21, 1999; A. D. Hopkins, "Walter Bracken: Company Man," in *The First 100: Portraits of the Men and Women Who Shaped Las Vegas*, ed. A. D. Hopkins and K. J. Evans (Las Vegas: Huntington Press, 1999), 20–21. See also Stanley W. Paher, *Las Vegas: As It Began—As It Grew* (Las Vegas: Nevada Publications, 1971); Ralph J. Roske, *Las Vegas: A Desert Paradise* (Tulsa: Continental Heritage Press, 1986); Gary E. Elliott, *The New Western Frontier: An Illustrated History of Greater Las Vegas* (Carlsbad, Calif.: Heritage Media, 1999).

4. K. J. Evans, "J. T. McWilliams: Battling the Big Boys," in *The First 100*, 22–24.

5. Eugene P. Moehring, *Resort City in the Sunbelt: Las Vegas, 1930–2000* (Reno and Las Vegas: University of Nevada Press, 2000), 174–75; Roosevelt Fitzgerald, "Blacks and the Boulder Dam Project," *Nevada Historical Society Quarterly* 24, no. 3 (Fall 1981): 255–60; Andrew J. Dunar and Dennis McBride, *Building Hoover Dam: An Oral History of the Great Depression* (Reno and Las Vegas: University of Nevada Press, 2001), 140–44, 306–7; Craig F. Swallow, "The Ku Klux Klan in Nevada during the 1920s," (master's thesis, UNLV, 1978); *Las Vegas Sun*, March 2, 1998, March 21, 1999.

6. Moehring, *Resort City in the Sunbelt*, 175–76; Gary Elliott, "The Moulin Rouge Hotel: A Critical Appraisal of a Las Vegas Legend" (unpublished paper, in the author's possession), 3; Roosevelt Fitzgerald, "Black Entertainers in Las Vegas, 1940–1960" (unpublished paper, Department of Special Collections, Lied Library, UNLV), 3; John M. Findlay, *People of Chance: Gambling in America from Jamestown to Las Vegas* (New York: Oxford University Press, 1986), 190; A. D. Hopkins, "Ernie Cragin: Flawed Vision," in *First 100*, 81–83.

7. Moehring, *Resort City in the Sunbelt*, 176–77; Roosevelt Fitzgerald, "The Demographic Impact of Basic Magnesium Corporation on Southern Nevada," *Nevada Public Affairs Review* 2 (1987): 27–38; Michael Coray, "African-Americans in Nevada," *Nevada Historical Society Quarterly* 35, no. 4 (Winter 1992): 250.

8. Moehring, *Resort City in the Sunbelt*, 177–78; Nefertiti Makenta, "A View from West Las Vegas," in *The Real Las Vegas: Life Beyond the Strip*, ed. David Littlejohn (New York: Oxford University Press, 1999), 110, 117; Fitzgerald, "Black Entertainers," 33.

9. Elliott, "Moulin Rouge," 3–4; Moehring, *Resort City in the Sunbelt*, 178–79.

10. James Goodrich, "Negroes Can't Win in Las Vegas," *Ebony*, March 1954, 5; Findlay, *People of Chance*, 189–90; James W. Hulse, *Forty Years in the Wilderness: Impressions of Nevada, 1940–1980* (Reno: University of Nevada Press, 1986).

11. Moehring, *Resort City in the Sunbelt*, 179–80; Findlay, *People of Chance*, 190; Littlejohn, *Real Las Vegas*, 117; K. J. Evans, "C. D. Baker: The Colonel," in *First 100*, 131–33.

12. Littlejohn, *Real Las Vegas*, 117; W. E. B. DuBois, *The Souls of Black Folk*, ed. David W. Blight and Robert Gooding-Williams (Boston: Bedford Books, 1997).

13. Ralph L. Denton and Michael S. Green, *A Liberal Conscience: Ralph Denton, Nevadan* (Reno: University of Nevada Oral History Program, 2001), talks about many of these figures. See also Grant Sawyer, Gary E. Elliott, and R. T. King, *Hang Tough! Grant Sawyer: An Activist in the Governor's Mansion* (Reno: University of Nevada Oral History Program, 1993); K. J. Evans, "Oran Gragson: Mayor Who Made His Mark," in *First 100*, 146–47; A. D. Hopkins, "Grant Sawyer: The Hang-Tough Governor," in *First 100*, 148–50; A. D. Hopkins, "Bob Bailey: Breaking the Color Line," in *First 100*, 151–52; K. J. Evans, "Ralph Denton: Good Citizen Ralph," in *First 100*, 155–56; Michael S. Green, "Hank Greenspun: Where He Stood," in *The Maverick Spirit: Building the New Nevada*, ed. Richard O. Davies (Reno and Las Vegas: University of Nevada Press, 1998), 74–95.

14. *Las Vegas Review-Journal*, January 18, 2000, August 18, 2001; *Las Vegas Sun*, December 29, 1999; Moehring, *Resort City in the Sunbelt*, 184; Fitzgerald, "Demographic Impact," 75; Elizabeth Nelson Patrick, "The Black Experience in Southern Nevada," *Nevada Historical Society Quarterly* 22, no. 2 (Summer 1979): 128–40; Patrick, "The Black Experience in Southern Nevada, Part II," *Nevada Historical Society Quarterly* 22, no. 3 (Fall 1979): 209–20; James B. McMillan, Gary E. Elliott, and R. T. King, *Fighting Back: A Life in the Struggle for Civil Rights* (Reno: University of Nevada Oral History Program, 1997), especially 77–90; Clarence Ray, Helen M. Blue, and Jamie Coughtry, *Clarence Ray: Black Politics and Gaming in Las Vegas, 1920s–1980s* (Reno: University of Nevada Oral History Program, 1991); Gary E. Elliott, "James B. McMillan: The Pursuit of Equality," in *The Maverick Spirit*, 44–57; A. D. Hopkins, "James B. McMillan: Fighting Racism," in *First 100*, 143–45.

15. Earnest N. Bracey, "The Moulin Rouge Mystique: Blacks and Equal Rights in Las Vegas," *Nevada Historical Society Quarterly* 39, no. 4 (Winter 1996): 272–88; Roosevelt Fitzgerald, "The Moulin Rouge Hotel: History in the Making," ed. Frank Wright (Las Vegas: Moulin Rouge Preservation Association, 1996); Patrick, "Black Experience—Part II," 219.

16. McMillan, Elliott, and King, *Fighting Back*, especially 77–90.

17. Ibid., 91–98.

18. McMillan, Elliott, and King, *Fighting Back*, 99–105, 126–35; Moehring, *Resort City in the Sunbelt*, 186–200; Sawyer, Elliott, and King, *Hang Tough!*, 103–4; Courtney Alexander, "Rise to Power: The Recent History of the Culinary Union in Las Vegas," in *The Grit Beneath the Glitter: Tales from the Real Las Vegas*, ed. Hal K. Rothman and Mike Davis (Berkeley: University of California Press, 2002), 145–74; A. D. Hopkins, "Charles Kellar: Fighting the Power," in *First 100*, 153–54; A. D. Hopkins, "Al Bramlet: The Organizer," in *First 100*, 196–97.

19. Moehring, *Resort City in the Sunbelt*, 191–95; Littlejohn, *Real Las Vegas*, 191–95; Mike Davis, "The Racial Cauldron," in *The Grit Beneath the Glitter*, 260–67.

20. Earnest N. Bracey, "Ruby Duncan, Operation Life, and Welfare Rights in Nevada," *Nevada Historical Society Quarterly* 44, no. 2 (Summer 2001): 133–46.

21. McMillan, Elliott, and King, *Fighting Back*, 137–38.

22. McMillan, Elliott, and King, *Fighting Back*, 83, 107–15 (McMillan both

praised and criticized Sawyer for his performance); Sawyer, Elliott, and King, *Hang Tough!*, 56–58, 95–106. Unless otherwise noted, the material in this chapter also comes from two sources: www.co.clark.nv.us, the Clark County Web site, which lists election returns over the past century, and Earnest N. Bracey, "The Political Participation of Blacks in an Open Society: The Changing Political Climate in Nevada," *Nevada Historical Society Quarterly* 42, no. 3 (Fall 1999): 140–59; *Las Vegas Sun*, May 17, 1959, May 19, 1959.

23. Bracey, "Political Participation," 143; Woodrow Wilson, Jamie Coughtry, and R. T. King, *Woodrow Wilson: Race, Community, and Politics in Las Vegas, 1940–1980s* (Reno: University of Nevada Oral History Program, 1990); A. D. Hopkins, "Mike O'Callaghan: The Popular Pugilist," in *First 100*, 227–29; Joseph N. Crowley, "Race and Residence: The Politics of Open Housing in Nevada," in *Sagebrush and Neon: Studies in Nevada Politics*, ed. Eleanore Bushnell (Reno: UNR Bureau of Governmental Research, 1973), 55–74.

24. www.co.clark.nv.us/election/Results; *Las Vegas Sun*, October 25, 2002; Bracey, "Political Participation," 140–59; Gary E. Elliott, "Law, Politics, and the Movement Toward Constitutional Equality in Nevada: The Revolution in Legislative Apportionment—Part I," *Nevada Historical Society Quarterly* 39, no. 1 (Spring 1996): 1–19; Gary E. Elliott, "Law, Politics, and the Movement toward Constitutional Equality in Nevada: The Revolution in Legislative Apportionment—Part II," *Nevada Historical Society Quarterly* 39, no. 2 (Summer 1996): 89–108; Eleanore Bushnell, "Reapportionment and Responsibility," in *Sagebrush and Neon*, 93–119.

25. www.co.clark.nv.us/election/Results, features useful information, as does *Political History of Nevada 2000* (Carson City: State Printing Office, 2001). Washoe County has elected two black state senators, Democrat Bernice Mathews and Republican Maurice Washington.

26. *Las Vegas Sun*, December 20, 1992, August 14, 2001.

27. McMillan, Elliott, and King, *Fighting Back*, 104; Bracey, "Political Participation," 140–59; *Las Vegas Sun*, December 29, 1999.

28. *Las Vegas Sun*, April 20, 2000; *Las Vegas Review-Journal*, August 28, 1996, September 4, 1996; McMillan, Elliott, and King, *Fighting Back*, 134–35.

29. *Las Vegas Sun*, March 21, 1997, June 4, 1997, July 3, 1997; *Reno Gazette-Journal*, May 9, 2003; *Las Vegas Review-Journal*, March 21, 1997.

30. These officials have been the subject of innumerable articles in the Las Vegas media, especially the *Sentinel-Voice*.

31. Boggs McDonald has been the subject of numerous local press articles, especially during her campaigns.

32. M. Gottdiener, Claudia C. Collins, and David R. Dickens, *Las Vegas: The Social Production of an All-American City* (Malden, Mass.: Blackwell, 1999), 103–6.

33. Earnest N. Bracey, "Anatomy of Second Baptist Church: The First Black Baptist Church in Las Vegas," *Nevada Historical Society Quarterly* 43, no. 3 (Fall 2000): 201–13; Moehring, *Resort City in the Sunbelt*, 174; Fitzgerald, "Evolution of a Black Community," 23.

34. This is gleaned from assorted articles in the *Las Vegas Review-Journal,* the *Las Vegas Sun,* and, especially, the *Las Vegas Sentinel-Voice.* See also *Las Vegas View,* August 7, 2002.

35. www.urbanchamberlv.org; www.lasvegasblackexpo.com; www.blacksinvegas .com; *Las Vegas View,* April 10, 2002.

36. James W. Hulse, Leonard E. Goodall, and Jackie Allen, *Reinventing the System: Higher Education in Nevada, 1968–2000* (Reno: University of Nevada Press, 2003), 130–31; *Las Vegas Review-Journal,* February 6, 2000.

37. *Las Vegas Review-Journal,* December 15, 2000, October 29, 2001, November 1, 2002, May 1, 2003; *Las Vegas View,* July 21, 1999.

38. This is based on examining copies of the *Las Vegas Sentinel-Voice.* The examples above are from the July 17, 2003, issue.

39. *Las Vegas Sun,* December 7, 1998, January 11, 1999, December 9, 1999; *Las Vegas Review-Journal,* August 26, 1998; *Las Vegas Mercury,* March 14, 2002.

40. *Las Vegas Sun,* December 17, 1998, May 31, 2000, October 24, 2001; *Las Vegas Review-Journal,* March 31, 2001, February 27, 2003.

41. *Las Vegas Sun,* April 24, 1997, August 4, 1999, December 10, 2001; *Las Vegas Review-Journal,* May 28, 2002.

CHAPTER 6

The Chinese

SUE FAWN CHUNG

Despite hardships and much discrimination, many Chinese Americans who have settled in Las Vegas have been able to fulfill their dream of achieving a good livelihood for themselves and their families and a promising future for their descendants. They succeeded by having a strong sense of belonging to Chinese cultural traditions modified by newly adopted American values and customs. Their unique ethnicity has been reinforced by their different physical appearance, their ties to their ancestral homeland, the hostility they have often encountered, and their membership in mutual-aid associations that emphasize cultural preservation. From 1875 until 1943 a scarcity of Chinese women due to American immigration laws made normal family life impossible.[1] After the 1940s all of this changed with the economic successes of the second- and third-generation Chinese Americans, the arrival of wealthier and better-educated Chinese immigrants, and the immigration of a larger number of females, resulting in an eventual gender balance in the 1970s. Additionally, the results of the 1964 civil-rights movement led to a broader acceptance of America's minorities. Chinese Americans experienced new opportunities and greater assimilation. At the same time they searched for their own identity and tried to determine whether they were Chinese, American, or both. There were neither simple answers nor any single solution.

Demographic Trends

The Chinese are the oldest and largest of the Asian groups residing in the United States. In Las Vegas they are second to the Filipinos. Dramatic changes have taken place in the size and makeup of Nevada's Chinese population in the last century and a half. Traits such as region or country of origin, spoken language, class, politics, sex ratio, and religion have become more diverse over this period. Chinese immigrants, primarily from southeastern China and particularly from Siyi (Four Counties) in Guangdong Province, entered Yinshan (Silver Mountain, the Chinese name for Nevada) in the 1850s. By 1880 they represented 8.6 percent (5,416) or more (many were not counted) of Nevada's population.[2] The 1875 Page Law, directed at prohibiting prostitutes from entering, effectively limited the number of Chinese women who could immigrate. The result was a predominantly male population with a miniscule number of females.

Discriminatory federal laws resulted in a decrease in the Chinese population. The 1882 Chinese Exclusion Act, which was amended several times over succeeding decades, prohibited Chinese laborers from immigrating and reduced the number of Chinese in the nation and state. In 1904–5, when the Bureau of Immigration (later renamed the Immigration and Naturalization Service [INS]) counted the Chinese in order to deport those without proper documentation, their number decreased again. In 1900 there were 1,352 Chinese (3.2 percent of the state's population), but by 1910 the number had dropped to 927 (1.1 percent). The 1924 Immigration Act established a quota allowing only 105 Chinese to enter the United States annually, so the population continued to drop. In 1943 the Chinese Exclusion Acts of 1882, 1892, and later were repealed. Nevada's Chinese population reached its lowest point in 1950, at 281 (0.2 percent). Because of the 1965 Immigration and Nationality Act, which ended the racial-origin quota, it gradually increased through 1970, when it reached 915 Chinese (0.2 percent), and it grew much faster thereafter, reaching 2,979 (0.4 percent) in 1980, 6,618 (0.5 percent) in 1990, and 18,387 (0.9 percent) in 2000.[3]

The post-1970 wave of immigrants came from Hong Kong, Taiwan, Southeast Asia, and the urban centers of the People's Republic of China. Like the population of the United States as a whole, the Chinese population was more diverse in its birthplace, and the new immigrants often had more education and better financial capabilities than earlier immigrants from China. The majority of the new immigrants were women, so that a gender balance was achieved. Between 1960 and 1990 the total U.S. Chinese American population increased by nearly one million. Census 2000 found Nevada's largest decennial increase in its Chinese population, not including those of mixed ethnicities. Based on demographic data, the Chinese American population in Nevada is expected to continue to increase rapidly in the early twenty-first century.[4]

Nevada had the largest increase in its Asian population of any state between 1990 and 2000: 207.4 percent. Growth of the Asian population of the Las Vegas MSA during the 1990s was even faster: 260.6 percent. During the same period, Las Vegas's Chinese population grew by 245.0 percent, reaching a total of 14,694 in 2000. Chinese Americans are second only to Filipinos among Las Vegas Asian groups.[5]

The small number of Chinese females in the state changed little during the first half of the twentieth century. There were 69 Chinese females in 1900 and only 76 in 1950. Thus, at midcentury, a significant gender imbalance persisted in the state, and most Chinese residents still remained separated from their wives and families. Those Chinese women who had immigrated were usually married to Chinese men in stable economic positions, primarily owners of restaurants, laundries, or other businesses. As a result of the repeal of the Chinese Exclusion Acts in 1943 and the later liberalization of laws regarding the admission of wives, the number of Chinese females increased from 76 in 1950 to 184 in 1960, and the sexual imbalance was eliminated by 1980. There was a greater number of families in the post–World War II Chinese American world, both nationally and in Nevada. New Chinese immigrants entered as family units: husband, wife, and unmarried children. The presence of women and families was important because it created a more settled community. It also established a family-centered society that expanded the market for Chinese goods and services not available from the larger society and diversified the services, such as beauty salons and medical facilities, that had not been present in the early decades.[6] This ultimately changed the character of the Chinese American community.

The post-1965 surge in the Chinese population led to another dramatic shift. Whereas the American-born Chinese had represented over 50 percent of the Chinese population nationally in 1940, the older pattern of a larger percentage of foreign-born Chinese reemerged. American-born Chinese regarded the new immigrants as less Americanized ("old fashioned"), and the recent Chinese immigrants looked down upon the ABCs (a derogatory reference to the American-born Chinese), who they believed were from poor rural, basically uneducated backgrounds and lacking in the proper respect for Chinese culture.[7] The stereotypes, though inaccurate, created divisiveness within the Chinese American community.

Another important new trend was the growing number of interracial and interethnic marriages. Nevada's miscegenation statutes originated in the 1861 territorial legislature and continued until the state legislature removed them in March 1959. After that date most of the interracial marriages were with other Asian Americans or Euramericans (the latter are estimated at 22 percent of all marriages among the younger generation in the United States). As the third generation came of age in the 1970s, 49.6 percent of Chinese Americans married non-Chinese in Los Angeles County, and a similar situation undoubtedly occurred in Las Vegas. The 2000 census enumerated the combination of Asians and non-Asians in general: 57,765 (Clark County), 19,397 (Las Vegas); and more specifically: 2,522 intraracial marriages between Asians and Hawaiians or Pacific Islanders (Nevada), 2,513 between Asians and non-

Asians (Nevada). Studies have shown that interracial marriages are less stable and less happy than intraracial marriages, especially among women, so Chinese American parents continue to discourage them.[8] The younger generation tends to ignore this, thinking that the common bond of American ideals, values, and customs makes them comfortable in their marriages.

Questions of identity and cultural preservation have plagued Chinese Americans both nationally and in Las Vegas, where their community is comparatively small and diverse. Sometimes traditions had to be invented in order to unify the group within their own context and then within the larger Asian American context. The American-born Chinese have had to deal with "ethnosclerosis, the hardening of the walls between ethnicities" so aptly described by Eric Liu in *The Accidental Asian: Notes of a Native Speaker,* a condition in which he or she not only has had to deal with prejudice and discrimination from Euramericans while growing up in a predominantly non-Chinese community, but also has asked whether it is wrong to affiliate with Asian American–only groups.[9] Liu also wondered if it was right to neglect one's own cultural heritage and marry outside of one's ethnic group—which he did. Just as Liu has no single answer, so the Chinese Americans in Las Vegas have taken a variety of paths in seeking their solutions to questions of identity while pursuing economic success.

Early Las Vegas

Settling in a frontier town like Las Vegas after 1905, the small number of Chinese had to interact with the Euramerican population at a time when, as historian John Higham has pointed out, there was an awareness of interdependence and a drive for assimilation, often called the "melting pot myth."[10] Most of the early Chinese in Las Vegas had already lived for several decades in the United States and had adjusted to American ways. Because of Chinese exclusionary laws, the arrival of new immigrants, who were more traditionally oriented, was minimal. Unlike their counterparts in many American communities that had a residential or occupational Chinatown, the Chinese in Las Vegas lived and worked in scattered parts of the town, so interactions with other ethnic groups were common. But acculturation and assimilation require degrees of tolerance and acceptance from the host community.[11] In the harsh environmental conditions of this frontier railroad town where services, including laundries, restaurants, and recreation, were needed, a frontier spirit of interdependence prevailed. Therefore their acculturation was faster than it was for those living in large western urban Chinatowns, and, for some, the achievement of the Chinese American dream became a reality sooner.

As in many Nevada towns, the Chinese moved into Las Vegas when it appeared that there was going to be a bright economic future. In 1905 Las Vegas became an important provisioning, fueling, and watering stop on the San Pedro, Los Angeles and Salt Lake Railroad line (later the Union Pacific). Visitors, travelers, and railroad employees needed lodging and food, and hotels and restaurants were built to meet these needs. Chinese Americans provided these and other services.

Very little is known about Las Vegas's early Chinese residents. A few came to start businesses, mainly laundries and restaurants—two occupations they filled in other parts of the state and region. One of the first Chinese residents was Ying Lee, who opened a laundry in 1905. His occupational choice was typical of his generation: between 1900 and 1930 approximately 25 percent of the Chinese in the United States were in the laundry business. Sociologist Paul Siu has described the hardships of the typical Chinese laundrymen; nevertheless, the work no doubt provided a good income for Ying Lee. In 1908 he formed a partnership with Man Ying and Chin Yee in order to purchase the Arrowhead Restaurant from Mrs. Albert Simmons, but after a few months he returned to the laundry business on an alley between First and Second Streets. In 1909 the partners sold the restaurant to Wong Kee, who had been working as a cook at the Colorado Hotel. The Arrowhead soon became a popular restaurant for railroad workers, following a pattern already established throughout the state. The railroad companies often paid a subsidy to restaurants to open twenty-four hours a day in order to serve their employees and passengers.[12] Chinese laundry and restaurant owners achieved a modicum of financial success through hard work in these early years, but a few also earned a bad reputation.

Wong Kee figured prominently in early Las Vegas newspaper stories that perpetuated negative stereotypes of Chinese Americans. In addition to the Arrowhead, he owned the Shady Cafe, which advertised "Chop Suey, Noodles, [and] China Goods" and had an opium den in the back.[13] Following a raid at the cafe in 1910, Slim Sin and Ah Sing were arrested under the 1881 Nevada law making the smoking of opium and possession of opium-smoking implements illegal. A hung jury saved both men from conviction. The following is one of many examples showing that the Chinese were not reluctant to go to court over disputes. In 1909 and 1911 Wong Kee was sued in justice court for $43.60, but he appealed the decision by taking the case to the Supreme Court of Nevada, which reversed the lower court's decision in 1914. He continued to have problems with the law. Shortly after his contract for providing food to prisoners at twenty cents per meal was canceled due to the poor quality of the food, he left Las Vegas.[14] His shady reputation cast aspersions on other Chinese Americans.

In 1909 this "tent town" became the county seat of the newly created Clark County. The 1910 census manuscript for Las Vegas recorded only two Chinese, Sing Chin, fifty, who had immigrated in 1880, and Sing Se, sixty-two, who had arrived in 1878. Both lived on Ogden Street and owned a laundry.[15] Like many other Chinese in Las Vegas, these men had lived for several decades in Nevada. Census records did not count all of the Chinese population; the notorious Wong Kee and two opium smokers, for example, were not listed.

The Chinese American community actually encompassed a larger group, including those living in outlying parts of the county. There were twelve other Chinese males living in Clark County in 1910, all either cooks, waiters, servants, or laundrymen, and, like the Chinese in other parts of the state, over half were married (with their wives presumably in China because of immigration laws) or widowed. The only person who appeared in both the 1910 and 1920 census manuscripts for Clark County, Charley Ching, worked for the prominent merchant/miner/hotel owner George Fayle and operated the Bullion boarding house in Goodsprings. Fayle employed Ching because, like other Nevada mine owners, he knew that this was one way to attract and retain his labor force—good food was a major incentive for staying on the job. Since Las Vegas was the closest large town, undoubtedly the Chinese men from around the county gathered there during their days off. This was certainly the case for California-born Sam Yet (1869–1932), a miner in Searchlight in the 1920s and 1930s who was a familiar figure in Las Vegas.[16] When he died, the Las Vegas Age noted in a laudatory tone that he was "considered a friend by many desert rats."[17]

By 1920 the only two Chinese listed in the census manuscript for Las Vegas were Guy Wong, fifty-three, and his partner, Quong Wong, fifty-five, both of whom had immigrated in 1877 and worked as cooks in a boardinghouse catering to railroad workers.[18] As was common in Nevada, these unmarried men lived with Euramericans, indicating an absence of rigid housing segregation among ethnic groups in this frontier town. Newspapers referred to other Chinese in town, but the census did not list them.

Despite the relatively wide-open nature of the new town, early Chinese residents recalled instances of prejudice. Teasing, hurtful remarks and rock throwing were commonplace in local schools according to several Chinese who recalled their experiences as schoolchildren. One example occurred in February 1921, when a Las Vegas grammar-school teacher beat a fourteen-year-old Chinese boy so severely that he lost the use of his legs.[19] However, instances of mistreatment or racial intolerance were seldom publicized in early twentieth-century Las Vegas newspapers. There was no report of anti-Chinese mob violence or anti-Chinese movements like the 1908 Reno burning of Chinatown. More subtle forms of prejudice were experienced: unavailability of housing and jobs, inequity in salaries, restrictions on memberships, and limited social activities.

Access to public education in the 1920s and 1930s did not necessarily mean equal opportunities for the Chinese in the Las Vegas area. The main focus of Chinese life, as in other parts of the state, was still home and family. Many Chinese students felt they were not welcomed but only tolerated at school. Even if one graduated, career opportunities were limited due to discriminatory hiring practices. For many decades to come, even for those with college degrees, small businesses, restaurants, and laundries continued to be the main sources of employment.[20] The most one could hope for was to own a business someday or achieve equity in salary.

The pace of life in the area remained slow until the early 1930s, when construction began on Boulder Dam. This enormous federal reclamation project eventually harnessed the mighty Colorado River and led to a large influx of workers and their families who needed services that the Chinese helped provide. State regulations governing construction of dams, which were written in 1902, prohibited the hiring of Chinese workers on the dam projects. Chinese residents, therefore, made a living in the traditional ways—restaurant, laundry, and hotel work. They also turned to entertainment and gaming for newcomers and visitors.

Gaming and Entertainment

The Chinese had participated in the gaming business since their first presence during the Comstock era. Following the statewide relegalization of gambling in 1931, Chinese entrepreneurs moved to participate in the industry. That year Woo Sing unsuccessfully applied for a gaming license in Clark County. He then launched the unique China Town, a supper club on South Main Street. The club featured gourmet cuisine prepared by Chef Leong, formerly of New York City, and entertainment by performers Bo Ling and Bo Ching, who had been on the Orpheum circuit and continued their careers in Hollywood for the next sixty years. A local newspaper described it as "one of the most attractive places—with myriad Chinese lanterns suspended from trees and numerous Chinese decorative art pieces on display, including textiles, embroidered silk robes and rare tapestries."[21] Although the nightclub closed in less than a year, China Town offered an elegant introduction to the more refined aspects of Chinese culture, helping to pave the way for future Chinese American entertainers, clubs, and restaurants.

Chinese Americans first attained gaming licenses in the 1930s, when Walter and Dorothy Tun opened their Star Club Casino in Reno. The most successful of the Reno enterprises was Bill Fong's New China Club on Lake Street, which operated with the help of the Bing Kong tong's rival, the Hop Sing tong, in the 1950s. All of the dealers at the New China Club had to pay the annual twenty-five-dollar dues to the Hop Sing tong.

In Las Vegas several Chinese Americans under the leadership of Harry Lee Fong and Rose Fong opened the West Side Club in the early 1940s to cater to African American customers, who were not welcomed in the major casinos. Others followed, most notably Zee Louie's Chickadee Club (later called the Louisiana Club), which closed its doors in 1957 when Louie moved to San Francisco. From 1954 until 1957 William Kee, born and raised in Hawthorne, Nevada, and his younger brother Frank owned and managed the El Rio Club, not far from the Louisiana Club. They targeted the same clientele and provided inexpensive games and good Chinese and American food. They had Chinese American and African American dealers, many of whom had to be trained by the casino. The casino business provided Chinese Americans with a comfortable living but not the wealth and prosperity of Downtown Las Vegas casino owners. When Bill Kee died, his younger brother Frank Kee briefly assumed the managerial position, then closed the club and eventually settled in Oakland, California, as an accountant.[22]

The civil-rights movement ended casino discrimination, making these Chinese-owned or -operated casinos for African Americans obsolete. Chinese Americans reentered casino ownership in 1985–99 with Richard Tam's Town Hall Motel and Casino (on Koval Lane near Flamingo) and in the 1990s with Theodore B. Lee's Eureka Casino (on East Sahara Avenue), both located off the Las Vegas Strip. Lee expanded his operations to Mesquite, building a casino and separate hotel facility there. While late-nineteenth-century Chinese gambling halls had been patronized largely, but not exclusively, by Chinese and, in the 1930s and 1940s, by African Americans, these post-1985 casinos have a broader audience. In 2003 Reno-born Bob Yee became the director of Bally's and Paris Hotel Casinos, major Las Vegas Strip enterprises. This century-and-a-half tradition of Chinese-operated gaming in Nevada has continued into the twenty-first century.

In the postwar era, major casino owners became interested in attracting Asian and Asian American gamblers to Las Vegas. In December 1946 Bugsy Siegel opened the Flamingo Hotel. In order to lure Asian customers, he hired

Chinese American entertainers, including Hawaiian-born Frances Fong, who continued her career in Hollywood for the next forty years.[23] Other Asian entertainers appeared in Strip casinos in the ensuing years, and by the 1970s major Asian entertainers appeared in famous casinos for a one- or two-night show during the Chinese lunar New Year (mid-January to mid-February). Asian gambling games, including keno (which had started in Chinese laundries during the mid-nineteenth-century Comstock era in Virginia City and Carson City), were introduced. By the 1970s *pai gow,* a type of domino game, and high-low, a dice game, were commonly found in Las Vegas casinos. The interest in bringing Asian gamblers, particularly those from California, New York, Hong Kong, Taiwan, and Singapore, led to the development of special departments within major casinos to target this market through advertisement, special entertainers, and Asian restaurants as well as cultural sensitivity training programs in the post-1960 era. Insiders referred to the Asian high rollers from the United States and abroad as "whales" and offered them free lodging, meals, show tickets, and discounted airfares as well as gifts.[24] Big losers even received luxury cars. Las Vegas casino owners continue to recognize the value of Asian and Asian American gamblers to the city's economy today.

Changes in casino policies allowed more Chinese American participation in gaming as dealers. In 1960 the Fremont Hotel and Casino in Downtown Las Vegas hired Ely, Nevada–born Moon Ong, the first of many Chinese American dealers. Ong had worked in an Ely casino for several years before moving to Las Vegas.[25] Arizona-born David Lum, a graduate of the University of Nevada, Reno, learned how to deal at Bill Fong's New China Club in Reno. In the early 1970s Lum was among the few Chinese American dealers on the Strip, and he worked for over thirty years at Caesars Palace. Other Chinese American dealers quickly followed. By the late 1990s Asian American female dealers outnumbered Asian American males, perhaps because of their sex appeal. By the turn of the twenty-first century, Chinese Americans had become an integral part of the Las Vegas gaming and entertainment scene.

Making the American Dream a Reality

No Chinese American family has achieved greater prominence in Las Vegas than the Fong family. The Fongs illustrate the common phenomenon of chain migration. Like many other early Chinese families, they emigrated from Taishan County, Guangdong Province. While searching for new opportunities, Wee Kin Fong sailed to Mexico and eventually joined the staff of Gen. John G. Pershing, commander of the U.S. Army forces pursuing Pancho Villa in 1916.

Since the army needed more cooks, Wee Kin Fong sent for his oldest son, Sui Mon Fong, to join him. A year later General Pershing applied to have Wee Kin Fong and his son admitted to the United States as exceptions to the Chinese Exclusion Acts. Younger son Sui Hui soon followed.[26]

Arriving in Las Vegas in 1922, Sui Hui Fong opened the Rainbow Cafe at First and Carson with a forty-dollar investment. In 1926 his older brother Sui Mon, who had been working in Watsonville, California, drying apples, joined him. A year later the two brothers sent for Gim Fong and another young brother to help them with the prospering business. As with the earlier Arrowhead, Union Pacific Railroad crews and passengers provided a steady stream of customers to the restaurant. During the Great Depression many locals were often short of money, so the Fongs served meals free of charge. As a result they developed a reputation for their kindness and generosity throughout the community. When Big Fong (Sui Mon) died, the local press paid him tribute: "He earned what he acquired by hard work, enterprise, and intelligence, and through the appreciation of the bounties available in his adopted country."[27]

The construction of the Hoover Dam between 1931 and 1935 brought a large number of workers to the area. Realizing the potential, the three brothers decided to expand their business, opening the Silver Café in 1934 on land leased from Mrs. Charles Morgan on North First and Fremont. One of only three "large restaurants" in town, it was noted for its all-electric kitchen and twenty-four-hour service. By 1938 the restaurant could accommodate ninety-four customers and even had slot machines for entertainment.[28]

In 1939 Sui Mon Fong sent for his thirteen-year-old nephew, Wing Fong (1925–), to help out at the restaurant. It was Wing Fong who eventually rose to prominence as a business leader and real-estate developer in the Las Vegas community. While working and living with his uncles and other restaurant employees, Wing attended the local elementary and high schools. He graduated from Woodbury College in Los Angeles with a bachelor's degree in business administration in 1950. Wing had achieved what many Chinese Americans desired: educational success.[29] This derived from following the Confucian adage of education as the "equalizer of mankind," giving him the credentials to launch his business career.

While in Los Angeles, Wing courted and married Superior, Arizona-born Lilly Hing Ong (1925–2002). The first Asian American teacher in the Clark County school system, Lilly taught for five years at Fifth Street School. In 1963 she organized and taught the first Chinese-language classes in Las Vegas, and she served as the state president of the Association of American University Women in 1972–73.[30] These experiences expanded her interest in the promotion of higher education. She served for ten years (1974–84) on the board of regents for the University and Community College System of Nevada, the first Asian American woman and the first Chinese American in the nation to be elected to such a prestigious position. As regent, Lilly supported a number of key initiatives: a program to encourage senior citizens and older students to return to college; scholarships for older, needy students at the community colleges; the introduction of the first courses in Chinese language; and the granting of awards for excellence in student teaching and to distinguished professors in the College of Education at the University of Nevada, Las Vegas (UNLV). Governor Paul Laxalt appointed her to the Commission on the Status of Women and Wing to the Equal Rights Commission. She and her husband were pillars of the First Presbyterian Church in Las Vegas.

Meanwhile Wing Fong's real-estate, banking, and restaurant business had made him a success. He was able to use his business connections in the Chinese community and the larger Las Vegas community—an example of the Chinese principle of *guanxi* (networking)—to move ahead economically, socially, and politically. In partnership with his two uncles, he opened Fong's Garden in 1955 on Charleston near Fremont. Beautifully decorated inside and out with a Chinese motif and seating two hundred people, the restaurant was one of the first businesses to advertise on the newest public medium, television. Eventually, Gim Fong's son took over Fong's Garden. In the 1960s Wing started Wing Fong Enterprises, which develops, builds, and owns office and commercial buildings and develops shopping centers. He and his associates started Nevada State Bank in 1962 and Frontier Savings and Loan two years later. Because of his skill as a businessman and his reputation for integrity, Wing Fong soon became a highly respected leader in the business community.

Wing and Lilly Fong received numerous awards for their many years of community service, their promotion of Chinese traditional arts and culture, and their donations, especially to UNLV. In recognition of Lilly Fong's contributions and her service as a regent, UNLV named the geoscience building in her honor in 1985. Two years later the university dedicated the Wing Fong and Family Computer Center, a state-of-the-art computer-science facility. In 1992 the Clark County School District dedicated the Wing and Lilly Fong Elementary School, the first public elementary school named after Chinese Nevadans. In 1998 the board of regents named both Wing and Lilly Fong Distinguished Nevadans.

The success of the Fong family, and especially Wing and Lilly Fong, was possible because of opportunities in education and business that had not been available to earlier Chinese residents. Wing and Lilly Fong recognized these opportunities and, through hard work and wise planning, were able to achieve economic, social, and political success. Their two children, Kenneth and Susan, both college graduates, continue the family tradition of economic success. For this Chinese Nevadan family, the American dream became a reality.

Another successful family exemplifies the tradition of merchandising and real-estate development, a field of activity for the Chinese since the Comstock era. Joe Shoong, one of the first Chinese American millionaires in the United States, started a chain of department stores called the National Dollar Store in California in the 1920s. Recognizing the potential in Nevada, Shoong added two more stores to his fifty-three branches. The Reno National Dollar Store had a short existence in the 1950s; however, the Las Vegas National Dollar Store, opened in March 1952, proved successful. At one time one of only two department stores in Downtown Las Vegas, the store continued in operation until the late 1970s. In recognition of Shoong's contributions to the community, a five-acre park in northeastern Las Vegas was named in his honor.

Hawaiian-born, Stanford University–educated Richard Tam (1916–99), Shoong's son-in-law, became active in property acquisition and real-estate development as well as the management of the National Dollar Store.[31] He built one of the early shopping centers, located at the intersection of Las Vegas Boulevard South and Sahara. Using his engineering background, he planned numerous commercial developments. In the 1990s he raised funds for the UNLV's Tam Alumni Center and received an honorary doctorate for all of his supportive activities, dating back to the 1970s.

Shoong's daughter, Doris, and her husband, Theodore B. Lee, continued the family's involvement in real-estate development through the Urban Land Company.[32] An attorney by training, Lee, with his wife, endowed the first chair in the university's law school. Their eldest son, Gregory, an attorney, sits on the board of The Meadows School in Las Vegas and is involved in several community organizations. The family also supports the Las Vegas Symphony. In 2003 Doris became chair of the board of the Asian Art Museum in San Francisco. The Shoongs are typical of several prominent Chinese Americans who make their home and business enterprises in both Nevada and California.

Since 1965 the wave of new Chinese immigrants and Chinese Americans has had a significant impact on the growth and development of Las Vegas as well as the Chinese American community. One area of professional growth has been that of Asian healing practices. Beginning in the 1850s Nevadans consulted Chinese doctors, especially when no Western-trained physician was conveniently available, but Chinese medicine declined in popularity when the 1892 restructuring of the Chinese Exclusion Act dropped Chinese physicians from the list of occupations eligible for immigration. In the 1920s there were a few scattered Chinese practitioners around the state but none in Las Vegas. In the early 1970s Dr. Yee-kung Lok moved from Hong Kong to establish the first acupuncture clinic in Las Vegas. He persuaded the state legislature to legalize traditional Chinese medical practices in 1973, thus making Nevada the second state in the Union to take this step.[33] He chaired the Nevada State Advisory Board on Oriental Medicine and established an acupuncture training center. Ten years later there were forty licensed acupuncturists in the state, and the number continues to grow. In 2003 Las Vegas had six acupuncture clinics.

Beginning in the mid-1960s, other professionals were attracted to the rapidly growing city. Due to the shortage of Western-trained physicians, Chinese and Chinese American physicians began to open Western-medicine practices, bringing skills in specialized fields such as radiology (Dr. James Lum and Dr. Douglas Wong), allergy (Dr. Clifford Lee), surgery (Dr. Malcolm Poon), gynecology (Dr. Fred Lee, born in Boulder City), and other specialties. Other professionals, including dentists and lawyers, followed.

Among the more prominent new Chinese American entrepreneurs are Buck Wong, his son, Lawrence "Timothy," and his daughter, Nancy, who broke ground for the North Las Vegas offices of their engineering firm, Arcata, Inc., in 1990. Started in 1975 in California, Arcata employs over three hundred people in North Las Vegas.[34] The firm has contracts with Nellis Air Force Base as well as the Federal Aviation Administration and the National Aeronautics and Space Administration. Buck Wong's role as a business leader led to his election as president of the North Las Vegas Chamber of Commerce in 1994. After Buck Wong's retirement, his son assumed the leadership of the company, playing an active role in the community and serving on the board of directors of the Clark County Library District, as treasurer of the Organization of Chinese Americans (OCA), and in other organizations.

Statewide opportunities opened up for Chinese Nevada residents in the public-service sector. In 1990 Hawaii-born attorney and music professor Cheryl Lau was elected secretary of state, and in 1994 she was the unsuccessful Republican gubernatorial candidate. Her political campaigns received strong support from Asian Americans throughout the state, especially in Las Vegas, with Chinese Americans crossing party lines in support of her candidacy. Lau, who has remained very active in state and national politics, has been an inspiration for other Chinese Americans, including educator Chopin Kiang and attorney Jerome Tao, to try for public office.

Chinese Americans have also gained international and national fame in fields outside of politics. Michael Chang, who lived for several years in Henderson, Nevada, is an internationally acclaimed tennis player. Poet Stephen Liu, artist

Bill Leaf, and physicist Victor Kwong also achieved international recognition in their respective fields. Bertha Au has represented the state in the National Education Association and, before her retirement, achieved the distinction of being the longest employed Asian American in the Clark County School District. Theodore B. Lee served as a member of Harvard University's board of overseers, president of the Harvard Law School's Alumni Association, and vice chair of the University of California, Berkeley Foundation, and has been active in other organizations related to the University of California, Berkeley, and its Boalt Hall Law School.

Organizations

Like many other ethnic groups, the Chinese community recognized the need to establish and adapt traditional organizations to their present situation. In the late nineteenth century in Nevada, several family and district associations, tongs (associations or brotherhoods), chambers of commerce, and other types of mutual-aid organizations were founded. These types of voluntary associations dominated the political, social, and economic life of Chinese Americans prior to 1965.[35] In Las Vegas a chapter of the San Francisco–based Chinese Consolidated Benevolent Association (usually called the Chinese Six Companies), an organization formed for recreational, economic, and mutual-aid purposes, catered primarily to the predominantly male population. It had a center on Fremont Street and sponsored traditional Chinese cultural events, such as the Chinese New Year. Whereas Reno had the Hop Sing tong, Las Vegas had the rival Bing Kong tong, a secret fraternal mutual-aid organization that promoted gambling and helped Zee Louie establish his casinos. Both traditionally oriented groups had declined in Nevada by the early 1970s.

The influx of new immigrants, including women, and the growth of families led to the establishment of more specialized organizations. In 1976 the Las Vegas chapter of the Ying On Merchants and Laborers Benevolent Association built its center on Carson Street before moving to East Sahara Avenue. Headquartered in San Francisco, Ying On has eight branches in three states: Los Angeles, Oakland, Fresno, Bakersfield, and San Diego, California; Tucson and Phoenix, Arizona, and Las Vegas, Nevada. Like the Chinese Consolidated Benevolent Association, the organization has an English- and Chinese-language secretary. In the 1990s approximately 85 percent of the Chinese casino executives in Las Vegas belonged to this organization, which boasted over one hundred male and female—including non-Chinese—members.[36] Its main goals are charity and welfare through fellowship and assistance, and it sponsors activities such as a Chinese New Year's festival and care for the elderly. Other business organizations include the Asian Chamber of Commerce and the Chinese American Chamber of Commerce of Nevada. Mutual-aid associations include the Chinese American Compassion Association and Help for Chinese in Crises.

Transnational groups have also formed through the years. Active in the 1970s, the Chinese American Association (CAA), which was closely tied to the politics of the Republic of China (Taiwan), was socially and culturally oriented, sponsoring traditional Chinese public events such as the Moon Festival Celebration each October. Most of the members were Chinese Americans or recent Chinese immigrants. A more narrowly delineated group along the same lines is the Taiwanese Association of Las Vegas. In 1976 the U.S.–Chinese Friendship Association, closely identified with the People's Republic of China, established a chapter in Las Vegas in an effort to disseminate information to the general public about China as well as to facilitate cultural exchanges. Both nationally and locally, the membership of this group is primarily non-Chinese. Like the CAA, its leaders and members are primarily older or retired, and unless younger members can be recruited, the organization will cease to exist.

Las Vegas's Chinese American community became politically active as it grew. One of its key organizations, the OCA, was established in the 1990s as one of forty-four chapters of the national OCA, founded in 1973. Attorney Jeannie Hua was its first president, followed by Shan O-Yuan. The organization works to strengthen the national and local influence of Chinese Americans and for Asian American political empowerment and civil rights. The OCA advocates voter registration and political activism, opposes hate crimes and discrimination, lobbies for civil rights causes, and has a youth-education program to train future leaders, reinforcing Chinese American identity at the same time. An older national organization, the Chinese American Citizens Alliance (CACA), a fraternal association founded in 1895 in California, established its eighteenth chapter in Las Vegas in 2002 under the leadership of San Francisco–born attorney Benson Lee.[37] The CACA takes political positions, supports candidates, works on immigration and discrimination issues, and sponsors patriotic and scholarship programs.

Like the Washoe County Chinese, the Chinese in Clark County have realized that becoming part of a pan-Asian coalition could strengthen their position on common political issues. Various Asian American organizations, including the Asian Pacific American Forum and Asian Chamber Political Action Committee, have been established. In 1995 the Clark County Commission, acting upon a directive from the Nevada state legislature, recognized the rapidly growing Asian American population by creating a Clark County Asian American Commission under the leadership of attorney Benson Lee. The purpose of the commission was to focus on the needs of the various Asian groups in Las Vegas and recommend solutions. However, after a year and a half, the county commissioners felt that the task had been completed and did not renew the commission.

Another important organization is the Pacific American Coalition for Education (PACE), established by Asian American educators in the 1980s. This organization was designed to help non-Asian teachers learn about Asian American culture so that it could be shared in the classroom. In addition to annual teacher-training conferences, PACE has provided videotapes, books, and other educational materials for Clark County teachers' use in support of the Clark County School District's adoption of multiculturalism and recognition of diversity in the classroom. Since 1987 the private Meadows School's kindergarten and two other classes have held annual Chinese New Year parades that include singing songs in Chinese. Recognition of the importance of retaining Chinese culture led to the establishment in the 1990s of the Las Vegas Chinese Cultural Foundation and the Nevada Chinese Academy. There is a drive to establish an Asian Cultural Center in the Downtown area of Las Vegas; as of 2000, approximately two million dollars had been raised for the project.

Chinese Americans are—and long have been—supportive when disaster strikes their countrymen in the United States and in Asia. When the San Francisco earthquake and fire of 1906 devastated Chinatown, Chinese from all over the United States donated relief funds. Similarly, when the 1999 earthquake claimed 2,101 lives in Taiwan, injured thousands, and destroyed many structures, Chinese Americans joined in an effort led by the Las Vegas Asian Chamber of Commerce and raised thirty thousand dollars.[38]

Language is a primary aspect of cultural heritage. Prior to 1965 the majority of Chinese spoke either Siyi and/or Sanyi dialects of Cantonese. Lilly Fong started the first Chinese-language classes for children in Las Vegas, but she discontinued them when her first child was born. Attempts to reestablish language training failed until the 1990s, when the Las Vegas Asian Chamber of Commerce sponsored a Chinese-language academy. Soon there were classes teaching traditional Chinese writing (as taught in Taiwan), spoken Cantonese (from Hong Kong and Guangdong), spoken Fujianese (from Fujian Province), and simplified Chinese writing (as taught in the People's Republic of China). Euramerican students and biracial children also attend the classes.

The teaching of culture and traditions, especially filial piety and ancestor reverence, does not necessarily include training in religious beliefs, for Chinese Americans embrace different religious faiths. Although many consciously or unconsciously adhere to the dictates of Confucius, a fourth-century BC philosopher, those who are religious have adopted some form of Christianity. In part this was the result of the federal government's 1892 reclassification of Chinese Christian, Daoist, and Buddhist religious leaders as laborers (which prohibited them from immigrating). Chinese Americans seeking spiritual guidance turned to American Christian churches beginning in the early twentieth century. Unlike Korean Americans, whose social life revolves around their own churches, the Chinese, in general, attend the majority community's churches. The exception are the Chinese Christians and Chinese Baptists, who have established their own churches, and the small number of Buddhists, who participate in Asian American Buddhist congregations (usually affiliated with Southeast Asian immigrants or Japanese Americans), which began to flourish in the late 1970s.[39]

In addition to organizations, a number of publications have developed to facilitate communication among Asian groups. By 2001 there were several local Chinese-language newspapers and magazines that supplemented the Southern California publications circulating in Las Vegas and catered to the growing number of new Chinese immigrants who are more comfortable reading in their native language. Among these are the *Las Vegas Chinese News* and *Southern Nevada Chinese Weekly.* Several Asian Pacific American newspapers, such as the *Asian Reader,* which began in the early 1990s, are also published in Las Vegas for the Asian—especially Filipino—local population. In 1996–97 the Las Vegas Chinese Chamber of Commerce began publishing an annual Chinese business directory to encourage the newcomers to patronize Asian American businesses and services. These publications help preserve cultural identity and traditional activities while promoting Asian businesses.

Chinatowns

Cultural and economic "Asiantowns" have evolved in Las Vegas to promote Asian traditions. These differ from urban Chinatowns, which have had a residential component. Fong's Garden on East Charleston attracted other Asian restaurants and grocery stores to the area, but by the 1990s only Fong's Garden remained in the area, and by 2000 the ownership appealed to a wider Asian clientele by offering Filipino dishes. Another Asian restaurant and shopping center had developed in Commercial Center on East Sahara in the 1950s, but Asian businesses began to be displaced by Hispanic enterprises after a distinctive Chinatown was built in the 1990s.

In February 1995 the new Las Vegas Chinatown development opened on Spring Mountain Road, west of the Las Vegas Strip between Wynn Road and Arville. This project, the only Chinatown in the state, represents a new concept combining both commercial and cultural attractions on ninety thousand square feet of land. It contains several Asian restaurants, a Chinese bakery, a pan-Asian supermarket, and a Chinese traditional medicine shop as well as a number of specialty shops. For five years was there even a Buddhist wedding chapel serving Asian tourists who wanted a Las Vegas–style wedding. James Chen, president of the JHK Investment Group, developed this nonresidential Chinatown, which was patterned after others throughout the United States. Taiwan-born Chen came to the United States in 1971, arrived in Las Vegas in the early 1990s, and recognized the potential for such a development after seeing the growing Asian population in Las Vegas and the large number of Asian tourists. Asian and Asian American tourists as well as schoolchildren tour this popular ethnic enclave and cultural center. The Las Vegas Chinatown has been the site of pan-Asian festivals and performances. The annual day-long Chinese New Year celebration has attracted local residents of different ethnic backgrounds and has helped to introduce the general population to Asian foods and culture. Chen's success led to the development of other Asian businesses along Spring Mountain Road so that "Asian Town" is now several blocks long east and west of Chinatown.

Conclusion

Founded in an era when discrimination against Asians was peaking, Las Vegas offered new opportunities to Chinese Americans because of its frontier nature. The harsh environment and small population made residents work together, and as the decades passed, mutual respect among the different ethnic groups developed. Negative stereotypes of men like Wong Kee had yielded to more positive ones by the post–World War II period, as Chinese American individuals and families achieved success. However, old negative images persevered when new events recalled the past. For example, the problem of Chinese prostitution, which led to the passage of the Page Law in 1875, resurfaced dramatically in 2000 when the FBI, the Immigration and Naturalization Service, and the Las Vegas police arrested several Chinese men in Operation Jade Blade for operating brothels in Las Vegas using smuggled Asian women. Old condemnations and images of enslaved, tortured young women have been revived and publicized in television dramas. Illegal immigration also brings back memories of the 1882–1943 era of Chinese exclusion, when "paper sons and daughters" tried to immigrate using false documents.[40]

As they achieved economic success and began to merge into the larger society, Chinese Americans strove to preserve their cultural heritage. By the 1960s and 1970s second-, third-, and fourth-generation Chinese Americans were comfortable in American society. At the same time, with the increasing influx of new immigrants and a broader weltanschauung, they sought their roots in Chinese traditions. For Chinese Americans, multiculturalism meant that the various national customs could coexist and that the white American- ism of the previous century was no longer the dominant force in education and society. An allegiance to American citizenship and cultural values could be combined with selective Chinese traditions, primarily found in festivals, language, foods, clothing, and long-held values—especially respect for elders and education as a gateway to success.[41] There was a renewed interest in China, Chinese history, and "things Chinese."

Since the 1970s, Euramericans have gradually accepted the concepts of multiculturalism and minority rights. The American public began to be in- terested in China through educational institutions, public forums, and travel. In 1992 President George Bush designated May as Asian Heritage Month, and in 2000 Governor Kenny Guinn proclaimed the same for Nevada.[42] Thus the Chinese Americans' search for their cultural traditions, reflected in the different types of organizations and activities they have developed in Las Vegas, has coincided with an American interest in Chinese culture and the Chinese ancestral homeland. This cultural symbiosis has helped Chinese Americans, in Las Vegas and throughout the country, to realize that while preserving as much of their culture as possible, they must participate in the larger community and in politics in order to make the American dream their reality.

Notes

1. For more details see George Anthony Peffer, *If They Don't Bring Their Women Here: Chinese Female Immigration Before Exclusion* (Urbana: University of Illinois Press, 1999); Huping Ling, *Surviving on the Gold Mountain: Chinese American Women and Their Lives* (Albany: State University of New York Press, 1998); Sucheng Chan, ed., *Entry Denied: Exclusion and the Chinese Community in America, 1882–1943* (Phila- delphia: Temple University Press, 1991), especially Chan, "The Exclusion of Chinese Women, 1870–1943," 94–146.

2. As ethnic Chinese from Southeast Asia, Taiwan, Hong Kong, the Philippines, and elsewhere began to settle in Nevada and brought with them different dialects of Chinese, communication often had to be in English. Prior to 1965 the majority of Chinese spoke either Siyi and/or Sanyi dialects of Cantonese. For an overview, see Sue Fawn Chung, "Destination Nevada, the Silver Mountain," in *Origins and Destina-*

tions: 41 Essays on Chinese America (Los Angeles: A Joint Project of the Chinese Historical Society of Southern California and UCLA Asian American Studies, 1994), 111–39. Several studies cover the restrictive immigration laws, for example, Bill Ong Hing, *Making and Remaking Asian America Through Immigration Policy, 1850–1990* (Stanford: Stanford University Press, 1993); Lucy E. Salyer, *Laws Harsh as Tigers: Chinese Immigrants and the Shaping of Modern Immigration Law* (Chapel Hill: University of North Carolina Press, 1995); Andrew Gyory, *Closing the Gate: Race, Politics, and the Chinese Exclusion Act* (Chapel Hill: University of North Carolina Press, 1998); Charles J. McClain, *In Search of Equality: The Chinese Struggle Against Discrimination in Nineteenth-Century America* (Berkeley: University of California Press, 1994).

3. Figures are from the U.S. Department of Commerce, Bureau of the Census, *Census of Population: Nevada* [title varies] (Washington, D.C.: Government Printing Office, 1880–2002). Census figures are only indicative—many Chinese are usually missed.

4. These numbers are based upon figures from the Chinese American Data Center, at http://members.aol.com/chineseusa/00cen3htm, and differ from the 14,694 in the Las Vegas, Nevada–Arizona Metropolitan Statistical Area and 3,239 in the Reno Metropolitan Statistical Area of Chinese ethnicity alone, at http://mumford1.dyndns.org/cen2000/AsianPop/AsianPopData/32st.htm for the state; http://mumford1.dyndns.org/cen2000/AsianPop/AsianPopData/4120msa.htm for Las Vegas MSA; http://mumford1.dyndns.org/cen2000/AsianPop/AsianPopData/6720cc.htm for Reno MSA. Taiwanese and Chinese of mixed ethnicities were counted separately. See also U.S. Census Bureau, *Census 2000,* Summary File 1, table P7 at www.census.gov; U.S. Department of Commerce, Bureau of the Census, *1990 Census of Population: General Population Characteristics: Nevada* (Washington, D.C.: Government Printing Office, 1992), table 26.

5. http://mumford1.dyndns.org/cen2000/AsianPop/AsianPopData/32st.htm; http://mumford1.dyndns.org/cen2000/AsianPop/AsianPopData/4120msa.htm. The rapid growth of Asian Americans in Las Vegas is noted in detail in M. Gottdiener, Claudia C. Collins, and David R. Dickens, *Las Vegas: The Social Production of an All-American City* (Malden, Mass.: Blackwell, 1999), 108–9.

6. L. K. Hong, "Recent Immigrants in the Chinese-American Community: Issues of Adaptations and Impacts," *International Migration Review* 10 (1976): 509–14. See also Xiaojian Zhao, *Remaking Chinese America: Immigration, Family, and Community, 1940–1965* (New Brunswick, N.J.: Rutgers University Press, 2002); Shehong Chen, *Being Chinese, Becoming Chinese American* (Urbana: University of Illinois Press, 2002). Min Zhou and John R. Logan, "Returns on Human Capital in Ethnic Enclaves: New York City's Chinatown," *American Sociological Review* 54 (October 1989): 816.

7. There is a large body of literature on this distinction between native-born and foreign-born Chinese. See, for example, Bernard Wong, *Chinatown: Economic Adaptation and Ethnic Identity of the Chinese* (New York: Holt, Rinehart and Winston, 1982); Leland T. Saito, *Race and Politics: Asian Americans, Latinos, and Whites in a Los*

Angeles Suburb (Urbana: University of Illinois Press, 1998); Susie Lan Cassel, ed., *The Chinese in America: A History from Gold Mountain to the New Millennium* (Walnut Creek, Calif.: AltaMira Press, 2002).

8. Philip I. Earl, "Nevada's Miscegenation Laws and the Marriage of Mr. And Mrs. Harry Bridges," *Nevada Historical Society Quarterly* 37, no. 1 (1994): 1–17; Morrison G. Wong, "A Look at Intermarriage Among the Chinese in the United States," *Sociological Perspectives* 32 (1989): 87–107. See also Betty Lee Sung, *Chinese American Intermarriage* (New York: Center for Migration Studies, 1990); Huping Ling, "Family and Marriage of Late-Nineteenth and Early-Twentieth-Century Chinese Immigrant Women," *Journal of American Ethnic History* 19, no. 2 (Winter 2000): 43–63; Yen Le Espiritu, *Asian American Women and Men: Labor, Laws, and Love* (Thousand Oaks, Calif.: Sage, 1997). Harry H. Kitano and Wai-tsang Yeung, "Chinese Interracial Marriage," *Marriage and Family Review* 5, no. 1 (Spring 1982): 35–48, contradicts Zhenchao Qian, Sampson Lee Blair, and Stacey Ruf, "Asian Americans' Marriage with Whites: Ethnic Differences in Educational and Nativity Assortative Mating" (paper presented at the American Sociological Association, 1999), which analyzed 1990 figures and found more Chinese immigrant–white marriages. The reason for the difference is the increased contact between China and the United States, 1980–2000. See also U.S. Census Bureau, *Census 2000,* Redistricting Data (PL 94–171), Summary File, table 1; Xuanning Fu, Jessika Tora, and Heather Kendall, "Marital Happiness and Inter-Racial Marriage: A Study in a Multi-Ethnic Community in Hawaii," *Journal of Comparative Family Studies* 32, no. 1 (Winter 2001): 47–60.

9. Published by Random House, 1998, and on the best-seller list that year.

10. John Higham has written numerous books and articles dealing with this subject. See, for example, "Current Trends in the Study of Ethnicity in the United States," *Journal of American Ethnic History* 1 (1982): 5–15. See also Leonard Dinnerstein and David M. Reimers, *Ethnic Americans: A History of Immigration,* 4th ed. (New York: Columbia University Press, 1999).

11. There is a wide range of literature on this subject. See, for example, Raymond Teske and Bardin H. Nelson, "Acculturation and Assimilation: A Clarification," *American Ethnologist* 1, no. 2 (May 1974): 351–68; Russell A. Kazal, "Revisiting Assimilation: The Rise, Fall, and Reappraisal of a Concept in American Ethnic History," *American Historical Review* 100, no. 3 (April 1995): 437–71.

12. See Loren B. Chan, "The Chinese in Nevada: An Historical Survey, 1856–1970," *Nevada Historical Society Quarterly* 25 (Winter 1982): 266–314; Sue Fawn Chung, "Destination Nevada, the Silver Mountain," 111–39; Paul Siu, *The Chinese Laundryman: A Study of Social Isolation* (New York: New York University Press, 1987); *Las Vegas Age,* February 1, June 13, 27, 1908, August 21, 1909, November 8, 1913. See also Chan, "The Chinese in Nevada," 273–74. This Wong Kee should not be confused with the wealthy miner Wong Kee of American Canyon who was a friend of "Death Valley Scotty." See David W. Valentine, "American Canyon: A Chinese Village," *Halcyon* (1999): 107–30; David W. Valentine, "Historical Archaeological Investigations at 26PE2137: American Canyon, Pershing County, Nevada" (master's thesis,

University of Nevada, Las Vegas, 1999), available on-line from the Lied Library Catalogue. John Fong, interview by author, Carlin, Nevada, July 2000. Fong owned such a restaurant in Carlin.

13. *Clark County Review,* October 22, 1910.

14. *Las Vegas Age,* April 2, 1910. On the matter of opium, see, for example, Gregory Yee Mark, "Opium in America and the Chinese," *Chinese America: History and Perspectives* (San Francisco: Chinese Historical Society of America, 1997), 61–74; R. K. Newman, "Opium Smoking in Late Imperial China: A Reconsideration," *Modern Asian Studies* 29, no. 4 (October 1995): 765–94. See *Las Vegas Age,* September 11, 1909, February 28, 1914. Wong Kee brought the case to the Supreme Court of Nevada, *Wong Kee* v. *Lillis, Justice of the Peace, 138 Pac Reporter, 1998,* February 18, 1914. See also Lucy Salyer, "Captives of Law: Judicial Enforcement of the Chinese Exclusion Laws, 1891–1905," *Journal of American History* 76, no. 1 (June 1989): 91–117, on the Chinese successes in court. *Las Vegas Age,* July 5, 1913; *Las Vegas Age,* November 8, 1913. The county commissioners then allowed the sheriff to spend twenty-five cents per meal from a Euramerican provider. This practice of complaining about the food prepared by a Chinese restaurant in order to change providers occurred frequently throughout Nevada in the late nineteenth and early twentieth centuries.

15. National Archives and Records Administration, U.S. Census Manuscript, 1910, Nevada, Clark County, Las Vegas, microfilm.

16. *Las Vegas Age,* January 22, April 15, 1916; *Las Vegas Age,* November 6, 1920, September 17, 1932; *Las Vegas Review-Journal,* April 22, 1973. A photograph of Sam Yet is on file at the University of Nevada, Las Vegas, Lied Library, Special Collections, Cashman Collection.

17. *Las Vegas Age,* September 17, 1932.

18. National Archives and Records Administration, U.S. Census Manuscript, 1920, Nevada, Clark County, Las Vegas, microfilm.

19. Author's interviews with several who wished to remain anonymous. The story of the boy's beating was even covered in the *Tonopah Bonanza,* February 16, 23, 1921.

20. These ideas were expressed by Ed Kim in Leslie G. Kelen and Eileen Hallet Stone, *Missing Stories: An Oral History of Ethnic and Minority Groups in Utah* (Salt Lake City: University of Utah Press, 1996), 208; Frank Chang of Lovelock, interview by Sue Fawn Chung and Mary K. Rusco, 1996, tape deposited in University of Nevada, Las Vegas, Lied Library, Special Collections. According to the 1970 census, 51 percent of the Chinese males and 57 percent of the Chinese females in Nevada over the age of sixteen had graduated from high school, and by 1980 they remained employed primarily in the service industry (941), with an increasing number in managerial and professional occupations (333) as well as in technical, sales, and administrative-support positions (329). Their median earnings were lower than those of their Euramerican counterparts. For more details, see Sue Fawn Chung, "The Chinese Experience in Nevada: Success Despite Discrimination," *Nevada Public Affairs Review* 2 (1987): 50.

21. *Las Vegas Review-Journal,* September 19, 1931. See also September 9, 26, Octo-

ber 1, 3, 9, 10, 15, 17, 23, 24, 1931, June 29, 1932. Photographs of Frances Fong are on file at the University of Nevada, Las Vegas, Lied Library, Special Collections, Asian-American file. Frances Fong, interview by author, Northridge, California, 1996. See *Las Vegas Review-Journal,* September 19, 1931, on the grand opening of China Town.

22. *St. Patrick Johnson* v. *Harry Lee Fong et al.* (April 1944) in Clark County Commission, *Book of Records,* 1944, Nevada Historical Society, Las Vegas; David Lum, interview by author, Las Vegas, 2001, transcript on file at the University of Nevada, Las Vegas, Special Collections, Asian American file; Clark County Commission, *Book of Records,* 1955, Nevada Historical Society, Las Vegas. Descriptions of gambling in these Chinese-owned and -operated casinos come from anonymous sources and a 2001 interview by the author in Las Vegas with David Lum, who worked at Fong's New China Club and, for over twenty years, Caesars Palace in Las Vegas. William and Frank Kee were the sons of Ah Cum Kee, who was born in Carson City. See Sue Fawn Chung, "Ah Cum Kee and Loy Lee Ford: Between Two Worlds," in *Ordinary Women, Extraordinary Lives: Women in American History,* ed. Kriste Lindenmeyer (Wilmington, Del.: Scholarly Resources, 2000), 179–96. For information about William Kee and the El Rio Club, see *Las Vegas Review-Journal,* March 6, 1956, January 24, 1957. A fire broke out at the El Rio, and William Kee extinguished it, but the stress led to his heart failure shortly thereafter.

23. Frances Fong, interview by author, Northridge, California, 1996.

24. There are many articles on this topic. See, for example, *Las Vegas Review-Journal,* January 25, 2001, Section D; *Las Vegas Review-Journal,* April 20, 2001. In a random survey on lifestyles of five hundred Chinese Americans in the San Francisco Bay Area in August 2000, 44 percent of the households queried had visited Las Vegas in the past year, and the percentage for Los Angeles, which is closer, is probably higher (*Jade Magazine* [San Francisco], September 2000).

25. Katherine Ong (Moon Ong's daughter), interview by author, Las Vegas, 1996.

26. *Las Vegas Review-Journal,* July 23, 1978, on Big Fong's death. This account differs from contemporary accounts on the dating of the events leading up to the opening of the restaurants.

27. Ibid., July 21, 1978.

28. Ibid., October 28, 1938.

29. Information on Wing and Lilly Fong was obtained from the Fong Biographical File and several oral histories of Wing, Lilly, and those who knew them on deposit at the University of Nevada, Las Vegas, Lied Library, Special Collections. See also Lisa Fremont [Williams], "Lilly Fong: Family, Community and University," unpublished student paper, 1992, University of Nevada, Las Vegas, Lied Library, Special Collections; Chung, "The Chinese Experience in Nevada," 49; John Cronan, *Nevada Men and Women of Achievement* (Las Vegas: n.p., 1966); *Nevada: The Silver State* (Carson City: Western State Historical Publishers, 1970), 1:223–26; Natalie Patton, "Fong, Former Member of Board of Regents, Dies," *Las Vegas Review-Journal,* March 21, 2002. The Fongs' was a typical Chinese employment family-living situation. See Andrew Sanchirico, "The Importance of Small-Business Ownership in Chinese Ameri-

can Educational Achievement," *Sociology of Education* 64 (October 1991): 293–304.

30. The importance of Chinese language for Chinese Americans is detailed in Him Mark Lai, "Retention of the Chinese Heritage: Chinese Schools in America Before World War II," *Chinese America* (2000): 10–31; Him Mark Lai, "Retention of the Chinese Heritage, Part II: Chinese Schools in America, World War II to the Present," *Chinese America* (2001): 1–30; see also Lai's bibliography for other works in this field.

31. Monica Caruso, "Las Vegas Developer Tam Dies," *Las Vegas Review-Journal,* July 8, 1999.

32. Adam Steinhauer, "Mesquite's Latest," *Las Vegas Review-Journal,* February 17, 1997, on Theodore B. Lee and his family. See also Natalie Patton, "Endowment Gives Law School Prestige Boost," *Las Vegas Review-Journal,* March 12, 2001. Doris and Theodore Lee, interviews by author, Las Vegas, 1998–99.

33. Anton Sohn, *The Healers of 19th Century Nevada* (Reno: Greasewood Press, 1997) gives background on Chinese doctors. See also F. P. Li, "Traditional Chinese Medicine in the United States," *Journal of the American Medical Association* 220 (1972): 1132–33; Haiming Liu, "The Resilience of Ethnic Culture: Chinese Herbalists in the American Medical Profession," *Journal of Asian American Studies* 1, no. 2 (May 1998): 173–91. Hawaii was the first state to legalize traditional Chinese medicine.

34. Information on Buck Wong comes from his daughter, Nancy Wong, of Las Vegas; *U.S.–Asian Chronicle* (June 1997): 2.

35. Paul Wong, Steven Applewhite, and J. Michael Daley, "From Despotism to Pluralism: The Evolution of Voluntary Organizations in Chinese American Communities," *Ethnic Groups* 8, no. 4 (November 1990): 215–34.

36. Lisa (Fremont) Williams interviewed several officers in 1992–93 and provided information about the organization. See also *Las Vegas Sun,* February 2, 1977.

37. Judy DeLoretta, "Asians Making Local Impact," *Las Vegas Review-Journal,* March 1, 2000; Sue Fawn Chung, "Fighting for Their American Rights: A History of the Chinese American Citizens Alliance," in *Claiming America: Constructing Chinese American Identities during the Exclusion Era,* ed. K. Scott Wong and Sucheng Chan (Philadelphia: Temple University Press, 1998), 95–126.

38. Debra D. Bass, "Asian Groups Come to Aid of Taiwan Quake Victims," *Las Vegas Review-Journal,* September 28, 1999.

39. The Bureau of Immigration made the definitive decision in 1899 to classify Chinese Christians as laborers as well. See the records of the Immigration and Naturalization Service, Record Group 85, Entry 132, Correspondence, Box 3, File 104, February 24, 1899; *Las Vegas Yellow Pages,* July 2001. The American Southern Baptists, Episcopalians, Methodists, Presbyterians, and Catholics were active in missionary work in China. See also *Las Vegas Chinese Business Directory, 2003,* in the University of Nevada, Las Vegas, Lied Library, Special Collections, Asian American File.

40. Carri Geer Thevenot, "Illegal Prostitution Ring," *Las Vegas Review-Journal,* September 19, 2000. On "paper sons and daughters," see, for example, Ko-lin Chin, *Smuggled Chinese: Clandestine Immigration to the United States* (Philadelphia: Temple University Press, 1999).

41. William Wei, *The Asian American Movement* (Philadelphia: Temple University Press, 1993) discusses this phenomenon. Lornita Yuen-Fan Wong, *Education of Chinese Children in Britain and the USA* (Clevedon, England: Multilingual Matters, 1992), 110, is one of many studies done in this area.

42. *Public Law,* 102–450.

The Italian American Social Club, E. Sahara Ave. Photograph by Jeanne Sharp Howerton

Temple Beth Shalom, Hazelwood Lane in Summerlin. Photograph by Jeanne Sharp Howerton

Fong's Garden, E. Charleston Blvd. Photograph by Jeanne Sharp Howerton

St. Joan of Arc, the first Catholic Church in Las Vegas and place of worship for early ethnic groups, including Italians, Irish, and Croatians, Casino Center Drive. Photograph by Jeanne Sharp Howerton

Soccer match between Hispanic teams, Bonanza Rd. in NE Las Vegas. Photograph by Jeanne Sharp Howerton

Jamia (Mosque) Masjid of Islamic Society of Nevada, E. Desert Inn Rd. Photograph by Jeanne Sharp Howerton

The Moulin Rouge, Las Vegas's first integrated casino resort, W. Bonanza Rd., 1955. Photograph courtesy of Nevada State Museum and Historical Society

Ecos de Chile folkloric troupe. Photograph by Hon. Paula B. Sparkuhl

Chinese New Year celebration, downtown Las Vegas, 1960s. Photograph courtesy of Sue Fawn Chung

Pinjuv Brothers' gas station, liquor store, and motel, an early Croatian-owned business, Fremont and 10th Streets, late 1930s. Photograph courtesy of Nevada State Museum and Historical Society.

Parade float of the Federation of Filipino American Organizations of Nevada. Photograph by Rozita Lee

Inauguration of the consulate general of El Salvador, N. Nellis Blvd., January 2004. Photograph by Thomas C. Wright

Scottish pipe bands on Fremont Street, 2002. Photograph courtesy of Deborah Sgambati

Super Mercado del Pueblo, one of many Hispanic markets in Las Vegas, Rancho Drive and Washington. Photograph by Jeanne Sharp Howerton

Temple of the Nevada Buddhist Association, S. Jones Blvd. Photograph by Jeanne Sharp Howerton

St. John's Greek Orthodox Church, El Camino and Hacienda. Photograph by Jeanne Sharp Howerton

Hindu temple of Las Vegas, Sageberry Drive, Summerlin. Photograph by Jeanne Sharp Howerton

Las Vegas Paiute Resort and golf course, U.S. Highway 95 Northwest of Las Vegas. Photograph by Jeanne Sharp Howerton

Second Baptist Church, Madison Avenue on the West Side. Photograph by Jeanne Sharp Howerton

CHAPTER 7

The Greeks

E. D. KARAMPETSOS & STAVROS ANTHONY

Between 1905 and 1922 almost half the able-bodied Greek men—nearly 450,000—left their homeland to find work in the United States. Almost a third came to the intermountain West, where work in mines and on the railroads was plentiful, and they were among the first to arrive in Las Vegas to help build and work on the railroad. The earliest record of their presence is an article in a 1905 *Las Vegas Age,* which complains that Greeks and other immigrant workers, who lived in tents near the tracks, made too much noise by staying up all night singing and shooting their guns in the air.[1] These Greek workers did not stay in Las Vegas once their work was completed but moved on, probably following the railroad to the next place where their labor was needed. The first Greeks to settle permanently in Las Vegas moved there in 1915. The community grew very slowly until the 1940s, when its growth began to accelerate.[2]

The earliest reference to Greeks in Nevada is in Myron Angel's 1881 *History of Nevada,* where two Greeks with the Americanized names of Henderson and John Fleming are listed as part of an ill-fated band of irregulars led by Major William Ormsby on a punitive expedition against the Paiute Indians in 1880. The Paiutes, falsely suspected of going on the warpath, killed most of their pursuers at Pyramid Lake. Whether the two Greeks survived is not mentioned.[3] The 1880 census counts two Greek families, Antipas and one with an Americanized name, Andrews, among the residents of Carson City. It would be surprising if there were more, because very few Greeks came to America before 1897.

People on the frontier might have been surprised to encounter flesh-and-blood Greeks, because, at best, they might have been familiar with the history of the ancient Greeks. Probably only historians would have known what came afterward, but the Greeks did survive. The Roman Empire absorbed the Greek world in the second century BC, and—as citizens of Byzantium, the Eastern Roman Empire—they learned to call themselves Romans. Even today, Greeks refer to themselves alternately as Hellenes, Grekoi, or Romioi. With the coming of Christianity, the Greeks entered a new multiethnic, multiracial empire of faith that stretched from Kiev to Ireland and as far away as India and Ethiopia. In 1453 Byzantium fell to the Turks, and the Greeks had to wait until the early nineteenth century to finally liberate a part of their land.

At the end of the nineteenth century, Athens, with a population of nearly 125,000, was the provincial capital of a country whose economy depended on farming and its merchant fleets, with important Greek communities in the Middle East and Africa. Constantinople (today's Istanbul) was the spiritual center of the Greek world, and Alexandria, with over 300,000 Greeks, its cultural capital.[4] Hundreds of thousands of Greeks lived along the Black Sea, in the south of Russia, in the Caucasus, and elsewhere. Nineteenth-century nationalism and ethnic cleansing put an end to this ancient Greek diaspora, sending uprooted Greeks to a homeland they had never known. Unfortunately Greece, suffering from crop failures and disastrous wars of expansion, was too poor to feed even its own inhabitants, who were compelled to join a monumental wave of emigration to America and other equally distant lands. Most of the early Greek immigrants, primarily males, had never ventured far beyond their native villages; they were virtually illiterate, knew little about the United States, and did not speak English.

White Pine County

In the early twentieth century almost all of the Greek immigrants coming to Nevada were drawn to White Pine County, where jobs were plentiful. By 1910 Greek immigrants were "the dominant labor force in the mines, mills and smelters of White Pine County, Nevada, and Salt Lake County, Utah."[5] In that year, for example, Greek immigrant workers (from 1,500 to 1,600 persons, virtually all men) comprised 5.8 percent of the population of Nevada and 10 percent of that of White Pine County. The Greeks lacked the training required for more skilled positions in an industrial economy, but like the Italians, Croats, Serbs, and other Slavs who arrived at about the same time, they willingly performed the menial, dangerous tasks native-born Americans disdained. They were housed twelve to sixteen in tents and received the lowest wages possible for their efforts. In addition foreigners such as the Greeks, who often had no idea they were being used as scabs, were frequently hired as a source of cheap, expendable labor to replace American workers who dared to go on strike.

Like most of the immigrant and American workers in the West at the time, the Greeks were almost exclusively young unmarried males, ranging from teenagers to men in their early thirties. There were three men for every woman, yet "white" women were off-limits to Greeks and members of other "undesirable" ethnic groups.[6] Without the example of their elders and the presence of women to soften their lives, their existence was often violent and brutal. The word *Greek* appeared almost daily in the headlines of White Pine newspapers. Sometimes the articles were not about Greeks, but the word was used as a synonym for *foreigner*. Most of the crimes involving Greeks reported by the papers were minor, involving unruly behavior and the violation of liquor laws. More frequently, however, the headlines noted the death of yet another young man or the loss of limbs in railroad accidents, mine explosions, or cave-ins.

The extent of the mistrust of Greeks can be found in the story of the shooting of Constable Davis in 1908, an event described by the Nevada historian Russell Elliott as the "climax of anti-foreign feeling in McGill."[7] Davis was in McGill looking for a load of stolen lumber when he came upon Tony Vasilopoulos, who was sawing lumber to build a stable. A few minutes later, he fled the scene seriously wounded by a bullet from the Greek's weapon. Soon afterward, law-enforcement officers and others acting as vigilantes swarmed through McGill's Greektown in search of Vasilopoulos and his alleged confederates. With an engine and crew, yard master James A. Smith pursued and mortally wounded Dimitris Kalampokas, who had no connection with the shooting. By the end of the day large numbers of Greeks had been rounded up and locked in boxcars, the intention being to expel them from White Pine County. In the end, however, the Nevada Northern Railway refused to haul the Greeks free of charge, and they had to be released the following morning.[8]

Wherever they settled in the United States, Greek immigrants attempted to reestablish the institutions of their homeland: the Greek Orthodox Church, Greek schools, the coffeehouse, and fraternal organizations. Greek-language newspapers appeared wherever they settled in large numbers. To better cope with life in America, the Greek immigrants organized local chapters of national organizations, such as the Panhellenic Union (established in 1907), whose main objective was to encourage their return to Greece, until—according to Steven Philips—it foundered on the eve of World War I as a result of accusations of fiscal mismanagement and its serving as an agent of the Greek government.[9] Later, in the 1920s, once immigrants realized their stay was going to be permanent, they joined the American Hellenic Educational and Progressive Association (AHEPA), whose main objective was to facilitate their assimilation while, at the same time, encouraging ethnic pride. The association had been founded by Greek American businessmen in Atlanta, Georgia, in 1922. The secret, male organization preached a doctrine of

Americanization and nonsectarianism. A year later the Greek American Progressive Association (GAPA) was founded with the goal of preserving the Greek identity of its members.

Although many Greeks came to the United States with the intention of making money and returning to Greece, almost 60 percent eventually decided to remain and become American citizens. Settling permanently involved getting married, starting families, and building Greek Orthodox churches. Built in 1910, St. Barbara's Greek Orthodox Church in McGill has the distinction of being one of the first Greek Orthodox churches west of the Mississippi. In 1930 St. Alexios Greek Orthodox Church was dedicated in Ely. The festivals of the Orthodox Church—in particular the Easter celebration, to which they invited the entire community—permitted Greek immigrants to present their best side to the American public, as they still do today.

On the eve of the great strike of 1912, the *Ely Daily Mining Expositor* estimated the Greek population of White Pine County at 1,600. The *Expositor's* informal census was provoked by a call to arms by the Greek government, which needed men for the Balkan Wars. Several hundred men left White Pine County to enlist in the Greek army, but most remained behind. Almost 90 percent of the men had already served once in the Greek army, as the *Expositor* found, and many were not interested in fighting again.[10]

The 1912 strike permanently changed the fortune of the Greek community in White Pine County. The Western Federation of Miners (WFM), which had organized the nonunion industry, went on strike demanding recognition of the union and a wage increase. On September 17, 1912, the strike started in Bingham, Utah, and on October 14 the WFM issued a general strike order in White Pine County. In order to break the strike, Nevada Consolidated exploited divisions among the workers and brought in professional strikebreakers. In the resulting violence two Greek strikers, George Prinaris and George Pappas, were killed and others were wounded. Nevada Consolidated finally agreed to give its workers the desired wage increase but refused to recognize the union, and in mid-November the strike ended with the union's defeat.[11]

As a result of the strike and the decline of the mining economy in White Pine County, many Greek immigrants moved to other parts of Nevada and the United States where their prospects were brighter. The entry of the United States into World War I in 1917 gave the Greeks who remained an opportunity to prove their loyalty to the country. They organized patriotic demonstrations at McGill and Ely, which brought them unaccustomed praise. The *Ely Record* reports that a meeting of Greeks in McGill raised almost nine thousand dollars—a huge sum for the time—in support of the war effort. On July 27, 1917, the *Ely Record* published the names of four hundred men listed by the local draft board. Almost a quarter of the names are Greek; many of the men named later enlisted or were drafted.[12]

The social and cultural barriers Greek immigrants encountered before World War I gradually weakened in the twenties and thirties and virtually disappeared as a result of World War II. According to William Flangas, whose father was one of the early Greek immigrants in White Pine County, all the young men went into the army to defend their country, and this prolonged absence from their ethnic communities had transformed them into Americans by the time they returned home at the end of the war, so that "we mixed with and married anyone we wanted."[13] Few Greeks now live in White Pine County. The children of the immigrants moved away a long time ago, going as far as their talents would take them and wherever there were new opportunities. Many now reside in Reno and Las Vegas, where some are active in politics and various other professions.

First Las Vegas Greeks

John Pappas, the first Greek to settle permanently in Las Vegas, came as part of a railroad construction crew. On leaving Greece as a boy, he went first to Chicago and later to Salt Lake City to work on the railroad. While still in his early teens, he found employment on the San Pedro, Los Angeles and Salt Lake Railroad construction line as a water boy. In 1905 the railroad came through Las Vegas, bringing Pappas with it. Although the railroad transferred him back to Salt Lake City, he eventually returned to become a permanent resident and community leader.[14]

In 1915 a group of Greek men working on the railroad in Idaho, among them George and Nick Sackas, moved to Las Vegas after hearing of better-paying work. For nearly fifteen years after that, the Greek population of Las Vegas fluctuated between five and eight men. Following the onset of the 1930s Depression, the railroad laid off many workers and, as a result, only two or three Greeks remained in Las Vegas.[15]

Putting Down Roots: Families and Businesses

The construction of Hoover Dam attracted hundreds of workers and softened the effects of the Depression. By the time the dam was completed in 1935, the Greek population had grown to over twenty, with three established families. The new arrivals did not come to Las Vegas to work on the dam or in the newly legalized casinos but to set up restaurants, a business traditionally associated with the Greek immigrants in America. In 1931 John Pappas, along with Sam Poulos, Jim Adres, and John Valache, opened the White Spot Cafe, Las Vegas's first Greek-owned restaurant. Located on Fremont Street, the White Spot served inexpensive American fare and had the distinction of being the first restaurant in Las Vegas to feature cloth napkins, air-conditioning, and a neon sign.[16]

During the 1930s and 1940s, other Greek restaurants appeared in Las Vegas. John Stathus opened the Busy Bee Cafe and Sam Poulos the State Cafe. George Tsouras opened the Las Vegas BBQ Restaurant in 1947. Tom Panos, who came to Las Vegas in 1939, bought and sold several restaurants, the last being the Melody Lane Restaurant at Third Street and Fremont, which was open from 1952 to 1972.[17]

Several Greeks operated small hotels, while others went into the wholesale food and beverage industry. Bill Cosulas came to Las Vegas in 1936 and founded Bonanza Beverage, a major liquor wholesale firm. In 1948 a Greek family in Las Vegas started Moran-Shetakis Wholesalers, a supplier of food to restaurants and casinos. John Moran eventually left the wholesale business to join the Las Vegas Metropolitan Police Department and eventually was elected sheriff.[18]

In 1931 George Sackas went to Los Angeles on vacation, where he met his future wife and got married. His wife, Lea, loved Las Vegas from the moment she arrived there, finding the small town pleasant and, unlike other parts of the state and the country, without any anti-Greek hostility. She immediately enrolled in an English language class and eventually went as far as seventh grade, which she did not complete because she was "short on math."[19] They had their first child in 1933, forming the first permanent Greek family in Las Vegas. In 1932 Sam Poulos met and married Venea in Salt Lake City. Tom Panos, a successful restaurateur in the 1940s, met Wilma in McGill, Nevada. The three Greek families all lived on Ninth Street between Fremont and Bridger.[20]

During the 1930s, in addition to the Greek families, there were, according to Lea Sackas, fifteen to twenty single Greek railroad workers, too few Greeks to sustain formal organizations. Instead, the women would visit each other's homes for coffee, while the men socialized primarily in Greek-owned restaurants; but these were difficult times and, as Sackas pointed out, the early Greeks were more inclined to work than socialize. Although the young wives were comfortable in Las Vegas, they were, as Lea Sackas put it, "so homesick for Greece, it was pathetic." Consequently, every two or three months the families would travel to Los Angeles or Salt Lake City in search of Greek company.

Unlike the stereotypical Greek immigrant in the first half of the twentieth century, Greek Cypriot Paul Ralli was well educated and held a law degree from the University of London. Ralli immediately fell in love with Las Vegas and recorded his experience in two autobiographical works, *Nevada Lawyer: A Story of Life and Love in Las Vegas* (1949) and *Viva Vegas* (1953). Ralli came to Las Vegas in 1933 after passing the bar examination in Reno. According to his account in *Nevada Lawyer,* he came into town with ten dollars in his pocket, but money started rolling in as soon as he hung out a shingle as a divorce lawyer. In search of a place to work, Ralli had the good fortune to ask for help from Bert Henderson, who lent him an office in exchange for occasional legal research. Ralli settled into his office the next day:

> While I was nailing pictures on the wall, a young woman came in and asked if I were an attorney.
>
> "Do you handle divorce cases?" she inquired.
>
> "All attorneys handle divorce cases," I said, halting my picture-hanging pastime.
>
> She then proceeded to write a check for one hundred and fifty dollars.
>
> "Will you take my case for that amount?" she inquired. "I understand that it is the minimum fee, and I can't afford more."
>
> "Very well then, the minimum it is," I agreed.
>
> That minimum was a fabulous fortune to me. It was remarkable, I thought, that so many things had happened to me in twenty-four hours, for in that short space of time I had obtained free office space to practice law, a connection with an old established law firm, and one hundred and fifty dollars of my own. I felt right with the world, rich and confident, capable of indulging in the contemptuous aloofness of the born rich toward the plebeians.
>
> That night I celebrated, not alone, but with my first client.
>
> Yes, Las Vegas was a wonderful place![21]

Although his education permitted him to fit seamlessly into the life of the community at large, Ralli did not forget his origins, for, as Lea Sackas recalled, "He loved his Greek customs."

Before coming to Las Vegas, Ralli had supporting roles in the movies *Married in Hollywood* (1929), *Montmartre Rose* (1929), *Show People* (1928), and *The Diego Water Hole* (1928). According to Jerry Giesler: "He appeared on the stage as Mae West's leading man in 'Diamond Lil,' . . . He served as Deputy District Attorney, and later was elected City Attorney of Las Vegas, Nevada, resigning in 1942 to enter the armed forces of the United States."[22] Ralli, who died in 1953 at the age of fifty, is a typical example of the Greek immigrants who came to America in increasing numbers in the second half of the century. Unlike their predecessors, many of these immigrants were educated and comfortable in modern, technological society.

Growth After Midcentury

From the 1940s through the 1960s, the Greek population of Las Vegas grew to almost 300. One reason for this growth was the passage of the Immigration and Nationality Act in 1965, which permitted greater numbers of Greek immigrants to enter the United States. Prior to 1920 there was virtually unrestricted access to the United States. However, after 1918 a series of federal immigration acts culminated in the 1924 National Origins Act, which increasingly limited immigration to the point of virtually cutting it off until the 1960s. Low wages, unemployment, and political instability in Greece drove nearly 200,000 Greeks to the United States between 1960 and 1980. As a consequence, the Greek community in Clark County increased from 300 in 1960 to 1,423 in 1980, 4,310 in 1990, and 6,704 in 2000. In 2000 the second largest Greek community in Nevada was in the Reno area, with 1,784 residents of Greek ancestry.[23]

The new immigrants of the 1960s and later came from a country that had more in common with the United States than the Greece left behind by immigrants at the start of the twentieth century. Fifty years of economic crises, wars, and foreign occupation had devastated Greece, but what emerged testifies to the indomitable Greek character. By the 1960s Athens had over four million inhabitants and Thessaloniki almost a million; Greece was no longer a rural society. The folk culture, which was dying even as the first great wave of immigrants came to America, was absorbed and transformed by the growing, cosmopolitan urban centers. No longer a nation with a largely illiterate population, Greece now boasts a literacy rate of 97 percent, one of the highest in the world, and has more doctors per capita than any other country in Europe. As there are more educated people than the Greek economy can absorb, they continue to emigrate.[24]

One of these immigrants is Evangelos Yfantis, a professor in the University of Nevada, Las Vegas, Department of Computer Science, who has a Ph.D. and three master's degrees. His siblings also have doctorates. One brother has worked for the aerospace firms Northrup and Lockheed and is now employed by NASA, another brother has taught at the University of California at Berkeley, and Yfantis's sister works for the Greek Ministry of Education. Yfantis recalls visiting a café in Lidhoriki, his hometown in Greece, and finding himself surrounded by old classmates who now hold teaching positions in the United States, Europe, and Australia but all call Lidhoriki, a little town with one thousand inhabitants, home. Obviously, not all recent Greek immigrants have advanced degrees, but there is a world of difference between them and their predecessors.

Starting in the 1960s, Greeks moved to Las Vegas to find employment in the food-related sectors of the casino industry as busboys, waiters, and cooks. At one point the entire staff of busboys and waiters at the Flamingo Hilton showroom was Greek. Some Greeks advanced into higher paying positions as bartenders, showroom captains, and food and beverage directors, while others became poker, baccarat, and craps dealers.[25]

Greeks made several attempts to break into the casino industry as owners and operators. After coming to Las Vegas in 1964, the Angelo Stamis family, along with Jerry (Gerasimos) Kalafatis Lodge, opened Jerry's Nugget, a small casino on Las Vegas Boulevard North, which has become a popular local establishment. The Stamis family also became active in the Greek community and was a driving force behind the completion of St. John the Baptist Greek Orthodox Church.

The most famous Greek in the gaming industry by far was Nick "the Greek" Dandolos, whose arrival in Las Vegas in 1955 is reminiscent of scenes in 1950s cowboy films in which a lone gunman rides crosses the city limit with the intention of shooting it out with the fastest gun in town. Benny Binion gave Dandolos a public stage at his newly opened Horseshoe Casino, from which Dandolos issued a public challenge for a no-limit poker game that would last until one of the two players went broke. Johnny Moss took up the challenge and a game of epic proportions began. Moss and Dandolos played for three months before the latter, having dropped five million dollars, finally gave in.[26] It was not the first or the last time Nick the Greek would go broke. By his own estimate, he was, according to Hank Greenspun, "alternately wealthy and busted seventy-three times." About the legendary gambler, Greenspun wrote: "There was a time in Las Vegas when the many thousands of visitors coming to the town were probably more fascinated by Nick the Greek gambling than the fabulous floor shows the hotels paid many thousands of dollars to produce."[27] Nick the Greek, born in 1893 in Rethymnon, Crete, and educated at the Greek Evangelical College in Smyrna, came to America when he was eighteen. During his marathon games, he would discomfit his opponents by "reciting verses, making inscrutable philosophical statements or reading virtually unknown books."[28]

Jimmy "the Greek" Snyder (Demetrios Giorgios Synodinos), another well-known Greek American, came to Las Vegas in the mid-1950s to make a new start after allegations of connections to organized crime, made during the Kefauver hearings, rendered him unwelcome in many states. In Las Vegas Snyder made a living from doing casino public relations and running a book-making business, the Vegas Turf and Sports Club, which he set up in the 1960s. As Stacey Hamilton notes in a December 1961 *Sports Illustrated* article, "The Greek Who Makes the Odds," Snyder drew national attention to his talents. "But," adds Hamilton, "his fame soon turned to notoriety." Snyder was indicted for violating laws against the interstate transmission of gambling information and forced to close his business, but he found a new outlet in *The Las Vegas Sun,* which hired him to write a column about politics and sports from his perspective as an odds maker. Later he started Sports Unlimited, a public-relations firm "whose clients," according to Hamilton, "included Caesar's Palace and Howard Hughes." In 1976 CBS hired Jimmy the Greek to comment on sports, a career that ended in 1988 when he was fired as a result of racist comments that "turned him into a pariah in broadcast sports, a casualty of the political correctness wars."[29]

Today Greeks are active in virtually all the professions and businesses found in Las Vegas. Greeks are found in the construction and insurance busi-ness; they are stockbrokers, financial planners, travel agents, and owners of apartments, shopping centers, and taxi companies. There are university pro-fessors, architects, doctors, physical therapists, and attorneys, several of whom have served as local judges. Bill Flangas was director of operations for the Nevada Test Site during the peak of nuclear testing at that facility, ninety miles north of Las Vegas.

As the Greek population of Las Vegas grew, chapters of national fraternal organizations were established. An AHEPA chapter was chartered in the 1940s with ten men, who met at the Eagles or Elks hall. During World War II Las Vegas Greeks, led by the local AHEPA chapter, showed their patriotism by holding a parade on Fremont Street. Later they organized a second parade to promote the sale of U.S. Savings Bonds.[30] Though it has gone through peri-ods of relative inactivity, the local AHEPA chapter has continued in Las Vegas to this day, spawning an offshoot in Henderson in 1988. Today the Las Vegas chapter has a membership of approximately fifty Greeks and serves primarily as a social organization.

Recently, as the Greek community of Las Vegas has grown, the Pan-Cretan, Pan-Arcadian, and Pan-Macedonian Societies have also set up chap-ters there. The establishment of AHEPA in the United States in 1922 was pre-ceded by these mutual-benefit societies, whose members came from specific regions of Greece and which were committed primarily to collecting money for public improvements in the home villages of their members. These organizations came late to Las Vegas, as its Greek population has grown large enough to support them only in the last forty years or so.

The Greek American Family and Tradition

The family structure most Greek Americans know is that of the folk culture brought to America by early immigrants. According to the values of this society, which were not so far removed from those of most Americans at the time, women were expected to stay home and focus their attention on the family and the church. Few women worked outside the home unless they worked in a family business. Greek women learned little English and, at first, had limited contacts with non-Greek neighbors. The husband, according to tradition, ruled the home. In practice, however, the wife had considerable freedom in the management of the home and raising of the children.[31] Many immigrants' children challenged their parents' values, though others embraced them. Like most young people, they felt great pressure to be like their classmates—to be American. Some rebelled against strong paternal and traditional ties, which they felt were irrelevant in the United States. There were conflicts over teenage dating, mixed marriage, and divorce. Many resisted learning Greek, which their parents felt was a key to preserving their Greek identity.[32]

The flourishing state of the Greek community of Las Vegas today is proof that the sense of Greekness has survived, though in varying degrees. Some speak of themselves as both Greek and American, others as Greek American, and still others who consider themselves fully American and refer to themselves as having a Greek heritage. These labels are not necessarily permanent but often depend on a person's age, friends, and current living circumstances. There are those who remember their Greek origins periodically at Easter or during the Greek Food Festival. Others become active in church and cultural activities when their children are growing up and need ethical orientation and a sense of their roots. Often a few language lessons, a few good books about Greek history and civilization, and a trip to Greece can inspire a new-found love and respect for the ancestral culture.

In many cases American customs replaced Greek ones in the lives of the Greek immigrants. For instance, the birthday party edged out the name-day celebration, the feast day of the saint after whom a person is named. In Greece Saint Basil's Day, January 1, is the traditional time of exchanging gifts and caroling, but in America the more colorful (and much more expensive) Christmas tradition prevailed.[33] Once adamant that their children find Greek spouses, parents learned to live with mixed marriages and to love their grand-children. Sons were given considerable personal freedom and encouraged to get as much education as they could. Daughters were expected to marry, and many parents believed that education would serve as an impediment. As a result young Greek men, free to study and socialize as they wished, frequently found wives outside the community, while daughters often neither married nor received educations.

Some Greeks moved to Las Vegas from elsewhere in the United States to escape the confines of their ethnic communities. Ironically, the kind of Greek society they were trying to escape exists mainly in stateside communities where immigrants have managed to preserve the way of life they knew prior to leaving Greece decades earlier. In Greece, especially after World War II, the strict, traditional ways of the villages rapidly gave way in the face of urban life, a growing sense of European identity, and the influence of American popular culture.

The Greek Orthodox Church

From the beginning the Greek Orthodox Church and its priests have played an important role in Greek American communities. The priest not only provides spiritual guidance but is also the focus of a community's aspirations. In the Greek Orthodox Church in America, a great deal of power is vested in the church councils run by the laity; thus, priests must use their informal influence and authority to guide their flocks. In the early twentieth century many Greek communities were torn apart by imported political quarrels between Greek royalists and modernizing Venizelist liberals. The vigorous leadership of Athenagoras, archbishop of North and South America (and later ecumenical patriarch) eventually put an end to these divisions. Many of the priests assigned to the first communities in the United States, especially the smaller and more isolated ones, were as poorly educated as their parishioners. Unprepared as they were, they were expected to defend the faith and inspire the faithful to remember their heritage.[34]

As the Greek American archdiocese grew, so did its auxiliary groups. The Greek Orthodox Youth of America (GOYA) was established in 1949 to bring second- and third-generation Greeks closer to the church. Greek language and youth religious education (Sunday school) programs were developed. The Ladies Philoptochos Society (Friends of the Poor) was organized by some of the first Greek immigrant women to assist needy immigrants and their families. Today, there is a Philoptochos chapter in every Greek Orthodox parish in the United States.

The first Greek residents of Las Vegas longed for a church, but their numbers were too small to support one in the 1930s and 1940s. This did not prevent them from practicing their beliefs or finding temporary alternatives. Religious services, especially at Christmas and Easter, were held in private homes, followed by a communal celebration. Las Vegas Greeks traveled to Los Angeles and Salt Lake City for weddings and baptisms for their children. In the 1950s Christ Episcopal Church, located at Maryland Parkway and St. Louis Avenue, allowed the Greek community to use its facilities. The liturgy was performed at noon, after Episcopal services, by a priest from San Bernardino.[35]

In 1957 the Greek women of Las Vegas, having formed a Philoptochos chapter with Georgia Adres as the first president, began a concerted effort, through dinner dances and other events, to raise funds for a Greek Orthodox church. Dr. Ernest W. Searles, who came to Las Vegas in 1958 to teach economics at the Community College of Southern Nevada, helped organize the Greek community. Searles persuaded a retired Russian Orthodox priest, the Rev. Sugmen Sergei Irtel, to become the priest of the Greek community. Knowing neither Greek nor much English, Reverend Irtel conducted the liturgy in Russian, while Searles chanted in Greek.[36]

In order to obtain the authority to sign a church certificate of incorporation, a general assembly of the Greek community was convened in March 1959. A parish council was selected, and John Pappas was asked to be its first president. Pappas, understanding that this was a pivotal moment for the community and feeling that someone better educated should lead it, declined the honor. Searles was then named president of the parish council.[37]

On April 9, 1959, assisted by George Franklin, a local attorney, the Greek community of Las Vegas was officially incorporated in the state of Nevada under the name Eastern Greek Orthodox Community of Las Vegas. In June 1959, Rev. Arcadios Arcadiou, a retired priest of Cretan heritage, became the community's first resident priest. In the meantime, while fund-raising for a new church went forward, services continued to be held at Christ Episcopal Church. On September 6, 1959, the first annual Religious Celebration Dinner Dance to raise money for a church took place at the Las Vegas Municipal Golf Course Country Club. The event was supported financially by over 150 Las Vegas businesses. Following Greek tradition, the privilege of naming the future church went to the highest bidder at an auction. John Pappas bid $5,000 and named the future church in honor of St. John the Baptist.[38]

The parish council purchased a two-and-one-half-acre parcel at Cashman and Oakey for $6,500 to build the church. However, in 1960, instead of erecting a new church, the parish council decided to purchase a Jewish synagogue at Carson and Thirteenth Street for $60,000, with a 10 percent down payment and interest free payments of $5,000 a year for ten years. When Reverend Arcadiou rededicated the former synagogue as St. John the Baptist Greek Orthodox Church, the community had nearly fifty active Greek members. In July 1962 the Greek archdiocese assigned the Rev. James Adams of Anchorage, Alaska, to be its first permanent Greek priest. The community flourished and within a couple of decades outgrew its new location.

By 1963 it was evident that a community center was needed for meetings and celebrations. A building committee—Bill Flangas, Michael Michelas, Francis Fuson, and Varthie Eliakis—raised funds and construction began, with the participation of members of the Greek community and outside contractors. When it came time to lay the roof of the community center, funds had been exhausted, so it was decided to auction the privilege of naming it to the highest bidder. Tom Panos won this honor, and the community center was named Panos Hall.[39]

In October 1970 the Reverend Adams was transferred to San Rafael, California, and was replaced by Rev. Steve Prodromides in June 1971. With contributions from the Greek community, especially donations from Jerry Lodge and Jerry Stamis, the last annual payment for the church was made and a mortgage-burning ceremony was held at the Stardust Hotel on December 5, 1971. In February 1978, the Rev. Apostolos Andrews replaced Reverend Prodromides. In 1982 Reverend Andrews retired for medical reasons, and the Las Vegas Greek community remained without a priest for almost a year, until Rev. James Karagas arrived from Texas.[40]

The Las Vegas Greek Food Festival

The popular Las Vegas Greek Food Festival originated in efforts to raise funds for a new church. The president of the Ladies Philoptochos Society, Janele Salon, proposed organizing a food festival not only to raise funds for the Greek Orthodox church but also to showcase Greek culture for the broader Las Vegas community. The first Greek Food Festival was held at the Stardust Hotel on March 29, 1972, and became an annual event, attracting larger crowds each year. In 1975 it was moved to the Sahara Hotel Space Center, where it remained for many years as a one-day annual event usually held on Mother's Day.[41]

Currently, the annual Greek Food Festival is held on the grounds of the Greek Orthodox church located at El Camino and Hacienda. By the end of the century this three-day event was drawing over twenty thousand non-Greeks to taste Greek cooking, pastries, and beverages; listen to Greek bands featuring the sounds of the bouzouki; and watch and participate in Greek dances. The funds raised from the event are used to continue the expansion of the church facilities.

St. John the Baptist Greek Orthodox Church

From the 1970s to the present, the Greek community of Las Vegas experienced rapid growth under the leadership of the late Nick Pandelis, who served an unprecedented seven terms as parish-council president. The church developed several parish programs such as Bible study, Sunday school, a folk-dance group, GOYA, Greek-language classes for adults and children, senior-citizen programs, and Panhellenic groups.

By the late 1980s it became evident the Greeks had outgrown their church at Carson and Thirteenth. Before the next step could be taken, an important and divisive issue concerning the ethnic identity of the new church and the community had to be dealt with. As the community grew, it also attracted a large number of converts to Greek Orthodoxy who desired a church that was fully American. In this they were supported by many American-born members of Greek descent. The objectives of the two groups could not be reconciled, and the community broke into two factions. One group, led by Father Nikolai, a Serbian priest who had been serving the Greek community, erected St. Paul Orthodox Church on Annie Oakley Drive in Green Valley, which is affiliated with the Orthodox Church of America. The Greek Orthodox Church of St. John remained in the hands of those who wished to preserve their Greek heritage. Although the break caused some bitterness at the time, relations between the two parishes are now amicable, and members frequently attend each other's services.[42]

The parish council and the Rev. Ilia Katre, who came to Las Vegas in 1988, led the effort to build a new church and community center on a larger piece of property. Tom and Wilma Panos located ten acres of land in the southwestern Las Vegas Valley at Hacienda and El Camino and suggested that the community purchase it. Once a mortgage was secured, the construction of a Byzantine-style Greek Orthodox church commenced, and on September 17, 1992, the new St. John the Baptist Greek Orthodox Church was opened. Soon afterward the construction of an administrative building and community center began under the leadership of Father Katre and laymen such as Angelo Stamis, George Filios, Nick Pandelis, and Nick Salon.

The Greek Orthodox Church of St. John induces a sense of joyful self-recognition for Greek Americans, as though they are looking upon a concrete manifestation of their communal inner landscape. It not only defines Greekness, but it also demonstrates in the most tangible way how Greek culture can contribute to America. The Byzantine church fits perfectly in the Las Vegas landscape, just as it would in Greece. It is not a fortress of Greekness, but an open part of a society to which it actively contributes. Certainly, the building itself will influence the way Las Vegans perceive architecture, history, and even the idea of beauty. Thus, the Greek community of Las Vegas makes a contribution by giving the community at large the best that it has; it actively changes and enriches the dynamic society of which it is a part.

In the spring of 2002, during a visit to the Ecumenical Patriachate in Istanbul, Father Katre was elevated to the episcopate of the Orthodox Church. Although his replacement, Father John Hondros, arrived from the Church of the Annunciation in Seattle in August, Bishop Katre did not completely sever his links with the community until the following spring. He wished to be present, along with the new priest and Gus Flangas, the president of the parish council, for the dedication of the St. John the Baptist Community and Education Center, a multipurpose structure and administrative building, in May 2003. Church offices, Sunday school classes, Greek school, Scouts, GOYA meetings, adult education, and the coffee hour that follows the Sunday liturgy are located there. Wilma Panos, who donated $1.5 million dollars to complete the center, named its great hall Panos Hall in honor of her late husband, Tom Panos. Panos Hall provides space for a variety of large functions, including banquets, ethnic and religious feasts, wedding receptions, and basketball games. In addition to ministries that meet at the community center, the classrooms will be available for courses about Greek culture and Greek American writers, and there is room for music recitals, art exhibitions, and dance performances.

Two dance groups, Argonaftes and Leondaria, which had previously been obliged to practice in borrowed and rented halls and, occasionally, in cold, poorly lit parking lots, will benefit from the community center's ample space. The dance ministry of the western diocese is one of the most important and unexpected defenders of Greek culture. In 1976, at the instigation of His Eminence Metropolitan Anthony, a folk-dance competition was established. The program has been extremely popular, and every year thousands of young Greek Orthodox dancers practice for months so they can participate. The dance groups from St. John the Baptist often do well and once came home with the sweepstakes prize. More important than the prize is the fact that young people establish a physical and emotional connection with the folk culture of their ancestors through dance.

In an important way, the new church and community center are the fulfillment of the dreams of Nevada's early Greeks. An article published in the

White Pine News on October 2, 1910, reported that the Greek community of Nevada would soon build a new church in central Ely. The church, it said, "will be after the style of the ancient Byzantine ecclesiastical architecture, with double towers topped by domes or cupolas, and surmounted by crosses." The article also promised that two chapels would be constructed, one at Copper Flat and the other in McGill. As anyone who has visited White Pine County knows, the modest Greek Orthodox churches there—St. Alexios in Ely and St. Barbara in McGill—do not approach the dreams described in the newspaper article. As for the chapel in Copper Flat, there is no proof that it was ever built. The members of the community, continues the article, "are looking forward with delight to looking upon a structure that will remind them of the home-land."[43] Indirectly, the article reveals something very important about the early Greek community—the immigrants who came to northern Nevada in the first decades of this century were capable of faith, dreams, and hope. When we consider what these Greek pioneers went through in order to establish themselves in a country where everything was new and often seemed very strange—the language, the customs, dress, the work they were expected to do—it becomes clear that the eighty years it took to build St. John the Baptist Greek Orthodox Church is not a very long time.

Greek Identity Today

Although this chapter is dedicated to the Greek American community of Las Vegas, it is important to point out that the Greek Orthodox Church is not an exclusively ethnic organization; while it contributes to the preservation of Greek culture, it has a wider constituency whose main concern is its Christian identity. In the cosmopolitan city of Las Vegas there are immigrants and descendants of immigrants from many countries where Orthodoxy is practiced, and many attend St. John. The diversity of the congregation is especially evident at Easter when the priest proclaims, "Christ is risen," and members of the congregation respond, "Truly He is risen! *Alithos anesti!* [Greek]. *Voistinu Voskrese!* [Church Slavonic]. *Hakku Kami!* [Arabic]. *Adevarat a inviat!* [Rumanian]. *Vertet u-ngjalll!* [Albanian]. *Krisdos haryan!* [Armenian]. *Hristos Aleemoutsos!* [Tigrinya]. *Kristos Tenea!* [Amharic]." At moments like this, the ancient ecumenical identity of the church manifests itself.

The children of Greek immigrants are familiar with the patriotic appeals from speakers on Greek Independence Day (March 25) and on October 28, which commemorates the Greek response to the Italian invasion of Greece in 1940. These contained impossible requests that they retain their ethnic purity, as though, one day, the entire community might return to Greece. Yet how many Greek immigrants to America have returned to Greece after twenty, thirty, or forty years to find a foreign country where they felt completely out of place? After a century of foreign occupation, a civil war, urbanization, and the plague of mass tourism, how could Greece and the Greeks not change? Many Greek Americans, however, felt relieved to escape the customs and values of their parents. Often the struggle was so bitter and prolonged that everything associated with the Greek world was set aside. It was the end of, as Maria Margaronis has described it, "a way of being that once held the world together from within—an indefensible, patriarchal, theocratic order."[44]

Even as they struggled with the world of their parents, the children of immigrants met great pressure in public school to become American. They learned to be ashamed of parents who spoke broken English and dressed, ate, and thought differently from their classmates and teachers. The road to self-esteem often entailed the successful effacement of one's ethnic identity. Schoolchildren, especially in their teens, felt an almost overwhelming pressure to fit in, to be like the rest of their classmates. Then came college, careers, marriage and families, and people were so busy getting along that for many Greekness was forgotten.

The historian and novelist Helen Papanikolas regrets the passing of the "*Romiosini* culture of the early immigrants."[45] The name-day celebrations, back when everyone in the community was welcome to drop by without having to be invited to wish the celebrant long life with a glass of liqueur, are gone. Gone are the days when the well-wisher would be served a piece of baklava or a *kourabie* and a demitasse of Turkish coffee and everyone was welcome because—according to the ancient Greek idea of hospitality— guests are sent by God.

Aspects of modern Greek culture rejected as too ethnic by the children of Greek immigrants often returned, however, as a result of changing American tastes. In the 1940s and 1950s, when the pressure to assimilate seamlessly into American culture was at its height, young Greek American women, wanting the svelte look of American movie stars, took up smoking and rejected Greek cooking. Olive oil, feta cheese, kalamata olives, home-baked bread, baklava, and *avgolemono* soup went out of favor. The products of the farm and the kitchen were replaced by American industry, which fed future Betty Grables with Wonder Bread, tasteless green olives stuffed with pimentoes, processed cheese, chocolate-chip cookies, and Campbell's chicken-noodle soup. But in the 1960s—as Americans became more open-minded about food and more particular—they learned to value Greek cuisine because it is healthy as well as tasty.

Even though many lament the loss of Greek identity through assimilation, the twenty-first century might have some surprises for the Greeks. In the first half of the twentieth century, Greece was far away, almost a month by boat and railroad. Good Greek schools were rare, and it was difficult to obtain books, newspapers, records, and other cultural artifacts from Greece. However, modern technology in travel and communication might well have given Greek culture in America a second breath. These days it takes less than a day to fly to Greece, and tickets are relatively inexpensive. Morever, whereas retaining one's ethnic identity was once considered un-American, contemporary Americans are more tolerant of diversity and, in many cases, encourage both assimilation and difference. As George Yannoulopoulos observes: "The line that divides a member of the Greek diaspora in the USA from the American of Greek origin is extremely hard to draw. Society in America is less homogeneous and more inclusive than in other countries and has the ability to assimilate new blood from overseas at a remarkable speed. On the other hand the absence of a clearly defined national identity tends to preserve a more or less pronounced sense of ethnicity which may rise to the surface."[46]

Many Las Vegas Greeks maintain second homes in Greece and travel back and forth regularly. Dr. Philipos Diamantis, who settled in Las Vegas after participating in javelin and acting as a trainer in the 1968 Mexico City Olympics, for several years provided the Greek community of Las Vegas with its only Greek-language radio program: a half hour Sunday nights on KLAV AM 1230. Now, a few hundred dollars a year bring the viewer three Greek television channels and one from Cyprus to Las Vegas by satellite.

Greece is accessible to those of Greek descent whose knowledge of Greek is rusty or nonexistent, because English is now spoken widely there. Further, many making a first visit realize that their relatives do not live in hovels but are quite up-to-date and likely have good educations, visit art galleries, go to the theater and the movies frequently, and love a night out on the town. A Greek American visitor from Las Vegas might find that the aunt she wanted to meet is in Brussels representing Greece at the European Parliament, while her cousins might be living in Melbourne, Johannesburg, or Buenos Aires. The heirs of Odysseus continue to go everywhere, while Greece remains at the center, an international nation. Once Greece was far away from America, but today it is virtually next door, and if one is ready and desires it, one's spark of Greekness can be ignited—or reignited—at the source at any time.

Notes

1. "A Nuisance," *Las Vegas Age,* September 25, 1905, 4.
2. Material on the Greek immigrants is derived from E. D. Karampetsos,

"Nativism in Nevada: Greek Immigrants in White Pine County," *Journal of the Hellenic Diaspora* 24 (1998): 61–95. Material concerning the Greeks of Las Vegas is drawn primarily from interviews in Stavros Anthony, "The Greek Community of Las Vegas" (master's thesis, University of Nevada, Las Vegas, 1987). As part of his research Anthony interviewed many members of the Greek community. Information and quotations from those interviews are used in this chapter. Further documentation can be found in Anthony's thesis. General studies of Greeks in the United States include: Thomas Burgess, *Greeks in America* (1913; reprint, New York, Arno Press, 1970); Dan Georgakas, ed., *New Directions in Greek American Studies* (New York: Pella Publishing, 1991); George Kourvetaris, *Studies on Greek Americans* (New York: Columbia University Press, 1997); Dimitris Monos et al., *The Greek Americans* (New York: Chelsea Press, 1996); Charles C. Moskos, *Greek Americans: Struggle and Success* (Englewood Cliffs, N.J.: Prentice-Hall, 1980); Helen Papanikolas, *An Amulet of Greek Earth* (Athens: Swallow Press–Ohio University Press, 2002); Harry Psomiades and Stavros Thomadakis, eds., *Greek American Community in Transition* (New York: Pella Publishing, 1993); Theodore Saloutos, *The Greeks in the United States* (Cambridge: Harvard University Press, 1964); Alice Scourby, *Greek Americans* (Boston: Twayne Publishers, 1984); J. P. Xenides, *The Greeks in America* (1922; reprint, San Francisco: R and E Research, 1972). Studies of Greek communities in the United States include: Anna Caraveli, *Scattered in Foreign Lands: A Greek Village in Baltimore* (Baltimore: Baltimore Museum of Modern Art, 1985); George P. Daskarolis, *San Francisco's Greek Colony: The Evolution of an Ethnic Community* (Minneapolis: Light and Life, 1995); Andrew T. Kopan, *Education and Greek Immigrants in Chicago, 1892–1973: A Study in Ethnic Survival* (New York: Garland Publishing, 1990); Helen Papanikolas, *Toil and Rage in a New Land: The Greek Immigrants in Utah,* 2d ed. (Salt Lake City: Utah State Historical Society, 1974); Helen Papanikolas, "Toil and Rage in a New Land: The Greek Immigrants in Utah," *Utah Historical Quarterly* 38 (1970): 97–206; George J. Patterson, *The Unassimilated Greeks of Denver* (New York: AMS Press, 1989); Nicholas M. Prevas, *History of the Greek Orthodox Cathedral of the Annunciation, Baltimore, Maryland* (Baltimore: Lucas Printing Co., 1982).

3. Myron Angel, *History of Nevada: With Illustrations and Biographical Sketches of Its Prominent Men and Pioneers* (Oakland: Thompson and West, 1881), 153.

4. Alekos, Lidorikis, "Greek Banking: A Century of Often Arduous Growth," retrieved 17/6/2003, from http://internet.ana.gr/hermes/1999/dec/banking.htm; Athanase G., Politis, *Contribution de l'Hellénisme au développement de l'egypt moderne,* vol. 2 of *L'Hellénisme et l'egypt moderne* (Paris: Félix Alcan, 1930).

5. Louis James Cononelos, *In Search of Gold Paved Streets: Greek Immigrant Labor in the Far West, 1900–1920* (New York: AMS Press, 1989), 174.

6. The American West at this time, as historian David T. Courtwright has shown, was essentially a society of young, unmarried men between the ages of seventeen and thirty, both American born and foreign, whose most outstanding characteristics were violence and instability. See his *Violent Land: Single Men and Social Disorder, from the Frontier to the Inner City* (Cambridge: Harvard University Press, 1996).

7. Russell Elliott, interview by E. D. Karampetsos, University of Nevada, Reno, June 12, 1992.

8. Details can be found in Karampetsos, "Nativism," 72–79.

9. Steven Philips, "The Ripples Will Not Cease: An AHEPA Story," n.d., retrieved January 10, 2002, from *http://www.mindspring.com/-ahepa.dist3/ahphist.html*).

10. "'Notice to the Public' by Greeks," *Ely Daily Mining Expositor,* October 5, 1912, 4.

11. Cononelos, *In Search of Paved Streets,* 208, 215–21.

12. "Greeks Buy Liberty Bonds," *Ely Record,* November 2, 1917, 17; *Ely Record,* July 27, 1917, 5.

13. William Flangas, interview by E. D. Karampetsos, Las Vegas, June 15, 1992.

14. Later the Los Angeles and Salt Lake Railroad, it was sold to the Union Pacific in 1918; Kalliope Pappas, interview by Stavros Anthony, Las Vegas, January 12, 1986.

15. Lea Sackas, interview by Stavros Anthony, Las Vegas, February 14, 1986.

16. Pappas, interview by Stavros Anthony, 1986.

17. Tom and Wilma Panos, interview by Stavros Anthony, Las Vegas, January 16, 1986.

18. John Moran, interview by Stavros Anthony, Las Vegas, February 12, 1986.

19. Lea Sackas, interview by E. D. Karampetsos, Las Vegas, April 15, 1992.

20. Sackas, interview by Stavros Anthony, 1986.

21. Paul Ralli, *Nevada Lawyer: A Story of Life and Love in Las Vegas* (Culver City, Calif.: Murray and Gee, 1949), 7–8.

22. Jerry Giesler, "Foreword," in Ralli, *Nevada Lawyer,* xii.

23. Stephan Thernstrom, *A History of The American People,* 2d ed., vol. 2 of *Since 1865* (New York: Harcourt, Brace Jovanovich, 1989), 633, 636; "Table DP-21 Profile of General Demographic Characteristics: 2000." Geographic area: Las Vegas, NV—AZ MSA, NV part. U.S. Bureau of the Census 2000, retrieved June 17, 2003, from p. 1, at http://censtats.census.gov/data/NV/390324120.pdf; "Table DP-2. Profile of Selected Social Characteristics: 2000." Geographic area: Reno, NV MSA. U.S. Bureau of the Census 2000, retrieved June 17, 2003, from p. 2, at http://censtats.census.gov/data/NV/390326720.pdf.

24. The Greek presidency of the European Union—eu2003.gr—education, retrieved July 26, 2003, from http://www.eu2003.gr/en/articles/2002/12/8/1149/; George Yannoulopoulos, "Beyond the Frontiers: The Greek Diaspora," in *In The Greek World: Classical, Byzantine and Modern,* ed. Robert Browning (London: Thames and Hudson, 2000), 297–98.

25. Nick Katris, interview by Stavros Anthony, Las Vegas, February 2, 1986.

26. Jesse May, "The Greatest Poker Hand Ever Played," 1999–2001, retrieved January 8, 2002, from http://pokerfaces.poker.com/jessemay/thegreatesrpokerhand everplayed.htm.

27. Hank Greenspun, "Nick the Greek Was Always Known as the King of the Gamblers." *Las Vegas Sun,* retrieved January 8, 2002, from http://wwwlasvegassun.com/remembers lo2700.html.

28. Ibid.

29. Stacey Hamilton, "Jimmy 'the Greek' Snyder," *American National Biography*, 2001, retrieved January 8, 2002, from http://www.anb.org/articles/19/19-00921.html.

30. The parade ended at the Busy Bee Cafe, where ten thousand dollars worth of the bonds were sold.

31. See Helen Papanikolas, "Greek Immigrant Women of the Intermountain West," *Journal of the Hellenic Diaspora* 16 (1989): 17–35.

32. Papanikolas, *An Amulet of Greek Earth*.

33. Ibid., 274–77.

34. Ibid., 78–85.

35. Sackas, interview by Anthony, 1986; Mike Michelas, interview by Stavros Anthony, Las Vegas, January 22, 1986.

36. Ernest Searles, interview by Stavros Anthony, Las Vegas, January 10, 1986.

37. Panos, interview by Anthony, 1986.

38. Peter Tsouras, interview by Stavros Anthony, Las Vegas, January 23, 1986.

39. Bill Flangas, interview by Stavros Anthony, Las Vegas, January 27, 1986.

40. Searles, interview by Anthony, 1986.

41. Janele Salon, interview by Stavros Anthony, Las Vegas, January 13, 1986.

42. Recent immigrants from Romania and Russia, who have joined the St. Paul parish in increasing numbers, have created pressures for the use of Romanian and Russian during the liturgy.

43. *White Pine News,* October 2, 1910.

44. Maria Margaronis, "Alexandros Papadiamantis," *Grand Street* (1989), 155.

45. Helen Papanikolas, interview by E. D. Karampetsos, Salt Lake City, Utah, May 26, 2001.

46. Yannoulopoulos, "Beyond the Frontiers," 297–98.

CHAPTER 8

The Italians

ALAN BALBONI

Few men and women of Italian birth or ancestry resided in Las Vegas from its founding in 1905 until the end of World War II. Always less than 2 percent of a Las Vegas population that grew from about one thousand in 1910 to over eight thousand in 1940, the Italian Americans were nonetheless well represented among those providing hospitality to travelers seeking good food, liquid refreshment, and a room for a night or two. A review of the 1910 Manuscript Census shows that most of the Italian surnamed came to the Las Vegas area either as railroad workers or as miners, as was the case with people of other ethnic backgrounds. Some came from farming or mining areas of northern Nevada, where several thousand Italian immigrants had settled in the 1860s and 1870s.[1] In this regard, Las Vegas was similar to many other western towns where railroads and mines were the major employers of immigrant labor.

A few entered the hospitality business directly. Foremost among the early entrepreneurs was Dominic Pecetto. The Italian-born Pecetto opened a liquor store in Las Vegas in 1905 and six years later built the Union Hotel across from the railroad station and near the present Union Plaza Hotel. Like so many immigrants who preceded and followed him, Pecetto relied on relatives to assist him. Joe Graglia, his brother-in-law, helped Pecetto manage the Union Hotel and then in 1923 built the Hotel National a few blocks south. Six years later Graglia leased the Union Hotel to John Vinassa, his wife's brother.[2]

More commonly, Italian Americans left their initial jobs as railroad workers or miners to start small farms, operate bars, or manage or own small hotels. After many years of working for railroads, Manuel Champo (né Ciampo) decided to support his family by growing fruits and vegetables to sell to Las Vegas residents and travelers. His daughter recalled that when a powerful summer storm produced a flood that completely destroyed the onions, lettuce, tomatoes, and other vegetables that her father had so carefully nurtured, he invested in a bar that provided his family with financial security during Prohibition.[3]

Wyoming bootlegger Berto Testolin made an even greater contribution to the demand for strong drink than did Champo. Testolin's nephew, Guido, recounted that when local law enforcement in Wyoming began taking Prohibition more seriously than the Italian-born Testolin thought appropriate, he moved his substantial bootlegging operation to the Las Vegas area, building a still about twenty-five miles northwest of the city in an area that is now a nature preserve, where water from underground springs was easily accessed. When passage of the Twenty-first Amendment in 1933 brought an end to Prohibition, Testolin bought the Cinnabar and Mission bars, in the present location of the Golden Nugget Hotel.[4]

The decision of the Nevada legislature to relegalize gambling in 1931 brought several Italian-born entrepreneurs to Las Vegas. Certainly the most controversial was Tony Cornero (AKA Tony Stralla). Like so many of the gambling entrepreneurs who built the Las Vegas Strip after World War II, Cornero had been a major bootlegger, often using motorboats to carry liquor from ships anchored just beyond the three-mile limit to usually deserted stretches of the California coast in the nighttime. He and his brothers were in Las Vegas planning construction of a casino some months before the Nevada legislature passed the laws allowing localities to license casino gambling. Initially it appeared that Cornero's investment in the casino and small hotel was a wise one, as both Las Vegans and visitors flocked to The Meadows, a plush casino built more than a mile from the center of the city. Yet within a few months Cornero saw that the effects of the Depression coupled with the small population and isolation of Las Vegas precluded realization of his dream. He sold the property to Jewish investors from Los Angeles and then put his capital and expertise into operating gambling ships off the California coast, near Santa Monica and Long Beach.[5]

Frank Detra was an Italian-born gambling entrepreneur whose experiences before arriving in Las Vegas in 1927 brought him into contact with major organized crime figures including Al Capone. Indeed, Frank's son, John Detra, told me that Capone himself, aware that Prohibition would eventually be repealed, had urged Detra to go west, particularly to Nevada, to check out opportunities to establish (illegal) gambling operations. John Detra recalled that his father operated a roadhouse on the old Highway 91, the Pair-O-Dice Club, which did not open to the public until repeal of Prohibition in 1933. The club served excellent Italian food and wine and provided diners an opportunity to play roulette, craps, and blackjack. In the late 1930s Guy McAfee, a former Los Angeles police captain who had amassed a small fortune soliciting payoffs from the bookmakers he was supposed to arrest, purchased Detra's roadhouse and renamed it the 91 Club.[6]

Pietro Orlando Silvagni, born in the impoverished region of Calabria,

Italy, and raised in Carbon County, Utah, made a more lasting contribution to the development of Las Vegas than did Cornero or Detra. A successful contractor until the Depression, Silvagni originally came to Las Vegas hoping that the Six Companies, building the Boulder Dam, would hire him as a subcontractor. His daughter Olga recalled that as soon as he saw Fremont Street, he put aside his initial goal and decided to invest every dollar that he could raise in building the largest and most fashionable hotel in Las Vegas. The Apache opened in March 1932, with the Las Vegas press lavishly praising Silvagni for not only providing elevators and swamp coolers (firsts for Las Vegas) but also including a drugstore, barbershop, ladies–wear shop, and the Apache Club Garden, which featured casual-style ballroom dancing.[7]

Of course the majority of the few score Italian Americans in Las Vegas were less likely than the individuals mentioned above to see their names in either of the two local newspapers. Included among them were restaurant owners and workers, bartenders, a gas-station owner, an apartment-house owner and manager, a co-owner of a liquor distributorship, and, as might be expected, table-game dealers and waitresses.

Unlike the cities and towns of the East Coast and Great Lakes areas, where the vast majority of the more than a million Italian immigrants who came to America between 1890 and 1924 settled, no neighborhoods dominated by descendants of a particular European ethnic group developed in Las Vegas (though African Americans were victims of de facto residential segregation). The Italian Americans were too few before the post–World War II influx to establish a Sons of Italy Lodge or any of the storefront clubs so common in the Little Italies of cities such as Boston, New York, and Philadelphia. Yet the children of the early pioneers report that they and their parents were conscious of their Italian heritage, and this was the basis of some socializing. Often members of the Champo, Detra, Graglia, Matteucci, and Vinassa families would gather at the home of one or another to enjoy Italian food and wine. In the winter they might travel to Death Valley and in summer drive the Mount Charleston road to a tree-shaded picnic area.

While the percentage of Italian Americans in the northern Nevada population was higher than in the Las Vegas–area population until the 1950s, Reno, the main city in northern Nevada, was more than four hundred miles from Las Vegas, and other mining or farming cities and towns with significant numbers of Italian Americans such as Elko, Ely, and Winnemucca were also distant. Contact between Nevada Italian Americans living in the Las Vegas Valley and the north was virtually nonexistent during the first half of the twentieth century and minimal during the second half, even with the remarkable improvements in auto and air transportation.

Assimilation was more rapid in the western United States than elsewhere. Immigrants from Europe often faced some discrimination, but it was generally neither as severe nor as long-lasting as that faced by their counterparts who settled east of the Mississippi. Ethnic enclaves were also less common in the West. Las Vegas Italian Americans faced virtually no economic or legal discrimination. They felt no need to seek the security that creation of an ethnic enclave would bring. The absence of physically and often emotionally limiting ethnic enclaves, together with the paucity of marriage-aged members of the opposite sex, ensured that the marriage of two Italian Americans was a rarity during the four decades preceding the post World War II influx of Italian Americans.[8]

The Mob Years

The Las Vegas area population grew from just under 9,000 in 1940 to almost 65,000 in 1960. During this time the percentage of Italian Americans in the population jumped from less than 2 percent to at least 10 percent. Thousands of Italian Americans left the ethnic enclaves of East Coast and midwestern cities, and to a lesser extent other western cities, to make a new life in what had been a dusty Mohave Desert town and was becoming the "Entertainment Capital of the World." Italian Americans (and Jewish Americans) were more than well represented among the men with experience managing gambling operations, restaurants, bars, and nightclubs.

As capital from mostly Jewish American and, to a lesser extent, Italian American investors poured into Las Vegas to build the Strip, Italian Americans were conspicuous by their numbers among the table-game dealers, bookies, bartenders, nightclub maitre d's, and food and beverage managers who flocked to Las Vegas. Of course some of the Italian Americans settled in Las Vegas to pursue the business and professional opportunities associated with a growing city in the Sunbelt.

In the twenty years between the opening of the Flamingo in late 1946 and Howard Hughes's arrival in late 1966, men of Italian birth, or more commonly Italian ancestry, were found in significant numbers in every aspect of Las Vegas's rapidly expanding resort industry except in ownership positions at Strip hotels. They were doormen, bellhops, dealers, floormen, boxmen at the craps tables, shift bosses, and casino managers. They opened, managed, and worked at restaurants, owned or tended bars, and dominated the ranks of the showroom maitre d's at a time when one did not get even a mediocre seat without greasing the palm of a maitre d' or his assistant. They came to the sunny and sparkling new city in the desert from the often-dreary cities of the

East Coast and Midwest to play in the showroom orchestras of the Strip hotels, to entertain in the lounges and showrooms, and to serve as entertainment directors of several hotels.

Two Italian Americans from the San Francisco Bay area, Emilio Georgetti and Italo Gelfi, were chief executives of Downtown (the Fremont Street area) casinos, the former rather briefly at the Westerner and the latter for several decades at the Golden Gate. Joe Canino, whose father, Antonio, had run an illegal casino in Denver, was the top manager of the relatively small Silver Slipper (located on the strip where The Mirage stands now) until Nevada Gaming Control Board agents discovered five shaved dice and closed the property on April 23, 1964. Had Tony Cornero, who invested every dollar he could raise to build the Stardust, not succumbed to a massive heart attack after shooting craps at the Desert Inn on July 31, 1955, he almost certainly would have become the chief executive officer of that hotel, which was about 70 percent completed when Cornero died.[9]

Men of eastern European Jewish birth or origin dominated the ranks of owners and chief executive officers of the Strip hotels in the twenty years following the end of World War II. Italian Americans were found in key positions at all the hotels with Jewish owners. Throughout the 1950s and 1960s Italian Americans, many from the same Great Lakes cities (Detroit, Cleveland, and Buffalo in particular) that owners Moe Dalitz, Sam Tucker, and Morris Kleinman hailed from, constituted a substantial segment of the Desert Inn's casino bosses and dealers. Frank Sennes, an Italian American associate of Dalitz in Cleveland and later in Newport, Kentucky, where Dalitz had invested in illegal casinos, served for several years as entertainment director at the Desert Inn and later at the Stardust, when Dalitz and his associates had financial interests in that property. At the Sands, whose principal investors included Jake Friedman, Jack Entratter, and Carl Cohen, Hank Saricola was the entertainment director for many years, and Nick Kelly (né Fiore) was showroom maitre' d. The pattern was repeated at the Riviera, whose major investors included Sam Cohen, Ben Goffstein, Harry Goldman, Dave Berman, and Jess Goodman. Italian Americans were found at all levels in the Riviera casino and hotel operations, with Tony Zoppa, entertainment director through the mid-1960s, the most prominent.[10]

The Tropicana, located on the east side of the Strip south of the Aladdin, provides a fine example of cooperation among men of Italian and Jewish ancestry who amassed considerable capital running gambling operations in the 1930s and 1940s. Ben Jaffe, chairman of the board of the luxurious Fountainbleu Hotel in Miami, was the Tropicana's president. Jaffe leased the casino to "Dandy" Phil Kastel, who had managed illegal casinos financed by Frank

Costello (né Franco Castiglia) and Meyer Lansky. Italian-born Joe Agosto was the entertainment director at the Tropicana for many years, until he was indicted on skimming charges in 1978.[11]

Italian Americans and Jewish Americans dominated the ranks of the owners (public and hidden) of the old-fashioned race books. These were often crowded, rather dingy establishments usually filled with cigar smoke, most unlike the comfortable and clean race and sports books that have appeared in virtually every casino in the past twenty years. The three most prominent Italian Americans were Frank Sala from Reno, George Ligouri from Hoboken, New Jersey, and Gaspare "Jasper" Speciale from New York City. All had run successful bookmaking operations before coming to Las Vegas, and all were associated with the Santa Anita Race Book in the 1960s, whose principal owner was Sammy Cohen. George Ligouri recalled that he immediately went to work as Cohen's assistant when he arrived in Las Vegas in 1960. Frank Sala was then the junior partner. Jasper Speciale, whose reputation for being associated with Carlo Gambino, allegedly a major figure in New York–area organized crime, was largely responsible for his being denied a gaming license by the Nevada Gaming Commission, operated what Ligouri termed a "concession area" at the Santa Anita.

The three prospered as Las Vegas grew rapidly in the 1960s. Sala, who had invested in residential and commercial property in the previous decade, became a licensed real-estate broker, sold his interests in the Santa Anita and in several casinos, and became a leader in the real-estate business, serving as president of the Las Vegas Board of Realtors in 1967 and as a member of the Nevada State Real Estate Board in 1970. Ligouri worked for Cohen for almost ten years before taking a position that he described as being "right–hand man" for Shecky Greene, a Jewish comedian of national renown whose name was found frequently on Strip marquees. Speciale was not as successful as Sala and Ligouri in making a transition to other businesses. Convicted of illegal sports bookmaking in 1965, a year later, and then again in 1973, Speciale owned and operated the Tower of Pizza on the Strip and then Jasper's Manhattan Florist, yet by most accounts he continued his bookmaking activities. He prospered in spite of the convictions, buying a home in the Scotch 80s, an exclusive neighborhood two miles west of the Strip.[12]

All of the scores of Italian Americans who arrived in Las Vegas between 1956 and 1966 and whom I interviewed were enthusiastic about working and residing in the city. Harry Merenda, who came from Newark in 1962 to work at the Desert Inn bar, best summed up the comments of many regarding their initial employment experiences, saying, "It was more like a party than a job." They were earning more money than they had previously, and in an environment that often included neighborhood friends and relatives. They saw that earlier arrivals from the Little Italies of their birth had quickly moved on to even more lucrative positions. Equally appealing for some of the young men was the absence of the constraints that accompanied life in the ethnic enclaves of cities such as Buffalo, Pittsburgh, Providence, and Chicago. No grandmothers peered out their windows to note how late Tony or Carmine returned home. Best of all was the availability of quite a variety of attractive young women, many working as cocktail waitresses or dancers, who did not regard marriage as a necessary prerequisite to sex. Some interviewees told me that being in Las Vegas in the 1950s and 1960s was like being in paradise. Of course they told friends from the old neighborhoods about their good fortune, which, in turn, brought more Italian Americans, especially single males, to Las Vegas.

Italian Americans contributed greatly to making the city an internationally recognized center of gambling and entertainment during the twenty years following the end of World War II. Las Vegas visitors could not help but notice how common Italian surnames were among the headline entertainers, lounge performers, orchestra conductors, and showroom maitre d's. If they got to know some of the dealers, pit bosses, and floor men in the casinos, they would inevitably converse with Italian Americans, many hailing from the Little Italies of East Coast and Midwest cities. Even if they only listened to the names of individuals being paged in the hotels, they would be aware of the Italian American presence in Las Vegas. The connection between organized crime and Italian Americans that had become part of the popular culture, especially following the meeting of more than two dozen reputed Italian American organized-crime leaders at a village in upstate New York in 1957, almost certainly drew tourists to the Strip resorts.

What could be more intriguing, more evocative of the mystery of Las Vegas, than the word *mafia?* The word conjured up images of swarthy men in silk suits, occasionally speaking a strange language in hushed tones and living by standards foreign to middle-class Americans. In Las Vegas, dreams could come true. The tired factory worker from Youngstown could hit the jackpot. The bored bookkeeper from Peoria could think that her companions at the craps table might include a famous entertainer, a high-rolling multimillionaire, or, most exciting of all, a mafioso—perhaps a hitman from Chicago.

Of course not all Italian Americans came to Las Vegas to work in the resort industry. Not surprisingly, given Americans' love of Italian food, quite a few Italian American men and women opened restaurants in Las Vegas. Anna and Angelo Barozzi settled in Las Vegas in 1931 and opened the Café Roma on the corner of North Second and Stewart Streets, the first of many Italian restaurants. They invested much of the profits from this venture in acquiring both vacant land and income-producing rental properties in the Downtown area. While the Barozzis had shifted their attention from the restaurant business to their investments by the 1940s, other Italian American cooks were responding to Las Vegans' love of Italian food.[13] Tom Vannozzi recalled in a 1994 interview that his Sicilian-born grandfather, Anthony Messina, after working many years in the food and grocery business in New Jersey and then California, opened an Italian restaurant, Tony's, on Fremont Street in the late 1950s. "Their pasta was renowned throughout the valley," Vannozzi said. "They were kings of pasta. It was wonderful stuff. Casino managers and businessmen frequented my grandfather's place."[14]

Two sisters from the Niagara Falls area also satisfied the appetites of both locals and tourists for fine Italian food. Maria Perri, Angie Ruvo, and their husbands, Albert and Louis, started the Venetian Pizzeria near the Downtown area in the mid-1950s. The pizzeria was quickly recognized for both quality pizza and tasty spaghetti dishes, and the owners soon added other Italian specialties. Almost ten years later, the Perris and Ruvos built the Venetian Restaurant about one mile west of the Strip. It was an immediate success.[15]

The Strip also caught the attention of Italian American culinary entrepreneurs. In 1951 two partners, one of whom, Louis Coniglio, was of Italian background, opened Louigi's, which quickly became the flagship Italian restaurant on the Strip. Frank Sala recalled that patrons there would line up four or five deep at the bar, waiting for an opportunity to dine. The Villa Venice, located near Louigi's and owned by an Italian American from Chicago, another of the better Italian restaurants on the Strip in the 1950s and early 1960s, was particularly popular with casino and hotel workers as well as with visiting Chicagoans with shadowy reputations.[16] As Las Vegas grew, more and more Italian Americans opened restaurants. By the mid-1950s 30 to 40 percent of Las Vegas's dining establishments were owned either by Americans of Italian background (most) or by Italians (a few). Throughout the latter part of the 1950s and into the next decade, more than half of the most renowned restaurants were owned or managed by the Italian surnamed.[17]

The extensive representation of Italian Americans among resort-industry workers and managers, entertainers, and restaurant owners and managers in Las Vegas during the twenty years of rapid growth following the end of World War II is no surprise if one considers the employment patterns of Italian Americans in the eastern and midwestern cities in which the great majority of migrants had lived. Employment in the service industries, as well as in construction and waste disposal, were attractive to many of the Italian immigrants who came to America largely from the most impoverished areas of Italy. Success in these fields was not dependent on formal education but was correlated with a willingness to work hard and smart, often in cooperation with family members and longtime neighborhood friends.

Although relatively few Italian American migrants to Las Vegas were skilled tradesmen in the construction fields, the ranks of post–World War II Las Vegas contractors always included Italian Americans. While the great majority of Italian American migrants to Las Vegas after the war came from east of the Mississippi River, the majority of Italian-surnamed contractors were born and/or grew up in California. Indeed, a few, most notably Mike Terlizzi, took their capital and expertise across the state borders several times in the 1950s and early 1960s, always assessing whether the usually booming economy of Southern California or that of southern Nevada would offer the better return on investment.

Italian American contractors were represented in all aspects of construction. Dominic Bianchi and Tony Marnell, masonry contractors who grew up in Southern California, were subcontractors in home building, commercial developments, Strip hotel construction, and Downtown casino renovations. As subcontractors, they often worked with other major Italian American builders such as Frank and Louis Miranti, Ray Paglia, and Gus Rapone. Rapone became one of three principal officers of Sierra Construction, a company that specialized in federal government projects in the 1950s and subsequently competed most successfully for gaming property construction.[18]

For more than four decades the Isola families dominated the waste-disposal business in the Las Vegas area. Members of both families, related by marriage, had operated a major garbage-disposal business in Oakland, California. When Al Isola visited Las Vegas in 1954, he saw the potential of the rapidly growing community and convinced other family members to join him in investing in a local disposal business, and in 1965 the Isolas assumed complete ownership. Both their close relations with key elected officials and their commitment to efficient use of the latest waste-disposal technologies ensured that they faced no serious competition in securing waste-disposal contracts with local governments in the Las Vegas Valley. The Isolas' role in waste disposal came to a quick end in 1997, when two family members were among several company employees convicted of tax evasion.[19]

Not all the thousands of Italian Americans who came to Las Vegas in the two decades following the end of World War II worked in the gaming, restaurant, construction, or waste-disposal businesses. A few were professionals—physicians, attorneys, and teachers. Some supplied food and beverages to the hotels; others worked in insurance, real estate, dry cleaning and a host of other medium–sized and small businesses. Still others were in the ranks of the several Las Vegas Valley police and fire departments. Italian-surnamed individuals were found among judges and other elected officials and among the leaders of the Culinary Union and the Las Vegas chapter of the American Federation of Musicians.

In the late 1950s initially small groups of Italian Americans began to plan the establishment of organizations that would bring men and women of Italian heritage together to preserve and, indeed, enhance their common culture. Some efforts foundered, while others led to the formation of Italian Catholic Federation (ICF) chapters at several Las Vegas–area parishes, the establishment of a Sons of Italy Lodge, and, most importantly, the creation of the Italian American Club of Southern Nevada (IAC). While most of the ICF chapters remained small but active even into the 1990s, the two other organizations flourished in the 1960s and the early years of the next decade. Hundreds of Italian American men and women joined one of the organizations, and some joined both. The IAC had a restaurant and bar, both of which were often packed on weekend nights and sometimes in between. Well-known Italian entertainers, including Frank Sinatra and Dean Martin, visited the IAC and, along with many other Italian Americans who performed in the Strip showrooms and lounges, contributed their time and talent to a variety of fundraisers. Some Italian Americans who moved to Las Vegas in the 1960s recalled that the IAC was a good place to meet people who were helpful in finding employment in the hotels. While the Sons of Italy Lodge had no permanent headquarters, its functions, too, were well attended and its fund-raising supported by some Strip entertainers.[20]

I interviewed scores of Italian Americans who arrived in Las Vegas between the time the Flamingo first opened its doors in 1946 and 1967, when Howard Hughes bought the Desert Inn. Each said Las Vegas was like paradise. Everything was new and shiny, so unlike the old and often depressingly dingy tenements found in the Little Italies of the East Coast and Midwest cities. Jobs were plentiful and well paying, often leading to contact with nationally known entertainers and other famous people. Advancement came to those who were intelligent and reasonably diligent. While there was no Italian neighborhood, Italian Americans often socialized with one another, even if they did not belong to an Italian American organization.

The Resort City in the Sunbelt Years

The mobsters, or to use a less negative term, "the boys," did not just pack up and leave town en masse when Howard Hughes began buying hotels and the Nevada legislature revised laws regarding the licensing of the potential owners of casinos to facilitate corporate ownership. Yet they became less important, and the flavor of Las Vegas did change, with Las Vegans far less likely to bring visiting friends and relatives to the Strip so that they might point to this or that property and assert that it was controlled by the Chicago Mob or Cleveland's Mayfield Road Gang. Italian American interviewees who worked in the gaming business during this time of transition reported that their lives changed little, noting that because Howard Hughes chose men with virtually no knowledge of gambling operations to manage his casinos, their experience and expertise were much needed, initially by Hughes's closest advisors and then by the corporate executives whose presence in Las Vegas hotels had become common by the end of the 1980s.

Las Vegas and adjoining areas continued to experience rapid population growth, existing Strip and Downtown hotels were expanded and refurbished, and new hotels were built. Italian Americans remained well represented among the new migrants. All areas of significant Italian American population contributed to the migration, though Great Lakes cities such as Buffalo and Chicago seemed to provide a disproportionate share. While many took positions in the hotels and casinos, opened restaurants or bars, or started small businesses, some came to pursue their professions as attorneys, physicians, accountants, or architects, and others, particularly during the 1980s and 1990s, came to enjoy their retirement.

Gaming remained an attractive business for ambitious and entrepreneurial Italian Americans, even as some noticed that the Italian-surnamed dominated the List of Excluded Persons (more commonly known as the "Black Book")—individuals whom the Nevada Gaming Commission banned from casinos. They also suspected that those with an Italian name seeking gaming licenses faced more than the usual scrutiny from Nevada regulators. Nonetheless, more Italian Americans were found at the hotel chief-executive level during the corporate years than in the 1950s and 1960s.

A brief review of Frank Fertitta's career provides examples of the opportunities in Las Vegas. Fertitta had come to Las Vegas from Galveston, Texas, in 1960 at the suggestion of his uncle, a floor man at the Stardust. He worked as a 21 dealer there, and then at the Tropicana, and was promoted to floor man a few months before Howard Hughes took residence in a Desert Inn suite. His intelligence and ambition soon brought him another promotion, then he took a baccarat-manager position first at Circus Circus and next at the Sahara in 1974. Fertitta recalled that he then began considering ownership of a casino. He pursued this goal during the almost two years that he was general manager of the Fremont, one of the larger Downtown hotels. In 1977 he and two partners negotiated the first of several loans from Valley Bank and opened the Bingo Palace about one half mile west of the Strip. Within a couple of years Fertitta had bought his partners' shares and was overseeing the upgrading and expansion of the property, which became the successful Palace Station.[21]

Fertitta correctly saw that the rapidly expanding Las Vegas population would be the basis of even more profitable suburban casinos. In August 1994 he and other family members opened Boulder Station several miles east of the Strip, and just eleven months later they opened Texas Station about five miles west of Downtown Las Vegas. Subsequently, the Fertittas built casinos in Henderson and purchased a casino adjacent to Texas Station.[22]

Other Italian Americans occupied hotel executive suites during the corporate era. Former Air Force General Ed Nigro was responsible for Howard Hughes's gaming properties, until he and his former college friend Robert Mayhew quarreled. Nigro was then employed in a similar position by Del Webb's Sahara Nevada Corporation until his sudden death from a massive heart attack in 1973 at age fifty-four. After serving as the chief executive officer of the Landmark, Frank Modica, who, like Fertitta, had begun his gaming career as a dealer, went on to serve as chief executive of the Showboat, located south of Downtown and east of the Strip. Al Casarotto, who also began his career as a dealer, served as chief executive officer of the Frontier and then the Tropicana before embarking on an unsuccessful effort to open a new casino with Italian American partner Nick Gullo.[23]

John Giovenco, John Chiero, Dan Cassella, and Paul Pusateri were four Italian Americans whose rapid rise up corporate ladders reflected their respective capacities to effectively analyze financial information. Giovenco was president of the Hilton's gaming division through most of the 1980s; Chiero was president of the Tropicana from the mid-1980s through the mid-1990s; Cassella left a top-level position at the Desert Inn to become the chief executive officer at the Stratosphere, Las Vegas's tallest hotel, in the mid-1990s and then in 1999 resigned to become a consultant for financier Carl Icahn. Paul Pusateri was named president of both Bally's–Las Vegas and the Paris shortly before the latter opened in September 1999.

The Las Vegas metropolitan area, with a population of over 1.5 million in the summer of 2003, remained attractive to entrepreneurial Italian Americans from other parts of the country and to those born in Italy. While the latter were few in number compared to the former, the Italian born owned or managed many of the finer Italian restaurants that had opened during the past thirty years. Probably no restaurant served more tourists than Battista's Hole in the Wall, situated near the intersection of Las Vegas Boulevard and Flamingo Road. Las Vegas was the land of opportunity for Battista Locatelli, who came to California in 1949. He worked as a farm laborer, miner, butcher, waiter, and oil truck driver before finding fame and fortune in Las Vegas. The restaurant business is a difficult one, and not all the Italian culinary entrepreneurs enjoyed success in their ventures, yet most did. In recent years chief executives of the major Strip resorts have often sought chefs trained at Italian culinary institutes for their gourmet restaurants.[24]

Las Vegas has continued to attract ambitious Italian Americans with knowledge and experience in construction. Not all were as successful as Buffalo native Angelo Cassaro, who came to Las Vegas in 1979 partly on the recommendation of another Italian American, a boyhood friend who had started a plumbing company two years earlier. Cassaro, soon joined by his brother Joe, also a plumber, began his own plumbing company. Successful in this endeavor and quite cognizant of the building boom throughout the Las Vegas Valley, Cassaro in 1983 joined with another upstate New York refugee of severe winters with experience in residential and commercial construction, Nick Montana, and established a company to build duplexes, fourplexes, and condominiums throughout the Valley. In the mid-1990s Cassaro (Montana had retired from the building company), taking note of the increasing number of suits being filed by home buyers against construction companies in southern Nevada, concentrated almost exclusively on commercial developments. At the same time, neither he nor Montana has lost sight of the potential profits associated with meeting the basic needs—food, drink, and gambling—of Las Vegas's rapidly expanding population. In August 2000 their applications for gaming licenses were approved by the Nevada Gaming Commission, which allowed them to open a sports bar/restaurant and adjacent convenience store near the Centennial Hills development in northwest Las Vegas.[25]

A brief look at the recent careers of three Italian American women, all of whom have served in elective office, provides additional information about the range of opportunities rapidly growing Las Vegas provided Italian Americans, and, of course, others. Soon after graduating from high school in Las Vegas, Lorraine Perri embarked on her fifteen-year singing career, which included Strip performances with Jerry Colonna, Roland DiIorio, and other members of Louie Prima's band as well as with Peter Anthony (né Laurino) and Pete Barbuti, two longtime Las Vegas comedians who began their entertainment careers as musicians. In 1972 she and her husband, Blackie Hunt, opened the Bootlegger, an Italian restaurant originally located about three miles east of the Strip (and more recently, just south of the Strip). In the years that followed, Lorraine Perri Hunt invested in commercial real estate and became a member of the board of directors of Continental National Bank. In 1994 she was elected a Clark County commissioner with strong support from

the business community, and four years later she was elected lieutenant governor of Nevada, once again with strong business support. She was reelected in
November 2002.

Kathy Alfano Augustine and Chris Giunchigliani, like the great majority
of Las Vegas Italian Americans, did not grow up in Las Vegas. Before settling
there, Los Angeles–born Kathy Augustine completed bachelor's and master's
degrees at Southern California universities. She was a teacher in a private
school when she successfully ran for a seat in the Nevada assembly in 1992.
Two years later, she was elected to the Nevada state senate, and then in 1998
she was elected comptroller of Nevada, thereby joining Lorraine Hunt and
attorney general Frankie Sue Del Papa (who had attended high school in Las
Vegas) as one of the three Italian-descent women holding 50 percent of the
elected executive-branch offices in Nevada from 1998 through 2002. Kathy
Augustine was reelected comptroller in November 2002 and was selected by
the Augustus Society as Nevada's Outstanding Italian American for 2003.

The Italian-born Giunchigliani grew up in Chicago, was impressed by the
opportunities in growing Las Vegas when she visited in 1979, and began her
career as a Clark County School District teacher the next year. She quickly
became active both in the teachers' union and local politics, advancing to the
union presidency in 1983 even before she celebrated her thirtieth birthday.
Subsequently, she served four years as president of the Nevada State Education Association before successfully seeking a seat in the Nevada assembly, to
which she has been reelected several times.[26]

The years of Las Vegas's emergence as a resort city in the Sunbelt brought
changes to Italian American organizations, with some declining temporarily
and then revitalizing, others just steadily declining, and new organizations
forming. In general the existing organizations—the IAC, the Sons of Italy, the
chapters of the ICF—declined in membership, because the men and women
of at least partly Italian ancestry who continued to settle in Las Vegas no
longer needed the types of socializing these organizations provided. As the
years passed it was more and more likely that the newcomers were of only
partly Italian background, had spent most of their lives in multiethnic suburban neighborhoods, had spouses who were not of Italian ancestry, and did
not expect their children to marry Italian Americans. New organizations that
were more in tune with the needs of well-assimilated men and women of at
least partly Italian ancestry grew in numbers and vitality as the more traditional organizations declined.

In the late 1980s Angelo Cassaro spearheaded an effort to revitalize the IAC.
Through the mid-1990s, whether serving as president or just as an active
respected member, Cassaro spent thousands of his own dollars to upgrade the

physical facilities and hundreds of hours working with a few other dedicated
IAC members (including Nick Montana) to develop new activities and recruit
new members. They experimented with amateur boxing matches, opera performances, and a three-semester series of conversational Italian courses
offered by the Community College of Southern Nevada. The morale of most
long-term members improved, membership increased, and monthly meetings were better attended—for awhile. Eventually Cassaro, as well as some of
the people who worked closely with him, had to turn their attention to other
matters. Recruitment lagged, as did attendance at monthly meetings, and the
financial health of the IAC became more precarious for a time. More recently
the financial picture improved, and IAC members and friends celebrated the
fortieth anniversary of the club's founding with a formal banquet in September 2000. Two years later, the club membership endorsed a bylaw change that
permitted women of Italian heritage to join the club itself rather than the
ladies' auxiliary.

Other traditional Italian American organizations also experienced problems in the last decade of the twentieth century. In spite of the efforts of Las
Vegas businessman and community activist Phil Carlino, the Sons of Italy
Lodge suffered an uninterrupted decline in membership, with only a handful
participating in meetings as the second millennium began. So, too, membership in ICF chapters declined, with only two parishes hosting chapters in the
summer of 2000 and only one, St. Francis DeSales parish, functioning three
years later.

New organizations—the Augustus Society, Nevada Society of Italian
American Lawyers (NSIAL), the Sun City Italian Club, and Club Italia—
formed by well-assimilated, successful Italian American men and women in
the 1980s and 1990s—have, not surprisingly, been more successful than the
traditional organizations in recruiting the active and retired business people
and professionals of at least partly Italian ancestry who continue to settle in
Las Vegas in the twenty-first century. In 1983 a small group founded the
Augustus Society, whose stated goals were improving the image of Italian
Americans, providing college scholarships to deserving high school graduates
of at least partly Italian ancestry, and assisting needy Italian Americans, especially seniors. Annual dues were set at $1,000. Membership initially grew
steadily, hitting a plateau of about seventy to seventy-five in the mid-1990s
and then reaching one hundred in 2002. The Augustus Society has been re-
markably successful in providing scholarships, with more than $550,000
awarded since 1983. Its leaders have not expended much time or effort to
improve the Italian American image, however, and the paucity of needy Italian American seniors in the Las Vegas Valley has made the third of the original

goals difficult to achieve. Most members have found the emphasis on scholar-ships to their liking.[27]

Angelo Cassaro was the most influential and effective Augustus Society member during the 1990s, its members often looking to him for guidance on how to proceed in many areas whether or not he was actually serving in a leadership position. Cassaro has almost always been a member of the board of directors, sometimes its chair, and has also served as president. In January 1989, with the assistance of other Augustus Society members who were also active in the IAC, Cassaro put together a working group that included formal leaders of all Italian American organizations to plan Las Vegas's first Colum-bus Day parade.

Subsequent parades, like the first one in 1989, provided examples of just how assimilated Las Vegas Italian Americans had become. Politicians of the Democratic, Libertarian, and Republican parties walked and waved to crowds lining Fremont Street; several marching bands played, gymnasts per-formed, a contingent of the Las Vegas Sons of Erin relaxed and drank beer on the back of a flatbed truck, and men and women of presumably Scottish heritage played the bagpipes. The only distinctly Italian aspect of the parade was the food served at a well-attended block party that followed. Organizing such a parade requires a good deal of time and effort, and everyone associated with it felt a sense of pride. Yet none whom I spoke with had stopped to consider how little of anything distinctly Italian was celebrated. The last Co-lumbus Day parade was held in 1995.[28]

The NSIAL, whose founder and first president was the Chicago-born and -raised Dominic Gentile, since its inception in 1987 has had a membership that includes both long-time Las Vegas attorneys and recent arrivals. Its mem-bership generally numbers thirty-five to forty, 20 to 30 percent of whom en-joy monthly lunches featuring Italian food purchased from one of several Italian delis in Las Vegas. These lunches give the lawyers an opportunity to exchange information on subjects ranging from legal community gossip to which Las Vegas restaurant has the best Italian food. Since 1990 NSIAL has cosponsored the Columbus Day Ball (initiated by the Augustus Society) and has raised funds for local community organizations, especially Child Haven.[29]

The Sun City Italian Club and Club Italia were founded by a former Los Angeles real-estate broker and businesswoman, Marge Russo, the first club in the mid-1990s and the second a few years later. Russo, an articulate and ener-getic retiree, drew upon her experience organizing Italian American groups in Southern California and recruited about two hundred members to the Sun City Italian Club. Many members, close to 50 percent, were not even of partly Italian heritage, as the rules of the Sun City retirement community prohibited sponsorship of any clubs not open to all residents. Rare indeed was the non-Jewish retiree who sought to join the Sun City Yiddish Club, but people of all backgrounds were anxious to immerse themselves in at least some aspects of Italian culture. Marge Russo found this situation displeasing and started Club Italia, which required that members be at least partly of Italian ancestry. Many Italian American members of the Sun City Italian Club followed their former president and joined Club Italia while also remaining members of the retirement-community group. By the summer of 2003 more than two hundred Italian Americans, still including a substantial number of Sun City Italian Club members, were enrolled.[30]

Both of the organizations founded by Marge Russo provide opportunities to socialize for the generally well-educated and well-traveled men and women who have enjoyed financial success. They can also learn as much, or as little, about Italian culture, food, wine, and language as they might desire. In contrast the IAC, even with its restaurant and bocce courts, has little to offer these recent arrivals to the Las Vegas Valley. It is too distant from their homes, and most of its members are actually older than the recent arrivals.

The organizations that adapt most effectively to the needs of an increasingly assimilated, rather affluent, and older population will survive into the second decade of the twenty-first century; the others will disappear. By the second quarter of this century, the rapid rate of assimilation will ensure that very few Las Vegans with some Italian ancestry will feel any need to socialize only with others of Italian ancestry. Recognizing this, yet anxious to preserve the best of both Italian and Italian American culture, Dominic Gentile began publishing *La Voce,* a monthly newspaper, in October 2001 with the goal of providing something of interest to the more than 120,000 men and women of at least partly Italian ancestry who reside in the greater Las Vegas area.

Noting the significant diversity among his intended audience, Gentile included information in each issue on Italian food, fashion, and travel, along with articles on a variety of subjects. With distribution of *La Voce* at over 13,000 only six months later, Gentile appeared well on his way to creating a virtual Italian American community in Las Vegas. Yet revenues lagged behind expenses through the summer of 2003, putting *La Voce'*s longer-term viability into question. Nevertheless, with or without *La Voce* and indeed with or without any of the organizations mentioned above, Las Vegas will remain an attractive city for Italian Americans—especially those approaching retirement age—who seek low taxes, sunny skies, golf courses, inexpensive buffets, and a chance to gamble.

Notes

1. U.S. Department of Commerce, Bureau of the Census, 13th U.S. Census, 1910 Abstract, 43, 582. Books that well record both the general experiences of Italian immigrants and the Italian American experience in particular American cities are many, yet Jerre Mangione and Ben Morreale, *La Storia* (New York: Harper-Collins, 1992), and Deanna Paoli Gumina, *The Italians of San Francisco* (New York: Center for Migration Studies, 1985), are particularly impressive.

2. *Las Vegas Age,* June 10, 1905, 1; April 1, 1911, 1; August 15, 1912, 2.

3. Elizabeth Patrick, "The Champos: An Italian Family Rose to Prosperity in the 1920s Las Vegas," *The Nevadan,* March 27, 1982, 6–7.

4. Guido Testolin, interview by author.

5. Alan Balboni, "Tony's Carpet Joint," *The Nevadan,* January 28, 1990, 125–35.

6. For information on Guy McAfee, see Eugene P. Moehring, *Resort City in the Sunbelt: Las Vegas, 1930–1970* (Reno and Las Vegas: University of Nevada Press, 1989), 42–43.

7. Alan Balboni, *Beyond the Mafia: Italian Americans and the Development of Las Vegas* (Reno, Las Vegas, and London: University of Nevada Press, 1996), 10–11.

8. Ibid., 6.

9. Ibid., 20–26.

10. Alan Balboni, "Southern Italians and Eastern European Jews: Cautious Cooperation in Las Vegas Casinos, 1940–1967," *Nevada Historical Society Quarterly* 38 (Fall 1995): 161–63.

11. Ibid., 164–65.

12. Frank Sala, interview by author; George Ligouri, interview by author; Phil Carlino, interview by author; Christine Fenton, interview by author.

13. *Las Vegas Evening Review-Journal,* October 18, 1931, 3; *Las Vegas Sun,* January 30, 1980; Mary Jean Barozzi, interview by author.

14. Tom Vannozzi, interview by author.

15. Balboni, *Beyond the Mafia,* 42.

16. Ibid., 41.

17. Based on a review of Las Vegas newspapers in the late 1950s and early 1960s and interviews by the author with numerous individuals who resided and dined in Las Vegas.

18. Balboni, *Beyond the Mafia,* 44–47.

19. Ibid., 44.

20. Ibid., passim.

21. Ibid., 32–33.

22. Ibid., 102–3.

23. Ibid., 65–71.

24. Battista Locatelli, interview by author; Giovanni Vanchieri, interview by author.

25. Angelo Cassaro, interview by author.

26. Lorraine Perri Hunt, interview by author; Kathy Alfano Augustine, interview by author; Chris Giunchigliani, interview by author. Additional information on the careers of Hunt and Giunchigliani can be found in Balboni, *Beyond the Mafia.*

27. Information on the IAC, Sons of Liberty Lodge, ICF chapters, and Augustus Society through 1995 can be found in Balboni, *Beyond the Mafia.*

28. Balboni, *Beyond the Mafia,* 127–28.

29. Interviews by author with attorneys Dominic Gentile; Paula Gentile (no relation to Dominic); Tony Montisano; and Donna Rosenberg.

30. Marge Russo, interview by author. (The author met many of the members when he addressed a March 1999 meeting of Club Italia.)

CHAPTER 9

The Jews

MICHAEL GREEN

The Las Vegas Jewish community reflects the city's uniqueness. No other city founded in the twentieth century reached a population of a million by the twenty-first or owed its growth so greatly to one industry, gaming, which Jews dominated. But as in eastern cities to which they immigrated from Europe, some local Jews held traditional jobs while others worked on the periphery of the law or outside it, facing a hard road to respectability. Their successes and failures revealed both the unusual nature of Las Vegas and its Jewish populace and their similarities to other Jews in other cities.[1]

Jews in the West: Trends and Themes

The story of Jewish immigration to the United States is older than the nation itself. "Secret" Jews who hid their religious identity lived in New Spain—now northern Mexico and the southwestern United States—in the sixteenth century. After the Mexican-American War added California and the Southwest to the United States and gold was discovered in 1848, Jews headed for the San Francisco/Sacramento area either from the East Coast or directly from Europe. The largest-scale Jewish immigration to the United States—and the one that would affect Las Vegas the most—occurred in the last two decades of the nineteenth century and first two decades of the twentieth: the migration from eastern Europe that came through New York's Ellis Island. A significant percentage of these Jews worked their way westward at the time or later. Jewish communities expanded throughout the western United States, but not until after World War II would Las Vegas become an important Jewish area.[2]

Amid mild anti-Semitism, Jews in the American West both maintained traditions and found acceptance and prosperity by taking part in the gentile community—especially in California, where Jews entered the economic and political elite. Offering few exceptions to historical rules about western Jews, Nevada Jews were socially mobile, free from outbreaks of excessive bias, and influential. Yet some Jews followed an eastern trend, forming their own neighborhoods and developing unity through their merchant class and civic groups, with synagogues following as their communities grew.[3]

No Jewish community formed in nineteenth-century Las Vegas. Save for Southern Paiutes, Mormons, and ranchers, Las Vegas lacked much population until 1905, when the new railroad auctioned off land. By 1910, of the 937 Las Vegans, the dozen or so Jews had no temple. Usually, Jews moved as families to cities and ran small businesses—thus their preference for Reno or mining towns and their absence in Las Vegas. And data on western Jews is limited until World War II due to the lack of census information and scholarship.[4]

The quickening pace of Las Vegas's development brought more Jews in the 1930s and 1940s. When Nevada legalized gambling in 1931, many Jews came from California's cruise ships and backroom games. As Hoover Dam construction began, Sallie and Mike Gordon bought liquor stores and, in 1932, began raising the town's first Jewish baby. Murray Wollman became identified with real estate, Mel Moss with banking, Sam Friedman and the Hechts with clothing. With brothers Louis and Harry, Nate Mack became the best-known Jewish resident. By the time of his death in 1965 he had owned casinos, moving and towing services, and restaurants. In the 1930s the Macks were among twenty families who formed the Sons and Daughters of Israel, met in a store, and taught their children the Torah. Las Vegas's Jewish population grew to around 100 by 1940, when the city's reached 8,400. The establishment of the Army Gunnery School (now Nellis Air Force Base) in 1941 was a major boost to Las Vegas's growth. During the war eastern gamblers descended on Las Vegas, creating a big enough Jewish populace to be active in civic affairs—and a big enough city for the Jewish community to flourish.[5]

Building a Resort City: Insiders and Outsiders

Las Vegas's Jewish arrivals in the 1940s sought to live as they had in the East, where many had been illegal gamblers, but with legitimacy: gambling was legal, the town small enough for Jews with trouble escaping their shady pasts to ply their trade legally. But while eastern European Jews going west often were second- and third-generation Americans, to those beyond Nevada's borders Jewish gamblers were outsiders. In Las Vegas, by contrast, Jews entered the local mainstream and affected Nevada's political economy and society far beyond their numbers.[6]

Though a small part of the populace, Jews ran almost every casino built in the 1940s, 1950s, and 1960s. Sunbelt growth and modern transportation widened their economic net. In the early 1940s Meyer Lansky and Bugsy Siegel drove from Hollywood—where Siegel had moved from New York City's Lower East Side to seek wealth and film stardom—to Las Vegas. Lansky foresaw the "most luxurious hotel casino in the world. . . . [and] after they had eaten and drunk all they could, there was only one thing left . . . gambling."[7] Siegel and his allies took over race wire concessions and bought the El Cortez, opened in 1941. From Minneapolis came "Icepick" Willie Alderman—named for his execution style—and Davie Berman, who allegedly tired of battling Siegel over splitting profits and whether to enter the international drug trade. They sold the El Cortez and Siegel turned to the Flamingo, begun by Hollywood publisher Billy Wilkerson. Piling up red ink and irking his Mob financiers, Siegel was killed in June 1947. Other Jewish gamblers entered the Flamingo, Lansky's biographer said, "with the steely precision of generals mopping up after a coup."[8]

New boss Gus Greenbaum's profitable leadership prompted more Mob investment and a Jewry disproportionately represented in gaming—with payoffs to Lansky. The Thunderbird opened in 1948, with hidden investors Lansky and his brother Jake. In 1950 the Desert Inn opened; needing money to finish it, Wilbur Clark gave control to the Mayfield Road Gang—Moe Dalitz and other midwestern gamblers. In the 1950s came the Sahara, Sands, Royal Nevada, Riviera, New Frontier, Dunes, Fremont, Tropicana, and Stardust, mostly run by Jews tied to Lansky. In the 1960s a Lansky ally, furniture supplier Al Parvin, bought several hotels. Jay Sarno built Caesars Palace, which thrived under Bill Weinberger and Harry Wald, both active in the Jewish community, and Circus Circus. Former Sarno lawyer and executive Burton Cohen became president of the Desert Inn, the New Frontier, and the new MGM Grand. In the 1960s, joining Major Riddle in reviving the Dunes was Sands co-owner Sid Wyman, a friend of Teamsters boss Jimmy Hoffa; its St. Louis link extended when lawyer and Hoffa crony Morris Shenker bought it. Downtown, in 1966, Greenbaum aide Ben Goffstein opened the Four Queens, named for his wife and daughters.[9]

By the 1970s organized crime was unraveling. Besides prosecuting "families" under the 1970 Racketeering Investigations and Corrupt Organizations Act, federal officials found several casino owners skimming for Lansky. In 1954 the *Las Vegas Sun* divulged Lansky's hidden interest in the Thunderbird—not coincidentally attacking Louis Wiener and his then-law partner—helping lead to the establishment of a Gaming Control Board to probe license applicants. The best-selling *The Green Felt Jungle* later called attention to Lansky and other Jewish gambling operators. In 1959 Governor Grant Sawyer backed a Gaming Commission to oversee licensing and the List of Excluded

Persons or "Black Book," which, critics have charged, targets Italians while few Jews are included, despite their frequent appearances in federal documents linking them to organized crime. When Nevada briefly added Desert Inn and Stardust investor Ruby Kolod to the list in 1965, Kolod reputedly donated $200,000 to Republican candidate Paul Laxalt, who beat Sawyer for governor.[10]

But change was imminent. Billionaire Howard Hughes bought the Desert Inn, Sands, and New Frontier from Jewish operators from Cleveland, New York, and Detroit; he tried to buy the Stardust, which might have removed Jews with the Chicago syndicate from its ownership. Nevada's Corporate Gaming Act of 1969 enabled publicly traded companies to buy casinos. Sawyer feared it would be a cover for the Mob, and he was right—for awhile. Laxalt believed it would cleanse Nevada's image as a Mob haven, and he was right—eventually. At first the difference was negligible. Allen Glick bought the Stardust and was the front man; Frank Rosenthal, a handicapper tied to the Chicago Mob, ran the casino and the skim. The state denied Rosenthal a license, later adding him to the "Black Book." Glick sold his interests and testified against the Chicago, Milwaukee, and Kansas City families receiving skim money from his casinos. Longtime Las Vegans Al Sachs and Herb Tobman, Stardust executives before Glick's purchase, bought the Stardust and the Fremont. Yet skimming went on, and in 1983 state officials revoked their licenses, although they never were convicted of wrongdoing.[11]

Jews not only owned many casinos but operated them as well. Already involved in entertainment and unions, both of which were tied to old illegal gambling, Jews held many top jobs, from casino manager to publicist. But no Jewish gambler affected Las Vegas more than Dalitz. Robbins Cahill, for many years Nevada's top gaming regulator, called Dalitz's group "silk glove men," doing legally in Nevada what they did illegally elsewhere. Dalitz's life reflected the experiences of many Jewish gamblers seeking to escape an ethnic enclave, enjoy wealth they found hard to make legally, and work with other ethnic groups. Dalitz often sought to take cash from illegal activities and launder it in legal businesses; Nevada's burgeoning gaming industry provided a perfect opportunity. With the Desert Inn profiting handsomely, in 1954 its operators put their money and know-how into running the casino at the Showboat on Boulder Highway; a quarter of a century later, its success prompted the building of newer, better hotel-casinos along that road. Besides running the Stardust, Dalitz also owned a Downtown property and leased it to other operators as the Sundance; it has since given way to Fitzgeralds.[12]

A source of unity, division, and vision, Dalitz symbolized the fact that while Las Vegas enabled Jewish gamblers to ply their trade legally, they never escaped a web of illegality. He told a friend, "I'll bet your grandpa drank whiskey. . . . I'm the guy who made the whiskey, and I'm considered the bad guy." But author and columnist John L. Smith said, "If you want to understand Las Vegas history, you must get to know Moe Dalitz." After Irwin Molasky and Merv Adelson formed Paradise Development, Dalitz and Desert Inn official Allard Roen joined them to build Sunrise Hospital and other buildings on Maryland Parkway. They developed malls, condominiums, and country clubs in southern Nevada and Rancho La Costa near San Diego; Molasky and Adelson helped start Lorimar, which produced *The Waltons*. Adelson's father, Nathan, ran Sunrise Hospital, and his death inspired them to start a hospice in his name. In 1999 Molasky bought out Adelson and developed Park Towers, an elite residential complex."[13]

The intersection of Jews with varied backgrounds continued when the Bank of Las Vegas opened in 1954. Prospering under the management of Mormon E. Parry Thomas, with Nate Mack and his son Jerome as two of Thomas's partners, it became the first bank to make loans to casinos; other bankers deemed gambling immoral and doubted that mobsters would repay loans. Thomas and Jerome Mack proceeded to invest widely. They merged with a Reno bank to form Valley Bank, now part of Bank of America, and built the city's largest office building. They bought land on Sunset Road, a leading 1990s business strip near the airport. They won control of New York electronics firm Continental Connector, which bought the Dunes and sold it to Shenker. Deeming local charities inbred, they began a United Way. Aware that UNLV owned only fifty-five acres on Maryland Parkway in the 1960s and that prices would skyrocket before it could buy more, they formed the Nevada Southern University Land Foundation, bought more land, guaranteed loans to UNLV, and recruited Molasky and Adelson to help. Appropriately, UNLV's arena for sports, concerts, and other events is the Thomas and Mack.[14]

These kinds of relationships characterized local Jewry generally. As in other 1940s western cities, Jews built the accoutrements of a community in Las Vegas, most notably a temple, which the local populace had grown enough to support. In 1943 Jews meeting in each other's homes and at St. Joan of Arc Catholic Church formed Temple Beth Sholom. The Gordons, the Macks, Arthur Brick, Ira Goldring, Sam and Dave Stearns, Al Salton, Harry Levy, Al Goot, Bill Mendlesohn, A. J. Schur, and Wollman, among others, built the Jewish Community Center (JCC) at Thirteenth and Carson. But they were not alone. Berman, usually not religious, recruited Alderman and Moe Sedway, fellow veterans of organized crime, to help, arguing that their children needed a Jewish upbringing. These developments marked a trend in Las Vegas Jewry: a convergence of the legitimate and the less legitimate. Nate

Mack invested in casinos; Siegel's partners and successors joined him in other businesses. The once-illegal gamblers were active in the community. Sedway donated to religious groups, mulled entering politics, and chaired the United Jewish Appeal, a post held by several casino bosses. Jack Entratter of the Sands and the Hotel Last Frontier's Jake Kozloff were temple presidents, followed by casino owner Mel Exber and lawyer Oscar Goodman.[15]

Goodman's defense work for alleged mobsters reflected links between the legal profession and gaming. Louis Wiener's family came to town in the early 1930s. After law school he represented several hotels; his partners included Neil Galatz and David Goldwater. David Zenoff, a temple president, went on to a judicial career. After introducing one of Nevada's first civil-rights bills in the legislature, George Rudiak represented the Teamsters and was part owner of Valley Hospital. A renowned advocate, Sam Lionel teamed with Grant Sawyer to form Nevada's largest law firm, which was noted for its real estate, gaming, and litigation practice. The legal community today includes many Jewish attorneys; supreme court justice Nancy Becker (her sister, Patricia, served on the control board and as a casino attorney); and such longtime district judges as Michael Cherry, Jeff Sobel, and Jack Lehman.[16]

Jews also entered politics. Greenbaum served in the largely honorary post of mayor of Paradise, a township created when Las Vegas tried to annex the Strip. When Sedway voiced ambitions, Siegel said, "We don't run for office. We own the politicians," and Dalitz spoke similarly. But Jews from outside gaming went into politics, often as Democrats. Legislators have included Sedway's optometrist nephew Marvin, a tax reformer who chaired assembly Ways and Means; Shelley Berkley, later a university regent, now a congresswoman; State Senator Valerie Wiener, Louis's daughter; William Hernstadt, who owned kvvu tv 5; David Goldwater, the attorney's son; longtime activist Eileen Brookman; contractor Bernie Posin, whose son and several relatives are lawyers; and veteran legislator and county commissioner Myrna Williams. Businessman Chic Hecht became Clark County's first Republican state senator in 1966 and in 1982 the only Jewish U.S. senator elected from Nevada. Ron Lurie, now general manager of Arizona Charlie's casinos, spent a term as mayor; his father, Art, a longtime boxing judge, ran stores and restaurants. Lurie won the election for mayor after two terms on the city council, where he served with realtor Al Levy, whose father, Harry, had been temple president. Pawn-business owner Michael Mack (no relation to Nate or Jerry) was appointed and then elected to the council, headed by mayor Oscar Goodman, who is considered Las Vegas's most popular politician.[17]

Other Jews wielded influence in the media. Morry Zenoff began a radio station, Channel 13, and newspapers in Henderson and Boulder City. He opened the weekly *Nevada Jewish Chronicle* in 1961 but closed it in 1965, when Jack Tell started the *Las Vegas Israelite;* Tell's family still publishes it. A co-owner of Channel 3, Wiener was active in philanthropy and politics. But no media figure—Jewish or otherwise—affected the area more than Hank Greenspun. Arriving after World War II and entering various enterprises, he also ran ammunition and guns to Israel, fighting to preserve its existence, and ended up pleading guilty to violating the Neutrality Act. He invested in the Desert Inn with his friend Clark but clashed with Dalitz. When locked-out *Las Vegas Review-Journal* typesetters opened a paper, Greenspun bought it with a loan from Nate Mack and turned it into the daily *Las Vegas Sun.*[18]

The *Sun* and its publisher were crusaders. Greenspun ardently defended Israel in print, and such leaders as Shimon Peres and Ariel Sharon were his close friends. He took on the power structure run by Senator Pat McCarran, his attacks prompting the senator and casino owners to mount an advertising boycott of the *Sun,* but Greenspun bested them in federal court. Civil libertarians hailed his attacks on the communist witch hunt and Senator Joe McCarthy. He also feuded with Dalitz when the *Sun* printed the latter's old mug shot and accused him of corruption. When Greenspun ran for governor in 1962 and said casinos spent $250,000 to beat him, Dalitz allegedly replied, "Hah, it cost almost twice that, but we got results!"[19]

Greenspun also got results. In 1953 he and other investors started Channel 8, the city's first television station. Years later, he built a cable television firm that his family sold to Cox Communications in 1998 for $1.3 billion. He built a country club (with a loan from the Teamsters and fellow Israel ally Hoffa), bought 8,000 acres that became Green Valley, and made Henderson, an industrial town, into an upscale city. His American Nevada Corporation, run by then-son-in-law Mark Fine, began selling homes in the late 1970s; Henderson almost overtook Reno as Nevada's second-largest city by 2000, and its population continues to rise toward 300,000. Greenspun's family owned parts of two casinos, The Hospitality Network, and weekly and monthly publications—giving them influence beyond the *Sun*'s small circulation; Greenspun's son Brian's ties to college friend Bill Clinton enhanced their national standing. In turn, Fine helped build Howard Hughes Corporation's development, Summerlin, including a Sun City. The result was an influx of retirees, a number of them Jewish, and two senior areas in Green Valley. And in 2001 Brian Greenspun and Del Webb Corporation bought Bureau of Land Management land for a master-planned community in North Las Vegas.[20]

Hank Greenspun was a key part of the Jewish community in an area in which Las Vegas reflected the nation: civil rights. In 1960, after many years of local segregation, Strip casino owners agreed to desegregate their resorts, and

Greenspun helped strike the deal. A key gaming figure in making the agreement, Dalitz, advised other casino operators to stop refusing black customers. Ironically, Greenspun and Dalitz wound up on the same side, even if they approached it from different directions.[21]

As in other areas, disparate local Jews came together for civil rights—not only Greenspun and Dalitz, but businessman Lloyd Katz. Arriving in 1951, he ran several movie theatres. Active in religious, political, and secular groups, his wife Edythe cofounded *The Jewish Reporter*. Lloyd Katz was active in civic affairs and business, from the university medical school advisory board to the Downtown Progress Association; he desegregated his theaters before he legally had to and lobbied Congress for civil rights; he was a charter member of B'nai B'rith and was temple president. With Jerome Mack and the Greenspuns, he and Frank Sinatra chaired a testimonial dinner for Entratter to benefit an Israeli nursery school and the temple school. Thus, Las Vegas Jews embodied many contradictions: on both sides of the law, yet politically and socially active; united and divided.[22]

United and Divided They Stand

In the 1980s then–Jewish Federation head Jerry Countess detected "as many divisions [among Jews as in] the general community, with the likelihood that on some issues there are more." The divisions were often personal—Greenspun's feuds with Dalitz, Wiener, and taxi, hospital, and cable television company owner Milton Schwartz. When Greenspun and Dalitz united—as in backing Laxalt over Sawyer—it had more to do with common enemies than common interests. Finally, an enemy united them: Joe Yablonsky, the Las Vegas FBI agent-in-charge from 1979 to 1983. Soon after arriving, Yablonsky joined Beth Sholom's board. But the FBI agent began criticizing local leaders tied to the Mob and investigated, among others, federal judge Harry Claiborne, a friend of the Horseshoe's Benny Binion, whom Greenspun called his best friend. As Senator Laxalt pressed the FBI to oust Yablonsky, Greenspun accused the agent of entrapment. Recalling unpleasant meetings at the temple, Yablonsky said, "The Jews treated me worse than anyone else." Finally, he reached mandatory retirement age, accused Greenspun of blackballing him from local jobs, and left Las Vegas.[23]

Between federal pressure, corporate gaming, local efforts to burnish the city's image, and age driving out old gamblers, Las Vegas had evolved by the century's end. From 1973 to 1989 no major Strip resort opened, but existing hotels grew, smaller ones sprouted, and local casinos became more popular. The next spurt was due to a new breed of Jewish casino owners, notably Steve

Wynn and Sheldon Adelson, who were politically important and controversial in the Jewish community and beyond.[24]

Wynn had a long history in Las Vegas. He visited in 1952 as a ten year old, returned in the 1960s, and tried several enterprises. Parry Thomas helped him get a $1.2 million loan to buy land that Caesars Palace wanted. Wynn made a large profit, took over and expanded the Golden Nugget, and built in Atlantic City. Appearing in his own commericals, he polished the image of casino owners, but Wynn was controversial, a perfectionist willing to use his power. And he was part of a Jewish combination that remade Las Vegas. Drexel Burnham Lambert trader Michael Milken helped finance his friend Wynn's Atlantic City property and The Mirage through junk bonds. As 1988 ended, The Mirage opened, made handsome profits, and elevated Strip resorts to another level of elegance. Like the Flamingo, it inspired other investors, creating another building boom that continues today, including Wynn's Treasure Island (now TI) next to The Mirage, and then the Bellagio.[25]

Already an economic power, Wynn wielded political power as well. While his substantial donations to candidates were nothing unusual, he based his political investments on scientific mailing and polling. Feuding with fellow temple member Berkley, then a regent, over UNLV's operations, he aided her opponents. When police tried to oust Mirage host Charlie Meyerson—a state official called him a "junket rep to the Mob"—Wynn accused Sheriff John Moran of getting even for his refusal to aid the careers of Moran's sons. Wynn won a libel suit against Lyle Stuart, publisher of a critical biography, but was unsuccessful in a case against its author, *Review-Journal* columnist John L. Smith.[26]

More controversial than Wynn, Adelson bought the Sands and, like Wynn, imploded his hotel to build another, the Venetian. Like Wynn, he offered high-end shopping and catered to high rollers, and he entered the art world, opening a Guggenheim Museum. Adelson shares his interest in politics but with more partisanship: a devoted Republican, he helped defeat a veteran county commissioner in 1996 but failed in 1998 to make a dent against several Democrats, including Berkley, who once worked for him as a corporate executive.[27]

Devoted to Judaism, Adelson and wife, Miriam, wed in Israel, where they own a home, and have eaten in the Knesset, joined by Benjamin Netanyahu, whose race for prime minister Adelson aided in 1996. Besides lobbying for gambling in Israel, Adelson has owned a movie theatre and an auto-parts firm and put up $500,000 for a helicopter training facility.[28] A victim of anti-Semitism growing up in Boston and cofounder of the Las Vegas Anti-Defamation League, he is a Jewish Federation board member and one of its top donors. Then-executive director Ronni Epstein has said, "If I had a hundred Sheldon Adelsons in town, we'd have the finest Jewish community in the United States."[29]

Opposed to Culinary Union efforts to organize his workers and politically involved, Adelson became controversial in the Jewish community. After someone soaped "Dead Jews" in his cabana, he asked the National Jewish Medical and Research Center to rescind an award to union leader John Wilhelm, "who obviously condones anti-Semitism." Two governors criticized Adelson; Berkley, an ex-Sands executive and local trustee of the medical center, said, "To accuse someone of anti-Semitism when it does not exist only undermines our ability to expose anti-Semitism when it does exist."[30] In 1999 Temple Beth Sholom planned a roast of Carolyn and Oscar Goodman at the Venetian, but the mayor would not cross the union picket line. Held elsewhere, the roast raised $200,000—$50,000 less than Adelson planned to donate. In turn he withdrew his pledge, threatened to end dealings with six congregants who attended, and called Rabbi Felipe Goodman unfit to head the temple.[31]

Historically, Las Vegas Jewry came full circle. Traditional arrivals and less-legitimate residents built the first temple, but they were later in controversy with Adelson, a casino owner of traditional origins. Wynn, another politically involved casino owner, became the victim of gaming's new respectability: MGM Grand engineered a hostile Wall Street takeover of his resorts. Wynn had risen with aid from Thomas, linked to early Jewish leaders through the Macks, who helped Jewish gamblers build, expand, and legitimize. Angry at accusations of organized-crime ties, Wynn now owned the Desert Inn after changing the street and the city Dalitz had helped build.[32]

Modern City, Modern Community

The development of the synagogues and groups comprising a community demonstrates the evolution of Las Vegas's Jewish populace. In 1987 Countess said, "The question is not why there are so many organizations but why there aren't more." He noted the lack of homes for the aged, a community center, and mental health services. Much of that is now present or planned, yet a visiting rabbi found "crosscurrents buffeting the community. . . . One group—by far the larger one—is drifting out of the Jewish orbit of life completely. The other group . . . is intently searching for ways to function as meaningful and committed Jews."[33]

Moving twice since its founding in the 1940s, Temple Beth Sholom reflects the city and its Jews. Katz, Levy, Dalitz, Molasky, and Zenoff led and raised money in the mid-1950s for the shift to Oakey and Sixteenth, an elite area at the time, with Kolod endowing a children's center. Later president Sandra Mallin called it "the center of Jewish life in Las Vegas," but its neighborhood declined as families living near it moved to planned communities. Looking west, the temple held services in a trailer and High Holy Days at a hotel before its Summerlin complex opened in September 2000 with a school, a sanctuary for 1,800, two ballrooms, the Sandra and Stanley Mallin Early Childhood Center, and the Fanny and Joseph Goldberg Education Building.[34]

Thirty years after Beth Sholom's founding, the populace had grown enough to sustain a reform temple, Congregation Ner Tamid, begun in 1975. In a year it included 100 families, but it went through a membership decline and several rabbis until Rabbi Sanford Akselrad arrived in January 1988; now it is the city's second-largest temple. Its religious school, named for Dalitz, began a special-needs program, an area of expertise of education director Jacqueline Fleekop, who created the program "Lessons Learned from the Holocaust," now used in two dozen school districts. Lois Steinberg Bergman came from Beth Sholom to run the preschool and kindergarten.[35]

Nothing better demonstrates the growth of southern Nevada and its Jewish community in the late twentieth century than the number of new temples: fifteen in twenty-five years. Like older congregations, they offer varied services, but they also try to appeal to younger Jews to draw new members. Yet the same temples cater to older Jews, especially in Sun City areas. They take part in community events, as sponsors or part of the traditional Jewish effort to be good citizens. And their locations and activities reflect Las Vegas's physical and demographic growth.

The number of Summerlin synagogues reflects northwest growth. Mel Hecht's Beth Am, which was built near Beth Sholom, planned a banquet hall, senior day care, learning center, and wedding garden. Reform Ahavat Torah began with couples praying and dining Friday nights; meeting at a Catholic church with religious school at an Episcopal church, membership reached 70 under Rabbi Craig Rosenstein. Yitzchak Wyne's Orthodox Young Israel AishHaTorah targeted younger Jews.[36] On the first and third Fridays of the month, Temple Bet Emet held Reform services at a Sun City Lutheran church, Herschel Brooks's Traditional Reform Bet Knesset Bamidbar at a community center. Yisroel Schanowitz's Orthodox Chabad of Summerlin held a Saturday B-L-T—Bagels, Lox, and Tefillah. Yaakov Wasser led the only Ashkenazic Orthodox daily minyan at Shaarei Tefilla.

Green Valley's synagogues have also grown. Six families began Midbar Kodesh; on March 26, 2000, the 200-family congregation opened a sixteen-thousand-square-foot temple with eight classrooms, a preschool, banquet rooms, a social hall, and a six-hundred-seat sanctuary; under Rabbi Jeremy Wiederhorn, new construction will nearly double its size. Rabbi Richard Schachet's Reconstructionist Valley Outreach met at Green Valley Ranch with a religious school, choir, bowling league, and adult Hebrew classes. Rabbi Simon Bergman's Reform Beth El met at Regis University's campus. Mendy Harlig conducts Chabad of Southern Nevada services, with Women's Group of Chabad Green Valley and youth and adult educational programs.[37]

The number of temples also grew in other parts of town. On South Jones, Reform Adat Ari El boasts 150 families, and Kabbalah Center of Las Vegas opened in February 2001. In 1990 the first Orthodox rabbinate, Chabad, began under Shea Harlig, who called himself "the only yarmulke-wearing Jew in town," and, a decade later, opened a center on Arville. Sephardic Orthodox Beit Nissim held daily services near Eastern and Desert Inn, close to Or-Bamidbar Orthodox, which met next to Ner Tamid as it built a new home. Conservative Temple Emanu-El met at Tropicana and Torrey Pines.[38]

Most synagogues offer varied programs. Almost all have singles', men's, and women's groups and Hebrew or Judaism classes. AishHaTorah courts young adults with a dating program, a "Wyne and Cheese" mixer, and "Invest in Torah" stockbrokering programs; Beth Sholom discusses Judaic issues and comedy in "Talmud and 'Friends.'" Services range from bereavement groups at Beth Am and Ner Tamid to overnight Shabbat facilities at Beit Nissim. The synagogues offer recreational activities: Beth Am offers a cruise; in keeping with rabbi and cantor Gary Golbart's background as a Strip entertainer, Adat Ari El hosts coffeehouses; and Ner Tamid hosts yoga classes. The synagogues also stress education. Adat Ari El's eighteen-week "Guide to Judaism" and Chabad's scholars in residence, programs on religious and family issues, and Jewish history classes appeal to adults. Beth Am has a preschool, kindergarten, and religious school; Midbar Kodesh a summer camp and fall semester; Or-Bamidbar a Hebrew school and Judaism class; Adat Ari El a youth choir and religious school. Chabad offers a day school, preschool, Hebrew school, teen groups, and Camp Gan Israel summer camp. Led by Orthodox Jew Jerome Kutliroff, the Jewish Community Day School opened in 1996, leasing space from Ner Tamid for classes 8:30 AM to 4 PM and participating in such events as a birthday bash for Israel, with a cake, singing, dancing, and a congressional proclamation from Berkley, represented by her husband, Larry Lehrner, a nephrologist and president of UNLV Hillel. To help the school start, Chabad's preschool dropped first grade and Beth Sholom closed its Solomon Schechter elementary school.[39]

Synagogues unite for special events. For National Jewish Outreach's Shabbat Across America, Adat Ari El offered a kosher meal and Ner Tamid a concert. The Jewish Community Center sponsored a concert by cantors from Beth Am, Ner Tamid, Midbar Kodesh, Beth Sholom, Valley Outreach, Adat Chavarim, and Ahavat Torah. Adelson's Sands Expo and Convention Center hosted a community Hanukkah celebration, because "in Las Vegas Jews make up about 7 percent of the population, so you don't walk into stores and hear Hanukkah music," said JCC executive director Laura Sussman.[40]

The Jewish Federation is crucial to the growth and activities of the Jewish community. Begun in 1966, it raises money, slates events, and publishes *The Jewish Reporter.* In 2001 it started www.jewishlasvegas.com, with a chatroom, e-cards, history, and news. Its Gertrude Sperling Resource Library for Holocaust Studies and Kronberg Media Center provide a library for Jewish and secular groups. The federation created a high-school curriculum on the Holocaust with the Clark County School District and Nevada Humanities Committee. It opened the Jean Weinberger Museum of Jewish Culture, with varied exhibits. Its Young Leadership Program emphasizes its commitment to the future. The federation chose from every Judaic branch—Orthodox, Conservative, Reformed, and Reconstructionist—for the program, which included twelve training sessions, charitable activities, and speakers.[41]

The federation promotes intrafaith and interfaith cooperation. It hosts a black/Jewish Passover Seder with UNLV's Interfaith Center, coordinates the Kallah Festival of Jewish Education, joins Ner Tamid on an annual Mission to Israel, and cosponsors a lecture series and the Jewish Bookfair. Its Community Relations Council seeks to aid "the rights of the members of the Jewish community . . . and promote Jewish community interests." The federation's endowment program sets up planned giving and fund-raising. It aids or sponsors the Brandeis Society for legal professionals and the Maimonides Society of medical workers. It hosts a monthly discussion of Yiddish culture, and its Women's Division holds and sponsors numerous events.[42]

While part of the federation, the JCC has its own administrators, events including bowling leagues, games, play groups, a friendship group for retired Jews from back east who winter in Las Vegas, a Teen Service Corps, Young Judaea, a Cub Scout pack, brunches, miniature-golf nights, early-childhood programs, potluck dinners, ballroom dancing, and Jewish geography classes. Its senior events include movies, golf, mah-jongg, and a talent show, "Viva Oy Vegas." Its Camp K'helah hosts college-age counselors and a camp specialist to demonstrate Israeli culture. It also raises funds and holds an annual gala honoring a local Jewish leader.[43]

The federation and JCC shepherded the Jewish Family Services Agency, (JFSA), created in January 1977, due mainly to the efforts of Combined Jewish

Appeal president Lloyd Katz and campaign chair Jean Weinberger. The JFSA's Child and Adolescent Programs feature a full-time therapist; full-service adoption, support, and socialization groups; psychological evaluations; testing for attention and learning disabilities; parenting workshops; and parental support groups. Its Senior Services Program provides psychotherapy, care plans, bereavement support, needs assessment, and living arrangements.[44]

Schools and camps serve children. Milton I. Schwartz Hebrew Academy, begun in 1980, offers classes up to middle school, with before-and-after care to 6 PM and a multimedia computer laboratory. Since 1999, Chabad of Summerlin's Desert Torah Academy has featured Judaic and general studies, a library, a computer lab, and a cafeteria. UNLV's Hillel hosts lectures, a monthly Shabbat ShaBang, a biweekly Hillel Happening, and a weekly Renaissance BYOL (bring your own lunch).[45]

Local Jewry's growth is also reflected in other local groups and branches of national groups. Las Vegas has five Jewish War Veterans posts, five Organization for Rehabilitation and Training chapters, two B'nai Brith and two Hadassah units, the Jewish Geneaology Society, Jewish professional singles groups, Brandeis study groups, and the Pomegranate Guild of Judaic Needlework. The Chanukah Store & More has artifacts. Antidiscrimination groups include the National Conference for Community and Justice, the Anti-Defamation League, and the Jewish Defense League of Nevada; their demonstrations and public press doubtless buttressed the state's decision in 1988 to fine Imperial Palace owner Ralph Engelstad over his Hitler memorabilia collection and Hitler birthday celebrations. In 2001 came Las Vegas's first Jewish mortuary, King David Memorial Chapel, near its first *genizah,* where sacred books are buried. No other Jewish community, said founder Allen Brewster, "has established both a mortuary and cemetery at the same time in the last 25 years."[46]

Conclusion

Las Vegas's growth has created challenges for its Jews. Most recent immigrants have come from eastern Europe, requiring both a further integration into the broader community and older Jews to reach out to new arrivals. Despite the proliferation of synagogues and organizations, the number of Jews belonging to temples or involved in religious or ethnic groups remains small, requiring continued efforts by Jewish organizations to publicize Judaic culture and events and attract interest. Making these goals harder to achieve is the way in which the city has evolved: while a power elite, including many Jews, still controls much of its political economy, Las Vegas has become more corporate and dispersed, reducing the possibility of achieving unity through neighborhoods or similar occupations.

Yet no religious or ethnic group has a greater claim on credit for the financial success of Las Vegas than its Jews. The founders of the Jewish community were leading businesspeople in a railroad town with big dreams; the next generation turned it into a gambling mecca; and the generation after that has turned it into a resort capital with an increasingly diversified economy. As the Jewish population creeps toward an estimated eighty thousand, it remains a political, cultural, economic, and social force to be reckoned with.

Notes

I am indebted to Alan Balboni and DeAnna Beachley of the Community College of Southern Nevada, Michael Brodhead of UNR's Department of Special Collections, and John Marschall of the UNR History Department for their help.

1. On Las Vegas, see Ralph J. Roske, *Las Vegas: A Desert Paradise* (Tulsa: Continental Heritage Press, 1986); Eugene P. Moehring, *Resort City in the Sunbelt, 1930–2000*, 2d ed. (Reno and Las Vegas: University of Nevada Press, 2000); M. Gottdiener, Claudia Collins, and David Dickens, *Las Vegas: The Social Production of an All-American City* (Malden, Mass.: Blackwell, 1998); Gary E. Elliott, *The New Western Frontier: An Illustrated History of Greater Las Vegas* (Encinitas: Heritage Media Group, 1999); A. D. Hopkins and K. J. Evans, eds., *The First 100: Profiles of the Men and Women Who Shaped Southern Nevada* (Las Vegas: Huntington Press, 1999); Sally Denton and Roger Morris, *The Money and the Power: Las Vegas and Its Hold on America, 1947–2000* (New York: Alfred A. Knopf, 2001); Hal K. Rothman, *Neon Metropolis: How Las Vegas Started the Twenty-First Century* (New York: Routledge, 2002).

2. See especially Ferenc M. Szasz and Margaret Connell Szasz, "Religion and Spirituality," in *The Oxford History of the American West*, ed. Clyde A. Milner, Carol A. O'Connor, and Martha A. Sandweiss (New York: Oxford University Press, 1994), 359–91, for a general history of religion in the western United States.

3. Moses Rischin and John Livingston, eds., *Jews of the American West* (Detroit: Wayne State University Press, 1991); Rischin, ed., *The Jews of the West: The Metropolitan Years* (Berkeley: University of California Press, 1979); Kenneth Libo and Irving Howe, eds., *We Lived There Too: In Their Own Words and Pictures—Pioneer Jews and the Westward Movement of America, 1630–1930* (New York: St. Martin's Press, 1984); Szasz and Szasz, "Religion and Spirituality," 359–69; John Marschall, "Jews in Nevada: 1850–1900," *Journal of the West* 13, no. 1 (January 1984): 62–72; John Marschall, "The House of Olcovich: A Pioneer Carson City Jewish Family," *Nevada Historical Society Quarterly* 41, no. 3 (Fall 1998): 169–90; Wilbur Shepperson, *Restless Strangers: Nevada Immigrants and Their Interpreters* (Reno: University of Nevada Press, 1970).

4. Eugene P. Moehring, "Profile of a Nevada Railroad Town: Las Vegas in 1910,"

Nevada Historical Society Quarterly 34, no. 4 (Winter 1991): 466–87; Leonard Dinnerstein, "From Desert Oasis to the Desert Caucus: The Jews of Tucson," in *Jews of the American West*, 136–63; Alan Balboni, "Southern Italians and Eastern European Jews: Cautious Cooperation in Las Vegas Casinos, 1940–1967," *Nevada Historical Society Quarterly* 38, no. 3 (Fall 1995): 154–55.

5. *Las Vegas Sun*, June 4, 1997; Moehring, *Resort City in the Sunbelt*, 236–37; Sandy Mallin, Dedication of Temple Beth Sholom, September 24, 2000, Jewish Emigration Archives, Department of Special Collections, Lied Library, UNLV; Nate Mack Biography File, ibid.; *Las Vegas Review-Journal*, December 3, 1997; Ivan Eisenberg, conversation with author, Las Vegas, March 31, 2001; Dinnerstein, "The Jews of Tucson," in *Jews of the American West*, 149; D. Asabi Aird, ed., *Official Ethnic Destination and Visitors Guide* (Las Vegas: Aird and Associates, 2000), 41; Moehring, *Resort City in the Sunbelt*, 1–30; Rischin and Livingston, *Jews of the American West*, 28.

6. Rischin and Livingston, *Jews of the American West*, 20; Dinnerstein, "The Jews of Tucson," 139. See "The Mob on the Run," a KLAS-TV-8 documentary aired in 1987, by Ned Day and Bob Stoldal; Alan Balboni, *Beyond the Mafia: Italian Americans and the Development of Las Vegas* (Reno and Las Vegas: University of Nevada Press, 1996); Denton and Morris, *The Money and the Power;* Ferenc Morton Szasz, *Religion in the Modern American West* (Tucson: University of Arizona Press, 2000), 81.

7. Balboni, "Cautious Cooperation," 153–59; Robert Lacey, *Little Man: Meyer Lansky and the Gangster Life* (Boston: Little, Brown, 1991), 51, 152; Ed Reid and Ovid Demaris, *The Green Felt Jungle* (New York: Trident Press, 1963), 13–15; Denton and Morris, *The Money and the Power*, 21–29, 49–58; Peter Wiley and Robert Gottlieb, *Empires in the Sun: The Rise of the New American West* (New York: G. P. Putnam's Sons, 1982), 191.

8. Susan Berman, *Easy Street* (New York: Dial Press, 1981), 18–23, 185–86; Reid and Demaris, *Green Felt Jungle*, 41; Denton and Morris, *The Money and the Power*, 49–58, 75–85; Lacey, *Little Man*, 152, 158; Dick Odessky, *Fly on the Wall: Recollections of Las Vegas' Good Old Bad Old Days* (Las Vegas: Huntington Press, 1999), 11; *Las Vegas Review-Journal*, July 31, 1995; Wiley and Gottlieb, *Empires in the Sun*, 193.

9. Reid and Demaris, *Green Felt Jungle*, 5, 13–15; Odessky, *Fly on the Wall*, 75, 151–59; Balboni, "Cautious Cooperation," 161–66; Moehring, *Resort City*, 74–76, 81–82; "The Mob on the Run"; A. D. Hopkins, "Benny Binion: He Who Has the Gold Makes the Rules," in *The Players: The Men Who Made Las Vegas*, ed. Jack E. Sheehan (Reno and Las Vegas: University of Nevada Press, 1997), 48–67; Denton and Morris, *The Money and the Power*, 30–37. See Ralph Denton and Michael S. Green, *A Liberal Conscience: Ralph Denton, Nevadan* (Reno: University of Nevada Oral History Program, 2001); Berman, *Easy Street*, 188–89; *Las Vegas Review-Journal*, September 5, 1954, January 18, 1956; Balboni, "Cautious Cooperation," 163–68; Lacey, *Little Man*, 320–21; Reid and Demaris, *Green Felt Jungle*, 221–34; Burton Cohen, conversations with author; Odessky, *Fly on the Wall*, 25–26, 31, 75–77, 87, 138–39; *Las Vegas Review-Journal*, October 28, 1993; Farrell and Case, *Black Book*, 47; A. D. Hopkins, "Jay Sarno: He Came to Play," in *The Players*, 92–103.

10. "The Mob on the Run"; Lacey, *Little Man,* 297–98, 320–21; Balboni, "Cautious Cooperation," 161–62; Odessky, *Fly on the Wall,* 174; Denton and Morris, *The Money and the Power,* 109, 132; Lacey, *Little Man,* 218; Farrell and Case, *Black Book,* 49–52; Reid and Demaris, *Green Felt Jungle;* Michael S. Green, "Hank Greenspun: Where He Stood," in *The Maverick Spirit: Building the New Nevada,* ed. Richard O. Davies (Reno and Las Vegas: University of Nevada Press, 1998), 84–85; Grant Sawyer, Gary E. Elliott, and R. T. King, *Hang Tough! Grant Sawyer: An Activist in the Governor's Mansion* (Reno: University of Nevada Oral History Program, 1993), 81–94; Farrell and Case, *Black Book,* 27, 37–38, 221–22, 228–29.

11. Among the works on Hughes, see Sergio Lalli, "Howard Hughes in Vegas," in *The Players,* 133–58, for a focused look. See also Denton and Morris, *The Money and the Power,* especially 266–90 for Hughes. Nicholas Pileggi, *Casino: Love and Honor in Las Vegas* (New York: Simon and Schuster, 1995) is useful but told mostly from Rosenthal's viewpoint.

12. Odessky, *Fly on the Wall,* 21, 75, 77–87; Balboni, "Cautious Cooperation," 159, 161, 169; Reid and Demaris, *Green Felt Jungle,* 37; Farrell and Case, *Black Book,* 26; John L. Smith, "Moe Dalitz and the Desert," in *The Players,* 35–47; Alan Balboni, "Moe Dalitz: Controversial Founding Father of Modern Las Vegas," in *The Maverick Spirit,* 24–43; Balboni, "Dalitz," 35–37; Smith, "Dalitz," 35–47. See also Pileggi, *Casino;* Denton and Morris, *The Money and the Power,* 224–82.

13. *Las Vegas Review-Journal,* December 3, 2000; ibid., June 10, 1990, in Farrell and Case, *Black Book,* 26; John L. Smith, "Double Life," in *The First 100,* 122; A. D. Hopkins, "The Developer's Developer: Irwin Molasky," in *The First 100,* 190–92; Moehring, *Resort City,* 120, 238–39.

14. *Las Vegas Sun,* June 4, 1997; John G. Edwards, "Banking on Success: E. Parry Thomas," in *The First 100,* 157–58; A. D. Hopkins, "Molasky," in *The First 100,* 192; Smith, "Double Life," 124; Moehring, *Resort City,* 227; Wiley and Gottlieb, *Empires in the Sun,* 199–20; *Las Vegas Review-Journal,* September 29, 1998; Denton and Morris, *The Money and the Power,* 149–69, 315–17.

15. Dinnerstein, "The Jews of Tucson," 145; Szasz and Szasz, "Religion and Spirituality," 385–86; Berman, *Easy Street,* 32–33, 187; Dedication of Temple Beth Sholom, September 24, 2000, Jewish Emigration Archives, Department of Special Collections, Lied Library, UNLV; *Las Vegas Sun,* January 27, 1963, May 27, 1965, Nate Mack Biography File, ibid.; Balboni, "Cautious Cooperation," 159–61, 172, n.18; Reid and Demaris, *Green Felt Jungle,* 15, 31–32.

16. *A Liberal Conscience*; *Las Vegas Sun,* November 6, 2000.

17. Reid and Demaris, *Green Felt Jungle,* 15, 36; *Political History of Nevada 2000* (Carson City: State Printing Office, 2000); Balboni, "Cautious Cooperation," 159–61; *The Jewish Reporter,* March 16, 2001.

18. Jake Highton, *Nevada Newspaper Days: A History of Journalism in the Silver State* (Stockton: Heritage West, 1990), 146–47, 233–52; Hank Greenspun and Alex Pelle, *Where I Stand: The Record of a Reckless Man* (New York: David McKay, 1966); Green, "Greenspun: Where He Stood," 74–95; Green, "The Las Vegas Newspaper

War of the 1950s," *Nevada Historical Society Quarterly* 31, no. 3 (Fall 1988): 155–82.

19. Highton, *Nevada Newspaper Days,* 241–43; Farrell and Case, *Black Book,* 28; Reid and Demaris, *Green Felt Jungle,* 132–33. Greenspun feuded with Milton Schwartz over cable television ownership and forced Schwartz to move his taxi company's propane tank out of the Downtown area, arguing it was a public health hazard. Schwartz sued Greenspun for libel, claiming it was all based on their financial battles, and lost.

20. Highton, *Nevada Newspaper Days,* 245; Gottdiener, Collins, and Dickens, *Las Vegas,* 129–53; *Las Vegas Sun,* May 11, 2001.

21. McMillan, Elliott, and King, *Fighting Back,* 95–98, 139–40.

22. Much of this comes from the Edythe Katz mss., Department of Special Collections, Lied Library, UNLV, and Edythe Katz Yarchever and Ralph Denton, conversations with author. See *Las Vegas Review-Journal,* April 8, 1986; *Los Angeles Times,* April 24, 1979.

23. Jerome D. Countess, "The Jewish Community of Las Vegas," September 1987, Elmer R. Rusco mss., Box 1, Folder 7, Department of Special Collections, Noble Getchell Library, University of Nevada, Reno, 1–2; Denton and Morris, *The Money and the Power,* 70, 331–44.

24. Gottdiener, Collins, and Dickens, *Las Vegas,* 224–29.

25. John L. Smith, *Running Scared: The Life and Treacherous Times of Las Vegas Casino King Steve Wynn* (New York: Barricade Books, 1995); Denton and Morris, *The Money and the Power,* 177, 318–22, 352–57, 376–81; Mark Seal, "Steve Wynn: King of Wow!," in *The Players,* 168–82; William N. Thompson, "Steve Wynn: I Got the Message," in *The Maverick Spirit,* 194–211; Hopkins, "Steve Wynn," in *The First 100,* 255–58; Gottdiener, Collins, and Dickens, *Las Vegas,* 36; *Las Vegas Review-Journal,* April 4, 1993.

26. *Las Vegas Review-Journal,* April 16, 1993; Hopkins, "Steve Wynn," 255–57.

27. *Las Vegas Review-Journal,* March 9, 1997, March 11, 1999.

28. *Las Vegas Sun,* April 28, 1999.

29. Ibid., April 20, 1998, December 14, 1998, April 28, 1999; *Las Vegas Life,* August 2000.

30. *Las Vegas Review-Journal,* September 18, 1997; *Las Vegas Sun,* December 4, 1997.

31. *Las Vegas Review-Journal,* December 27, 1999.

32. Gottdiener et al., *Las Vegas,* 224–29; Smith, *Running Scared,* 308–9; Hopkins, "Steve Wynn," 255–57; Denton and Morris, *The Money and the Power,* 318–22, 352–57, 376–81.

33. Countess, "The Jewish Community of Las Vegas," 15–17; *Jerusalem Post,* June 1, 2000, at www.jewishdestiny.com. I regularly consulted the *Las Vegas Israelite,* which publishes bimonthly, and *The Jewish Reporter,* which appears monthly. Both the *Las Vegas Review-Journal* and the *Las Vegas Sun* also list various events. Unless otherwise noted, I have used these sources.

34. Dedication of Temple Beth Sholom, September 24, 2000, Jewish Emigration

Archives, Department of Special Collections, Lied Library, UNLV; *The View,* September 8, 1999; *Las Vegas Review-Journal,* November 15, 1998, January 15, 2001; www.beth sholomlv.com; *Las Vegas Life,* August 2000; *Las Vegas Sun,* September 10, 1999.

35. www.uahc.org; *Las Vegas Review-Journal,* April 5, 1997, July 29, 1999.

36. www.weddingofficiantslasvegas.com; *Las Vegas Review-Journal,* April 5, 1997, November 15, 1998; *The Jerusalem Report.Com; Las Vegas Review-Journal,* July 29, 1999; *Las Vegas Life,* August 2000; www.aish.com/branches/las_vegas.

37. uscj.org/pacsw/lasvegas/mkt/news.htm; www.Midbarkodesh.org; *The View,* January 23, 1999; adatariel.com; chabadlv.org; *Chabad of Southern Nevada Newsletter,* January 2000, Jewish Emigration Archives, Department of Special Collections, Lied Library, UNLV.

38. adatariel.com; *Las Vegas Review-Journal,* July 29, 1999; www.kabbalah.com; *L'Chaim* 143, December 28, 1990; *Las Vegas Life,* August 2000; *Las Vegas Review-Journal,* May 10, 2000; chabadlv.org; *Chabad of Southern Nevada Newsletter,* January 2000; Book of Remembrance, 2000-5761, Bet Knesset Bamidbar, Jewish Emigration Archives, Department of Special Collections, Lied Library, UNLV; www.levhashem .org; *Las Vegas Review-Journal,* July 7, 1998, October 13, 2000; *Las Vegas Sun,* June 21, June 22, 2000.

39. uscj.org/pacsw/lasvegas/mkt/news.htm; www.Midbarkodesh.org; *The View,* January 23, 1999; www.aish.com/branches/las_vegas; adatariel.com; www.aish.com/ branches/las_vegas; www.levhashem.org.

40. uscj.org/pacsw/lasvegas/mkt/news.htm; www.Midbarkodesh.org; *The View,* January 23, 1999, April 25, 2001; www.kabbalah.com; *Las Vegas Review-Journal,* May 30, 2000, June 10, 2001; *Las Vegas Sun,* December 14, 1998; adatariel.com.

41. Countess, "Jewish Community of Las Vegas," 11–14; *The Jewish Reporter,* December 1976, Edythe Katz mss., Department of Special Collections, Lied Library, UNLV; Jewish Federation of Las Vegas, *Guide to Jewish Life in Southern Nevada 2000– 2001,* 7; www.jewishlasvegas.com; Countess, "Jewish Community," 1–3; *Las Vegas Review-Journal,* December 23, 1997; *Summerlin View,* June 8, 2001.

42. *Las Vegas Sun,* October 3, 1997, April 20, 1998; *Las Vegas Review-Journal,* September 20, 1997, April 11, 2000; Jewish Federation of Las Vegas, *Guide to Jewish Life in Southern Nevada 2000–2001,* 39–40; Countess, "Jewish Community of Las Vegas," 15; www.jewishlasvegas.com.

43. Jewish Community Center brochure; www.mishmash.virtualave.net/usa-nev -vegas.html; www.lasvegas.com; *The View,* August 18, 1999; Jewish Federation of Las Vegas, *Guide to Jewish Life in Southern Nevada 2000–2001; JCC Singles Newsletter,* February 2001.

44. *The Jewish Reporter,* January 1977; Countess, "Jewish Community of Las Vegas," 13; Jewish Family Service Agency brochures.

45. Jewish Federation of Las Vegas, *Guide to Jewish Life in Southern Nevada 2000– 2001,* 23, 44; www.lvhebrewacademy.com; www.unlv.edu; *Las Vegas Review-Journal,* April 11, 2000, June 10, 2001.

46. jewishvegas.com; Countess, "Jewish Community of Las Vegas," 10–11; www

.lasvegas.com; communities.msn.com/littledabsingles; *Las Vegas Review-Journal,* April 5, 1997, December 23, 1997, January 27, 2001; *Las Vegas Sun,* October 23, 1996, July 15, 1998, April 19, 1999, October 8, 1999; Jewish Federation of Las Vegas, *Guide to Jewish Life in Southern Nevada 2000–2001,* 48–49; Jeff Burbank, *License to Steal: Nevada's Gaming Control System in the Megaresort Age* (Reno and Las Vegas: University of Nevada Press, 2000), 55–79; *Summerlin View,* June 8, 2001.

CHAPTER 10

The Croats

JERRY L. SIMICH

The Croats are a South Slavic people found mainly in Croatia and Bosnia-Herzegovina. Over the last two centuries, hundreds of thousands of Croats immigrated to the United States, Latin America (especially Chile and Argentina), Canada, and elsewhere. The largest number—approximately 500,000—arrived in the United States between 1880 and 1914. The numbers dwindled after restrictive immigration laws were enacted in the 1920s. Post–World War II arrivals numbered over 100,000, as Croats left Yugoslavia for the United States. Exact numbers are difficult to ascertain, because for many years Croats were listed in immigration records variously as Slavonians, Austrians, Hungarians, Italians, Turks, or Yugoslavs—their nationality assigned on the basis of the empire or state under which the unfortunate Croats happened to fall. The 2000 U.S. Census indicates that 374,241 nationwide reported that they were of Croatian ancestry, a figure significantly below older figures. The numbers for Nevada are 2,742 and for Clark County, 2,320. Some Croats likely claimed to be of Yugoslav ancestry.[1]

Reasons for Leaving Home

Explanations for Croatian immigration to the United States involve a number of push and pull factors. In the case of the earliest arrivals there was often a desire of the coastal Dalmatian Croats for adventure and economic opportunity. For those who came during the great migration, approximately 1880–1914, push factors included economic deprivation: poverty, lack of land, crop failures, and heavy taxation levied by the Austro-Hungarian government. In addition the mostly peasant Croats were unhappy with what they considered to be political oppression—measures taken by the authorities to deny Croats self-determination, instruction in their native language, and representation in the government, to name a few. Contributing to the exodus was the Austro-Hungarian policy that actually encouraged Croats to emigrate, thereby freeing up land to be repopulated by those more amenable to the ruling class.

The pull factors were also both economic and political. Thousands of returnees from the United States to Croatia, the *Amerikantsi,* reported on the availability of jobs as well as the freedom to be enjoyed in "Amerika." Chafing under the harsh political conditions in Austro-Hungary, many Croats from the wealthier eastern counties, who had no economic reason to leave, tartly expressed their feelings in the refrain, *Mi idemo traziti li jos pravica na svietu* (We are going to find out whether there is still justice in the world).[2] As was often the case with other immigrants during these times, the men arrived first, to be joined later by women and children.

The post–World War II immigrants left for similar reasons. Most of them were highly antagonistic toward the communist regime that took power in Yugoslavia in 1945. Unlike the earlier immigrants, the newer arrivals portrayed themselves as refugees rather than immigrants and, on the whole, were better educated than their predecessors—professionals, teachers, scientists, and skilled workers. These *novidoslih* (newcomers) were understandably drawn to the established Croatian settlements in the United States but were often misunderstood by the older immigrant generation. Conflicts between them were not uncommon. While many of the newcomers established their own organizations, others integrated quickly into the older ones. Likewise, the children of the post–World War II generation assimilated into the American social scene more easily than did those of the pre–World War II generation.[3]

Arrival and Settlement in the United States

The earliest arrivals were from the Dalmatian Coast. These men were sailors, fishermen, and craftsmen, many of whom jumped ship and settled along the Gulf Coast of today's Louisiana, Mississippi, and Alabama in the seventeenth and eighteenth centuries, before the United States came into existence.[4] Within a few decades they had established settlements in and around New Orleans, Biloxi, and Mobile. Many of these pioneer Croats took to oyster cultivation in the Mississippi Delta, where their descendants continue to pursue the trade of their ancestors. Interestingly, their numbers are maintained even today, reinforced by newcomers from the same regions of the Dalmatian Coast.

Drawn by news of gold discoveries, many Dalmatian Croats quickly set sail for California. Finding the climate similar to that of their homeland, those who did not strike it rich opened saloons, coffeehouses, fruit stores, and restaurants in San Francisco, while others later turned to agricultural pursuits in the outlying Bay Area. Within a few years, Croatian settlements had been established in San Francisco, Sacramento, and adjacent cities and towns.[5]

In the period from roughly 1880 to 1914, Croats, by the hundreds of thousands—largely from the interior of Croatia—poured into the mines, mills, and factories of the rapidly industrializing northeast United States, especially Pennsylvania, West Virginia, Ohio, Michigan, Indiana, and Illinois. Others became miners in Minnesota, South Dakota, Wyoming, Montana, Colorado, Washington, Utah, New Mexico, Nevada, Arizona, California, and Alaska. Still more started fishing businesses and worked in the lumber industries in California, Oregon, and Washington.

Croats Come to Nevada

Croatian arrivals in Nevada coincide roughly with the beginning of large-scale mining operations. The vast majority of the Croats immigrated originally from Dalmatia, and many had spent time working as miners and in other jobs in the San Francisco Bay Area and gold country of California. Census records, directories, official documents, newspaper articles, and other sources indicate that hundreds of Croats were employed in various activities in Virginia City, Carson City, Reno, Austin, Tybo, Hamilton, Sherman Town, Treasure City, Gold Hill, Eureka City, Pioche, and other Nevada locations.[6]

Croats, sometimes in partnerships with Serbs from Montenegro and Herzegovina, incorporated mining companies bearing names such as Slavonian Gold and Mining Company, Adriatic Mine, Servia [*sic*] and Slavonia Mine, Bajazet and Golden Era Consolidated Gold and Silver Mining Company, and Austria Gold and Silver Mining Company. While some of the immigrants mined for precious minerals, others sought opportunities related to mining. For example, Marko Medin, in addition to filing papers to mine, opened the San Francisco Fruit Store on 14 N. C St. in Virginia City in 1865. A little later Nikola Barovich, also from Dalmatia, opened first the Alhambra Saloon and then the Sazerac Saloon in Austin. Vincent Milatovich, from Dubrovnik, Dalmatia, operated the Milatovich Grocery Store and a nearby saloon on N. C St. in Virginia City, while Martin Brazzanovich built a hotel and bathhouse at the hot springs in Soda Springs (Mineral Co.) in the 1870s. Pavlak, a former post office and now only a pile of logs situated two miles north of Jarbidge in Elko County, is named after Mike Pavlak, one of the discoverers of the Pavlak Mine.[7]

Few of these pioneers sank roots in the hard rock of Nevada. Most returned to northern California and, in some cases, to their country of birth. Soon after the discovery of large deposits of minerals in and around Tonopah, Goldfield, Ely, Delamar, and Las Vegas at the turn of the twentieth century, even greater numbers of Croats, along with immigrants from numerous other countries, flocked to the mines and smelters and the railroads that were built to transport whatever the mines produced. The majority of Croats settled in McGill and Ruth, near Ely, to work the copper mines, while smaller numbers went into the mines in Nye County, especially in Tonopah and Goldfield.[8] A few found employment in Las Vegas, Sloan, Goodsprings, and Searchlight.

The 1910 Federal Census for Clark County records that William Wallace, an "Austro-Slavonian," was employed in Las Vegas as a stonemason. The 1920 Census indicates that John Stipcic was living in Arden, just south of where Blue Diamond Road crosses the Union Pacific Railroad tracks, a transfer point for a now-abandoned narrow-gauge railroad that hauled gypsum mined in the hills above what is now the Rhodes Ranch development. Listed in the same census were men surnamed Evanovich, Martinovich, Medjugorac, Peich, Vesich, and Zubovich, all working in the lime quarry at Sloan. The 1920 Census also shows that Sam Mikulich and Mijo Pinjuv were living in Las Vegas. Of the aforementioned individuals, it appears that only the latter two established permanent residence in Las Vegas.

Pioneers

The beginning of a Croatian community in Las Vegas can be traced to the arrival and settlement, in the second and third decades of the twentieth century, of the Mikuliches, Pinjuvs, Malnars, and Trinaystiches. There was extensive intermarriage among them, resulting in a large number of children, grandchildren, and beyond. Many of the immigrants' children, now in their seventies and eighties, still reside in the Las Vegas Valley. While these families established no Croatian organizations, they nonetheless formed a community. They socialized, worshipped together, married, baptized their children, and mourned the deceased at St. Joan of Arc Catholic Church in Downtown Las Vegas. In the areas on and near Ogden, Fremont, Eighth, Ninth, and Tenth Streets, Croatian-owned businesses soon sprang up in the young Las Vegas.[9] As will be shown, these pioneers, along with those of other ethnic groups, contributed in no small way to the development of Las Vegas.

One of the first to settle permanently in Las Vegas was Sam M. Mikulich. Born in Kocerin, Herzegovina, in 1888, Mikulich arrived in New York City in 1907 and quickly set out for Los Angeles, which by that time had a fast-growing Croatian community, many from Herzegovina. After operating a restaurant for several years, he moved to Las Vegas in 1914 and within a few years opened the Nevada Grill on Fremont Street near Main Street. In 1920 he married Slava (Lily) Malnar at St. Joan of Arc Church, the city's first Roman Catholic Church, located on Second Street. In 1922 Mikulich opened the Las Vegas Cafe inside the Nevada Hotel, later known as the Sal Sagev—or Las Vegas spelled backward—now the Golden Gate Casino.[10]

In 1929 Mikulich built the Ambassador Egyptian apartments, later named the Ambassador Auto Court, at Ninth and Fremont. In 1948 he expanded the business and renamed it the Ambassador Hotel. Mikulich also operated a service station and liquor store at Fremont and Tenth during the 1930s. For years Mikulich; his wife, Slava; sons, John and Joseph; and daughters, Francis, Rosemary, and Lily Patricia tended to the family business. Five years after Sam's death in 1973, the family opened the Best Western affiliated Ambassador Motel East at Tenth and Fremont Streets.[11]

Arriving in Las Vegas about the same time as Sam Mikulich was Mijo (Mike) Pinjuv. Born in Listica, Herzegovina, in 1889, Mijo Pinjuv came to the United States as a teenager and worked for awhile in Albany, New York, and then spent some time in Los Angeles. He eventually found work with the San Pedro, Los Angeles and Salt Lake Railroad and was transferred to Las Vegas in 1917 to work as a machinist in the railroad shop at what is now the site of the Union Plaza Hotel. In the same year Pinjuv married Frances Malnar. Soon thereafter he decided to go into business for himself.[12]

In 1921 Pinjuv purchased the Las Vegas Transfer Company and hauled goods mainly from the railroad station to points around the then-small Las Vegas. Three years later he sold the business to Sebastian Mikulich and George Markich. Within two weeks Pinjuv, along with Sam Mikulich and Tony Mikulich, established the Nevada Oil Company at Main and Bridger Streets at a cost of twelve thousand dollars. The distribution plant featured a pump house and machinery capable of delivering eight thousand gallons of gasoline per hour from railroad cars into tanks to supply the city's growing number of motor vehicles. A particularly proud day for Pinjuv and Las Vegas was April 17, 1926, when Pinjuv's company refueled the inaugural flight of Western Air Express contract air-mail service to Las Vegas. In May 1928 Pinjuv sold his Nevada Oil Company to the Richfield Oil Company, and on January 31, 1929, he opened the Pinjuv Cash Grocery at Ogden Avenue and Eighth Street. Mike and Frances had six sons and two daughters: Charles Pinjuv worked for years at the Stardust Hotel, Ed was a longtime employee of Centel, Walter and John became metal contractors, Fred a real-estate appraiser, and Mike Jr. an insurance agent. Frances Pinjuv died in 1954, Mike Sr. in 1957.[13]

Mike Pinjuv's cousin, Ivan P. Pinjuv, also born near the town of Listica, married Ana Lalich in Los Angeles before arriving in Las Vegas in 1929. Ivan quickly purchased the Desert Iron Works at 209 Eleventh St., which became a major supplier of iron products and wrought-iron fencing. Ivan's son George graduated from Las Vegas High School in 1943 and then piloted B-17s, B-24s, and B-29s during a military career that spanned three decades, including combat missions during World War II and the Korean War. A highlight of George's service occurred in 1949, when he piloted a B-29 from Castle Air Force Base near Merced, California, to McCarran Field for the airport's formal dedication. Pinjuv retired from the U.S. Air Force as a colonel in 1973 and moved to Reno.[14]

One of George's sisters, Lina, who was born in Los Angeles and baptized at St. Anthony's Croatian Catholic Church, arrived with her family in 1929. After graduating from Las Vegas High School, she attended the University of Nevada in Reno, completed a two-year normal program, and was certified as a schoolteacher. Jobs were scarce in the cities and towns, so Lina took a job at the Blue Eagle Ranch in Railroad Valley in 1940. She taught about ten children in the one-room wooden school, grades one through eight. After a year she married rancher Jim Sharp, a grandson of Henry Sharp, who had immigrated to the United States from England and settled in Nevada in the late 1860s. Lina, after teaching at Blue Eagle Ranch and at Currant, Duckwater, and Tonopah, is now retired and living at Blue Eagle.[15]

Lina and George's sister, Evelina (Pinjuv) Dunton, now residing in San Mateo, California, recalled growing up during the 1930s and 1940s on the family's property about five miles west of Downtown near what today is Del Monte Avenue, just south of Charleston Blvd. Living in a yet-to-be-developed area, the Pinjuv children amused themselves playing games such as kick-the-can and hide-and-seek. Picnics took the family to Mount Charleston, Red Rock Canyon, and later to Fourth of July festivities at Jean.[16]

Another Croat, Tony Mikulich—not related to but a close friend of the other Mikuliches and the Pinjuvs—was involved in various businesses in Las Vegas, most notably his partnerships with Mike Pinjuv and later with pipeline contractor Nick Bebek of Los Angeles. With the latter he opened a petroleum distributorship and service station in the early 1930s at Tenth and Fremont Streets, close to several other Croatian-owned businesses.[17]

Yet another example of the varied business ventures involving the circle of Croatian immigrants was that of George Markich. In January 1924 he and Sebastian Mikulich (not related to Sam or Tony Mikulich) purchased the Las Vegas Transfer Company from Mike Pinjuv. Aside from owning the Las Vegas Liquor Store at 812 Fremont, a local fixture for several decades, Markich built what was known as the Markich Block, a large business building on Fremont between Eighth and Ninth Streets. On October 18, 1931, the *Las Vegas Age* noted that the "block, owned by George Markich, who has been long established in business in this city, has had an almost lightning like growth for the past six months." The Markich Block quickly became home to several businesses.[18]

Young Sebastian F. Mikulich was well traveled before he finally established a niche for himself in Las Vegas. Born near Mostar, Herzegovina, Mikulich arrived in New York at age seventeen. He soon found work in a Camden, New Jersey, shipyard and three months later was laying telephone wires in Chicago. In 1911 he moved to Los Angeles, taking various jobs; two years later he was in Las Vegas working for the railroad. Not satisfied, he set out for San Francisco, where he worked in a saloon and then in a shipyard. He then left for the state of Washington and found employment as a fireman in a sawmill. Back in Las Vegas, Mikulich married Mary Ann Yelanc at St. Joan of Arc Catholic Church in 1921. His new wife would become a diligent worker, astute business partner, and mother of the family's five children.[19]

Mikulich and Markich bought the Las Vegas Transfer and Taxi Company from Mike Pinjuv, and before long Sebastian began delivering mail, groceries, supplies, and occasional passengers over dirt roads to Goodsprings, Nelson, and Moapa. In the late 1920s he was delivering lumber and supplies to the short-lived mining company at Wahomie, thirty miles east of Beatty, now in the Nevada Test Site. It was during the long hauls to Wahomie that Mikulich realized there was a need for a transportation system from Las Vegas to Tonopah. Selling the transfer company in 1927, he secured a franchise to start the Las Vegas–Tonopah Stage Line. Mikulich later recalled that some people were skeptical about the prospects of a bus line operating out of Las Vegas. "One day," Sebastian predicted, "Las Vegas will have 25,000 persons and the roads to Tonopah will be paved."[20] Sufficient passengers and mail contracts insured further growth, and in 1935 Mikulich extended service to Reno; the line now became the well-known Las Vegas–Tonopah-Reno Stage Line (LTR). In the 1940s LTR opened lines to Death Valley and Phoenix. By this time Sebastian's sons, Frank, Sebastian, and Andrew, and daughters, Alice and Amelia, were active in the family business.[21]

By 1966 LTR was a very busy company, the largest privately owned bus company in the United States, with more than 115 pieces of modern equipment, 1,500 route miles, and 50,000 passengers transported monthly, many of them between the Nevada Test Site and Las Vegas. Well known locally as one of the city's pioneer businessmen, Mikulich earned national recognition by serving on the board of directors of the National Bus Traffic Association. He was also a director of the National Truck Association, and LTR received the National Safety Council award many times over the years.[22]

Sebastian Mikulich died in 1977, thousands of miles from his native village in Herzegovina, a part of the world little known in the United States until the bloody events leading to the disintegration of Yugoslavia in the early 1990s. Starting with a horse-drawn wagon and then a Ford Model T truck, Mikulich built a transportation system that was doing a multimillion-dollar business at the time of his death. He left 20 percent of the company to each of his five children, but by 1984 a feud regarding the operation of LTR prompted two of his sons to sell their shares to outside interests. A year later the other son and two daughters followed suit, thus ending the enterprise the immigrant and his family had worked so diligently to build.[23]

The Croatian Community Grows

Other Croats continued to follow the pioneers to Las Vegas during the city's formative years, often from other established Croatian communities across the United States, including Los Angeles and the settlements in and around Ely. The Smilanick brothers—Dan, George, and Pete—illustrate this process of adapting to Las Vegas. Born in Croatia in 1881, Dan came to the United States at age twelve. According to the 1920 Census for White Pine County, brothers George and Pete were born in Illinois. The same census listed no father, but the mother Ella was entered as a hotel keeper. Most likely she ran a boardinghouse for Croatian miners in Ruth, a common practice among Croatian wives and widows. All the Smilanick brothers were listed as laborers in the copper mines.

Dan served in the U.S. Army during World War I, surviving seventeen months of frontline action in France, where he was wounded. After moving to Las Vegas in the 1930s, he was employed by the Nevada Highway Department and was active in the affairs of the Disabled American Veterans, Veterans of Foreign Wars, American Legion, as well as the Elks and the Eagles. Brother George worked as a manager with the Boulder City Company Stores during construction of Boulder Dam. Active politically, he was elected Chairman of the Boulder City Democratic Club in 1934; a year later, he was serving as a member of the Clark County Democratic Central Committee. His political networking must have paid off, as he was appointed inspector for the Nevada Public Service Commission in 1935 and moved to Carson City to assume his new duties. He returned to Las Vegas as assistant area manager for the 1940 census and in 1943 became a legal investigator for the Office of Price Administration. Brother Pete, who drove a bus for Sebastian Mikulich's stage line for several years, was also involved in Democratic politics in Clark County and ran unsuccessfully for the state assembly in 1934.[24]

Articles and notices gleaned from newspapers as well as information from directories, interviews, and other sources provide glimpses into the lives and activities of the growing number of Croats in Las Vegas. In 1929 John Victor Trinaystich, son of immigrant John Trinaystich, married Mary Malnar at St. Joan of Arc. George Skala of Los Angeles moved to Las Vegas in 1932 to purchase the Fremont Bakery on Fremont and Eighth Streets; associated with Skala was William Yankovich. The same year, Dan Bogich, who had been working on Boulder Dam, lost his home to a fire.[25] In 1934 J. J. Malnar, the proprietor of Rio Rita Oil Company, opened the Daily Ice Service at the corner of Tenth and Fremont Streets, advertising "only first class ice."[26] In a recent interview Rudy Crnko recalled arriving in Las Vegas in the mid-1930s to work for the Civilian Conservation Corps, which included a stint building a reservoir and digging a water well on the Rex Bell/Clara Bow Ranch outside town. Charles Pinjuv, a son of Mike Pinjuv, married Ruth Vukojevich of Los Angeles at St. Joan of Arc in 1939. J. J. Malnar in 1946 was operating the Signal Oil Company at 1812 Stanford Street and in the same year was elected to the North Las Vegas Town Board, which was seeking to incorporate North Las Vegas as a city. Josephine Trinaystich, age eighty-five, mother of John Trinaystich and native of Croatia, died in 1946. Two years later her grandson, John Trinaystich, graduated from Las Vegas High School and won a four-year scholarship to study chemistry and mathematics at Stanford University. After earning his degree, John worked for three decades at Titanium Metals in Henderson. Now retired, he still resides in the home built by his father, John Victor Trinaystich, on Third Street in Downtown Las Vegas. Two of the three daughters of John Victor and Mary Malnar—Frances Trinaystich and Mary Ann Costello—also reside in town. Frances still volunteers at St. Joan of Arc Catholic Church, a short distance from the original family home.[27]

Organizing Begins

For decades the Las Vegas Croats tended to business, raised families, and enjoyed each other's company. Unlike their cohorts in larger settlements, they made no attempt to organize fraternal benefit lodges or social clubs. Although there was a sufficient number of Croats as early as the 1930s to found a local lodge of the Croatian Fraternal Union (CFU), apparently there was little interest in doing so, despite the fact that CFU lodges had been established in the mining communities of McGill and Ruth, near Ely, and in Tonopah during the first two decades of the last century.[28] Many years would pass before a Croatian organization would appear in Las Vegas.

For some years Croats had been moving to Las Vegas from such places as Pennsylvania, Illinois, and Los Angeles. In their older neighborhoods they could hear mass in their language, eat in Croatian restaurants, and participate in myriad activities sponsored by Croatian organizations, including soccer leagues. Even in Southern California, which had a Croatian neighborhood before its residents dispersed throughout the Southern California basin, Croats retained their original church (St. Anthony's) and could socialize with four thousand of their friends at annual picnics and cultural festivals. In Las Vegas, because neither a neighborhood nor familiar cultural events were available, newcomer Croats turned to organizing.

Meeting May 13, 1983, at the Center for the United Campus Ministry on the University of Nevada, Las Vegas, campus, Jerry L. Simich, a UNLV political-science professor, Nik Skrinjaric, a UNLV student at the time, his mother, Biserka Skrinjaric, and her sister, Nada Trstenjak, along with Matt Bebic, Ratko Soda, Nedo Elezovic, John Musa, and Francine Sansota, organized, on an informal basis, the first Croatian American Club (CAC) in Las Vegas.[29] Members of the small club have continued to meet, recruit new members, and schedule an occasional picnic or dinner.

After corresponding with the national office of the CFU, members of the CAC decided to form a CFU lodge. Meeting on March 30, 1985, with national CFU president Bernard Luketich attending, Las Vegas Croats signed up for insurance policies and/or individual retirement accounts, thus becoming members of the national organization.[30] The local lodge was designated number 1985 and was named "Herzegovina," given that many of the Croats in Las Vegas had some connection to that region. The name of the lodge notwithstanding, some of its new members had ties to various regions of Croatia proper as well. By joining the CFU, members receive a bilingual weekly newspaper, the *Zajednicar* (unionist or fraternalist), informing them of events not only across the United States and Canada but also in *stari kraj* (the old country). Some Croats, members of CFU lodges across the United States, have moved to Las Vegas and transferred to Lodge 1985. Jerry Simich has served as lodge president for many years.

In order to involve Las Vegas Croats who for one reason or another did not join the CFU, it was decided to formally incorporate the Croatian American Club. On January 26, 1994, a group met at the home of Frank and Goldie Zrna and began the incorporation process. A board of directors was chosen, including Nik Skrinjaric (now an attorney), John Krmpotic, Jerry Simich, Frank Zrna, and Nada Trstenjak.[31] Goldie Zrna became the president and driving force of the club, assisted by Agnes and Carl Katalenic, Bruno Turkovic, and, more recently, Charles and Katica Cule.

Since the formal establishment of the CAC, it has operated jointly with Lodge 1985 in sponsoring different activities. The CAC sends a newsletter to approximately three hundred families in Clark County informing them of various events. About half of CAC's members are first generation (foreign born); the others are mainly second generation, born of earlier immigrants. Relations among the foreign-born and second-generation members are very cordial. Friendships between the two cohort groups have blossomed, and at any CAC event one can hear both English and Croatian spoken.

Besides enlisting new members, another task the club faces is keeping older ones active. A common complaint is that the twenty-four-hour, seven-day-a-week nature of the Las Vegas economy makes it difficult or even impossible for members and potential members to attend club functions. Another obstacle to recruitment and retention is the absence of a clubhouse where people might socialize and conduct business. Planning meetings have taken place invariably at the home of Frank and Goldie Zrna, who were exceedingly gracious and generous hosts. A bright sign is the fact that many young Croats, most of them refugees from Bosnia, attended the club's 2001, 2002, and 2003 Christmas dinners. No doubt the continued viability of the CAC depends on the participation of younger people, as the majority of the club's leadership is in the sixties to eighties age group.

Group Maintenance: Charitable, Cultural, Social, and Recreational Activities

The above problems notwithstanding, the Croatian community has an impressive record of accomplishments. Under the leadership of lodge 1985, Croats meeting in March 1992 at the Zrna residence raised several thousand dollars for the Croatia Humanitarian Aid Fund to assist victims of Yugoslavia's war on Croatia. In April 1993 the lodge sponsored a dinner at the Guardian Angel Cathedral hall, again raising thousands of dollars to assist displaced and orphaned children in Croatia and Bosnia-Herzegovina.[32] In September 1998 the lodge and the CAC, in collaboration with the Croatian consulate in Los Angeles, again contributed money and assistance to help rebuild the Croatian city of Vukovar, which was devastated by the Yugoslav army. Charitable assistance to war victims in Croatia and Bosnia-Herzegovina continues to be a priority for Las Vegas Croats.

Local Croats have also been involved in bringing several outstanding folk-culture groups to Las Vegas from Croatia.[33] In 1989 the CFU sponsored a nation-wide tour of the folk-music and dance company Milica Krizan from Osijek, Croatia. The company performed at the Las Vegas High School auditorium in February of that year, much to the delight of those attending. The forty-member song and dance company Matija Gubec from Karlovac, Croatia, met an enthusiastic response at the Flamingo library in July 1996. The CAC, in concert with the Croatian consulate in Los Angeles, brought Histrion, an outstanding stage group from the Croatian National Theatre of Zagreb, to the Circus Circus Hotel in February 2001 to recite poetry, drama, and prose, accompanied by music. While local Croats were not involved in bringing the string orchestra I Solisti Di Zagreb to UNLV's Ham Hall in April 1994, many attended the concert. In addition many Croats attend the annual performances of Pittsburgh's Duquesne University Tamburitzans (players of plucked string instruments), where they can enjoy folk songs and dances from Croatia, Bosnia-Herzegovina, and other countries.

Local Croatian organizations are fortunate to have live music performed at dinners and picnics by the Yeseta Brothers Orchestra of Los Angeles. Tom Yeseta, the group's organizer and leader, has a degree in music from Loyola University and is nationally acclaimed not only for his musical talents but also his knowledge and love of the folk and popular music of the different regions of Croatia and Bosnia-Herzegovina.

The Croatian Fraternal Union and Las Vegas

The Croatian Fraternal Union of America traces its origins to 1894. With headquarters in Pittsburgh, it has hundreds of affiliated lodges throughout the United States and Canada, and in recent years several lodges in Croatia itself have joined the organization. In its peak membership years, the organization boasted over 100,000 members; with the passing of older persons, the CFU's membership has declined to about 69,000.[34]

With all its attractions, Las Vegas is a very popular destination for members of the CFU nationwide. The national office frequently awards "grand prizes"—airline tickets and rooms at Strip hotel-casinos—for members who recruit a sufficient number of new members. The first of these endeavors was the Las Vegas Holiday cohosted by the CFU national office and lodge 1985 and held at the Tropicana Hotel and Casino in October 1986. Over 400 CFU members attended the four-day event, most flying into town from the eastern United States. Additional events followed: Campaign 88 rewarded recruiters with a stay at the Flamingo Hilton in October 1988, and Campaign 89 was celebrated at the Golden Nugget. Campaign 91 was held in conjunction with the CFU's Eighteenth Quadrennial National Convention at The Mirage Hotel and Casino. In January 1993 grand-prize awards for recruiters found them again at the Golden Nugget.[35]

The CFU national leadership recognizes that Las Vegas excursions are a powerful inducement to recruitment efforts. Joseph Brigich, national CFU vice president, put it this way: "Trips to Las Vegas always stir excitement among our volunteer recruiters as do excursions to the Old Homeland. Trips to Las Vegas and Zagreb have proven to be among the most popular Grand Prizes that our Society has offered over the years."[36] Las Vegas has also been chosen for two National cfu Adult Tamburitza Festivals or TamFESTS, musical extravaganzas staged annually throughout the United States and Canada. TamFEST IX was held in November 1995 at the MGM Grand Hotel and Casino, providing an opportunity for Croats and their friends to celebrate Croatian culture, meet old friends, and make new acquaintances. The cfu's national president, Bernard Luketich, described the event as follows:

> Mixed in with the glitter and slot machines, beautiful showgirls and the aura of excitement, the music of Croatia as presented by the 14 ensembles was more than equal to the challenge as the cfu members and friends came to the ballroom early and stayed late. Everyone expressed appreciation and heart-felt happiness for the performances presented by all of the ensembles.
>
> The entire weekend built to an exciting crescendo and nothing could have been more awesome and heartwarming than the finale presented by the Granicari ensemble of Milwaukee, who in their first appearance at a TamFEST brought the audience of more than 2,000 to their feet with their rendition of "Boze cuvaj Hrvatsku" [God Watch over Croatia]. And there wasn't a dry eye in the house as the curtain rang down on a most beautiful Croatian happening in the desert town of Las Vegas, Nevada.[37]

A second TamFEST, number XIV, came to the Riviera Hotel and Casino in November 2000. Again, over two thousand people from the United States, Canada, and Croatia attended and were thrilled by the nineteen tamburitza music and dance groups from Pennsylvania, Ohio, Indiana, Michigan, Illinois, Wisconsin, California, and Canada. In addition to music and dance events, the cfu sponsors ski, golf, basketball, and bowling tournaments. On three occasions the national leadership designated Las Vegas as the venue for national bowling tournaments—the first at the Gold Coast Hotel and Casino in 1995 and the second and third, cohosted by lodge 1985, at the Orleans Hotel and Casino in 1999 and 2003.[38]

Religion

The vast majority of Croats are of the Roman Catholic faith, and their Croatian Catholic parishes are found in most of the larger Croatian settlements in and around New York City, Pittsburgh, Chicago, Milwaukee, St. Louis, Kansas City, Kansas, Los Angeles, and the San Francisco Bay Area. A notable exception is New Orleans, which—despite its sizable Croatian population—has no Croatian church. In early Las Vegas Croats attended services at St. Joan of Arc with other Catholic families, including Irish and Italian Americans.

Perhaps the first Croatian-language mass in Nevada was celebrated by Monsignor Felix Diomartich of St. Anthony's Croatian Catholic Church of Los Angeles at Floyd Lamb Park on June 19, 1994, prior to a picnic sponsored by lodge 1985 and the CAC. The second Croatian mass was given on May 7, 2001, at St. Bridget's Catholic Church.[39] In September 2001, Father Mate Bizaca from St. Anthony's began offering monthly masses at St. Bridget's. Lacking the numbers to sustain a parish, it appears unlikely that local Croats will realize the dream of having their own church.

Croatian Lives in Las Vegas

After nearly one hundred years in southern Nevada, Croats are found in a wide array of occupations. Not surprisingly, the majority are employed in the hotel-casino industry as managers, pit bosses, dealers, chefs, cooks, and waiters. There are physicians, attorneys, architects, research scientists, engineers, professors, teachers, and librarians as well as dancers and musicians. Others have found opportunities in contracting, small businesses, real estate, and property management and as government employees. There is little to distinguish Croats from other middle-class participants in the Las Vegas economy. Perhaps the only marks of distinction are the often difficult-to-pronounce (for non-Croats) surnames and the accents of the foreign born. The following biographical sketches represent the variety of the Croatian experience in Las Vegas. Readers familiar with the city's recent history might recognize a few of the names.

A Las Vegas entertainer beginning in the 1950s and resident from 1981 until his death in 1999, singer-actor Guy Mitchell was a popular Strip performer at many hotel-casinos. Born Albert Cernick to immigrant parents in Detroit, Mitchell began his career in Los Angeles, successfully auditioning for Warner Brothers Studio. His greatest achievement, however, was as a popular singer and recording artist. Following service in the U.S. Navy at the end of World War II, Mitchell performed with the Carmen Cavallero Band, won an Arthur Godfrey talent contest, and then caught the attention of Mitch Miller of Columbia Records, who advised him to change his name.[40]

Cernick, now Mitchell, had a string of popular hit songs in the 1950s, including "Singing the Blues," "Heartaches by the Numbers," "My Heart

Cries for You," "(There's a Pawnshop on a Corner in) Pittsburgh, Pennsylvania," "Truly, Truly Fair," and "Chica Boom," which was featured in the 1953 musical western *Those Redheads from Seattle,* starring Mitchell, Rhonda Fleming, and Agnes Moorehead. He also appeared in *Red Garters* (1954) and *Wild Westerners* (1962). Mitchell's last public performance was at the old Hacienda Hotel and Casino in 1994. About a month before he became ill and died, Mitchell and his wife, Betty, were exploring the possibility of opening the Guy Mitchell Buffalo Ranch, where troubled and disabled children might find happiness by caring for animals and enjoying the outdoors.[41]

Dancer, choreographer, teacher, founder, and artistic director of the Nevada Dance Theatre Vassili Sulich is well known internationally as well as locally. Sulich was born in 1930 on the island of Brac, just off the Dalmatian Coast. After classical dance studies in Zagreb and London, he joined the Ballet de France de Janine Charrat (1953) and later attained the stature of Danseur Etoile with the Ballet des Etoiles de Paris and other companies. Sulich partnered such dance luminaries as Ludmilla Tcherina, Zizi Jeanmarie, and Collete Marchand, and by 1960 he was the principal dancer at the Lido de Paris. He later turned his talents to choreography, staging the *Suite Lyric, The Wall,* and *Oedipus the King,* the latter with Jean Cocteau and composer Maurice Thiriet. Sulich went to Broadway in 1964 with the Folies Bergère as principal dancer and, while there, studied dance with Martha Graham.[42]

In New York Sulich was offered a three-month contract by the producer of the Folies Bergère at the Las Vegas Tropicana Hotel, an agreement that turned into a nine-year engagement. He described his first days in Las Vegas as follows:

> On Albert Avenue, a small apartment cost $90 a month. With a salary of $250 a week, which was ten dollars more than I made on Broadway, I opened a savings account at Valley Bank. Employees' cafeteria meals were seventy-five cents, and my dog got plenty of juicy bones for free. My apartment was furnished with secondhand furniture. I bought two nightstand lamps with blue chip stamps. When dancers visited one another, we knew who worked in which hotel by the silverware, glasses, dishes, and towels. Mine were furnished by the Tropicana.[43]

In 1972 Sulich began a twenty-two-year career as a dance teacher at UNLV; he also founded the Nevada Dance Theatre (NDT), which he directed for twenty-five years, thus giving Las Vegas its only resident ballet company. Sulich and the NDT staged fifty-one ballets, including the venerable *Nutcracker,* for appreciative Las Vegas audiences. For NDT's fifteenth-anniversary season, Sulich created two new ballets, the antiwar *Walls in the Horizon* and a full-length production of *Cinderella.*

Sulich has been very active outside Las Vegas as well. In 1998 he presented his ballet rendition of *Oedipus the King* for the National Theatre of Croatia at the Dubrovnik International Summer Festival, and he choreographed *Queen of Spades, La Gioconda, Boris Gudunov, Adriana Lecouvreur* and *Eugene Onegin* for the San Francisco Opera. Sulich has staged his *Mantodea* in Brazil, Bulgaria, Canada, New Zealand, Singapore, Hong Kong, and Hungary as well as the United States, and he has also choreographed *War and Peace* for the Seattle Opera during the Goodwill Games of 1972.[44]

Sulich's talents as dancer, teacher, choreographer, director, and manager have been widely recognized. He has received the Distinguished Nevadan Award from the University of Nevada System Board of Regents, the Governor's Arts Award as Outstanding Individual Artist, and the Las Vegas Chamber of Commerce award for Achievement in Arts and Entertainment. In 1992 U.S. Senator Harry Reid presented Sulich an Artistic Achievement Award for his efforts with the NDT, and in 1999 he was inducted into the Casinos Legends Hall of Fame, a salute to his dancing at the Tropicana Hotel in the Folies Bergère.[45] Still active creatively, Sulich published his autobiography, *Vision in the Desert: A Dancer's Life,* in 2001.

Though ballet and pipeline construction would appear to have little in common, both require ambition, determination, and hard work. Not far inland from the Island of Brac lies Herzegovina, the hilly, rocky, dry landscape that sent many young men to Southern California in search of work, often as laborers digging trenches and laying pipelines. Martin F. Kordick, a former St. Mary's College of California football star and coach and the son of such an immigrant, eventually entered the pipeline-construction business in the 1940s. In 1971 Kordick and his son, Martin A. Kordick, the third generation of Kordicks involved in pipeline work, in partnership with Nick Artukovich of Los Angeles, completed a twenty-six-mile section of pipeline that brought Lake Mead water to the growing Las Vegas Valley. Before moving to Las Vegas in the 1990s, the Kordicks built many pipelines in Southern California and several in Ecuador. Both father and son and their wives, Peggy and Arline, are active in the CAC.[46]

After moving to Las Vegas from Chicago, Matthew Matanovich, along with his partner Rudy Novosel, operated the Crow-Bar (Croatian Bar), a tavern at 1000 Boulder Highway, for years before they retired in 1984. Older southern Nevada sports fans might remember Chuck Razmic and John Tartan (Trtanj), former football coaches and teachers at several local high schools. Basketball fans will remember Las Vegas resident Tim Grgurich, UNLV assistant coach during the Jerry Tarkanian years. Grgurich also served briefly as head coach after Tarkanian's departure and is now an assistant coach

for the Phoenix Suns. Tony Trudnich, the former owner of Cal Vada Volks-
wagen and BMW and a past president of the Southern Nevada New Car and
Truck Dealers Associations was well known to boxing fans for his Las Vegas
Sports Promotion cards at such venues as the Sahara, Aladdin, and Showboat,
Arizona Charlie's, and the Orleans. Many of the matches he promoted were
telecast on the Sports Channel and the USA Network. Trudnich died in
March 2002.[47]

A recent arrival from Bosnia, Ana Puljich works for the Migration and
Refugee Service of Catholic Charities of Southern Nevada finding jobs for
the many refugees coming to Las Vegas to begin new lives. A former refugee
herself, Ana has joined the CAC and is active in recruiting recent Bosnian
Croat refugees into the club. She says that assisting other refugees to settle in
Las Vegas is "very satisfying."[48]

Conclusion

After nearly a century in southern Nevada, Croats continue to make significant contributions to the Las Vegas community. While their numbers are not
great compared to those of other ethnic groups in the area, the Croats have
established themselves as a recognizable entity. This presence will be reinforced as Croats from the eastern and northern cities, western mining towns,
Southern California, Croatia, and Bosnia-Herzegovina continue moving to
Las Vegas, drawn by the same opportunities for work, entrepreneurship, and
retirement that have made the city a magnet for peoples around the globe.

Notes

The author thanks David Millman of the Nevada Historical Society and Museum, Duane Mosser, Melanie Young, and Jennifer Simich for their assistance in the
preparation of this chapter.

1. Ivan Cizmic, *Hrvati u Zivotu Sjedinjenih americkh drzava* (Zagreb: Globus,
1967), 418; see http://factfinder.census.gov/servletQTTable?_ts=7497579273Q.

2. George J. Prpic, *The Croatian Immigrants In America* (New York: Philosophical
Library, 1971), 161–62.

3. Prpic, *The Croatian Immigrants in America*, 406–12.

4. "Croats," in *Harvard Encyclopedia of American Ethnic Groups,* ed. Stephen
Thernstrom (Cambridge, Mass,, and London, England: Harvard University Press,
1980), 247.

5. Prpic, *Croatian Immigrants,* 62.

6. Adam S. Eterovich, *Yugoslavs in Nevada, 1859–1900* (San Francisco: R and E
Associates: 1973), 173–241.

7. Adam S. Eterovich, "Silverminers and Mineowners in Nevada," unpublished manuscript in the possession of Jerry L. Simich; Eterovich, *Yugoslavs,* 22–51; David F. Myrick, *Railroads of Nevada and Eastern California,* vol. 1, *The Northern Roads* (Reno: University of Nevada Press, 1962), 186; Helen S. Carlson, *Nevada Place Names: A Geographical Dictionary* (Reno: University of Nevada Press, 1974), 188.

8. Lenore M. Kosso, "Yugoslavs in Nevada, Part 1," *Nevada Historical Society Quarterly* 27 (Summer 1985): 69–89; "Yugoslavs in Nevada after 1900: The White Pine Community," *Nevada Historical Society Quarterly* 27 (Fall 1985): 158–74.

9. Ed Pinjuv, interview by Jerry L. Simich, Las Vegas, August 24, 2001.

10. *Las Vegas Age,* November 10, 1917, 2; Rosemary (Mikulich) Pisani, interview by Jerry L. Simich, Las Vegas, February 16, 2002.

11. Pisani, interview by Simich, February 16, 2002; *Las Vegas Sun,* March 26, 1978, 3C.

12. Pinjuv, interview by Simich, August 24, 2001.

13. *Las Vegas Age,* March 20, 1920, 1; *Las Vegas Age,* January 19, 1924, 1; *Las Vegas Age,* January 12, 1924, 1; Fred Wilson Collection, no. 01710230, Special Collections, Library, UNLV; *Las Vegas Age,* May 8, 1928, 1; *Las Vegas Age,* January 3, 1929, 1; *Las Vegas Sun,* May 20, 1983, 21.

14. *Las Vegas Age,* December 24, 1931, 2; *Las Vegas Sun,* May 1, 1986, 3B.

15. Robert D. McCracken and Jeanne Sharp Howerton, A *History of Railroad Valley Nevada* (Tonopah: Central Nevada Historical Society, 1996), 229–33. Howerton is the daughter of Lina Pinjuv Sharp.

16. Evelina (Pinjuv) Dunton, interview by Jerry L. Simich, San Mateo, California, March 27, 2002.

17. *Las Vegas Age,* April 1, 1933, 3.

18. Ibid., January 19, 1924, 1; Las Vegas Telephone Directory, April 1, 1926; *Las Vegas Age,* October 18, 1931, 3.

19. John Cronan, "Sebastian F. Mikulich," *Nevada Men and Women of Achievement,* vol. 1, *Southern Nevada Edition* (Las Vegas: John Cronan, 1966), 106.

20. Cronan, "Sebastian F. Mikulich," 106.

21. *Las Vegas Review-Journal,* April 10, 1977, 4–5.

22. Cronan, "Sebastian F. Mikulich," 106.

23. *Las Vegas Review-Journal,* May 15, 1988, 1AA.

24. Ibid., January 21, 1935, 3; *Las Vegas Review-Journal,* May 15, 1988, 1AA; May 4, 1950, 3; January 21, 1935, 3; September 22, 1935, 1; *Las Vegas Evening Review-Journal,* October 11, 1934, 1; June 25, 1935, 1; December 28, 1939, 1; March 26, 1943, 2; August 4, 1934, 1.

25. *Las Vegas Age,* May 4, 1929, 6; April 26, 1932, 1; June 15, 1932, 1.

26. *Las Vegas Evening Review-Journal,* April 10, 1934, 5.

27. Rudy Crnko, interview by Jerry L. Simich, Las Vegas, October 22, 2001; *Las Vegas Age,* December 23, 1939, 1; *Las Vegas Evening Review-Journal,* January 30, 1946, 2; September 15, 1948, 3; Frances Trinaystich, telephone interview by Jerry L. Simich, August 12, 2001.

28. Ivan Mladineo, ed., *Narodni Adresar, Hrvata-Slovenaca-Srba: The National Directory of the Croat-Slovene-Serb Organizations, Institutions, Business, Professional and Social Leaders in the United States and Canada* (New York: Ivan Mladineo, 1937), 418.

29. *Las Vegas Sun,* May 11, 1983, 59.

30. *Zajednicar,* May 1, 1983, 1.

31. Some members of the CAC belong to the nationwide Croatian Catholic Union, a fraternal-benefit organization similar to the CFU. Some wish not to pay yearly insurance premiums; others are not interested in joining either of the national organizations. CFU minutes, January 26, 1984.

32. *Zajednicar,* March 4, 1992, 1; June 3, 1993, 1.

33. Information regarding these cultural events is found in the minutes of the CAC.

34. CFU staff in Pittsburgh, telephone interview by Jerry L. Simich, January 24, 2002.

35. *Zajednicar,* July 2, 1986, 1; October 24, 1988, 1; February 15, 1989, 1; September 25, 1991, 1; November 4, 1992, 1.

36. Ibid., March 4, 1992, 1.

37. Ibid., November 15, 1995, 2.

38. Ibid., November 1, 2000, 1; *Zajednicar,* March 29, 1995, 1; *Zajednicar,* November 1, 2000, 1; March 29, 1995, 1; May 5, 1999, 1.

39. CAC minutes, June 3, 1994; CAC minutes, May 1, 2001.

40. *Las Vegas Review-Journal,* July 13, 1999, 2B.

41. Ibid., April 24, 2001.

42. Vassili Sulich, *Vision in the Desert: A Dancer's Life* (San Francisco: Robert D. Reed Publishers, 2001), 253.

43. Ibid., 254.

44. Ibid.

45. Ibid.

46. Martin F. Kordick and Martin A. Kordick, interview by Jerry L. Simich, Las Vegas, February 9, 2001.

47. Evelyn Matanovich, telephone interview by Jerry L. Simich, August 20, 2001; *Las Vegas Sun,* March 1, 2002, 8B.

48. Ana Puljich, interview by Jerry L. Simich and Thomas C. Wright, Las Vegas, February 6, 2002.

CHAPTER II

The Poles

TED G. JELEN

To the casual observer the Polish community in Las Vegas is virtually invisible. Unlike other national groups in southern Nevada and in contrast to their conationals in other large cities in the United States, Las Vegas Poles are geographically dispersed, occupying no distinctive or identifiable neighborhood.[1] Polish Americans in the Las Vegas Valley bear no discernable stigma of discrimination, and members of the Polish American community are not concentrated in any particular industry or occupation. Thus, a visitor to Las Vegas might well be forgiven for overlooking the Polish presence in the city.

Nevertheless, there *is* an identifiable Polish community in Las Vegas, whose members have a strong consciousness of national roots and origins. The leaders of this community are engaged in the dual tasks of assisting their Polish counterparts in becoming socially and economically integrated into the larger Las Vegas community and at the same time preserving and transmitting a distinctive Polish culture. Indeed, the existence of a large pool of new arrivals from Poland and other American cities in the last two decades has occasioned something of a renaissance of Polish national identity in the Valley, with two new organizations being created within the past eight years. This recent increase in national consciousness and ethnically based activity has created new and more formidable resources for the Polish community as well as tensions between different Polish groups and organizations. All of this is to be found within a polyglot community in which strong assimilationist pressures exist. The energy, pride, and rivalries that have recently emerged among Poles in Las Vegas, as well as limitations imposed by the external social environment, provide the foci for this chapter.

A Note on Method

Most of the material that follows was based on interviews with leaders of the major Polish American organizations in Las Vegas as well as with active members of these organizations and participants in the activities that the groups organize. The chapter's views reflect those of active, self-conscious members of the Polish community of the Las Vegas Valley and do not offer a representative sample of the values, attitudes, and actions of the Polish American population as a whole.

I derived my list of respondents from a series of snowball samples with different starting points. I began my search using such mundane sources as the Internet and the telephone directory to find my initial set of community leaders and organizations. After making initial contact with a respondent, I would ask him or her whether there was anyone else to whom I should speak. Virtually all respondents were quite forthcoming, on at least two occasions calling the person in question to arrange the interview. While I have no way of knowing whether this informal convenience sampling procedure produced anything resembling a comprehensive overview of the Polish American community in southern Nevada, I was able to view a variety of perspectives. In particular, the fact that I was easily able to unearth certain tensions between rival organizations purporting to represent Polish values in this southwestern setting provides me with some confidence that I was able to obtain multiple viewpoints and observations.

With only a few exceptions, the people I contacted were extraordinarily cooperative.[2] I was able to conduct a number of interviews in private homes, and, less frequently, in places of business or at the sites of organized group activities. Most of the interviews were tape-recorded, and they typically lasted sixty to ninety minutes. A few of the respondents declined to be taped due to embarrassment about their accents, usually requesting that I take my notes in longhand instead.

To some extent the ease with which I gained access to these respondents can be attributed to my own ethnic credentials. Although I speak no Polish (a source of continual frustration during the data-gathering phase of this study), I bear a Polish surname and was able to display a strong familiarity with, and approval of, Polish cuisine.[3] The facts that I originally hale from Chicago, which is something of a center for Polish culture in the United States, and that I had recently returned from a trip to Warsaw and Krackow helped establish my bona fides with several of the respondents. Indeed, for many respondents Chicago was virtually considered "the old country,"[4] and my familiarity with particular neighborhoods and, especially, Polish Catholic churches was an occasional source of instant rapport.[5] Throughout the study, I was quite amazed and delighted by the extensive and spontaneous hospitality displayed by virtually everyone I encountered. Every ethnographer should be as fortunate.

Patterns of Migration

The Polish community in the United States has a long history; indeed, there has been a visible Polish presence in the area since well before the American Revolution.[6] This means that Polish American family histories vary enormously in length as well as in other respects. However, it is helpful to regard contemporary Polish Americans as belonging to one of three cohorts.

The oldest and most imprecisely defined of these can be considered the pre–World War II cohort, the bulk of which arrived in the late nineteenth century through the beginning of World War I. Most of these first-generation immigrants came to the United States for economic reasons, and many of them planned to earn money in the New World then return to Poland with their newly acquired wealth. While many of these "temporary" immigrants did exactly that, a number of them remained in the United States, becoming permanent residents and, eventually, citizens. The descendants of members of this early wave of immigrants have obviously been in the United States for several generations, and most of them are fully assimilated into American culture. Mobility, intermarriage with non-Poles, and weakening ties with the Catholic Church have all contributed to a declining distinctively Polish identity for this group.

A second and somewhat more visible group of immigrants arrived in the United States during and after World War II. While a few of these immigrants fled Poland during the ascendancy of the German Third Reich, a large majority arrived in the country during the "Iron Curtain" phase of the Cold War, in which the Soviet Union asserted hegemony over Eastern and Central Europe in the immediate postwar period. The descendants of this World War II cohort, now in their second and third generations, are to some extent defined by the circumstances surrounding their arrival in the United States. Indeed, I was struck by the frequency and ferocity with which members of this group condemned the Yalta agreement (or the "Yalta betrayal," as some of my more polite respondents described it) between the United States, the USSR, and Great Britain near the end of World War II.

Members of this cohort settled in large cities in the Great Lakes region (Buffalo, Syracuse, Detroit, Cleveland, Rochester, Milwaukee, Gary, and especially Chicago), where they found work as laborers in industries such as steel and automobile manufacturing and coal mining and in the stockyards of midwestern cities such as Chicago, Omaha, and Kansas City. The immigrants and their descendants tended to form homogeneous urban communities in each of these cities. Such communities were rather complex social organizations, generally centered around a Catholic parish, a parochial school, and numerous cooperative "self-help" organizations such as savings-and-loan associations. These communities, which often had very large populations (although they tended to be geographically compact), formed a critical mass within which important aspects of the Polish culture such as language could be preserved and transmitted. Through the local Catholic Church, a local Polish-language press, and (somewhat less frequently) the school system, a Polish linguistic community could be maintained in a multicultural urban environment and a sense of national identity could be sustained.

The most recent cohort of Polish immigrants to the United States can be termed the Solidarity cohort. In the late 1970s and early 1980s, a Polish trade-union association known as Solidarity (*Solidarnosc*) challenged the hegemony of the Communist Party in Poland, and, by extension, the dominance of the Soviet Union in Polish politics. Led by shipyard worker Lech Walesa, who won the Nobel Peace Prize in 1983, and inspired by the election of Polish pope John Paul II in 1978, Solidarity is often credited with a crucial role in the collapse of the Soviet Communist bloc during the Reagan administration.

Of course the unconventional and often illegal political activity organized by Solidarity was not conducted without cost or risk. A substantial number of politically active Poles, fearing reprisal from either the Communist regime in Poland or from the Soviet Union itself, immigrated to the United States as a result of their participation in the Solidarity movement. The members of this cohort tend to be considerably younger than members of the World War II generation (although I observed substantial variation in the ages of members of this cohort in Las Vegas), and—for obvious reasons—much less assimilated than members of earlier cohorts of Polish immigrants. For most of these people Polish is their first language, and many have struggled to find roots and employment in the United States.[7]

The arrival of the two most recent cohorts in Las Vegas took place by different and varied routes. Members of the World War II cohort migrated to the Southwest individually and generally came from a Polish community in one of the larger cities in the Great Lakes region. The reasons for these individual migrations varied, including health considerations, employment prospects in times of economic downturn in the Rust Belt, and the desire for a warm climate in which to enjoy retirement. Interestingly, a substantial number of migrants to Las Vegas were initially employed in circuses and arrived for the first time in southern Nevada as part of touring entertainment troupes. The arrival of the World War II cohort and its descendants has taken place gradually over a number of years, coinciding with the spectacular growth of Las Vegas generally.

By contrast the arrival of the Solidarity cohort has been somewhat more abrupt, and for many members of this group Las Vegas was their initial destination in the United States. The strong anti-Communist stance of the Reagan administration was quite compatible with support for the Solidarity movement, and immigration to the United States from still-Communist Poland was rather easy during the decade of the 1980s. Immigrants from the Solidarity cohort were settled wherever sponsors could be located in the United States. While many Polish immigrants in the 1980s had relatives in the declining Polish communities of the East and Midwest, many others did not, and they often settled in unlikely locations such as Las Vegas, Salt Lake City, and Los Angeles.

Poles in Contemporary Las Vegas

Figures from the U.S. Census show that the Polish population of Clark County has been growing in absolute terms. In 1990 the census reports that 24,939 residents reported their ethnic identification as Polish. This rose to 36,150 for the 2000 census, representing an increase of approximately 69 percent.[8]

As a check on the census data, I asked local Poles to estimate Las Vegas's Polish population. Since Poles are one of the older ethnic groups in the United States, and since there has been at least a nominal Polish presence in Las Vegas for several generations, my respondents had some difficulty with this request. Estimates ranged from 10,000 to 30,000, with most respondents expressing some frustration over their inability to formulate more precise estimates. As one respondent sighed, "What do you mean by Polish? Do you mean people like us [Polish-speaking recent immigrants] or people like you [people of Polish ancestry but with few remaining ties to the language or culture]?"[9] Across most of the organizations I examined, members of the activist Polish American population agreed that members of the Solidarity cohort comprised a large portion of the visibly Polish population. My own observations confirmed that—despite strong opinions to the contrary—the older members of the Solidarity cohort provided a disproportionate number of leaders for all of the organizations described in this chapter.

Unlike the Polish communities in the Great Lakes cities from which most of the older local Poles migrated, the Polish community in Las Vegas is quite geographically dispersed. My interviews took me to several different sections of the greater Las Vegas Valley and provided a marked contrast with the ethnically homogeneous neighborhoods of my native Chicago. In my youth people in the Garfield Ridge neighborhood on the city's Southwest Side would sit on their front porches on warm evenings and converse with neighbors who came by. Several Las Vegas respondents shared my nostalgia for this practice, and one older woman wryly observed that "where we used to have front porches, now we have cell phones."[10]

This impression of psychological as well as geographical dispersion was reinforced by a subtle linguistic phenomenon. In more concentrated communities of Polish Americans, the Polish community in the United States (indeed, the Polish community outside of Poland) is termed "Polonia."[11] However, despite a strong commitment to retain connections with their Polish roots, none of the respondents in this study employed that term to describe their ethnic group.

Both the imprecision of estimates of the Polish community's size and the geographical dispersion of its population in Las Vegas are regarded by leaders of the Polish community as symptoms of the same underlying maladies—division within the ranks of the local Polish population and a lack of physical space within which the Polish community can interact and reaffirm its commitment to the Polish language and culture. Some of the members of local organizations attribute this unfortunate state of affairs to personal rivalries among the leaders of competing Polish organizations. However, many respondents attributed the lack of Polish cohesion in Las Vegas to a more fundamental cause: the independence of the Polish residents of the city. As one respondent told me:

> You have to understand that these are very independent people. After all, they [voluntarily] left their communities in Poland or in the East [meaning the eastern seaboard and Great Lakes regions of the United States]. It's hard to get people who have [voluntarily] left one community to make deep roots in another."[12]

Clearly, respondents who are active members in one or more Polish American organizations are more likely to bemoan the lack of community and cohesion among Poles living in Las Vegas than those who do not participate in such clubs. However, to an extent that I found remarkable, the respondents agreed that having a physical location around which Las Vegas Poles could converge would do much to alleviate the problem. As one woman told me, "We need a *place* we can call our own; where we can get together, do business, speak Polish, and just 'hang out,' like the kids say."[13] I was told of various attempts to establish a Catholic parish with a Polish identity (a move several respondents informed me was vetoed by the local bishop some years ago), a school, or a shopping center. The Chinatown area of western Las Vegas was frequently cited as an example of the sort of community focal point people had in mind.[14]

Although more modest than a parish, a neighborhood, or a school, a focal point for social interaction among local Poles has appeared recently. The

Polonez Restaurant, with a sizable bar, opened in 2002 east of the Las Vegas Strip. Several visits to this establishment showed me that it has become a popular place among some Las Vegas Poles, where conversations in Polish and English can be heard at almost any hour.[15] A new Polish restaurant, the Polonia, with an attached market, opened in 2004 on South Eastern Avenue.

Leaders of the Las Vegas Polish community are also eager to maintain contact with Polish communities in other parts of the United States and, more recently, in Poland itself. While some individual Poles residing in Las Vegas retain ties to more established and internally cohesive Polish communities in Los Angeles, for the most part Las Vegas Poles look to Chicago. Not only do many Las Vegas Poles have relatives living in the Windy City, but all of the organizations described below maintain correspondence with the Polish National Alliance, which is headquartered in Chicago. Moreover, members of both the Polish-American Social Club and the Polish American Center have had opportunities to appear on Polish-language radio programs in Chicago.

Lacking a physically rooted community or ethnically homogeneous institutions such as churches or schools (which provide a basis for community in other parts of the United States), Polish Americans in Las Vegas have formed formal fraternal organizations as a means by which they can interact with one another and can preserve and transmit Polish culture and identity. The three most important of these are the Polish-American Social Club, the Polish American Center, and the Solidarity Generation Foundation.

The Polish-American Social Club

The oldest and perhaps the most venerable Polish organization in Las Vegas is the Polish-American Social Club (PSC). Founded in 1968, the club has as its stated purpose the promotion of Polish culture, history, and language. Like all the Polish fraternal organizations in Las Vegas, the PSC lacks a formal structure or headquarters; nevertheless, the group is quite active, with monthly meetings in hotel meeting rooms or in the private homes of various members.

In comparison with other Polish American organizations in southern Nevada, the PSC lacks a highly visible public presence in the Las Vegas Valley. Indeed, I only learned of the organization's existence through my interviews with members of other clubs. Although the PSC does not have either a Web site on the Internet or a listing in the telephone directory, the group maintains a mailing list of three hundred to five hundred members, who are regularly invited to dinners, dances, and other social activities conducted under the club's auspices.

Conversations with the club's leaders reveal that an important latent purpose of the Polish-American Social Club is networking. The club has as a stated purpose providing assistance to new Polish immigrants in Las Vegas. Moreover, the meetings appear to be pleasant social occasions, in which alcoholic beverages (such as beer and vodka imported from Poland) and national foods are consumed in moderate quantities and at which business cards are exchanged and business opportunities are discussed. Henry Gee, a longtime member and informal leader of the club, describes with pride the number of prominent business and political leaders who are, or have been, members.

Both members and critics of the PSC report that this older organization largely attracts members of the post–World War II cohort, who came to the United States in the later 1940s and early 1950s. The membership of the PSC is regarded by Poles outside the organization as being comprised of Poles who have "made it" in the competitive Las Vegas economy and are not particularly interested in preserving central aspects of Polish culture. Indeed, members of the Polish American Center occasionally speak disparagingly of members of the Polish-American Social Club as Poles "who do not even speak Polish" and who are "not interested in doing anything."[16]

Naturally, the leadership of the PSC does not accept these stereotypes, and it largely attributes tensions between Polish American organizations to personality conflicts caused by leaders of the Polish American Center. Indeed, several members of the PSC's leadership are members of the Solidarity cohort and appear to share a sense of group membership and pride in this generation of immigrants. However, it was apparent to an outsider such as myself that some members of the PSC appear to embody an assimilationist ethic, in which certain practices that are regarded as distinctively American are explicitly embraced. In addition to providing contacts for business and employment opportunities, leaders of the PSC seek to emulate what they take to be the best practices from American culture. For example, two leaders of the PSC, in separate interviews, pointed with pride to the organization's highly developed bureaucratic (in the Weberian sense) manner of conducting business. As one of the leaders of the PSC thundered:

> We have bylaws, a written constitution, a budget, an annual report. We do things by the *book,* and by the *law!* This is America, where things are done—always—by the rules. Those of us from Poland remember when decisions were made in secret, by a small group of secret leaders. We run our affairs openly, in public, and without any cliques. We don't want to be like the police in the old country.[17]

As I continued to conduct my interviews, I came to suspect that this emphasis on "the rule of law" was a not-so-thinly veiled slap at the leadership of the Polish American Center. The self-image of the Polish-American Social Club is, to some extent, syncretistic. The leadership seeks to combine the best features of Polish culture and American society and to provide resources by which Las Vegans of Polish ancestry can prosper in the American Southwest.

The Polish American Center

The Polish American Center (PAC) is a much more recent addition to the roster of nationality-based organizations in southern Nevada. The center was founded by Paul Krowicki (pronounced crow-VIN-skee) in 1997. Krowicki, a building contractor, moved to Las Vegas in 1994 in order to take advantage of the construction boom taking place in Clark County during the 1990s. While living in Los Angeles, he had been quite active in a number of organizations in the Polish American community in that city. Shortly after arriving in Las Vegas, Krowicki became a member of the Polish-American Social Club and an officer in that organization.

Krowicki informed me that he soon became impatient and disillusioned with the bureaucratic (in the pejorative sense) inertia of the PSC. In particular he became frustrated with the lack of a physical facility to be shared by the local Polish community, and he reported disappointment with the PSC's apparent unwillingness to take on new projects. In response, along with some other members of the PSC, Krowicki formed the PAC.

According to accounts offered by members of both groups, the membership of the PAC consists largely of younger, more recent immigrants of the Solidarity cohort. Again, my own observations suggest that the generational stereotypes of the membership of both the PSC and the PAC are somewhat exaggerated, and, indeed, I spoke to a number of people who were members of both organizations.[18] However, what does seem clear is that there are substantial differences in the scope and purposes of the two.

First, it is quite clear that the PAC, as a new organization, is considerably more aggressive in pursuing its goals than is the PSC. The PAC has a monthly newsletter and a Web site, both of which facilitate communication with members and potential members. In addition the PAC, and Krowicki in particular, were quite active in attempting to create the physical location so desired by most active members of the Polish American community. As a contractor, Krowicki had planned a combination strip mall and community center. This was to have included a Polish delicatessen, a bakery, restaurants, a real-estate office, and a savings and loan. In addition it was hoped that a public space, such as a small park and auditorium, could be included as well. Although Krowicki reports expending substantial time, energy, and money on the project, he informed me that it is "on hold" at this writing due to a lack of financing.[19]

In addition to the physical community center, PAC actively attempted to create civic institutions that would permit the preservation and transmission of Polish culture. Since Polish communities in larger cities are often clustered around Catholic parishes, the PAC spent considerable time and energy investigating the possibility of establishing a Polish-language parish somewhere in the Las Vegas area. According to several of my respondents, the creation of a new parish was rejected by the local bishop. However, the PAC retains an ethnic/religious connection by flying in a Polish-speaking priest once a month to say mass at a Catholic church (incongruously located on the Las Vegas Strip).

Having experienced a setback in attempting to establish a Polish church, the leadership of the PAC turned to another venerable civic institution: schools. While it seems clear that the Polish community in Las Vegas lacks the numbers, financial resources, and cohesion to sustain a full-fledged private alternative to the public schools, the PAC has established a Polish-language school for children of elementary school age that meets on Saturday mornings. The White Eagle School (named after an important Polish national symbol) has no permanent facility, but classes are held on the campuses of local colleges. My observation of one of these classes was quite interesting. I saw about a dozen small children, ranging from about six to nine years of age, watching videotapes of Polish-language cartoons and laughing at (apparently) appropriate points in the program. The students' desks were generally free of the paraphernalia associated with elementary schools, such as paper, pencils, crayons, and other tools of the trade. Clearly, the White Eagle School is presented to its students as a recreational rather than an educational institution. Nevertheless, the parents of these children, with whom I spoke while the class was in session, attach enormous importance to the school as a resource for preserving central aspects of Polish culture and transmitting a sense of Polish national identity to future generations.

The PAC also sponsors several major balls and concert events throughout the year and maintains a mailing list of about eight hundred names. Members of the center regard their organization as more inclusive and authentically Polish than the PSC. Moreover, the widespread belief among members that the PAC is the organization which best serves immigrants of the Solidarity cohort is thought to provide the PAC with a certain high level of moral authority. While such characterizations are certainly controversial and are not shared by leaders of the PSC, it does seem clear that the emphasis of the PAC is much more on the preservation and transmission of Polish culture than on integration with the larger Las Vegas community. While the PSC does sponsor activities such as soccer games and dances for younger people, my interviews made it quite clear that the socialization of the young, especially including the transmission of the Polish language, is a very high priority for the PAC. Several of the group's publications are written in Polish only, and members feel a strong need to resist excessive assimilation on the part of their children.

It is perhaps noteworthy that no one with whom I spoke considered the possibility that both organizations might have distinctive but complementary roles to play in the social life of southern Nevada. At the leadership level, most respondents (with the notable exception of Paul Krowicki) argued that their organization was the one most authentically representing the Polish community. Members of both organizations who were not part of the leadership decried the lack of unity in the Polish community and attributed the apparent discord to personality conflicts among the leaders.

My own observations led me to consider the possibility that the two organizations serve different purposes and, perhaps, different clienteles and that the current arrangement might serve most parties reasonably well. To summarize, the Polish-American Social Club tends to look outward and to provide an environment in which members of the Las Vegas Polish American community can survive and thrive in the dominant culture, while offering resources to prevent complete assimilation and abandonment of the Polish culture. By contrast the Polish American Center seems to look inward and to place the preservation and transmission of Polish culture at the center of its priorities. The PAC devotes substantial resources to the socialization of the young, perhaps recognizing that peer pressure is most intense among elementary and high-school students. It seems reasonable to suppose that if Las Vegas Poles are to retain a culture that is authentically Polish and to prosper in the multicultural economy of southern Nevada, the services provided by both organizations are of considerable importance. The public roles played by the PSC and the PAC might well be complementary rather than oppositional.

The Solidarity Generation Foundation

This chapter would not be complete without some mention of the Solidarity Generation Foundation (SGF). The organization was founded in August 2000 (just four months before the initial interviews for this study took place) and had an extremely ambitious agenda. The foundation was created by members of the Solidarity cohort, many of the founding members having ties with the PSC. By 2003 the organization was apparently defunct. Though a president, mailing address, and telephone number were listed on the Web site for the Polish consulate in Los Angeles, a conversation with the person listed as president (Josef Niezgoda) revealed that the organization is no longer functioning "because no one would help."[20] Both the facts that the organization was founded and that it did not survive have important implications for the future of the Polish community in southern Nevada.

The foundation sought to capitalize on the moral authority and international cooperation that they regard as the hallmark of the Solidarity movement. The founding members of the SGF believed the Polish Solidarity movement to be the prime cause of the fall of Communism in the eastern bloc and thought that the liberation of nations such as Hungary and East Germany is derivative of a social movement that began in Poland. At the same time the foundation's mission statement acknowledged that the success of the original Polish movement could not have been achieved without the assistance of the United States. The overthrow of Polish (and, ultimately, European) Communism was thus regarded as an exemplar of Polish American cooperation, and the foundation sought to continue that spirit in the post-Communist era.

The mission of the SGF was generally philanthropic, with its philanthropy directed toward recipients in both Poland and the United States. The foundation sought to provide assistance to disadvantaged people in Poland in order to ease the transition from Communism to democratic capitalism there. Conversely, the foundation attempted to maintain philanthropic activities in the United States in order—in the words of Henry Gee (the foundation's secretary)—to "give something back" to the United States. The American side of the SGF's activities was intended to be dedicated to recognizing U.S. assistance in liberating Poland.[21]

The SGF sought to provide assistance to children in both nations; indeed, the organization's slogan is "Children Are Our Future." One activity in which the organization attempted to engage was the creation of a Vitamins for Kids charity, in which vitamins, food, milk, medicine, and toys would be distributed directly to children in poverty areas in both Poland and the United States. As this program was described to me, the disdain that the SGF's leadership had for "politics" became very clear. The Vitamins for Kids program was intended to be a form of *direct* philanthropy, without the intervention of intermediaries such as government or private charities such as the United Way in the United States. Another program intended for the children of the United States and Poland was the Christmas Tree Charitable Program, which was intended to provide toys for disadvantaged children. Unlike the Vitamins for Kids Program, the Christmas Tree Charitable Program was specifically designed to use existing organizations such as the Toys for Tots program sponsored by the U.S. Marine Corps to distribute the Christmas presents.

Aside from its primary goal of assisting disadvantaged children, the SGF also hoped to create a "Polish-American Solidarity and Friendship Promotion Committee," which was intended to provide public information about the role of Poles in American society and history. This committee planned a wide range of ambitious activities, including the creation of awards and grants to individuals and organizations that would exemplify the ideals and values of the foundation. The creation of a Crystal of Solidarity Award for individuals who embody the principles of Solidarity was a specific aspiration of the foundation. Other planned activities included the establishment of a Web site on the Internet and the creation of a Polish-American Solidarity Festival as well as a Polish-American Solidarity and Friendship Museum. This ambitious agenda was abandoned due to a lack of participation by the Poles of southern Nevada.

As I conducted the interviews with leaders and members of the SGF, another goal of the organization became apparent. Several of the people with whom I spoke expressed deep disappointment with the transformation of the Polish Solidarity Organization from spearhead of a continent-wide social movement to "mere" political party in post-Communist Poland. Lech Walesa himself was singled out for criticism by several group leaders, who criticized him severely for becoming "just another politician." As one member of the foundation's leadership told me:

> Solidarity [Walesa's organization] has lost its way. They used to be a worldwide organization, promoting freedom and friendship. They helped liberate not just Poland, but Hungary, the Czech Republic, and Russia itself. Now, they're just one of a group of thieves, trying to get power for themselves. I don't like to criticize Walesa, but I think he's gotten more selfish, and has forgotten the ideals which made Solidarity what it used to be.[22]

Two members of the leadership of the SGF told me that they hoped the foundation could provide a good example for the original organization. These respondents considered one of the roles of the SGF to be prophetic, to bring the Polish movement back to its senses and to its original purpose. The SGF leadership hoped to create a highly visible, binational organization that could influence social and political life in both Poland and the United States.

Conclusion

Members of the Polish American community in Las Vegas appear to experience few difficulties with respect to integration into the larger culture of southern Nevada. As immigrants and descendants of immigrants from northern Europe, Poles experience virtually no racial discrimination and do not appear to constitute a salient outgroup for other ethnic communities. Further, in the linguistic polyglot that is southern Nevada the fact that some of the more recent arrivals from Poland speak heavily accented English does not seem to be an insuperable handicap to social acceptance and economic success.

Rather, the daunting challenge for the activist members of the Polish community with whom I spoke is maintaining a distinctive cultural identity in the face of strong assimilationist pressures. Indeed, the social forces that make cultural preservation and transmission difficult are formidable. The failure of the SGF to achieve any of its social or philanthropic goals, or even to survive as an organization, is perhaps only the most visible manifestation of these forces.

To a large extent the identity of Las Vegas Poles is not defined by any distinctive set of *American* experiences but rather by political events that took place on the other side of the Atlantic. As the experiences of Communist rule and successful resistance to Communism fade from the memories of subsequent generations, it is difficult to imagine a set of common historical memories that can sustain a self-conscious national identity of Polish Americans as *Poles.* The fact that many Las Vegas Poles are recent immigrants and members of the Solidarity cohort undoubtedly provides a sense of energy and commitment to Polish cultural values. As these new arrivals are replaced by their children, who lack direct experience of participation in the glorious efforts of Solidarity, maintaining such a sense of national identity may be difficult.

Moreover, many members and descendants of older immigrant cohorts may be self-selected for their lack of interest in maintaining a cohesive Polish community. By and large, members of the pre–World War II and World War II cohorts voluntarily left the homogeneous ethnic enclaves of the large cities of the American East and Midwest. This supposition is admittedly speculative, since I did not interview peripheral members of the Las Vegas Polish community. However, it seems plausible to suppose that people of Polish ancestry who chose to leave the cohesive ethnic communities east of the Mississippi might have limited interest in reviving such communities in their new southwestern surroundings. The arrival of the Solidarity cohort in Las Vegas may constitute a brief interruption of the disintegration of a cohesive national community, but in the long run such disintegration may prove to be inexorable.

The theme of generational replacement has another component as well. Given the dispersion of Poles throughout the Las Vegas Valley and the lack of stable community organizations with fixed locations, it seems inevitable that intermarriage with members of other national groups is likely to increase over time. In larger, more established Polish communities in cities such as Chicago and Detroit, intermarriage has been both a cause and an effect of the gradual breakup of ethnically homogeneous neighborhoods. I can see no reason why such trends would not be accelerated in the cultural mosaic that constitutes the Las Vegas area.

Finally, the absence of a specifically Polish American Catholic parish, combined with a more general secularization of American society, seems likely to weaken the connection between Catholicism and Polish national identity.[23] The lack of a religious focal point for the community denies Las Vegas Poles the opportunity to reaffirm their common ethnic origins in a setting that "sanctifies" one's Polishness and one's Catholicism. Traditionally, Catholic churches have served as centers of Polish communities, and Catholic priests as local leaders of national groups. The lack of such an institution in Las Vegas may be one source of disunity between the rival groups I have described and may contribute to a disjunction between ethnic and religious identifications.

Thus, I would hazard the cautious and perhaps pessimistic prediction that the impressive efforts of members of the Polish community in Las Vegas to maintain a distinctive Polish identity and presence are likely to be unsuccessful. Indeed, the strenuousness of the efforts expended by the activists I interviewed suggests the magnitude of the challenge. For centuries the Poles have resisted the yoke of tyranny and have retained a sense of nationhood despite a history of occupation and oppression. However, efforts at cultural preservation and transmission may not survive the less obvious—but perhaps more effective—pressures of American pluralism.

Notes

Thanks are due to the people I interviewed, including: George Kalelak, October 1, 2000; Elizabeth Kawaka, October 7, 2000; Paul Krowicki, October 8, 2000; Henry Gee, November 9, 2000; Joseph Niezgoda, November 9, 2000, June 16, 2003; Wesley Fyda, November 9, 2000; Malgorata Fyda, November 9, 2000; and Janusz Mowak, November 9, 2000.

1. See Steve Kaniger, "Asians Lead Minority Shift Into Suburbs," *Las Vegas Sun,* July 20, 2001, www.lasvegassun.com/sunbin/.

2. One exception to this generalization was a Polish American veterans organization. Despite repeated attempts, I was not able to gain access to the group.

3. In most settings my last name is pronounced JEL-en. However, in Polish-speaking circles the original (and correct) pronunciation is YAY-lan. In addition I often reverted to the Polish version of my first name (Tadeuzs, pronounced tah-DAY-oos) when making initial contact with respondents whose first language was Polish. The

culinary aspect of the study had the unfortunate result of adding to my already ample waistline. It is virtually impossible to escape from a Polish home without partaking of a variety of national delicacies. I know readers will appreciate this demonstration of my dedication to scholarship.

4. See Victor Green, *For God or Country: The Rise of Polish and Lithuanian Ethnic Consciousness in America, 1860–1910* (Madison: The State Historical Society of Wisconsin, 1975).

5. Several respondents were particularly impressed with my familiarity with Five Holy Martyrs Catholic Church in the Brighton Park neighborhood on the South Side of Chicago. This parish was the site of several demonstrations of support for the Solidarity Movement in Poland during the Reagan administration.

6. See W. S. Kuniczak, *My Name Is Million: An Illustrated History of the Poles in the United States* (New York: Doubleday, 1978); Victor Greene, "Poles," in *Harvard Encyclopedia of American Ethnic Groups,* ed. Stephan Thernstrom (Cambridge, Mass.: Harvard University Press, 1980), 787–803.

7. See Mary Patrice Erdmans, "Recent Political Activism on Behalf of Poland: The Interrelationship Among Polonia and Cohorts" in *Polish-Americans,* ed. Helena Znaniecka Lopata, 2d ed. (New Brunswick, N.J.: Transaction, 1994), 213–42.

8. U.S. Bureau of the Census, 1990 Census Population: Social and Economic Characteristics: Nevada, table 137, 159; http://factfinder.census.gov/servlet/QTTable ?_ts=7497579273.

9. Elizabeth Kawaka, interview by author, Las Vegas, October 7, 2000.

10. Malgorzata Fyda, interview by author, Las Vegas, November 9, 2000.

11. See Green, *For God or Country;* Lopata, *Polish-Americans.* These scholarly sources are consistent with my own observations in Polish American communities in the Great Lakes region of the United States.

12. Janusz Nowak, interview by author, Las Vegas, November 9, 2000.

13. Elizabeth Kawaka, interview by author, Las Vegas, October 7, 2000.

14. Several analysts have noted the importance of real property to Poles living in Poland and the United States. See Greene, "Poles"; Norman Davies, *Heart of Europe: A Short History of Poland* (New York: Oxford University Press, 1986). My conversations with Las Vegas Poles provided striking confirmation of this generalization.

15. The Polonez changed its name to The Euro Place in 2004.

16. Interview by author with respondent who requested that her/his name not be used with respect to this issue.

17. Henry Gee, interview by author, Las Vegas, November 8, 2000.

18. It also became clear in the course of my interviewing that Paul Krowicki is held in very high regard by the other members of the Polish American Center. I believe it was to some extent Krowicki's popularity that occasioned the PSC representative's emphasis on rules and procedures.

19. www.polishcenterlv.com; Paul Krowicki, interview by author, Las Vegas, October 8, 2000.

20. Josef Niezgoda, interview by author, Las Vegas, November 9, 2000.

21. Henry Gee, interview by author, Las Vegas, November 9, 2000.

22. Ibid.

23. Recent scholarship has suggested that the extent of secularization in the United States is controversial and may not be as great as previously imagined. However, work in the sociology of religion in the United States does suggest that religion is increasingly compartmentalized into specialized segments of individual lives and does not provide an overarching context within which social life is conducted. See especially Jose Casanova, *Public Religions in the Modern World* (Chicago: University of Chicago Press, 1994); Roger Finke and Rodney Stark, *The Churching of America, 1776–1990* (New Brunswick, N.J.: Rutgers University Press); Gene Burns, *Frontiers of Catholicism: The Politics of Ideology in a Liberal World* (Berkeley: University of California Press, 1992).

CHAPTER 12

The Filipinos

ART D. CLARITO, HEATHER LAWLER,

& GARY B. PALMER

The Filipinos, Las Vegas's largest Asian ethnic group, are an active community of citizens who make significant contributions to the health, welfare, and education of the city. More than forty-two thousand persons of Filipino origin or descent now live in Las Vegas. They are predominantly Catholic in religion but very diverse in their particular Filipino ethnic origins. The number of distinct languages and ethnic groups indigenous to the Philippines surpasses eighty and may run as high as two hundred.[1] Among the languages and/or dialects spoken by Filipinos in Las Vegas, we find Tagalog, Kapampangan, Pangasinan, Ilocano, Bikol, and the Visayan dialects of Boholano, Cebuano, Ilonggo, and Waray. The people come from the north, central, and south Philippines; from Luzon, Visaya, and Mindanao. They have formed many associations based on ethnicity or province of origin, common interests, and social causes. They find many venues and opportunities to associate with their ethnic fellows, but they make independent residential choices based primarily on economic and social factors other than ethnicity. While they are found in many occupations, those who go into business often choose the food industry, especially the "oriental market," which provides foods and goods preferred by Filipinos and other Asians.

Though Filipinos have been in Las Vegas since the construction of Hoover Dam, the majority—like most other residents of Las Vegas—arrived only recently. During the second half of the twentieth century, Filipinos in Las Vegas organized many associations based on ethnic or regional origins and common interests, such as profession and military service. In organizing, they seek the company of their peers and the comfort and stimulation of conversation in home languages and dialects; they seek political influence; and they promote social recognition, education, and socio-economic advancement as well as equal opportunity in public service and humane and impartial treatment within the country's criminal justice system for their members. Their talent for organizing is bearing fruit in terms of membership and positions on local and national boards and agencies, both governmental and nongovernmental. The process of group formation is dynamic, with new groups emerging from older ones, which either continue or realign themselves. Many people belong to several Filipino associations. By drawing together people of varied interests, abilities, resources, and connections in common enterprises, Filipino groups in Las Vegas will likely provide a steady source of new solutions to Filipino community problems. Furthermore, this process allows the community to identify those with leadership ability and to raise persistent important issues in public forums.

Global Distribution of Filipinos

Although the United States is the preferred destination for most Filipino migrants, they can be found in many other countries, often working on temporary contracts as Overseas Contract Workers (ocws). Nearly one million work in the Middle East, including Saudi Arabia, Kuwait, Iraq, and Iran, where they are employed as manual laborers, domestic servants, construction engineers, doctors, and nurses. In Hong Kong, Japan, and Singapore they find work as domestics and entertainers. In Spain and Italy approximately fifty thousand, mostly women, work as domestics. Though ocws contribute about six billion dollars annually to the Philippine economy, they suffer from homesickness and sometimes appalling working conditions. Several films have dramatized the case of Flor Contemplacion, a Filipino mother who was hanged in Singapore for the alleged killing of a young boy in her charge when she was working there as domestic servant. Flor is seen as a modern heroine, and her death has sparked organizations espousing women's rights worldwide. One of our own consultants in Las Vegas described working in debt bondage in a nightclub in an Arab country. Her freedom was purchased by an American serviceman, whom she subsequently married.[2]

Filipino Migrations to the United States

The arrival of Filipinos on this continent dates from surprisingly early times. The people of the Philippines (named for Felipe II, king of Spain 1558–98) lived under Spanish colonial rule from 1565, when Miguel Lopez de Legazpi established a colony on the island of Cibu, until 1898. "Manila Men," as they were popularly called, arrived on ships of the Manila-based Spanish galleon trade that traveled between the Philippines and Spanish Mexico until 1815. In 1833 deserters from the Spanish galleons established the village of St. Malo, numbering about one hundred persons, on the Mississippi River outside of New Orleans.[3] These former crew members represent the earliest recorded U.S. immigrant community from the Philippines.

In 1898, following the Spanish-American War, the United States denied independence to the Philippines and waged an imperialistic war, killing hundreds of thousands and subjugating the islands by 1901. American rule lasted until 1946. American businessmen fostered an agricultural export economy emphasizing sugar and paid for with imports of rice and textiles, both of which were already produced in abundance in the Philippines. As happened to many other peoples around the globe, the displacement of indigenous small-scale subsistence industries by an export economy based on plantation agriculture or mining had the effect of fostering economic dependency. The Americans introduced universal public education based on the American model; instruction was conducted mainly in English, using textbooks from the United States. Consequently, Filipino students schooled in U.S. culture and values began to aspire to visit the United States and seek the opportunities described in their textbooks.[4]

The first group of students arrived in the United States as *pensionados* (scholarship holders) in 1903. Most graduated and returned to the Philippines, though many—often for lack of funds to continue their education—left school to become unskilled laborers and remained in America.[5] Between 1910 and 1938 approximately fourteen thousand young male students, both sponsored and unsponsored, migrated to the United States. At the high point of pre–World War II Filipino enrollment in U.S. schools, between 1920 and 1925, two thousand attended high school or college. This dropped to three hundred toward the end of the Great Depression in 1939. Yen Le Espiritu wrote: "Stranded by the Great Depression and lost ambitions, most of these 'unintentional migrants' lived out their lives as laborers in the United States."[6]

Another avenue for entrance into the United States was provided by service in the merchant marine and the U.S. Navy. Following World War I Filipinos were allowed to work as stewards and mess boys, but after service on board ship they were permitted to remain in the United States, a policy that lasted until 1936. During the 1920s and 1930s, the number in the service "hovered around 4,000," but recruitment increased with the onset of the Korean War.[7] Prior to 1965, even more than the pensionado movement and the rights accorded by naval service, it was the need for agricultural laborers that drew the largest group of Filipinos to this country. Filipino laborers worked in the fields of Hawaii and the West Coast, primarily in California. Their struggles have been immortalized by Carlos Bulosan in his moving autobiography, *America is in the Heart.*[8]

In Hawaii the majority of the new labor recruits were Japanese, but numerous Filipino workers also arrived. By 1930 over sixty-one thousand Filipinos remained in permanent residence after their contracts expired, some ten thousand of them women. About two-thirds of the migrants to Hawaii were Ilocano *sakada* (migrant workers), who had seen their indigenous textile industry displaced by imports. The second largest group was from the eastern Visayas. Following the Hawaiian plantation strikes of the 1920s, about eighteen thousand Filipino laborers moved from Hawaii to the mainland United States to continue as field laborers in California and Washington, but some found work in the Alaskan canneries. By the end of the 1920s over forty-five thousand Filipinos resided in the mainland United States, mostly in California, where they performed harsh stoop labor in the fields for low wages. The migrant housing available to them was unsanitary, crowded, and even dangerous. To cope with difficult conditions, Filipino laborers cherished networks of family and friends and established strong cultural, religious, and community organizations, including fraternal organizations with elaborate rites of initiation. In the 1930s they organized labor unions and were granted charters in the American Federation of Labor. Though most people think of the farmworkers' movement as a Mexican American phenomenon that began with the historic 1965 Delano grape strike in the San Joaquin Valley, the movement was actually launched in the 1930s with the Filipino Workers Association, the Filipino Labor Union, and the Filipino Agricultural Laborers Association. The 1965 grape strike was itself launched by the Filipino Labor Union, headed by Larry Itlong, and was joined a week later by César Chávez and his National Farm Workers Association UFW. The two unions were merged into the United Farm Workers of America with the assistance of Philip Vera Cruz, who became a vice president of the UFW.[9]

As jobs became scarce in the Great Depression, resentment of Filipino workers led to race riots. In Watsonville, California, according to Espiritu, "four hundred white vigilantes attacked a Filipino dance club, beating dozens of Filipinos and killing one."[10] Other race riots occurred in California and Washington. California and twelve other states enacted laws against marriages between Filipinos (then called "Malays") and whites. Immigration came to a near halt in 1932, when the Great Depression severely curtailed recruitment of Filipino workers abroad. In 1934 the passage of the Tydings-McDuffie Act by the U.S. Congress defined Filipinos as aliens and limited their entry into the United States to fifty per year. It was not until 1946, when the United States granted Philippine independence, that immigration restrictions were eased and rights and privileges of naturalization were allowed to Filipino residents in the United States.

Veterans of World War II

At the outbreak of World War II, there were thousands of Filipino Scouts with the U.S. Expeditionary Forces in the Far East (USEFFE) under Gen.

Douglas MacArthur. The scouts were called by President Franklin Roosevelt to defend Corregidor and Bataan in a vain attempt to repel the invading Japanese. They fought side by side with the American troops, and after the fall of Bataan they were forced to undergo the infamous Bataan Death March to the Japanese garrison at Camp O'Donnel in Capas, Tarlac, where those who survived endured severe hardships, deprivations, and cruelties.

After the the war, in recognition of their gallantry, many of these soldiers were granted special visas to settle with their families in the United States. Some fortunate ones were compensated for disabilities sustained in military service, but only after intense and constant lobbying of Congress. A greater number were denied benefits, and succeeding legislation cut the entitlements in half. The veterans are now in their twilight years and, having survived the horrors of World War II, must still suffer the indignity of being denied equity in medical and hospitalization benefits with veterans from other ethnic groups such as Mexican Americans. During a state visit to the White House on November 20, 2001, Philippine president Gloria Macapagal-Arroyo joined a rally organized by the American Coalition For Filipino Veterans and the San Francisco Veterans Equity Center. Participants urged President Bush to give full recognition to U.S. Filipino war veterans.[11] On December 13, 2003, Bush signed a veterans bill that included "full war-related disability pension and burial benefits to about 100 Filipino veterans and 400 dead soldiers' widows living in the United States."[12] Earlier in the month he had extended health benefits to about seven thousand surviving Filipino World War II veterans living in the United States.

Recent Arrivals and the Distribution of Filipinos in the United States

The distribution of Filipinos in this country reflects the history and character of Filipino immigration throughout the twentieth century. For the first half of the century the vast majority of Filipinos could be found in the Pacific Rim states of California, Washington, Alaska, and the territory of Hawaii. The wartime heroics of Filipino soldiers and nurses caused many Americans to revise their estimation of Filipinos. Some sixteen thousand were drafted in 1942 alone. Those drafted into the war were naturalized in mass ceremonies. Many non-Filipino servicemen brought home Filipino wives. Filipino men who had served with the U.S. armed forces also gained eligibility for citizenship. Many of them brought their families to the United States and settled in major cities scattered across the midwestern and eastern states. Between 1946 and 1965 there was a 44 percent increase in the number of Filipinos in the United States.[13]

Under the Immigration Act of 1965, professional employment status as college-degree holders and family reunification became valid reasons for immigration. During the 1960s and 1970s Filipino immigrants increased their numbers in major U.S. cities. Although the Pacific Rim states still prevailed in sheer numbers, by 1970 sizable Filipino populations were established in New York, Illinois, New Jersey, Virginia, Maryland, Florida, and Pennsylvania. Many of those settling in the cities were doctors and nurses, who were overrepresented among Filipino migrants to the United States during the 1960s and 1970s. They went disproportionately to the inner cities and rural areas, where medical personnel were scarce.

In 1984 the United States had twenty-six thousand registered nurses (RNs) who had been trained in the Philippines. In 1989 three out of four foreign-trained nurses in the United States were Filipinos. Filipino nurses tend to earn more money than nurses from other ethnic groups in the United States, because they are willing to work longer hours and accept less desirable shifts in order to meet family obligations. They are only half as likely as nurses from other ethnic groups to reach management positions (9 percent, versus 18 percent of all employed nurses). Higher income targets rather than glass ceilings seem to provide a partial explanation. Nurses working double shifts or working with nursing registries may earn more than a head nurse, so there is an incentive to avoid promotion.[14]

The geographical distribution of Filipino nurses in the United States differs somewhat from that of earlier Filipino immigrants, as many nurses were recruited to Chicago and even more to New York, where 18 percent of the RN staff is Filipino. When their contracts expire, many relocate to Los Angeles, even though they must take another licensing exam. It seems likely that some of the relocaters have eventually settled in Las Vegas, which is accessible from Los Angeles, also has a warm climate, and offers a somewhat similar lifestyle.

The population arriving after 1965 was more diverse than that in previous decades, consisting of both educated urban professionals and the lower echelons of the working class. In the early 1970s Filipino enlistees in the U.S. Navy, now numbering over 16,000, were granted the right to enter any occupational rating. Filipino communities developed in San Diego and other U.S. cities with naval facilities. About 300,000 relocated to the United States during the fourteen years of martial law imposed during the Marcos regime from 1972 to 1986. As is the case for recent arrivals in Las Vegas, the new professionals tended to settle in the suburbs and join associations. In the 1990s, according to the U.S. Census of 2000, the U.S. Filipino population grew by 31.5 percent to 1,850,314. The Lewis Mumford Center puts the 2000 total at 2,196,952. Currently, over 63 percent reside in the western United States. Four western states also have the highest concentration relative to other populations within the state. Hawaii remains the highest (14.1 percent), followed by California (2.7 percent), Alaska (2.0 percent), and Nevada (2.0 percent). The fastest-growing Filipino community in the United States is that of Nevada, which surged a phenomenal 337 percent in the 1990s. Currently, Filipinos in the United States are 70 percent foreign born and 60 percent female. The Philippines is the largest source of Asian migration to the United States and second only to Mexico among all nations.[15]

Filipinos and Filipino Americans in the United States have gained fame in several spheres of life. Among those who have gained national prominence in politics or government service are Carlos Bulosan, the 1930s writer and labor organizer, and Benjamin Cayetano, the recent governor of Hawaii. Noted writers, in addition to Bulosan (*America is in the Heart,* 1946), include Jessica Hagedorn (*Dogeaters,* 1990) and poet Jose Garcia Villa ("The Anchored Angel"). Prominent Filipino entertainers and celebrities include Lou Diamond Phillips, Tia Carerre, and Lea Salonga, star of the Broadway hit *Miss Saigon.* Miss America for 2001, Angela Baraquio, is a Filipina from Hawaii. Prominent scholars include the linguist Teresita Ramos at the University of Hawaii at Manoa and critical theorists Epifanio San Juan Jr. of Washington State University and Vicente L. Rafael of the University of Washington, Seattle. And the visual-development artist for Pixar's animated film *Monsters, Inc.* is Ricky Nierva, a Filipino American from San Diego.[16] With Filipino Americans gaining national prominence, it is not surprising that local Filipinos and Filipino Americans are also contributing to the life and culture of Las Vegas.

The Filipino Population of Clark County

To the best of our knowledge, the first Filipinos to arrive in Las Vegas came during the Depression. Two uncles of Leo Nanat—Simplicia Pajatin and Maximo Gusalo—left California to escape discrimination and low wages of five cents an hour and also came to work as laborers on the construction of the Hoover Dam. A few years later they obtained work as busboys at the El Rancho Hotel, holding these jobs for the remainder of their lives. The hotel soon urged them to invite more Filipinos to come. In later decades many Filipinos found work in the Hughes-owned Silver Slipper and Sands.[17]

Another very early arriver was Rudy Roque Legaspi Oquendo, who came to Las Vegas in the 1930s. Working as a deputy sheriff by day and a bartender at night at the old Thunderbird, he bought property on south Eastern Avenue, and the east-west street where his land was located was named after him. Ven Manaois, also early arriver, studied accounting in Los Angeles before World War II. After the war he came to Las Vegas and found work in the U.S. Post Office. At that time he was known as the most-educated Filipino in Las Vegas.[18]

In 1952, at the age of sixteen, Rudy Crisostomo—born in Corregidor, Republic of the Philippines—came to the United States, where he eventually studied fine arts at the University of Texas. After a stint in the army, he became a sign designer in Detroit. In 1963 he was hired by Federal Signs in Las Vegas (later purchased by YESCO). In the course of his career Cristostomo designed several bright spots in the glittering Vegas skyline, including the neon marquee signs for the former Sands Hotel and Dunes and for Circus Circus, Binion's Horseshoe, the Luxor, and Whiskey Pete's at Primm. He also designed the spectacular pylon of the Rio Hotel and Casino. One of only ten Las Vegas Filipinos currently active in the Masons, Rudy is a past Master of Mt. Moriah Lodge #39.[19]

In 1954 Rudy Santos, a sixteen-year-old boy born in Corregidor, came to San Francisco with his father, a retired Filipino Scout from Castillejos Zambales, about seven and one-half miles from Subic Bay in the Philippines. For fifteen dollars each, they took passage in the USS *Sultan,* a cargo ship that carried five thousand troops from Manila to the Golden Gate, making the crossing in a little over two weeks.[20] In San Francisco a friend of Rudy's father called him about a job as a busboy in Las Vegas, which he understood to mean he would be taking tickets on a bus. Arriving in May 1955, he found a city of forty to fifty thousand people with perhaps one hundred Filipinos. His job as a busboy was not on a bus but in the showroom of the Flamingo, where he worked with another retired scout named Aberin. He also remembers Tommy Bolo and Rudy Oquendo as first acquaintances. When the Royal Nevada opened in 1955, Rudy worked in the showroom as a waiter and later became a bartender, a promotion that was not easily come by in those days. He stayed with the Royal Nevada for twenty-seven years.

From 1957 to 1958 Rudy lived with fourteen or fifteen other Filipino young men, Kapampangans and Ilocanos, in a three-bedroom house at 114 Fourth Street. Calling themselves "The Untouchables," they socialized by playing mah-jongg or poker and bowling at Las Vegas Bowling at St. Louis and Las Vegas Boulevard. Their meals of chicken or pork, which were cheap, were cooked by one of the group. At work they made tips of seven or eight dollars a night, which seemed a lot of money, as it cost only five dollars to bowl and buy beer. Most sent their paychecks of fifty dollars a month home to the Philippines. At that time there were few Filipino females in Las Vegas, so they socialized with non-Filipino girls. As the hotels opened, they needed workers. Filipinos were known as quiet, diligent workers who came to work on time and did not talk back to their bosses, so Rudy was asked to recruit friends and relatives. He found farmworkers near Los Angeles and other parts of California. The hotels put the workers in dormitories, which the Filipinos called "barracks," consisting of one long apartment connected to the hotel. Rudy's brother-in-law lived in one such barracks at the Riviera. The Flamingo had one for dining-room workers.

Rudy later married a Euramerican woman, saved his money, and in 1978 purchased the Jade Garden restaurant in Commercial Center at Sahara and Maryland Parkway, keeping it for three years. He is now retired, divorced, and living in Henderson. Rudy says a few of his buddies married nurses seeking green cards in the 1960s, but the girls soon divorced them and went back to their sweethearts in the Philippines. Rudy's story of arriving in San Francisco, finding work in the hotel-casinos of Las Vegas, helping to recruit other Filipinos for the hotels, finding promotion in work difficult or impossible, yet staying with a hotel for decades and marrying a non-Filipino is replicated in the experiences of other early arrivers. Other Filipino Scouts who established families in Las Vegas were named Padillo, Salazar, Deyro, Barban, Guinto, and Benito. The Santos and Benito families were the largest Filipino families in the city in the early 1960s. At one time there were 120 Santos and Benitos, all cousins. The Vicuña, Patolo, and Cunanan families also arrived about this time.

Leo Nanat, originally from Agno, Pangasinan, had been a school principal in Quezon City, which is now a part of metropolitan Manila. When he arrived in America in the late 1960s on a degree-holder preference, he found work as a bellman at the Holiday Inn in San Francisco. When a new Holiday Inn opened in Las Vegas in 1972, Leo was the only Filipino to come to Las Vegas to help open the new hotel, which later became Harrahs. He was probably the first Filipino bellman in town. When he went to the post office to send money to his wife in San Francisco, he met Ven Manaois. The hotel asked Leo to recruit more Filipinos, so he wrote letters to California, and they came.[21]

The subsequent growth of the Filipino population in Nevada and in Clark County parallels that of Las Vegas, which is to say that significant growth occurred during the 1980s, followed by massive increases throughout the 1990s. In 1970, 573 Filipinos lived in Clark County, but by 2000 there were

42,596 Filipinos residing in the Valley, constituting over a third of the Asian population. Washoe, with 7,583, is the only other county in Nevada with a significant number of Filipinos. Breaking down the figures by ethnicity or by state or country of origin is difficult. A local realtor has tracked the growth of the Hawaiian population in Las Vegas since 1988 by using records from the Internal Revenue Service and the Department of Motor Vehicles. He places the current Hawaiian Filipino population at 5,000 to 6,000, most arriving since 1995.[22]

There appears to be no exclusively Filipino residential neighborhood in Las Vegas. The early arrivers in the 1950s and 1960s settled along east Charleston Boulevard from Sixth and Seventh Streets to Nellis Avenue, and many Filipinos still live in that neighborhood (but there are also other Asians, Hispanics, and Euramericans there). Most of the early arrivers found work in the casinos, and it is still the case that many Filipino businesses are located along East Charleston.

Today, newcomers are settling in the Westside between the Alta corridor and Flamingo Road, where they find new developments with relatively cheap housing. Retirees coming from California and Chicago and some of those working in the casinos have accumulated enough money for down payments on houses in the $150,000 to $200,000 range. Asian Americans in general, including Filipinos, are buying in the western suburb of Spring Valley, where three-bedroom homes sell for $20,000 to $30,000 more than in the northeast Valley. Crime is relatively low, and there is convenient access to the Las Vegas Strip, where many work in the hotel-casinos.[23] Asian Americans are also moving into the suburbs of Green Valley and Summerlin, where they constitute 10 percent of the population. The move to the more affluent suburbs relates to educational levels. As Kate Recto, president of the Philippine Chamber of Commerce of Southern Nevada (PCCSN), points out: "It's just expected of the children to be able to finish high school and go on to college."[24]

Organizations

Filipinos in Las Vegas are actively organizing in and across a number of social dimensions, including ethnicity, region of origin, religion, and other common interests. Often, organizations from these various domains have officers in common and plan cooperative events, as when the ethnically based Aguman Capampangan cooperates with the Agila Lions Club, which we characterize as a common-interest organization.[25] Whatever their basis, the organizations typically have a constitution and an agenda consisting of community service, fellowship, remembering the needs of the homeland by sending food and money for education and for the alleviation of natural disasters, and the perpetuation of Filipino culture in America. Lately, they have become increasingly involved in politics by supporting candidates in elections, conducting voter-registration drives, and sponsoring their own candidates for school board and state assembly.

Perhaps the first Filipino organization in Las Vegas was "The Untouchables," the self-named group of fourteen or fifteen young men who lived in a house at 114 Fourth Street from 1957 to 1959 and worked as busboys. An early formal organization was the Filipino Community (FC), which was established in 1973 under president Mel Salazar to assist new residents in the legalization process. About the same time, the Filipino American Association of Nevada, Inc. (FAANI) was organized, with Rudy Crisostomo as its first president. Also in 1973, the FC split and the Filipino American Senior Citizens of Southern Nevada (FASCSN) was organized, with Ven Manaois as its first president.[26] Manaois held the position until 1997. The formation of the senior citizens' group was followed shortly by the Aguman Capampangan, the Ilocano Association, and the Visayan Association.

There are two umbrella groups, the Nevada chapter of the National Federation of Filipino American Associations (NaFFAA) and the Filipino American Federation of Nevada (hereafter The Federation). The member groups of these organizations may belong to both groups, as is the case with the Aguman Capampangan. The NaFFAA, Nevada includes fourteen member organizations, including the Philippine Nurses Association of Nevada and three other health-related organizations, six ethnic or regional associations (Bikolanos, Bulakeños, Bisayans, Boholanos, Ilocanos, and Luzon), and organizations for servicemen, youth, and the technical professions. Among the issues on the agenda of NaFFAA, Nevada are seniors, youth, Filipino immigration status, World War II veterans' status, a Filipino community center, cultural and social adult classes, and computer and information-technology classes.[27]

The Federation was established in 1993 in a hotly contested election as a reorganization of the former Filipino Services of Nevada, but it could also be seen as a successor to the FAANI, which subsequently disintegrated and endorsed its funds over to The Federation. Influential groups coming into the new Federation included the Aguman Capampangan, the Agila Lions Club, and the Senior Citizens. The Federation encouraged the formation of many new organizations, such as the local chapter of Kahirup International. In all, twenty-one associations now belong to The Federation. Among other things, it sponsors or cosponsors the celebrations of Filipino Week, Independence Day, and the Catholic festival of Santacruzan. Filipino Week and Independence Day have been celebrated since 1993, Santacruzan since 1996. The Federation supported the current Las Vegas mayor, Oscar Goodman, in both his elections. The Federation, the PCCSN, the Agila Lions Club, and the Golden Agila Lions Club were all founded by one person—Tonie Sison.[28]

Ethnic Associations

The Philippine Bisayan Society of Nevada, Inc., founded in 1990, has a membership of over one thousand, with over four hundred active members. It operates a scholarship program for college-bound Filipino American high-school students in southern Nevada and for students in the Philippines. The society also supports Filipino American youth organizations in Nevada and makes donations of food and clothing to the needy and homeless through the Salvation Army and the St. Vincent Shelter as well as making donations to calamity victims in the Philippines and sponsoring cultural presentations. A computer-literacy program for middle-aged Filipino Americans was scheduled in 2001.

The Aguman Capampangan of Las Vegas (ACLV), an organization based on origins in the province of Pampanga, sponsors an annual celebration in honor of St. Anthony de Padua, with a fiesta and a grand raffle draw located at the Christ Episcopal Church.[29] The ACLV is working with the Agila Lions Club to raise funds for the renovation of the San Antonio de Padua Church in Barangay San Antonio, Guagua, Pampanga. It also supports the ABS-CBN Bantay Bata (Guard the Children) Foundation.

The first association of Bicolanos was the Bicolanos of Nevada, Inc., which has about sixty members, many of whom also belong to the Ilocano and Bisayan associations (in some cases because a spouse or parent belongs to one of these ethnic groups). A more recent association of Bicolanos is the Bikolnon. The Luzon (Phil) Association, whose basis of recruitment is origin on the main island of Luzon rather than ethnicity per se, has about forty members. Some people who belong to the Ilocano or Capampangan associations also belong to the Luzon (Phil) Association, which is composed of a mixed group of Bicolanos, Ilocanos, Tagalogs, and Visayans. The main celebration of the Luzon Association is the Santacruzan, held in May.[30]

Kahirup International (KI) limits its regular membership to natives of the islands of Panay and Negros (Occidental), so it also has an Ilonggo ethnic base. Sixty percent of its membership is in the medical fields, including medical technicians, nurses, and doctors. The KI sponsors family picnics, a scholarship program, and a medical program and is one of the sponsors of the Flores de Mayo festival held at Our Lady of Las Vegas Catholic Church. It donates medical books and equipment to the University of San Augustine, Iloilo City, has made donations to Shade Tree Shelter (a local shelter for women and children), participates in the cultural diversity training program for the city police, and is one of the sponsors of the National Conference for Community and Justice.[31] The activities of KI are sponsored by local branches of two national corporations.

The Ilocano-American Association of Nevada, Inc. (IAANI) has about four hundred members, of whom three hundred are active.[32] Every second year, on odd numbered years, the IAANI holds a "Filipiniana Affair" at the Castaways Hotel and Casino, featuring the wearing of traditional *terno* gowns with "butterfly" sleeves by the women and *barong* formal shirts by the men. There are also *sunka* games and performances of traditional folk dances in native costumes by the Pearl of the Orient cultural dance company, Ilocano folk songs by IAANI officers, and a formal exhibit of antique costumes. This group is active in politics as well, making courtesy calls on Nevada elected officials and obtaining the support of U.S. senator Harry Reid to cosponsor the Filipino World War II Veterans Bill in Congress. During the presidential election of November 2000, the IAANI initiated a nonpartisan Get-Out-The-Vote (GOTV) project, with participation from members of Samoan, Chinese, Vietnamese, Japanese, and Hispanic communities. They enlisted young families to distribute flyers and made eighty-one thousand phone calls to potential voters, offering rides if needed.

The IAANI has also addressed the excessive use of force by Las Vegas and Henderson police, as seen particularly clearly in the case of Jerry Waje, an Ilocano victim of a fatal police shooting on September 15, 1996.[33] Weekly candlelight vigils held at the city hall were instrumental in motivating the establishment of the Citizens' Review Board. The immediate past president of the group, Rozita Lee, is regional vice chair of the Southern California/ Nevada Region IX of the National Federation of Filipino American Associations (NaFFAA) and was also the chair of the NaFFAA's 4th National Empowerment Congress. She is a former producer and host of the PBS KLVX-TV 10 program *Spectrum*, a former special assistant to the governor, and a former president of the Women's Democratic Club of Clark County.

Common-Interest Associations

Other associations are based on significant common interests, such as health and military service, culture, and place of employment. They vary from formally organized and registered groups to very informal ones, which meet only occasionally. One of these is the Filipino American Club, which participates in celebrations such as the International Food Festival and sponsored parties. The club also conducts contests for Miss Philippines of Las Vegas. Other groups conduct contests for Miss Zamboanga, Miss Mindanao, and Miss Luzon.[34]

The Philippine Medical Association of Nevada (PMAN) was founded in 1995 with 25 members. Its membership has grown to 150 members, of whom about a third are retired physicians from all over the United States. The association was founded with three objectives: "community service, to foster camaraderie among Filipino physicians in the Nevada area, and the promotion of continuing medical education of its members by keeping abreast of advances in the field of medicine."[35] The PMAN conducts annual health fairs, with sponsorship from hospitals and pharmaceutical companies. It works with the Philippine Bisayan Society of Nevada in giving scholarships to deserving high-school students of Filipino heritage.

The Philippine Nurses Association of Nevada (PNAN), with 120 active members, was founded in 1991 with the objective of promoting and honoring the profession. The PNAN lobbies for employment benefits, job security, reasonable work shifts, nondiscrimination, recognition, and respect. It also provides continuing education seminars and lectures for its members and for nursing students, administers free breast exams and blood-pressure checkups at health fairs, and conducts other charitable activities as well as holding the annual Philippine Nurses Valentine's Ball.[36] Among the issues of concern for PNAN are the high rates of suicide and teen pregnancy among Asian youths. Another issue involved a bill introduced in the state legislature in the early 1990s that proposed allowing Canadian nurses to practice in Nevada without taking the licensing exam required for all others. The PNAN, led by founding president Belen Gabato, fought the bill, arguing that it was illogical to assume that a nurse is competent because of the country of origin. The bill failed.

The Filipino-American Servicemen's Association (FASMA) was founded in 1991 by U.S.-born Filipino servicemen returning from Clark Air Force Base. The functions of FASMA include monthly family-oriented get-togethers, fund-raisers, and participation in the Asian American Heritage celebration at Nellis Air Force Base. The group recognizes all Asian Americans. The Technical Organization of the Philippines (TOP) was formed in 1998 by a group of Filipino technical professionals in Las Vegas (architects, engineers, medical technologists, computer users, electricians, and members of other technical trades). The Web site of the group states: "The organization pursues educational, employment and financial opportunities for its members and the Filipino community." One of TOP's priority projects is to provide free classes on the use of computers for e-mail and access to the Internet. A branch of the Philippine American Youth Organization (PAYO) conducts programs for students of high-school and middle-school age. Classes in leadership, driving, and Philippine culture are conducted in donated space.[37]

In addition to these groups there are also the Filipino Music & Cultural Arts Foundation, the Filipino Association of Senior Citizens of Southern Nevada, the Agila Lions Club, and the Golden Agila Lions Club. The Association of Senior Citizens has plans to promote voter registration. The Desert Toastmasters Club, though open to all who wish to improve their skills in public speaking, was founded mostly by Filipinos.[38] At the University of Nevada, Las Vegas (UNLV), there is a branch of the Filipino American Students Association (FASA) and of LEO, which is a youth branch of the Lions Club. There are also informal associations, such as the lunch group of about a dozen Filipino employees at UNLV.

Businesses and Occupations

Thousands of Filipinos in Las Vegas work in law, education, retailing, entertainment, medicine, and service industries. They own businesses, organize associations, support charities, and sponsor festivals and educational events. Many contribute their time to advisory boards of local and state governments. In a list we made of over forty Filipino businesses in Las Vegas, we found that roughly half of the establishments are in the business of selling food.[39] We found twelve restaurants, ten food markets, and two bakeries, one of which is also a restaurant. Most of the markets are self-labeled as "oriental markets." We also found three publications, four businesses related to travel and the sending of goods and money overseas, and a variety of other service businesses. We know of no manufacturing or computer-related businesses with Filipino ownership in Las Vegas. The accommodation of different languages can be quite impressive in Filipino businesses. For example, Dental Care of Las Vegas, Inc., accommodates "English, Spanish, Tagalog, Ilocano, Kankanaey, Capampangan, etc."[40]

In addition to the business owners, many Filipinos and Filipino Americans work in the casinos as bellhops, dealers, sports and race book writers, change persons, restaurant/buffet staff, and security. One is a marketing manager for customers from the Far East. Outside the casinos they work in retail foods, restaurants, real estate, insurance and accounting firms, travel agencies, beauty parlors, auto-repair shops, and mortuary services. One is a boxing referee, another a boxing manager. Some are doctors, nurses, engineers, and lawyers. The director of case management at the University Medical Center (UMC) is Filipino, and a high percentage of the staff is as well. There are two Filipino American judges, one in family court and the other in municipal court. Filipino singers, musicians, and entertainers have performed in the major casinos. Some of the recognized talents are singers Jonathan Potenciano, who performed at the Palace Station; Bert Nievera; the Reycard Duet, who performed at lounges on the Strip and at Jackie Gaughan's Union Plaza Downtown during the 1960s and 1970s; Rudy Genasky, who was billed at the Roadhouse Casino on the Boulder Highway; and the Far East Band, which performed at the Excalibur Hotel and Casino. Singer Martin Nievera performed at the Golden Nugget in 2003.[41]

Religious Activities and Affiliations

Religion plays an important part in the daily lives of most Filipinos.[42] Prior to contact with Europeans, Filipinos believed in the supernatural deity called Bathalà, who rules over the earth. Traditional religion (*anito*) emphasizes worship of ancestors and otherworldly spirits, such as those of animals and natural objects, and there are also beliefs in ghosts (*multo*), witchcraft (*kulam*), a vampire that splits in two and develops wings on the upper body (*manananggal*), and a host of other spirits. It is believed that a person (*tao*) should comply with the laws and biddings of Bathalà or Diyós lest he or she incur the deity's ire. There is also traditional faith in the efficacy of psychic healers, midwives (*manghihilot*), herb doctors (*herbolaryo*), and fortune-tellers (*manguulat*).

Many Filipinos maintain both traditional and Christian beliefs. The Christian Spiritists Union of the Philippines has some fifteen thousand registered members and eighty psychic surgeons—the most notable of whom is Dr. Tony Agpaoa. Some local Filipinos patronize traditional fortune-tellers and spiritual healers, especially when Western medical practices prove ineffective.

Three centuries of Spanish rule over the islands established Catholicism as the predominant religion practiced by 83 percent of the population. Nine percent of Filipinos are Protestants, including fundamentalists and Mormons. The Protestants include Aglipayans, Baptists, Methodists, and Presbyterians, while the fundamentalists include Jehovah's Witnesses, Seventh-day Adventists, and Iglesia ni Cristo. Muslims make up 5 percent, and the remaining 3 percent are Buddhists, Taoists, Hindus, Jews, and "other" (which may include "no religion").[43]

During fiesta celebrations, especially in the provinces, Catholics hold religious processions in which images of Christ the Nazarene, Mary, and various saints are paraded along the major streets from and back to the church. Filipinos observe the national religious holidays of Holy Thursday, Good Friday, Easter Sunday, All Saints' Day, and Christmas Day. The reigning Roman Catholic prelate, Cardinal Jaime Sin, is one of the most influential religious leaders in recent Filipino history. During the Marcos dictatorship, Sin publicly denounced political corruption and the exploitation of the poor by the rich and landed families in the Philippines. Upon his bidding, nationalistic Catholic priests and nuns lent their support during the EDSA (Epifanio de los Santos Avenue) People's Power Revolution of 1986, which brought down Marcos.[44]

The majority of Filipinos in Las Vegas are Catholic, but unlike other areas that have large Filipino populations, such as Chicago, the Las Vegas diocese lacks a Filipino ministry and official Filipino organizations. However, through popular devotion a number of distinctly Filipino celebrations and prayer groups function at the parish level. These may use church facilities and request the participation of a Filipino American associate pastor.

In addition to observing all Catholic holy days and rites, many Filipino Catholics in Las Vegas also celebrate the feasts of Santo Niño de Pastor, St. Monica, St. Lorenzo Ruiz, the Mother of Perpetual Help, Santacruzan, Our Lady of Fatima, All Souls Day, and Simbang Gabi. Most feast days are celebrated by a mass, procession, and potluck. A few, such as Santo Niño (Holy Child), Our Lady of Fatima, and Santacruzan, also involve a house-to-house prayer rotation, as in the Philippines. Santo Niño is celebrated in January at Our Lady of Las Vegas, St. Anne, and St. Bridget Catholic Churches. The occasion for the celebration is the miraculous recovery of the unblemished white statue of Santo Niño, the child Jesus, which Magellan gave to the chief of the island of Cebu in 1521. According to legend, on a return expedition in 1565 the Spanish burned the village that held the statue to the ground, but by divine intervention the Santo Niño survived unmarked.[45]

Santacruzan is the reenactment of the quest of St. Helena, the mother of the fourth-century Roman Emperor Constantine. In Jerusalem, St. Helena gathered together eight crosses claimed to be the cross of Christ. A cross from Syria, which healed the lame and blind, was determined to be the true cross. In the Philippines, Santacruzan is celebrated on May 15. Each of the participants represents a figure in the Bible. In Las Vegas, where Santacruzan has been held since 1996, it has evolved in a secular direction, merging with Flores de Mayo and becoming a pageant featuring young women participating in evening gowns.[46]

The Feast of the Mother of Perpetual Help is celebrated the last Wednesday of June at Our Lady of Las Vegas. St. Monica, the mother of St. Augustine, is venerated for her perseverance. For twenty years she prayed for her wayward son Augustine, who did not believe in God. Augustine converted to Catholicism and became a bishop in Africa. Both saints' feast days fall in August, and both enjoy wide and popular observance in the Philippines. In Las Vegas a special prayer-group gathering marks the feast of St. Monica. St. Lorenzo Ruiz is the first Filipino saint. He was martyred in Japan during the persecutions of Filipino workers by Spanish priests. St. Lorenzo is celebrated by a mass and procession at Our Lady of Las Vegas in September. Our Lady of Fatima is celebrated with a mass and procession on the 13th of every month from May through October. The Blessed Mother appeared each of these days in Fatima, Portugal, in 1917. Our Lady of Fatima is recognized by all Catholics, but in Las Vegas it is predominantly Filipinos who attend the mass and organize processions. Simbang Gabi (Worship at Night) is the nine days of masses before Christmas. In Las Vegas the masses take place in the evenings at Our Lady of Las Vegas.

Religious groups organized by church members in Las Vegas include the Bible study group Banál na Pagaaral and Santo Niño, which brings the Virgin Mary to each house. Some Filipino Catholics in Las Vegas are also members of the Knights of Columbus, an officially sanctioned international Catholic fraternal benevolent association. We know of no Las Vegas chapter that is exclusively Filipino.

In the event of the death of a Catholic, private family masses are sometimes held to celebrate the fortieth day.[47] Others may be invited to attend in order to commiserate with the bereaved. After the mass, the house of the deceased is blessed by the priest to ensure that the spirit will not return to disturb the surviving relatives. The officiating priest first blesses the family altar by sprinkling the image of Santo Niño with holy water, then he blesses the room of the deceased, the living room, the main door entrance to the house, and, finally, the food on the table, which is shared by the entire family and their guests. Privacy and solemnity are the hallmarks of these events.

In Las Vegas there is a local chapter of El Shaddai, which is affiliated with El Shaddai in the Philippines. El Shaddai is a Catholic-sanctioned charismatic group with creationist and millennial doctrines. Weekly prayer meetings are held at the Knights of Columbus hall adjunct to the Prince of Peace Catholic Church. A meeting that we attended included a worship service in song led by a non-Filipino Pentacostal minister from Toronto, followed by a sermon in English and Tagalog by a minister from Los Angeles.[48]

Among other Christian religious organizations with substantial membership in the Philippines and some following in the United States are the Philippine Independent Church (Aglipayan), founded in the 1900s by Bishop Gregorio Aglipay and labor leader Isabelo de los Reyes of the Union de Los Obreros de Filipinas, and the Iglesia ni Kristo; neither appears to have an established congregation in Las Vegas. Though there is a large Muslim population in the southern Philippine islands of Mindanao and Sulu, there are few, if any, Muslim Filipinos in Las Vegas.

Wider Ties

The national chair of NaFFAA, Alex Esclamado, lives in Las Vegas and is active in the affairs of the local chapter. The fourth national convention of NaFFAA, held at Bally's Hotel in September 2000, was chaired by Rozita Lee, the immediate past president of the IAANI. In December 2001 the Nevada chapter sponsored a talk by Vicki Garchetorina, the chief of the presidential management staff for Philippine president Gloria Macapagal-Arroyo. Lee was also involved, with Paul and Vilma Gorre, in the establishment of the legislatively created Asian American Cultural Commission in 1993, becoming one of the fifteen commissioners. The bill establishing the commission, Assembly Bill 525, was supported by Gene Segerbloom and Dina Titus.[49]

The officers and directors of The Federation and the PCCSN also sit at the center of a wider network of regional and international contacts. The PCCSN in Las Vegas is a member of the Federation of Philippine American Chambers of Commerce (FPACC), which is based in Berkeley, California, but includes other regions. Kate Recto, president of the PCCSN, was vice president for the FPACC national conference, held in Las Vegas in 2000. Tonie Sison, a director of The Federation, is chair of the FPACC political-action group, vice chair of the Tourism Advisory Council of Las Vegas for the Philippines, and regional chair of the Lions International. The NaFFAA and The Federation cooperate with the Tourism Advisory Council of the Philippine Consulate in San Francisco and also maintain contacts with the mayor of Manila and the Manila Chamber of Commerce.[50] Prominent members of associations in both federations also have memberships on the mayor of Las Vegas's "kitchen cabinet," the Community Development and Recreation Board, the Nursing Board for Consumer Interests, the newly formed Las Vegas Asian American Foundation, the Concerned Asians of Nevada Development Association (CANDO), the Community Development Review Board, the Nevada Board of Health, and the Nevada Board of Chiropractors.

Ben Torres was appointed by Mayor Oscar Goodman as arts commissioner for the City of Las Vegas and will head the Las Vegas Centennial Celebration Committee. Dr. Rena Nora, a former president of the PMAN, is a member of the Nevada Commission on Mental Health and Developmental Service. Dr. Joey Villaflor, the current vice president of PMAN, is a member of the Nevada State Board of Health. The current president, Dr. Manuel B. Gabato, looks forward to establishing a medical mission to alleviate health problems among the needy in the Philippines. He anticipates working through UPLIFT Foundation, a nonprofit organization in Colorado with experience in volunteer work. In 2001 Nadia S. Jurani, a Filipino American CPA and law student at UNLV, was appointed by the governor to the Nevada Equal Rights Commission. Cheryl B. Nora-Moss, a Filipino American, was sworn into the Eighth Judicial District Court, Family Division, Clark County, an elective office. Nita Lopez-Tongson, a Filipino American, is the business-development coordinator at Clark County. She was awarded the Business Minority Advocate of the Year 2001 by the Nevada Minority Purchasing Council (NMPC). She also serves on a variety of other local and international organizations. Kahirup International, under President Haydee Florentino, supports programs in Iloilo, the Philippines. It also has ties with Tambalan U.S.A. and helps to sponsor the National Conference of Community and Justice. The Filipino American Students Association at UNLV is affiliated with the national students' organization. The Philippine Nurses Association coordinates with the American Heart Association and the American Stroke Association.[51]

Wider ties sometimes also involve Filipino youth. A senior-bound student at Clark High School, Paul "PJ" Gorre II, took part in the Presidential Classroom Scholars' program held at Georgetown University, Washington, D.C., in June 2002. The program gives 450 students from around the United States the opportunity to meet members of congress. PJ had one-on-one meetings with Nevada members of congress Shelley Berkley and Jim Gibbons and with senators John Ensign and Harry Reid, was a youth delegate to the NaFFAA 4th Empowerment Congress in 2000, and attended the Area Eleven Hawaii Leadership Academy of the Naval Junior Reserve Officers Training Corps NJROTC in 2001.[52]

When considering wider ties, it should not be forgotten that the Catholic Church, to which the majority of Filipinos belong, is a global institution. As we have mentioned, El Shaddai, itself an international organization sanctioned by the church, has ties to Pentacostalism, also a global institution.

Perhaps more important than any of the institutional ties to the Philippines are the active family and commercial ties maintained by many, if not most, Filipinos in Las Vegas. Many Las Vegas Filipinos fit the definition of the transnational citizen. Some commute to the Philippines at intervals of months or years to visit families, see to businesses, or occupy professional positions during certain months of the year. Some are able to sponsor family members to come to Las Vegas. Many send money and "*balikbayan* boxes" ("return to country boxes") full of American goods back to their relatives in the Philippines. These remittances and gifts make a crucial contribution to the Philippine economy. Economic exchanges and human movements between Las Vegas and the Philippines have not yet been quantified.

Conclusion

The network of Filipino organizations in Las Vegas directly involves a significant minority of Filipinos as members and connects other Filipinos by drawing them into festivals and other activities. These groups may split and form new groups, sometimes leading to the gradual demise of the original. In spite of the occasional fissioning of groups, there is widespread agreement that all Filipinos in Las Vegas are ready to unite behind common causes. The process has culminated in the current organization in which the NaFFAA, Nevada and The Federation serve as umbrella groups for over two dozen ethnic, regional, and common-interest groups. These groups form a network of multiple intersecting memberships at both the group and individual levels. The public events sponsored by the groups provide evidence of Filipino community and identity as well as opportunities for socialization through enjoyment of traditional foods, music, dance, and language. Programs such as voter registration, instruction in the use of computers, and the organization of nurses that are sponsored by the Filipino associations exert an important constructive influence on the Las Vegas community.

Due to rapid population growth in the 1980s and 1990s, Filipinos now constitute the largest Asian population in the city. Many live in the ethnically diverse neighborhood along East Charleston, and many new arrivers are purchasing houses in the upscale suburbs of Spring Valley, Summerlin, and Green Valley. Filipinos run over forty businesses, including many markets and restaurants. While few Filipino Americans have found management positions in the hotels and casinos, members of the educated and professional classes settle in the city with increasing frequency, either to retire or to work in their professional capacities. The Filipino American community in Las Vegas is predominantly Catholic, growing rapidly, and organizing vigorously, both socially and politically. Filipino Americans are striving for economic, educational, and social advancement and are bringing a distinctly island flavor to their enthusiastic participation in the community.

Notes

We wish to acknowledge the generosity and hospitality of the many Filipino Americans who provided interviews and other forms of assistance and welcomed us into their homes, offices, worship services, and social functions. Thanks especially to Sampaguita (Sammy) Alcedo, Rudy Crisostomo, Haydee Florentino, Belen and Manuel Gabato, Paul and Vilma Gorre, Teresita "Bing" Legaspi Janjua, Tessie and Pete Landas, Rozita Lee, Lolita Lopez, Leo Nanat, Pam Otado, Toots Parnell, Mrs. Mel Salazar, Rudolpho Santos, Diana Shoup, Tonie Sison, Adelfa Sullivan, Albert Vergara, and Father Frank Yncierto. Rozita Lee was particularly helpful in the final stages of editing. Due to limitations of time and the vagaries of chance, we have almost certainly omitted some important persons and stories from this account. We hope that someone, perhaps a Filipino scholar or graduate student, will follow up this small study with a major research project and a book. Thanks also to A. D. Hopkins for terrific editorial assistance and to Eugene P. Moehring for valuable information and to Miguel Llora for a careful reading.

Art Clarito, Heather Lawler, and Gary B. Palmer are equal coauthors of this chapter. Lawler got the ball rolling with a draft of the section on history and population. Clarito wrote the sections on religion and veterans, made contributions to other sections, provided essential perspectives based on his own lifetime experience as a Filipino, and used his knowledge of the Filipino community to arrange several interviews. Palmer edited and augmented the contributions of Lawler and Clarito, added sections on organizations, and integrated the final paper.

The spellings of some languages and ethnic groups vary, particularly with respect to the use of the letters *c* and *k*. The use of *c* is the older Spanish spelling. Thus we have Bikol and Bicolano, Kapampangan and Capampangan. We have used the spelling in our most recent source, which varies with context and personal preference.

1. Metropolitan Racial and Ethnic Change—Census 2000, at http://mumford1 .dyndns.org/cen2000/AsianPop/AsianPopData/4120msa.htm. The Lewis Mumford Center for Comparative Urban and Regional Research at the State University of New York at Albany makes estimates that are higher and probably more accurate than the U.S. Census count for most Asian, Latin American, and African American groups in the United States. Lawrence A. Reid listed "more than 80 indigenous languages" in *Philippine Minor Languages: Word Lists and Phonologies* (Honolulu: University of Hawaii Press, 1971), vii. Fe Aldave Yap cited "the 150 to 200 or more languages of the Philippines" in *A Comparative Study of Philippine Lexicons* (Manila, Philippines: Institute of National Language, Department of Education and Culture, 1977), xii. Many of the larger languages have several dialects. Languages coincide roughly with ethnic groups.

2. Luciano Mangiafico, *Contemporary American Immigrants: Patterns of Filipino, Korean, and Chinese Settlement in the U.S.* (New York, Westport, and London: Praeger, 1989), 41. See, for example, *The Flor Contemplacion Story* (Manila, Philippines, and Walnut Creek, Calif.; Viva Video, 1995) and *Modern Heroes, Modern Slaves*

(New York: Filmmakers Library, 1997). See *The Sara Balabagan Story* for a similar case (Manila, Philippines, and Walnut Creek, Calif.: Viva Video, 1997). See also Anne-Marie Hilsdon, "The Contemplacion Fiasco: The Hanging of a Filipino Domestic Worker in Singapore," in *Human Rights and Gender Politics in the Asia-Pacific,* ed. Anne-Marie Hilsdon et al. (New York: Routledge, 2000), 172–92. On debt bondage, name withheld, interview by Gary Palmer, Las Vegas, 1997.

3. Yen Le Espiritu, *Filipino American Lives* (Philadelphia: Temple University Press, 1995), 1. For a contemporary perspective on these events, see Vicente L. Rafael, *White Love and Other Events in Filipino History* (Durham, N.C.: Duke University Press, 2000). On St. Malo, Mangiafico, *Contemporary American Immigrants,* 31.

4. Espiritu, *Filipino American Lives,* 3.

5. Mangiafico, *Contemporary American Immigrants,* 32.

6. Espiritu, *Filipino American Lives,* 4.

7. Mangiafico, *Contemporary American Immigrants,* 36; Espiritu, *Filipino American Lives,* 15.

8. Carlos Bulosan, *America Is in the Heart: A Personal History* (Seattle/London: University of Washington Press, 1943).

9. Espiritu, *Filipino American Lives,* 10, 11; Bulosan, *America Is in the Heart,* 195; Veltisar Bautista, *The Filipino Americans from 1763 to the Present: Their History, Culture, and Traditions* (Farmington Hills, Mich.: Bookhaus Publishers, 1998); Bautista, *The Filipino Americans,* 135, 240.

10. Espiritu, *Filipino American Lives,* 13.

11. The information on veterans is from the lead article in the *Filipino Guardian* (San Francisco), November 30–December 13, 2001, 1; Richard Simon, "Filipino Veterans See Gains in Fight," *Las Vegas Review-Journal,* July 7, 2003, 10A.

12. Richard Simon, "Filipino Veterans Gain More Benefits," *Las Vegas Review-Journal,* December 17, 2003.

13. Espiritu, *Filipino American Lives,* 9. Filipinos from the United States infiltrated the Philippines and sabotaged Japanese communications equipment. This Filipino role in the war went entirely unnoted in the Hollywood film *An American Guerrilla in the Philippines,* made in the postwar years and starring Tyrone Power as an American who infiltrated Leyte and provided information on the movements of Japanese ships. On Filipinos in the United States, John M. Liu, Paul M. Ong, and Carolyn Rosenstein, "Dual Chain Migration: Post–1965 Filipino Immigration to the U.S.," in *Asians in America: The Peoples of East, Southeast, and South Asia in American Life and Culture,* ed. Franklin Ng (New York and London: Garland, 1998), 35.

14. On immigration, Epifanio San Juan Jr., *The Philippine Temptation: Dialectics of Philippines—U.S. Literary Relations* (Philadelphia: Temple University Press, 1996), 95; on doctors and nurses, Espiritu, *Filipino American Lives,* 21; Paul Ong and Tania Azores, "The Migration and Incorporation of Filipino Nurses," in *The New Asian Immigration in Los Angeles and Global Restructuring,* ed. Paul Ong, Edna Bonacich, and Lucie Cheng (Philadelphia: Temple University Press, 1994), 164–95; Ong and Azores, "The Migration and Incorporation of Filipino Nurses," 184–85.

15. On diversity, San Juan, *The Philippine Temptation,* 116. See also Gary B. Palmer, "*Sana'y Maulit Muli:* The Grammar of Agency and Emotion in a Tagalog Transnational Cinematic Melodrama," *Habi: Journal of English Studies and Comparative Literature* (Quezon City: UP-Diliman, forthcoming); Espiritu, *Filipino American Lives,* 22, 16; on 1972–86, Rick Bonus, *Locating Filipino Americans: Ethnicity and the Cultural Politics of Space* (Philadelphia: Temple University Press, 2000); San Juan, *The Philippine Temptation,* 15; Espiritu, *Filipino American Lives,* 19–20, 22. Lewis Mumford Center for Comparative Urban and Regional Research, "Asian Population Sortable List by Country Origin (Filipinos)" lists the populations of 331 U.S. cities. The sum of this list for the year 2000 is 2,196,952, at http://mumford1.dyndns.org/cen2000/AsianPop/AsianSort/filSort.html. The U.S. Census 2000 figure of 1,850,314 is disputed by Gloria Caoile, vice president of NaFFAA. She claims a more accurate number would by "2.5 million nationally." On Nevada Filipinos, Cherie M. Querol Moreno, "1,850,314 U.S. Filipinos," *Philippine News,* June 13–19, 2001, A1, A21. The article mistakenly estimates the increase shown in the Nevada census to be 236 percent. On migration to the United States, Ong and Azores, "The Migration and Incorporation of Filipino Nurses," 171.

16. Bulosan, *America Is in the Heart;* Jessica Hagedorn, *Dogeaters* (New York: Pantheon Books, 1990); Jose Garcia Villa, "The Anchored Angel," in *Brown River, White Ocean: An Anthology of Twentieth-Century Philippine Literature in English,* ed. Luis H. Francia (New Brunswick, N.J.: Rutgers University Press, 1993), 227–30. ("Death Comes to Doveglion / From Manila Enfant Terrible to Manhattan Writer, Mentor and Thinker, Jose Garcia Villa Lived for poetry," *Asiaweek.com,* August 1, 2001).

Profiles of other prominent Filipino Americans can be found in Bautista, *The Philipino Americans.*

17. Leo Nanat, interview by Art Clarito and Gary Palmer, Las Vegas, July 18, 2001. The Silver Slipper and the Sands were purchased by Hughes in 1967 and 1968, respectively. The Sands was built in 1952. Eugene P. Moehring, *Resort City in the Sunbelt: Las Vegas, 1930–1970* (Reno: University of Nevada Press, 1989).

18. Information on Oquendo was provided by Teresita "Bing" Legaspi Janjua, a niece of Rudy Oquendo. The Thunderbird, established in 1948, was later called the Silverbird, El Rancho. Manaois is pronounced [ma-NA-wis].

19. Crisostomo is currently Ambassador of the Zelzah Shrine Temple. Masters and past Masters of Masonic lodges are accorded a status of utmost reverence and respect by members of the fraternity. Only one other Filipino, Ben Racelis, current Master of Silver Cord Lodge #51, has attained such status.

20. We have been unable to verify the existence of a ship called the USS *Sultan,* but neither have we any reason to doubt Santos's account.

21. Leo Nanat, interview by Gary Palmer and Art Clarito, Las Vegas, July 18, 2001.

22. U.S. Census Web page, at http://www.census.gov/Press-Release/www/2001/tables/redist_nv.html#demoprofile, August 13, 2001; http://mumford1.dyndns.org/cen2000/AsianPop/AsianPopData/4120msa.htm; Steven Lum, No Ka Oi Realty, interview by Heather Lawler, Las Vegas, March 2001.

23. The information in this paragraph is based on interviews with Tonie Sison, who has been a realtor in Las Vegas since 1991, by Art Clarito and Gary Palmer, Las Vegas, June 26 and October 22, 2001. On Spring Valley, Steve Kaniger, "Asians Lead Minority Shift into Suburbs," *Las Vegas Sun*, July 22, 2001, 1D, 5D.

24. Kaniger, "Asians Lead Minority Shift," 5D.

25. The information in this section is based on previously cited interviews with Haydee Florentino, Leo Nanat, and Tonie Sison, as well as interviews with Rudy Crisostomo (June 24, 2001) and Albert Vergera (July 18, 2001) conducted in Las Vegas by Art Clarito and Gary Palmer, and with Vivienne Kerns and Father Frank Yncierto, who were interviewed by Heather Lawler in Las Vegas in 2000 and 2001. Additionally, it is based on observations and conversations at festivals; articles in the *Asian American Times, FIL Living in Las Vegas,* and *Asian Reader;* and the personal experience of coauthor Art Clarito. Region of origin and ethnicity are, of course, closely related. The current president of ACLV is Romy Ibe. Ernie Guiao, current president of the Agila Lions Club, is a past president of ACLV.

26. On "The Untouchables," Rudy Santos, interview by Art Clarito and Gary Palmer, Las Vegas, September 19, 2001. Assistance for the FC was received from U.S. Senator Howard Cannon and then District Attorney Harry Reid. Advisors for the organization were UNLV professor Antonio Lapitan, Father Jose Rico, and Al Hernandez, a decorated U.S. World War II veteran. A later president was Ven Manaois. The second president of the FAANI was Bert Kilates, the third Mellie Santos. Also active in the FAANI were Ven Manaois, Willie Vicuña, Gene Micu, Mel Salazar, Andres Santo Tomás, and Albert Vergara. Leo Nanat later served as president for six years. Some meetings were held in the Jade Garden from 1978 to 1981, when it was owned by Rudy Santos. The current president of FASCSN is Albert S. Vergara.

27. Meeting announcement in the possession of Gary Palmer. In 2002 Rozita Lee was the president of NaFFAA, Nevada.

28. Until 1999 there was a parallel Confederation of Filipino Americans of Nevada (COFAN) that was formed at the same time as the Federation. Organizations that were under COFAN evolved into the NaFFAA. The current president of The Federation is Art Macaraeg.

29. "2001 Feast of St. Anthony of Padua, June 9, Grand Raffle Draw for a 2001 Dodge Caravan," *Asian Reader,* June 2001.

30. The president of the Luzon Association is Bambi Quijano.

31. Kahirup International used to get ample write-ups in the society pages of the major metropolitan dailies in Manila. It used to be an elite club whose members came from the landed families of Iloilo and Negros provinces in Western Visayas. They held elaborate gala balls at the bigger hotels in Manila, where society matrons wore exquisite gowns made by well-known Filipino couturiers. Its president is Haydee Florentino.

32. Ilocano-American Association presidents are Rozita Lee, 2000–2001, and Amie Belmonte, 2001–2002.

33. Tanya Flanagan, "Two Officers Cleared in Fatal Shooting," *Las Vegas Review-*

Journal, October 15, 1996, 1B, 3B. Salli Fune, "Jury Rules Justifiable Homicide in Vegas Slaying," *Philippine News* 36, no. 13, November 20–26, 1996, 1–14. See also "Media Advisory," "Pilipino Americans for Justice," and "A Yellow Ribbon for Gerry," all October 1, 1996, press releases in possession of Gary Palmer. The inquest was perfunctory; copy in possession of Gary Palmer.

34. Rudy Crisostomo, interview by Art Clarito and Gary Palmer, Las Vegas, June 24, 2001. Crisostomo, who was elected president of the club shortly after his arrival in Las Vegas in 1963, says that his efforts to direct the club were hampered by arguments among the different ethnic groups, with divisions falling along the lines of "mountain, central, and southern." Being only twenty-seven years old at the time, with little experience of the different regions of the Philippines, he felt himself ill equipped to resolve the differences. Our interview was a memorable event, because it was followed by a dinner at a Chinese restaurant, during the course of which an armed robbery took place within ten feet of our table. Crisostomo was the only one present able to provide a useful description of the perpetrator.

35. "Philippine Medical Association of Nevada," *FIL,* March 2001, 24. The current president of FMA is Manuel B. Gabato, M.D.

36. "Philippine Nurses Association of Nevada," *FIL,* March 2001, 15.

37. The founder of FASMA was Edgar Balagtas, the first president, Bay Tumbocon. The current president is Nolan T. Fajota, who is the first native-born Filipino American to serve in that capacity. On TOP, Romy Jurani, interview by Gary Palmer, Las Vegas, August 2001. The organization's chairman is Sony Loreto. *Payo* means "counsel" or "advice" in the Tagalog language. The chair of the board of trustees of PAYO is Manuelita Patricio.

38. One of the founders of the Desert Toastmaster's Club was Las Vegas Municipal Court judge Cedric A. Kerns.

39. Without our having the resources for a thorough survey, the list is likely to be incomplete. We apologize to any business that has been inadvertently omitted. The list may be consulted at www.nevada.edu/ngbp/filipinos.

40. According to a brochure handed out at the Independence Day celebration at Lorenzi Park, June 10, 2001.

41. On the UMC, Belen Gabato, interview by Gary Palmer, Las Vegas, November 27, 2001. The UMC's director of case management is Haydee Florentino. On Filipino American judges, Cheryl B. Moss, 8th Judicial District Court, Family Division I, and Cedric A. Kerns, Las Vegas Municipal Court, Dept. 5. The information on performers is collated from numerous interviews, conversations, Filipino publications, and the personal experience of Art Clarito. On the Golden Nugget performance, see "Neon Up Front," *Las Vegas Review-Journal,* May 30, 2003, 1.

42. The information in this section is based on an interview with Father Frank Yncierto by Heather Lawler, the personal experience of Art Clarito, attendance at services as indicated, and Philippine ethnography. For the latter, see A. L. Kroeber, "The History of Philippine Civilization as Reflected in Religious Nomenclature,"

Anthropological Papers of the American Museum of Natural History, vol. 19, pt. 2 (1918): 35–67; Damiana L. Eugenio, ed. *Philippine Folk Literature: The Myths* (Quezon City: University of the Philippines Press, 1993).

43. *CIA World Factbook,* July 2000, at http://www.cia.gov/cia/publications/fact book/geos/rp.html.

44. This information and much of what follows concerning the Catholic Church was provided by Father Frank Yncierto, interview by Heather Lawler, Las Vegas, 2000. On Cardinal Jaime Sin, AFP, "Sin: We Have Become People of the Light," *Philippine Daily Inquirer,* January 22, 2001, 1; Benedict Anderson, "Cacique Democracy in the Philippines," in *Discrepant Histories: Translocal Essays on Filipino Cultures,* ed. Vicente L. Rafael (Philedelphia: Temple University Press, 1995), 3–47; also, personal knowledge of Art Clarito.

45. Santo Niño is the Filipino version of the Holy Infant Jesus of Prague. See Santo Niño de Cebu Association International, at http://www.santoninodecebu.org/history/default.html. According to the SNCAI Web page, the expedition of 1565 was led by the Augustinian priest Andres Urdaneta and was the occasion of fighting. According to Agoncillo and Guerrero, Urdaneta was the chronicler of the Loaysa Expedition in 1536. The expedition of 1565 was led by Miguel Lopez de Legazpi, and no fighting occurred. However, they mention Portugese attacks that occurred two years earlier. See Teodoro A. Agoncillo and Milagros C. Guerrero, *History of the Filipino People,* 5th ed. (Quezon City, Philippines: R. P. Garcia Publishing, 1977).

46. Father Frank Yncierto, interview by Heather Lawler, Las Vegas, 2000.

47. Ibid., telephone interview by Thomas C. Wright, Laughlin, Nevada, June 18, 2004.

48. *Nevada Examiner,* June 22–28, 2001, 26; August 1, 2001.

49. Unless otherwise stated, all listed officers of organizations held these offices in 2001.

50. Chairperson for TACLVP is Rita Vasuani; the first director of the AACC will be Tonie Sison. On the medical mission, "Philippine Medical Association of Nevada," *FIL,* March 2001, 24. On Nadia Jurani and Cheryl Nora-Moss, "Political Awareness Persons of the Year" and "Judge Moss Swears In," *Asian Reader,* June 2001. On Nita Lopez-Tongson, "A Woman for All Seasons," *Asian Reader,* June 2001, 14. Lopez-Tongson is also vice president of the Golden Agila Lions International Club, Nevada Chapter, and a member of the International Association of Business Communicators.

51. Tambalan@aol.com

52. Undated press release, "Presidential Classroom, Alexandria, Va.," and materials supplied by Paul Gorre Sr.

CHAPTER 13

The Salvadorans

THOMAS C. WRIGHT & JESSE DINO MOODY

The presence of a Salvadoran community in Las Vegas is a recent phenomenon. The 1990 census, the first to identify Salvadorans in Las Vegas, found 2,076 people of Salvadoran origin, making them the fourth largest Hispanic group in Las Vegas after Mexicans, Cubans, and Puerto Ricans. By 2000 Salvadorans had become Las Vegas's second largest Latino population. The 2000 census identified 7,180 Salvadorans living in the city. However, official figures for both years are not credible owing to the inconsistent, often confusing categories used by the Census Bureau and to immigrants' distrust of government intrusion. An independent research center places the number of Las Vegas Salvadorans at 12,242 in 2000, while local Salvadorans estimate between 25,000 and 40,000.[1]

Even the casual observer might detect growing signs of the Salvadoran presence in Las Vegas in the restaurants featuring *pupusas,* delicious, plump stuffed tortillas that are the signature Salvadoran dish. One also notices remittance services for sending money to El Salvador and vehicles bearing bumper stickers or decals proclaiming their owners' Salvadoran origin and identity. A bit of probing reveals more: a Salvadoran civic club, soccer teams, and businesses serving the needs of one of Las Vegas's fastest growing ethnic communities.[2]

Salvadoran Immigration to the United States

Salvadoran immigration to Las Vegas mirrors the broader U.S. trends. A small Central American country of 8,292 square miles, approximately the size of Massachusetts, El Salvador has a population of 6.6 million, making it the most densely populated country in the Western Hemisphere. Its per capita income in 2003 was estimated at $4,800, placing it behind Mexico and all South American countries except Bolivia and Ecuador, and in the middle range of the Central American republics. El Salvador was conquered and settled by the Spanish beginning in the 1520s, and it remained a Spanish colony until 1821. The great majority of Salvadorans are mestizos, people of mixed Indian and Spanish descent. The Salvadoran economy came to be dominated by coffee for export in the late nineteenth century; to enter the coffee-export market, the elites stripped the rural population of much of its land, thus proletarianizing most of the Salvadoran peasantry. Land reform has been a major issue since the 1960s and was a driving force behind the 1979–92 civil war.[3]

Historically, Salvadoran immigration to the United States has been very low. Neighboring Honduras absorbed much of El Salvador's excess population through the 1960s; a much larger and less populated country, Honduras had extensive vacant lands in its western half, abutting El Salvador, which Salvadorans colonized informally. Tensions over this phenomenon came to a head in the 1969 Soccer War, so called because it followed a series of hotly disputed games between the two countries' national teams. The Soccer War drove thousands of Salvadorans back across the border to their own over-crowded country, increasing pressures for the Salvadoran poor to migrate further afield. The 1980 U.S. census counted some 94,000 Salvadorans.[4]

The 1979–92 civil war was the major push factor that launched massive Salvadoran emigration. Thwarted in their attempts to democratize the corrupt, elite-dominated, repressive political system, leftist activists turned to guerrilla warfare in the late 1970s to effect change and improve the lives of common people. Following the 1979 Sandinista triumph in neighboring Nicaragua, the U.S. government viewed the Salvadoran left with suspicion and, under President Ronald Reagan, with hostility. Declaring the insurgency a Communist plot directed by a Moscow-Havana-Managua axis, the Reagan administration liberally supplied the Salvadoran military with training and weaponry, which the government turned against the civilian population as well as the guerrillas. Caught in the war between guerrillas and government troops, terrorized by paramilitary death squads, and further impoverished by the destruction of the economy, a large part of El Salvador's population was internally displaced, driven to neighboring Central American countries, or launched on the long and desperate trek to the United States. By the time peace was achieved in 1992, over 75,000 people, primarily civilians, had been killed and over a million had become refugees.[5]

From a nearly insignificant presence in the United States, Salvadorans by 1990 had become the fourth largest Latino group in the country; after growing by 92 percent in the 1990s, the Salvadoran population reached 1,117,959 in 2000, although it fell behind the faster-growing population from the Dominican Republic (1,121,257) to fifth place among Hispanic groups. Salvadorans were also outnumbered by Mexicans (23,060,224), Puerto Ricans (3,640,460), and Cubans (1,315,346). Roughly one sixth of El Salvador's population resides

and works in the United States. The Los Angeles area hosts the largest Salvadoran community, followed by the Washington, D.C., and Houston metropolitan areas, but Salvadoran immigrants are dispersed across the United
States.[6]

During the period of escalating immigration provoked by the civil war, the
U.S. Immigration and Naturalization Service (INS) very rarely granted asylum status to those fleeing the violence, including those with legitimate fears
of political persecution or worse in their homeland. Observers attributed this
to U.S. support of the Salvadoran government, whose forces were responsible
for the great majority of human-rights violations, including several that made
international news: the assassination of Archbishop Oscar Arnulfo Romero
(1980), the rape and murder of four American churchwomen (1980), the mas-
sacre of over one thousand villagers at El Mozote (1981), and the execution-
style slaying of six Jesuit priests in 1989.[7] This negative attitude toward Salvadorans contrasted with the favoritism shown Cubans leaving the Castro
regime, who automatically qualified for political asylum and hence legal residency.

Blatant discrimination against Salvadorans as well as Guatemalans fleeing
civil war and state terror in their country gave rise to the church-based sanctuary movement, which sheltered undocumented Central American immigrants and, in 1985, sued the government for violating the 1980 Refugee Act.
The 1990 settlement of the sanctuary suit as well as several legislative and
executive measures allowed many, but far from all Salvadorans in the United
States to legalize their status. At present, however, thousands of Salvadorans'
legal status in the United States is still based on short-term extensions of their
Temporary Protected Status (TPS), which includes permission to work.[8]

The war's end in 1992 did not end immigration, legal or illegal, to the
United States. The peace accord that ended the fighting stipulated democra-
tization, agrarian reform, and other measures designed to implement some of
the changes that the guerrillas had fought for. Despite progress in some areas,
poverty persisted into the new century and crime—even against the poor—
increased. The Salvadoran economy was crippled in 2001 by major earthquakes, drought, and a precipitous decline in coffee prices due to a glut in the
world market. While these developments made the journey to "El Norte"
obligatory for many of El Salvador's poor, the U.S. economy moved toward
recession; in the wake of the September 11, 2001, terrorist attacks, efforts to
ease immigration standards were suspended.[9]

Another important push factor that drives the continuing immigration
stream to the United States is El Salvador's "culture of immigration." This
culture is reflected in ubiquitous signs for "coyotes" (guides who charge for

the service of getting Salvadorans into the United States without papers) and remittance firms and a statue outside the capital's airport dedicated to "our distant brothers." The consumer goods and cash that returning Salvadorans bring with them confer status and stimulate others to follow their example. It has become almost a rite of passage for young men to migrate to the United States. The culture of immigration, the high percentage of Salvadorans living in the United States, the two-way cultural transmission, and the ease with which Salvadorans having legal papers travel back and forth have created a transnational community among Salvadoran immigrants.[10]

In the 1990s, as a result of the growing numbers of Salvadorans authorized to live and work in the United States, the means of immigrating have changed for many Salvadorans. Those joining established family members in the United States and in possession of papers can fly or take buses to the North. But for the majority, the passage to the North is even more perilous and daunting than it was in the 1980s as a result of the U.S. crackdown on illegal immigration and similar measures enacted by Mexico. Salvadorans without papers normally engage coyotes who charge between $3,000 and $10,000 to deliver immigrants across the U.S. border—if all goes well. This journey across two countries and three borders is recounted in the ballad "Tres Veces Mojado" (Three Times a Wetback), a reference to the rivers separating El Salvador from Guatemala, Guatemala from Mexico, and, along much of the border, Mexico from the United States. Death along the way is not uncommon, as the immigrants often have to cross deserts or are locked in airless trucks or trailers; thirteen of a group of thirty Salvadorans died of exposure in the Arizona desert in 1980, and the story has been repeated many times. Many undocumented immigrants experience abuse, robbery, and/or detention by Mexican authorities or bandits who prey on Central Americans. Women are sometimes sexually abused. If successful in crossing into the United States, the immigrants are sometimes held in detention by the coyotes until additional money is paid by family or friends as ransom. Even if the journey goes smoothly, the new arrivals start their new life deeply in debt to the relatives or friends who loaned the money for the coyote.[11]

After arriving in the United States, legally or illegally, Salvadorans follow patterns established in the 1980s. As did their predecessors in the great transatlantic migration to the United States, Salvadorans go to places where they have relatives or friends in order to find work, housing, and assistance in overcoming the language barrier. Those receiving the new arrivals are normally from the same hometown, be it a small village or the capital, San Salvador. This settlement pattern replicates Salvadoran societies at home and gives rise to hometown associations—an important form of social organization for Salvadoran immigrants. These associations send money or goods for projects in their hometowns; they were very active in providing relief for the 2001 earthquakes. Larger U.S. metropolitan areas have Salvadorans from multiple sending locations, while smaller locales might have Salvadorans from a single sending town.[12]

Finding work is the primary objective of Salvadoran immigrants, and the booming U.S. economy during the 1990s provided an abundance of jobs. Usually lacking education beyond the primary level, skills other than those associated with agriculture, the use of English, and papers, Salvadorans necessarily settle for whatever is available when they arrive at their destination. These jobs vary from place to place according to the local economies, but they have in common insecurity, low pay, and a lack of benefits. In short, newly arrived Salvadorans must take the jobs that no one else wants. When between jobs, some join the ranks of immigrants and native born at the casual labor-pickup points, and sometimes they become homeless.[13] The title of a book chapter on Central Americans in Los Angeles aptly describes the situation of many Salvadorans—particularly the most recently arrived—in the United States: "At the Bottom; Struggling to Get Ahead."[14]

Salvadorans follow the general pattern of immigrants settling into new lives in the United States. After starting at the bottom, they tend to move to better paying, more secure jobs, although normally remaining in the construction, manufacturing, and service sectors where English is not required and skills can be learned on the job. Salvadorans have a reputation for being hard, reliable workers, which appears to give them an edge in employment. They have done particularly well in the Washington, D.C., area, owing to an early presence there and a prolonged construction boom.[15]

Despite their struggles to survive and move up the economic ladder, most Salvadorans save money to send home to support their families. In the mid-1990s remittances from the United States were estimated conservatively at between seven hundred million and one billion dollars per year; by 2002 the figure may have reached two billion dollars, or two thousand dollars for every Salvadoran man, woman, and child in the United States. A major Salvadoran bank has opened branches in several U.S. cities to facilitate the flow of funds. Remittances are the leading source of foreign exchange, far exceeding the value of Salvadoran exports and accounting for over 10 percent of the gross domestic product. There is no part of El Salvador that does not benefit from remittances. As is the case for Mexico and several Central American and Caribbean countries, El Salvador has become absolutely dependent on the export of labor to the United States. Without many of their people holding jobs in the United States and subsidizing the poor at home, these countries would face imminent disaster.[16]

While individual transmission of money to families back home accounts for most of the remittances, another form of remittance is the collective donation of material improvements by hometown associations to the villages and towns they left behind—such things as funds to pave a road, build a school, refurbish a church, or support a clinic. This massive transfer of resources—both individual and collective—is generated not only by established immigrants with steady jobs but also by recent arrivals working at the bottom of the occupational pyramid. For them, supporting their families at home is accomplished only by persistence, frugality, the holding of several jobs when possible, and the pooling of resources for housing, food, and transportation.[17]

A look at Nombre de Jesús, a town of some 1,500 inhabitants in Chalatenango Department northeast of the capital on the Honduran border, confirms this general pattern. Nearly all the young men and several young women of this town have worked in the United States or are there now. Some migrate with papers, others the old-fashioned, dangerous way—hiring a coyote and taking their chances. They go where they have contacts to help with getting settled and finding work. In the case of Nombre de Jesús, the primary migration destination is the Washington, D.C., area, with the greatest concentration in Alexandria, Virginia. The new arrivals take the usual kinds of jobs: the least skilled, the lowest paid, the least secure.[18]

The effects of migration are very visible in this remote corner of El Salvador. Those who succeeded and returned live in cement-block houses with concrete floors, in sharp contrast to the prevailing adobe houses with dirt floors; they have U.S.–style appliances and may own a vehicle. Some have bought land, herds, or stores. Some residents of Nombre de Jesús have attained legal residency in the United States, which allows them to go back north when cash is needed. A main subject of conversation is the movement of fellow townspeople and their lives in Alexandria and vicinity. A visible reminder of absent family and friends is the new Ford ambulance parked in the town plaza, a collective remittance from the absent sons and daughters of Nombre de Jesús.

Salvadoran Immigrants in Las Vegas

Salvadorans in Las Vegas have much in common with their compatriots across the United States, while being influenced by the peculiarities of the local setting. The arrival of the first Salvadorans in Las Vegas is unrecorded, but by the early 1970s there was a tiny nucleus of what would become a recognizable and growing community by the 1980s. By 2000 Salvadorans were gaining recognition as a distinct national group among Hispanics, although still overwhelmed numerically by southern Nevada's burgeoning Mexican and Mexican American population—the only Hispanic group to outnumber them in Las Vegas.[19]

In common with Salvadoran immigrants throughout the United States, Las Vegas Salvadorans are drawn largely from the urban and small-town working class and from the impoverished peasantry. The immigrants tend to have less than a full primary education, and some are illiterate. A substantial number had migrated from small towns to San Salvador before coming to the United States. Like the U.S. cities with large Salvadoran populations, Las Vegas draws from all parts of the country, although several informants have the impression that Usulután Department is disproportionately represented. This pattern contrasts with some smaller U.S. cities, whose Salvadorans may arrive through migration streams from one or a few specific towns or regions. There is also a minority representation in Las Vegas of persons of middle-class background who lived above the poverty level and attained at least a partial high-school education.

Both economic and political motives underlie Salvadoran migration to Las Vegas. Before the escalation of violence in the late 1970s, economic motives drove the migration, as changing patterns of production pushed campesinos off the land and the aspirations of middle-class people were frustrated by a stifling lack of socioeconomic mobility.[20] In the words of a Las Vegas Salvadoran who immigrated to Los Angeles in 1972, "I came to this country for the money."[21] From the late 1970s onward, as the country descended into violence and further impoverishment, emigration was fueled by political concerns often underpinned by economic necessity.

Some Las Vegas Salvadorans prudently decided to emigrate in order to escape the escalating violence. Several had family, friends, or classmates assassinated at the hands of police or paramilitary units. One man who left in his teen years because of crackdowns on high school students reported: "It was dangerous to be a young person." Expressing a common sentiment, another local Salvadoran said simply: "I was afraid of being killed."[22]

Others were literally driven out of El Salvador by the violence. José Vargas, a small farmer who sought to avoid participating in the conflict, was caught between pro-government and guerrilla forces and forced to flee when neutrality became impossible. Marina Vargas, his wife, stayed behind with the children, but in 1981 residents of her rural zone were given twelve hours' notice to get out before a major government air and ground campaign was to begin against local guerrilla units. Having never left home, she fled with her year-old son, a fifteen-year-old niece, and only the possessions she could carry.[23]

Manuel Franco was a leader of the transport workers' labor confederation at a time when that position marked one for death at the hands of the notorious death squads; forced to flee San Salvador, he joined the FMLN (Frente Farabundo Martí de Liberación Nacional) guerrillas. After a year he could no longer endure his "suicide" assignment of driving supply trucks through numerous government checkpoints to guerrilla territory. At that point, "the solution was to get out, to the United States."[24]

A few of our informants, primarily middle-class persons with family already in the United States, were able to fly north and enter legally, although in some cases they subsequently became illegal by overstaying their visas. For the majority the journey was much less pleasant, as they came overland without entry papers, following the many variants of the "Tres Veces Mojado" script. Some relied on relatives in the United States to loan them money for a coyote to arrange the entire journey. Others, with fewer resources, took their chances, setting off on their own through Guatemala and Mexico and engaging a local coyote in Tijuana or Ciudad Juárez to get them across the U.S. border. Whether transnational or local, the coyote was a key figure for everyone. In an arranged trip, emigrants pay the coyote an all-inclusive fee reaching the $10,000 range. The coyote obtains exit papers, buys the bus and train tickets, pays the required bribes along the route, and, if all goes well, delivers the travelers safely inside the United States. Those lacking the funds for a transnational coyote must cross the Guatemalan and Mexican borders at unguarded places, make their way north by bus or train, and hire a local coyote at the U.S. border for a reported minimum fee of $300.[25]

While the long trip went smoothly for a few, for most it was plagued with inconveniences, misfortune, or worse. Those with arranged trips sometimes arrived at the U.S. border only to be detained and deported. Those who crossed safely often faced the additional trauma and danger of getting past INS checkpoints on highways leading north from the border. As a child of eleven, Manuel Rivas arrived in Los Angeles in a refrigerated truck with 155 others. Héctor García was abandoned by his coyote in Ciudad Juárez, detained in Las Cruces, New Mexico, and subsequently deported on the second of his three crossings.[26]

Those people lacking the resources for an arranged trip usually faced greater hardships and spent a longer time en route. When forced to flee her home in 1981 with her infant son and adolescent niece in tow, Marina Vargas crossed Guatemala and then made the acquaintance of another Salvadoran and three Guatemalans on a bus to Mexico City. They engaged a taxi at the bus station, but the driver took them to some abandoned buildings on the out-skirts of the capital, where several police with drawn pistols joined the driver in taking the little money they had. Following that, "gracias a Dios," a passing bus driver took pity on them and carried them north to Querétaro, where Marina had a contact who provided shelter but had no money to offer. By begging for used clothing in wealthy neighborhoods and selling it in poor districts, she raised passage money to the border but, with child at breast, had to stand the three days on the train. After living two weeks in the open in Tijuana, she engaged a local coyote who left the three in a San Diego garage for four days with insufficient food and water. Eventually, she was able to join her husband in Las Vegas.[27]

Felipe Umaña was a student when he fled El Salvador in 1980 to escape death threats after some fellow students had been killed. He found that cross-ing Guatemala was easy, but Mexico was a challenge. He was assaulted, robbed, and reduced to begging. Despite paying the usual bribes to police, on another attempt to reach the United States he was jailed, robbed again, and deported to El Salvador. He made it across the U. S. border on his fifth try.[28] Marina Vargas, Felipe Umaña, and other Salvadorans in Las Vegas and throughout the United States are the lucky ones. For countless others, the description given by Father Flor María Rigoni, director of a Mexican shelter for Central Americans, tells the grim story of the trek: "The migrant's route is a cemetery without crosses."[29]

Marina and José Vargas are among the minority of our informants whose initial destination in the United States was Las Vegas. Almost all Salvadorans who came directly to Las Vegas after crossing the border had family in the city, some of whom date back to the tiny community that existed by the mid-1970s. A few had good contacts in Las Vegas through family members. The majority of Las Vegas Salvadorans, however, reached southern Nevada through secondary migration from Los Angeles. Los Angeles was a natural and comfortable destination for arriving Salvadorans without legal status for several reasons. From the 1960s on, it hosted the largest Salvadoran commu-nity in the United States, so almost everyone had a relative, friend, or towns-man there; it is close to a border that was relatively easy to cross until the crackdown of the 1990s; and with its millions of Mexicans and Mexican Americans, Los Angeles provided a sanctuary for Central Americans, a place where one's whole life could be conducted in Spanish and, broadly speaking, within one's cultural norms. Most of these secondary migrants spent a few years in Los Angeles and moved to Las Vegas upon learning of the opportuni-ties provided by the burgeoning economy and cheaper cost of living.[30]

Like those direct from El Salvador, most of those coming from Los Angeles to Las Vegas counted on family or friends for help in adjusting. Given the strength of family ties among Salvadorans, those with close family normally fare better than those with more casual contacts in Las Vegas. Since many established Salvadorans in Las Vegas own homes, arriving family members are often accommodated for a year or more while they find work. Migrants lacking such binding ties usually go into shared, inexpensive apartments featuring low move-in costs and small deposits in neighborhoods such as the area around Clark High School, the area west of the Boulevard Mall, and the Naked City area just west of the Strip. For those needing it, assistance is available through the Nevada Association of Latin Americans (NALA) for finding housing and work and for learning English.[31]

The essential thing to do upon arrival is to find work. Since Salvadorans in the United States have the reputation of being hard, reliable workers, it may be easier for them than for some others to find jobs.[32] Entry into the local labor force is normally at the bottom in low-paying, non-union positions: kitchen help, unskilled construction jobs, house and office cleaning, landscaping, car washing. These jobs are normally secured through an informal recruitment pattern in which workers themselves recommend their friends or relatives, saving employers the expense of formal labor recruitment. The majority of our informants indicate that their relatives or friends took them to work with them when a vacancy occurred or, in some cases, placed them in jobs that they were vacating for better positions. In these first jobs for arriving Salvadorans, a leveling of the home country's strict social stratification occurs. People who were teachers, accountants, medical doctors, or business owners at home mop floors or fold sheets side by side with peasants and laborers. As a former dishwasher put it, "An engineer there has to wash dishes here with peons."[33]

Like other workers, Salvadorans in Las Vegas normally progress beyond these initial jobs into positions that require more skill and responsibility and pay considerably above the minimum wage. Some remain in their initial positions and move up the wage scale on the basis of hard work, skill, and longevity. Others take advantage of Las Vegas's expanding economy by shifting to other lines of work and learning the needed skills on the job. Despite this mobility, the situation of the majority of Salvadorans who are not union members is aptly summarized by a long-term restaurant busperson: "The boss always requires more of the 'Hispanic' and pays less." As for job security, in the words of another informant: "Do the job right. Security is a result of Salvadorans' being good, hard workers and doing tasks others might not do."[34]

Construction companies and hotel casinos are the largest employers of Salvadorans in Las Vegas. By most calculations, work in the strip and downtown hotel casinos that have contracts with the Culinary Workers Union, Local 226, is the best available to unskilled workers with minimal English. The union, moreover, has an impressive training program that since 1993 has placed some 2,500 people per year, many of them immigrants, in these jobs. Most work behind the scenes in kitchens, as housekeepers, and in other jobs that do not require interaction with guests. At The Mirage, of the primarily Hispanic noncooking kitchen staff of 292, 112 are Salvadoran. Of The Mirage's total 7,000 employees, some 500 are Salvadoran; collectively, other hotel-casinos employ thousands of Salvadorans. Under contract with the Culinary Workers Union, kitchen workers at the big resorts earn an average of $12.90 per hour, housekeepers $11.35, and both receive health, pension, and vacation benefits as well as free meals during their shift.[35] A Salvadoran (or any other) couple working at a resort hotel can make approximately $50,000 per year, save on the grocery bill, and—if they lack family members to care for the children—can avoid child care expenses by working different shifts. This is a ticket to home ownership and the consumer culture that typifies Las Vegas.

Alongside these stories of realizing the American dream, there is a large pool of Salvadorans who have not progressed beyond entry level. Many are recently arrived from El Salvador, and many of these are among the individuals lacking legal status—perhaps between 5 and 10 percent of all Salvadorans in Las Vegas.[36] They cannot be hired in businesses associated with gaming, because these require a special sheriff's work card, which in turns requires legal papers. It is difficult to obtain a driver's license without legal status, shutting off another area of employment. As a result, they take jobs that pay minimum wages or less and may be forced to work two or more jobs.

The construction industry illustrates the difficulties of the recent, undocumented Salvadoran immigrant. Bosses reportedly prefer to hire legals, but when demand for labor is high, they hire the undocumented for the least skilled positions. Whereas Salvadorans with papers who have learned skills and acquired some seniority can make $12 per hour or more, the undocumented make around $6—although neither group receives benefits. Moreover, there are ways to cheat entry-level workers out of their modest wages, such as requiring them to sign blank time sheets that are later filled in by a supervisor and starting and stopping their time clocks at the construction site although two or more additional hours may be spent in the company yard and en route. Thus for a ten-hour day, they may be paid at $6 per hour for eight hours or less.[37] These are the Salvadorans who, along with Mexicans,

Guatemalans, and others, live twelve or fifteen to an apartment, with one sleeping in the bathtub and several on the floor, in the cheapest areas of town. Yet most of them have wives and children, and/or parents and siblings to support at home, and they normally make their contribution to the nearly $2 billion remitted annually by Salvadorans in the United States.

There is a small group of Salvadorans who do not do manual labor in Las Vegas, although most of them graduated from entry-level jobs to the positions they now hold. Among the owners of small businesses are restaurateur Sabino Abrego; computer service owner Walter Serrano; concrete company owner Felipe Umaña; market and courier service owners Blanca and Manuel Orellana; Dalia Merino, proprietor of a beauty salon; and travel agency owner Francisco (Frank) Canales. Salvadorans in management positions include Zoila Panameño, executive steward at the Mirage Hotel and Casino, and Héctor García, general manager of Carbon Block Technology, a water filter manufacturing plant that employs nearly three hundred people. The list of Salvadoran professionals is small; it includes a dental assistant, Rosario García; attorneys José and Soveida Cornejo; a medical doctor, Dr. Carlos Anaya; civil engineer Erick Mendoza; and Professor Francisco Menéndez, chairman of the film studies department at the University of Nevada, Las Vegas, whose recent film, *Medio Tiempo,* deals with the same themes covered in this chapter.[38]

While this is far from an exhaustive list, it is notable that the Salvadoran business and professional community is in its embryonic stage. Among the reasons for this is the difficulty of passing examinations for licensure, required in many professions and businesses and given only in English. Felipe Umaña says of the contractor's license exam, which he took five times in California and four in Nevada before passing it: "It's very hard and tricky for Spanish speakers." A number of cosmetologists are limited to being beauticians' assistants because of the language barrier.[39] Obtaining credit on favorable terms is another obstacle facing Salvadorans interested in starting businesses.

This small business and professional group and the much broader, maturing group of Salvadorans who hold steady and remunerative jobs, own homes, and enjoy the normal American amenities constitute a solid, permanent Salvadoran community in Las Vegas. While many express dismay at being forced out of their homeland and bitterness about their initial treatment in the United States, including discrimination that began at the border crossing, they are also thankful for the chance to put their lives back together and help family in El Salvador. They have adjusted to the realities, opportunities, and problems of Las Vegas and the United States. Most visit El Salvador periodically but admit the impossibility of adjusting to life there after a decade or even less in the United States.[40] Many have acquired U.S. citizenship. Children are a major focus of their lives. Some express worry about gang influence and a high dropout rate from school, while they recognize and value their children's educational opportunities and have high aspirations for their careers. In short, Salvadorans in Las Vegas are following the trajectory of immigrants in general.

Community Institutions

While the Salvadoran population is growing rapidly and sinking roots in Las Vegas, it lacks some of the community institutions of its counterparts in other, larger U.S. cities. Missing in Las Vegas are hometown associations, found among Salvadorans in other American cities, that provide a sense of community while aiding the areas from which their members emigrated. Unlike many Las Vegas immigrant groups, Salvadorans apparently have no folkloric organization to perform Salvadoran music and dance.

Although various Salvadoran clubs have been formed over the years, none has lasted. The latest version, the Fundación Salvadoreña (Salvadoran Foundation), was established in 1998. The foundation promotes voter registration among citizens, assists with the legalization of the undocumented, bestows achievement awards, and coordinates activities with visiting Salvadoran officials and dignitaries. It maintains contact with other western Salvadoran organizations and with the new national organization, the Comisión Nacional de Salvadoreños (CONASAL), and lobbied for the establishment of a Salvadoran consulate in Las Vegas. Despite the Salvadoran Foundation's efforts to raise community consciousness, most local Salvadorans either ignore its existence or, if they are aware of it, do not know what it does.

Although lacking broadly supported voluntary associations, Salvadorans have other community institutions through which they socialize and affirm their culture. Las Vegas has around ten Salvadoran restaurants, some of which identify themselves as Mexican and Salvadoran, following the normal pattern of purveyors of a cuisine that is little known to the broader public. Besides serving food and drink from home, they play Salvadoran music and videos and have available the local Spanish-language newspapers and the weekly *El Salvador* from Los Angeles. There is only one Salvadoran market, but a few Salvadoran products may be found in the more numerous and larger pan-Hispanic and Mexican markets. Since almost all Salvadorans send money home to relatives, either regularly or sporadically, they may meet at one of the many money remittance agencies such as Urgente Express or the Tienda El Salvador, whose owner is also a courier who competes with the money wire services by traveling twice monthly to El Salvador, where, in his automobile, he delivers money, letters, and packages to the remotest hamlets reachable by road.[41]

Salvadoran musical groups, including Los Hermanos Flores, Grupo Algodón, and Fiebre Amarilla, play to large crowds, often at Jerry's Nugget casino in North Las Vegas or El Rey Night Club on Twain Avenue, while touring U.S. cities with sizable Salvadoran populations. This provides opportunities for camaraderie and dancing several times annually.

Soccer is a central institution for Las Vegas Latinos, including Salvadorans. Las Vegas has six organized soccer leagues with nearly three hundred teams; at an average of eighteen players per team plus coaches and referees, organized soccer includes some six thousand men, over 90 percent of them Hispanic. Many teams are of mixed nationalities, with Mexicans normally dominating, but there are approximately twelve Salvadoran teams, including Once Lobos, ADET, and Atlético Cabañas, which play in the Liga Centroamericana de Fútbol. The leagues' season unfolds during the cooler months, September through May, although games continue over the summer despite the notorious Las Vegas heat. The season culminates with the interleague Copa Univisión in June, sponsored by television channel 15. In 2001 the champion was a Mexican team, Real Autlense; the following year, Inter United, largely Mexican with some Salvadoran players; in 2003, Cruz Azul, primarily Mexican American.[42]

Soccer is much more than a game. On Saturdays and particularly Sundays, the soccer fields in Las Vegas parks and schools are filled with players, families, vendors, and fans—even in summer, despite a shortage of bleachers and shade. For many players and coaches, and sometimes their families, Sundays revolve around soccer. After their game they may watch other games and often will repair to someone's home for a barbecue or to a Salvadoran restaurant. The day may include an excursion to Lake Mead, Red Rock Canyon, or Mount Charleston and watching international soccer on television. From a coach's perspective, soccer is a tool for building discipline and morality among young Salvadoran workers, especially those who experience low-paying jobs and overcrowded living conditions. Liga Centroamericana founder and director Abel Cuevas and Atlético Cabañas coach Manuel Rivas are proud of their roles in providing alternatives to the drinking, drugs, and violence that would tempt poor young men in an alien environment.[43]

Soccer team sponsorship provides another insight into the centrality of soccer in Salvadoran and Latino culture in Las Vegas. Restaurants, sporting-goods stores, hotels, and other businesses sponsor teams, providing the shoes and uniforms with their logos and paying the teams' league dues and referee costs. Construction companies sponsor many of the teams, consisting of their own workers, although the companies' role is often invisible because—while underwriting all the costs—they allow the players to name their teams for their hometown or region or for professional teams in their home countries. Construction company sponsorship does not necessarily spring from interest in soccer or, in many cases, from concern for their workers' needs; rather, it is a tool for building employee loyalty in a setting of constantly expanding demand for good construction workers. In one expert's view, "workers regard the man who gives them shoes and uniforms as a god."[44] It is also suggested that through team sponsorship, construction companies make their workers loyal and happy enough so that they are less likely to ask for raises or be upset if denied.

Many Salvadorans indicate that religion is an important part of their lives. Traditionally Catholic El Salvador has recently become more religiously diverse, as Protestant missionaries have enjoyed wide success in the country. Those Salvadorans who have embraced Protestantism, either in the home country or in the United States, generally belong to the fundamentalist denominations that encourage participation in several events per week. For some, the Spanish-language churches they attend become the primary locus of social life. Catholic Salvadorans attend mass at one of the several parishes that offer mass in Spanish. Whether Protestant or Catholic, Salvadorans mix with other Latinos at worship. Thus, rather than institutions that reinforce Salvadoran culture, Spanish-language churches are institutions of the broader Hispanic culture of Las Vegas.

Several factors may explain why Las Vegas Salvadorans do not have more community institutions. Unlike their countrymen in Los Angeles and the Washington, D.C., area, Salvadorans do not have a core residential and business area of their own. Rather, they live and patronize restaurants and other businesses throughout the greater Latino district of North Las Vegas and central and eastern Las Vegas. Salvadorans as well as other Las Vegas Hispanics live their lives within the extensive Spanish-speaking community largely created and dominated by Mexicans. Given the relatively small differences in language and the general cultural affinity between the two nationalities, it may be difficult for Salvadorans to assert themselves so as to establish a separate identity in concrete, formal ways.[45] Finally, there are the factors that dampen participation in all ethnic organizations in Las Vegas: the twenty-four-hour, seven-day work schedule in which many Salvadorans participate and the individualistic culture that is a Las Vegas hallmark.

Recent developments are likely to have an impact on Las Vegas's Salvadorans. In April 2002 the Central American Coalition of Nevada was founded to "serve and empower the Central American communities" of Las Vegas and the state. Joining forces under the slogan "Seven countries, one voice," the Central American Coalition has already made a mark; thanks to its lobbying, Governor Kenny Guinn proclaimed April 1 as Central American Day in Nevada. The ceremony marking the first Central American Day, April 1, 2003, was attended by the Los Angeles–based consuls of four of the countries. In 2004 and beyond, the coalition plans to hold a joint celebration of the independence day common to all Central American countries except Panama and Belize, September 15, complete with a pageant that will crown the "Miss" of each country.[46]

The second and third developments were closely linked. On January 16, 2004, the Banco Salvadoreño, one of El Salvador's largest banks, opened a branch in Las Vegas. The following day, Salvadoran foreign minister María Eugenia Brizuela de Avila inaugurated a consulate general on North Nellis Boulevard, in a heavily Latino district. This is the second Latin American consulate established in Las Vegas, following the Mexican consulate, which opened in 2002. With jurisdiction over Nevada, Arizona, Utah, and part of Colorado, the consulate will pursue international business contacts and promote Salvadoran community activities and organizations. Because it issues passports and other important documents, it will attract visits by Salvadorans from within its four-state purview. The consulate and the bank may become magnets for Salvadoran businesses, foster the growth of small groups of professionals, and contribute to the formation of a Salvadoran spatial community presently absent in Las Vegas.[47]

The continued growth of Las Vegas's Salvadoran population, combined with the potential impacts of the consulate, the bank, and the Central American Coalition, will likely give Salvadorans a heightened profile within both the Hispanic and the broader Las Vegas communities. At present, however, Salvadoran culture is best experienced within the family and in the home. There, values are preserved and transmitted, traditions are enacted, and immigrants long for the homeland and the relatives and friends left behind, even as their children grow up much the same as other hyphenated Americans, past and present.

Notes

The authors sincerely thank everyone who shared with us their knowledge of Salvadorans in Las Vegas. These individuals and the dates of our interviews with them in Las Vegas, in alphabetical order, include: Sabino Abrego, July 20, 2000; Dr. Carlos Anaya, August 2, 2001; Jennifer Angel, July 9, 2003; Francisco (Frank) Canales, July

13, 2000, June 21, 2001; Clarissa Cota, September 7, 2000; Abel Cuevas, July 12, 2001; Manuel Franco, August 9, 2001; Zullie Franco, August 3, 2000; Héctor García, June 22, 2001; Rosario García, June 22, 2001; Eduardo López Rajo, July 20, 2000, July 19, 2001; Efraín Martínez, June 21, 2001; Dalia Merino, August 4, 2001; Vicenta Montoya, August 17, 2001; Modesto Neftalí Gómez, August 6, 2001; Blanca Orellana, June 19, August 7, 2001; Salvador Panameño, August 2, 2001; Zoila Panameño, August 2, 2001; Margarita Rebollal, July 24, 2000; Manuel Rivas, August 6, 2001; Elías Samarano, July 25, 2000; Walter Serrano, July 19, 2001; D Taylor, May 23, 2001, July 9, 2003; Felipe Umaña, June 28, 2001; José Vargas, June 24, 2001; Marina Vargas, June 24, 2001.

1. *The New York Times,* June 27, 2001, 21A and July 1, 2001, 21, 23, addresses problems with census categories and data. See census and estimated figures from the Lewis Mumford Center for Comparative Urban and Regional Research, State University of New York at Albany, at http://mumford1.dyndns.org/cen2000/HispanicPop/HspPopData/4120msa.htm. The 25,000–40,000 range is widely accepted among local Salvadorans. Sarah J. Mahler, *American Dreaming: Immigrant Life on the Margins* (Princeton, N.J.: Princeton University Press, 1995), finds disparities between census figures and credible estimates of the Salvadoran population on Long Island, New York, that are roughly equivalent to the gap between census figures and community estimates for Las Vegas.

2. These are the authors' observations.

3. The statistics are from CIA, *The World Factbook 2000,* at http://www.cia.gov/cia/publications/factbook/fields/. For an overview of El Salvador's history, see Tommie Sue Montgomery, *Revolution in El Salvador: From Civil Strife to Civil Peace,* 2d ed. (Boulder, Colo.: Westview Press, 1995), 23–126.

4. For the Soccer War and its background, see Thomas P. Anderson, *The War of the Dispossesed: Honduras and El Salvador, 1969* (Lincoln: University of Nebraska Press, 1981). 1980 census figures are reported in Cecilia Menjívar, *Fragmented Ties: Salvadoran Immigrant Networks in America* (Berkeley: University of California Press, 2000), 6.

5. Montgomery, *Revolution in El Salvador;* Americas Watch, *El Salvador's Decade of Terror: Human Rights Since the Assassination of Archbishop Romero* (New Haven: Yale University Press, 1991).

6. Menjívar, *Fragmented Ties,* 6; Sarah J. Mahler, *Salvadorans in Suburbia: Symbiosis and Conflict* (Needham Heights, Mass.: Allyn and Bacon, 1995), xiii; Terry A. Repak, *Waiting on Washington: Central American Workers in the Nation's Capital* (Philadelphia: Temple University Press, 1995), 23–71; Nora Hamilton and Norma Stoltz Chinchilla, *Seeking Community in a Global City: Guatemalans and Salvadorans in Los Angeles* (Philadelphia: Temple University Press, 2001); John R. Logan, "The New Latinos: Who They Are, Where They Are," Lewis Mumford Center, at http://mumford1.dyndns.org/cen2000/HispanicPop/HspReport/MumfordReport.doc. Correspondent Salvador Castellanos of Univisión national news on August 12, 2001, put the number of Salvadorans in the United States at two million.

7. Americas Watch, *El Salvador's Decade of Terror.*

8. Susan Bibler Coutin, *The Culture of Protest: Religious Activism and the U.S. Sanctuary Movement* (Boulder, Colo.: Westview Press, 1993). The same author's *Legalizing Moves: Salvadoran Immigrants' Struggle for U.S. Residency* (Ann Arbor: University of Michigan Press, 2000) explains Salvadorans' changing legal status. See also Victoria Rader, "Refugees at Risk: The Sanctuary Movement and its Aftermath," in *Illegal Immigration in America: A Reference Handbook,* ed. David W. Haines and Karen E. Rosenblum (Westport, Conn.: Greenwood Press, 1999), 325–45. Jeffrey S. Passel, "Undocumented Immigration to the United States: Numbers, Trends, and Characteristics," in *Illegal Immigration,* 38, estimates that there were 335,000 undocumented Salvadorans in the United States in 1996, a number second only to Mexico's estimated 2.7 million. The authors wish to thank immigration attorney Vicenta Montoya for deciphering the complexities of Salvadorans' changing legal status.

9. Montgomery, *Revolution in El Salvador,* 213–69; *Las Vegas Review-Journal,* January 18, August 4, 2001; *El País* (Madrid), September 9, October 7, October 10, 2001; *Las Vegas Sun,* January 9, 2002.

10. Sarah J. Mahler, "Vested in Migration: Salvadorans Challenge Restrictionist Policies," in *Free Markets, Open Societies, Closed Borders? Trends in International Migration and Immigration Policy in the Americas,* ed. Max J. Castro (Miami: North-South Center Press at the University of Miami, 1999), 157–73, describes the "culture of immigration." See also Montgomery, *Revolution in El Salvador,* 213–69. A 2002 survey found that one of three Salvadorans would emigrate if they could (*The Washington Post,* March 24, 2002). Nicholas Van Hear defines a transnational community as one having activities, networks, and patterns of life "encompassing both the host and home countries," in *New Diasporas: The Mass Exodus, Dispersal and Regrouping of Migrant Communities* (Seattle: University of Washington Press, 1998), 2–3.

11. *Las Vegas Review-Journal,* May 24, 2001. The U.S. Border Patrol claimed that 106 people died in attempting to cross Arizona's desert in 2000. The number rose to 145 in 2002. *Las Vegas Review-Journal,* July 28, 2003. Menjívar, *Fragmented Ties,* 58–76; Mahler, *Salvadorans in Suburbia,* 47–52.

12. Menjívar, *Fragmented Ties,* 77–114; Repak, *Waiting on Washington,* 23–71; Hamilton and Chinchilla, *Seeking Community; Las Vegas Review-Journal,* August 18, 2001.

13. Mahler, *Salvadorans in Suburbia,* 53–103; Menjívar, *Fragmented Ties,* 115–243; Repak, *Waiting on Washington;* David E. López, "Central Americans: At the Bottom, Struggling to Get Ahead," in *Ethnic Los Angeles,* ed. Roger Waldinger and Mehdi Bozorgmehr (New York: Russell Sage Foundation, 1966), 279–304.

14. López, "Central Americans."

15. Repak, *Waiting on Washington.*

16. Mahler, "Vested in Migration," 159; Menjívar, *Fragmented Ties,* 99–100; Benjamin Rider Howe, "Getting Used to the Greenback," *The Atlantic Monthly* 287, no. 5 (May 2001): 23–28. In 2001 the Salvadoran ambassador to the United States esti-

mated remittances at $2 billion (*The Washington Post,* March 24, 2002). The Salvadoran government consistently lobbies the U.S. government to extend the TPS for Salvadorans in the United States to preserve the flow of remittances and to prevent the return of hundreds of thousands of people for whom there are no jobs.

17. Menjívar, *Fragmented Ties,* 107–9; Repak, *Waiting on Washington.*

18. Information on Nombre de Jesús found in this and the following paragraph is from coauthor Wright's visit to the village October 19 through 21, 2000, and interviews with the following individuals during that period: Luis González Sánchez; Germán Escalante; Oscar Rodríguez; Romeo Calderón; Guillermo Rodríguez Chávez; and Peace Corps volunteer Kevin Baltz. Wright thanks Baltz for facilitating the visit and the interviews.

19. http://mumford1.dyndns.org/cen2000/HispanicPop/HspPopData/4120msa .htm. Our information about Las Vegas's Salvadorans comes from interviews and observation, since there is almost no published material on them. See the list of interviews at the head of the notes. Specific sources are cited only for quotations. It should be noted that almost without exception, sometimes after an initial hesitation, our informants were enthusiastic about being interviewed. Most thanked us for simply paying attention to them, as they are little known to the broader Las Vegas community, which, as several told us, consider anyone with dark hair and features who speaks Spanish a Mexican.

20. Montgomery, *Revolution in El Salvador,* 56–59.

21. Zoila Panameño interview. This and all subsequently noted interviews were conducted by the authors in Las Vegas on the dates listed at the head of the notes.

22. Walter Serrano and Felipe Umaña interviews.

23. Marina and José Vargas interviews.

24. Manuel Franco interview.

25. Mexican authorities deported some 10,000 illegal Central Americans in 1980; then, with the escalation of war and repression, particularly in El Salvador and Guatemala, these numbers ballooned to 100,000 in 1990. Meanwhile, by 2000, the United States was deporting some 1.5 million people who had crossed the border with Mexico illegally. *Excelsior* (Mexico City), April 5, 2001, 1A, 16A. For a study of coyotes serving Mexican clients, see Ted Conover, *Coyotes: A Journey Through the Secret World of America's Illegal Immigrants* (New York: Vintage Books, 1987). In his interview with the authors, Manuel Franco aptly summed up the central role of the coyote for Salvadorans: "Thinking about coming to the U.S. means thinking about the cost of a coyote."

26. Manuel Rivas and Héctor García interviews.

27. Marina Vargas interview.

28. Felipe Umaña interview.

29. Father Rigoni is quoted in *Time* (August 13, 2001): 6.

30. Hamilton and Chinchilla, *Seeking Community.*

31. Zullie Franco interview.

32. Repak, *Waiting on Washington*, 123–24, refers to Salvadorans' "positive typification" as workers. Several of our interviews confirm that Salvadorans in Las Vegas are aware of their good reputation as workers and believe that this helps them find jobs.

33. Walter Serrano interview.

34. Marina Vargas interview; Blanca Orellana interview (August 7, 2001).

35. The Mirage may be something of an exception, since the executive steward in charge of this staff, Zoila Panameño, is Salvadoran. Layoffs following the post–September 11, 2001, decline in tourism affected some Salvadorans employed in hotel-casinos. Interviews with D Taylor of the Culinary Workers Union, Local 226, May 23, 2001, and July 9, 2003. The union also has an immigrant citizenship program that prepares members for naturalization. For a history of the Culinary Union in Las Vegas, see Courtney Alexander, "Rise to Power: A Recent History of the Culinary Union in Las Vegas," in *The Grit Beneath the Glitter: Tales from the Real Las Vegas,* ed. Hal K. Rothman and Mike Davis (Berkeley: University of Caliornia Press, 2002), 145–75.

36. Estimates vary greatly, and most are higher than this figure proffered by immigration attorney Vicenta Montoya. She points out that as of August 2001, only Salvadorans who entered the United States after February 15, 2001, are denied the possibility of applying for permission to work and hence to stay. The cost of processing the paperwork through a notary is a minimum of $250, usually higher (Vicenta Montoya interview).

37. Abuses of undocumented construction workers were noted at a hearing by the state labor commissioner and reported in the *Las Vegas Sun,* February 18, 2002, and the *Las Vegas Review-Journal,* February 19, 2002.

38. The making of "Medio Tiempo" is chronicled in the *Las Vegas Sun,* August 7, 2001.

39. Felipe Umaña and Dalia Merino interviews. In 2001 the Nevada legislature enacted Senate Bill 153 to make the cosmetologist's exam available in Spanish and, if future demand warrants, in other languages.

40. Dr. Carlos Anaya, who sees many Salvadorans in his medical practice, believes that "eighty percent of Salvadorans are not happy in the U.S.," but "after five years or so it is hard to readjust to El Salvador" (Dr. Carlos Anaya interview).

41. Other examples of advertising two cuisines, found as new cuisines enter the United States and before they establish their own identity and clientele, include Cuban with Mexican, Peruvian with Mexican, Thai with Chinese, and Vietnamese with Chinese. The courier service was explained in the interview with Blanca Orellana, wife of the courier.

42. Soccer is so important to some sponsors that they recruit players, usually semi-professionals, including some recently retired from those leagues, in Mexico. The recruitment is normally by word of mouth. Typically, a current player reports someone from his hometown or someone he has heard of to the sponsor. The sponsor, again through informal channels, then offers the player a job and the loan necessary to pay the coyote. Efraín Martínez, sports director of Univisión channel 15, was recruited in this fashion from Mexico to play for the Caesars Palace team in 1976. Our sources

told us that the recruitment process reached as far as El Salvador, but we could not confirm this allegation (Efraín Martínez interview).

43. Efraín Martínez, Abel Cuevas, and Manuel Rivas interviews.

44. Efraín Martínez interview.

45. El Salvador was conquered and heavily settled by Nahua Indians from Central Mexico several centuries before the Spanish conquest, and the country has many place names reflecting this cultural legacy. Except for Brazilians and Haitians, linguistic and cultural differences among Latin American immigrant nationalities certainly pale compared to those among Asian, European, and African immigrant groups.

46. *El Mundo,* May 3, 2003; *El Tiempo Libre,* May 30, 2003; interview, Central American Coalition president Jennifer Angel.

47. *Las Vegas Sun,* May 5, 2003. Coauthor Wright attended the inauguration of the consulate, where the opening of the bank was announced.

CHAPTER 14

Peoples from the Indian Subcontinent

SATISH SHARMA

A prominent scholar has remarked: "People migrating are changed by their travel, but remain marked by the places of origin." Just as the roots remain an integral part of a tree even when the tree is transplanted, immigrants retain their characteristics of origin no matter how long they live in a foreign country. The longer the immigrants stay in their new home, the more the culture and social practices of the place grow on them, bringing inevitable changes in values, attitudes, behaviors, personalities, and modes of living. This chapter deals with immigrants to America and Las Vegas from the Indian subcontinent, specifically from India, Pakistan, Bangladesh, and Sri Lanka.[1]

The Indian Subcontinent

The densely populated Indian subcontinent is heavily influenced by its geography. The basins of the Indus and Ganges Rivers form one major division to the north and the Deccan Plateau another to the south. The Himalayas to the north and Hindu Kush/Karakoram ranges to the west erect formidable barriers, while the Brahmaputra River and the mountains beyond provide barriers to the east. The subcontinent is framed by the Bay of Bengal to the east and the Arabian Sea to the west. It becomes a peninsula to the south, with its southern tip ending in the Indian Ocean. Twenty miles southeast of the southern tip is Sri Lanka, with a unique history of own.[2]

The river basins supported the rise of two urban civilizations in ancient times: the Indus Valley Civilization in the third millennium BC and the Ganges Valley Civilization in the first millennium BC. The Indus Valley Civilization was at its peak between 2300 and 1700 BC, before the Vedic Aryans migrated to India from the northwest frontiers between 1300 and 1200 BC. This civilization declined and disappeared at one point but has been recently rediscovered. The Ganges Valley Civilization flourished and declined, but it has remained a part of the historical tradition of the subcontinent and continues to inspire its culture, trade, and social life.[3]

Foreign domination of the subcontinent began with the rule of northern

India by Hun tribes between 500 and 527 BC. Arabs started invading the subcontinent in the seventh century, and in AD 711 an Arab invader conquered the Sind region. Arab attacks continued, with more and more areas coming under their rule, until AD 1526, when Baber defeated the Delhi Arab sultanate and laid the foundation of a Mughal rule in India. The Mughal rule lasted into the eighteenth century, and its legacies are many and everlasting.

Parts of India came under British rule through the British East India Company, which was founded in 1600. In 1858, when the East India Company was dissolved, India came under the direct rule of the British Crown. Nearly a century passed before India freed itself from the British rule in 1947; the nation of Pakistan was subsequently carved out of it. Pakistan was, in turn, divided into Pakistan and Bangladesh in 1971. Sri Lanka won its freedom in 1948, after 150 years of the British rule.

Marks of foreign domination on the Indian subcontinent are deep and easily visible on the land and its people. Economic and political development are presently crucial concerns, but resources within the subcontinent are few, economies are small and population pressures are great, income disparities are large, corruption and religious strife are widespread, and human misery is rampant. The modern subcontinent has been influenced by industrialization, urbanization, and westernization, together with the combined effects of physical mobility, formal education, wider labor participation, and consumerism. Urban culture shows massive modernization trends, but villages have been isolated and maintain traditional culture. A majority of the people live in villages, follow agricultural pursuits, and lead simple lives.

With a population of more than a billion people and a total area of 1,222,550 square miles, India is the largest nation in the subcontinent, bordering China, Pakistan, Bangladesh, Nepal, Bhutan, and Myanmar (Burma). India has twenty-eight states and seven union territories, each with a rich cultural history and unique traditions of its own. Hinduism, Buddhism, Jainism, and Sikhism were born in India; Islam came to India with the Arab invaders; and Christianity, Judaism, and Zoroastrianism came across the seas to the south. Eighty percent of the population is Hindu, 11 percent Muslim, and the remaining 9 percent follow other faiths. Caste and joint family systems are fundamental to social organization and determine behaviors, marriage practices, power distribution, lifestyles, and roles and responsibilities within and outside the home.[4] Marriage is nearly universal in India, having children and raising them properly are considered important, and the divorce rate is low. Age and gender play significant roles in social settings and day-to-day dealings. Life expectancy is fifty-nine years, the literacy rate is 52 percent, and the per capita national product is $2,540. The diversity of the nation is readily visible in its races, sects, castes, tribes, religions, family patterns, marriage practices, sociocultural conditions, physical environment, and spoken languages. The north and central parts of India are home to Aryan culture and Indo-Aryan languages; the south is home to Dravidian culture and language; and tribal people have their own rich history, traditions, and languages. Hindustani and English are the linguas francas, with English used widely in official business.[5]

Pakistan covers 307,374 square miles, has a population of 148 million, and borders Iran, Afghanistan, China, and India. Its four regions are the Great Highlands, the Balochistan Plateau, the Indus Plain, and the desert areas. The people are descendants of Aryans, Persians, Greeks, Arabs, and Mughals. A substantial part of the population is of indigenous origins. In terms of languages and regional cultures, 55 percent of the population of Pakistan identify themselves as Punjabis, 20 percent as Sindhis, 10 percent as Pathans and Mujahirs, 5 percent as Balochs, and 10 percent as others. Spoken languages in Pakistan include Urdu, Punjabi, Sindhi, Pashto, Balochi, and Brahui, each with a strong regional basis, while Pakistan's official languages are Urdu and English. Most people are Sunni Muslims, although there is a significant presence of Shi'tes and Ahmadiyahs, or Quadianis. A majority of Pakistan's inhabitants live in villages and follow agricultural pursuits. The family is patriarchal, and *beradari* (patrilineage) is important. Agriculture employs more than half of the working population. Life expectancy is fifty-eight years, the literacy rate is 35 percent, and the per capita national product is $2,100.[6]

Bangladesh, with a population of 133 million and an area of 55,598 square miles, is bounded by India, Myanmar (Burma), and the Bay of Bengal. Racial stocks include Vedas, Aryans, Armenoids, Arabs, Persians, Turks, and indigenous people. More than 85 percent of the nation's population is Muslim, while 10 percent are Hindu and the rest follow Buddhism or animism. Bengali and English are Bangladesh's official languages. Other organizational features mimic those of India and Pakistan. The country is densely populated, very poor, and one of the least urbanized nations in South Asia. Eighty percent of the population of Bangladesh live in villages and follow agricultural pursuits. Life expectancy is fifty-five years, the literacy rate is 35 percent, and the per capita national product is $1,750.[7]

Sri Lanka, a densely populated island country in the Indian Ocean, has an area of 25,332 square miles and a population of more than 18 million. Sinhalese (80 percent), Tamils (12 percent), and Muslims (7 percent) predominate, and Burghers, Parsis, and Vedas comprise the remaining 1 percent of the population. Sinhalese speak Sinhala; Tamils and Muslims speak Tamil. More than 90 percent of the Sinhalese are Buddhists; Tamils are predominantly

Hindus; and the remaining population follows Islam, Christianity, or animism. Sri Lanka is diverse, with most of its people living in rural areas, poor and dependent on agriculture. From ancient times, there have been many Indian influences on Sri Lankan culture and tradition. The nation is famous for preserving the Thervada (Hinayana) Buddhist tradition and for inventing a sophisticated irrigation system for drier lands over two thousand years ago. Life expectancy is seventy-two years, the literacy rate is 88 percent, and Sri Lanka's per capita national product is $3,190.[8]

India, Pakistan, Bangladesh, and Sri Lanka have always had close ties for historical, economic, political, and cultural reasons, with relations among these countries varying from harmonious to conflicted. India and Pakistan, particularly, have had a hostile relationship over the years due to the ongoing Kashmir issue. Since independence from the British rule in 1947 the two nations have fought two wars, and another one has loomed during the past several years. Irrespective of such tensions at home, as immigrants the people from these nations get along well with one another, interact socially and culturally, and downplay the hostilities affecting their native countries.

Immigration Patterns

The Indian subcontinent has had trade relations with much of the world since ancient times but little immigration until the British promoted it within the British Empire to areas such as Myanmar (Burma), Fiji, Trinidad and Tobago, Malaysia, Mauritius, British Guinea, Kenya, Uganda, South Africa, the West Indies, and later, Great Britain and other commonwealth countries. In the new lands the immigrants worked in agriculture and manufacturing, on railroads, as artisans and clerks, and in other jobs. After the subcontinent's independence from British rule, the pattern of immigration widened, and Australia, Canada, the United States, and the Middle East became popular destinations.[9]

The first recorded immigrant from the Indian subcontinent to the United States was counted in the 1820 census. Immigrant numbers remained miniscule until after World War I, when a group of Sikhs from Punjab settled in Vancouver, British Columbia, and later moved south to work in the lumber mills of Bellingham and Everett, Washington, and in agriculture in California, first as laborers and then as innovators and entrepreneurs in rice and cotton cultivation. After reaching some 6,000 in the mid-1920s, the number of immigrants from the subcontinent declined in the 1940s then rose to 6,000 again only in the 1950s.[10]

Beginning in the 1950s, American universities sought foreign students in professional and technical fields and offered financial aid and visas. This launched a steady and growing immigration from the Indian subcontinent that continues to the present day. The trend was also abetted by the U.S. immigration reforms in the 1960s, which removed ethnic and racial barriers and emphasized professional qualifications. The data show that in 1990, there were 815,447 immigrants in America from India, 81,371 from Pakistan, 11,838 from Bangladesh, and 10,970 from Sri Lanka, totaling 919,626 from the Indian subcontinent. Figures from the 2000 census indicate that there was a 133 percent increase from 1990 in the Indian population in the United States, totaling 1,899,599.[11]

Immigration from the Indian subcontinent has been driven by push and pull factors. The push factors include high unemployment rates, poor wages and salaries, poor working conditions, a lack of upward mobility, economic corruption, bureaucratic red tape, political and religious instability, and overall poor living conditions. Pull factors are good educational and professional opportunities, the availability of well-paying jobs, the possibility of upward mobility, better working conditions, more amenities, better life chances for children, and opportunities for family reunification. In the case of Las Vegas, some additional pull factors include strong state and local economies, agreeable climate, reasonably priced housing, good facilities for children's education, availability of recreational facilities nearby, and the glamour of the city.[12]

Informants indicate that immigrants from the subcontinent started arriving in Las Vegas in the late 1960s. By the early 1970s there were several bachelors and twenty to twenty-five families from the subcontinent. Among them were a couple of physicians (Dr. Toni Ram and Dr. Javed Anwar), a couple of professors at the University of Nevada, Las Vegas (UNLV) (Dr. Sadanand Verma and Dr. Satish Bhatnagar), two architects (Himansu Shroff and Pravin Bakrania), a couple of motel owners (Babubhai Patel and Ishwarbhai Patel), several casino workers from the Sindhi community (Tony Punjabi, Mangu Jasnani, Mannu Punjabi, and Ramesh Khitri), one engineer with the Xerox company (Murli Motwani), one structural engineer at the Nevada Test Site (Kirti Kumar), one or two students at UNLV, and a few others. One informant, who came to Las Vegas in 1973, recalls that the city at that time was quite small, the minimum wage was $1.15 per hour, and there were just a few people from the Indian subcontinent. More vigorous immigration from the subcontinent to Las Vegas occurred in the late 1970s and early 1980s, when Dr. Bhagwan Singh, Dr. Nasim Dil, Dr. Satish Sharma, Dr. Ashok Iyer, and Dr. Naranapiti Karunaratne joined the UNLV faculty and many others joined the community. Immigration to the city has continued to accelerate. According to the estimate of the Lewis Mumford Center, the Las Vegas Metropolitan

Statistical Area (MSA) had some 4,800 Indians and 2,100 people from Pakistan and Banglidesh combined. There is no census figure for Sri Lankans.[13]

Distribution and Characteristics

Although one occasionally finds doctors and other professionals from the Indian subcontinent in small towns around the country, immigrants have largely settled in metropolitan areas, particularly New York, Chicago, Los Angeles, San Jose, Long Beach, Houston, and Washington, D.C. The pioneer immigrants who had served in the British army were farmers, artisans, and laborers in civilian life. They were generally illiterate, came from the rural areas of Punjab, India, and followed the Sikh religion. Through the 1950s immigration remained narrowly based, drawn from a few states of India, then beginning in the 1960s the pattern of immigration widened to include people from all parts of the subcontinent, especially well-educated urban professional men with homemaker wives and grown children. By the 1970s dual-earner couples with teenage children were common. Recent immigrants have included older parents and younger relatives as well, many of whom are less well educated and are finding it difficult to adjust to American economic and social conditions.[14]

Both Nevada and Las Vegas have attracted relatively few immigrants from the Indian subcontinent in comparison with those coming to the United States as a whole, and most immigrants who do settle in Las Vegas come from India and Pakistan. All major languages and religions of the subcontinent are represented in the city, and the same is true of caste and regional backgrounds. To an outsider the immigrant group may appear homogeneous, but its diversity is easily recognized by the insiders.[15]

Parmatma Saran has offered an overview of Indian immigrants in the United States during the 1980s, and this profile applies to the Indian, Pakistani, Bangladeshi, and Sri Lankan immigrants in Las Vegas with a few exceptions, which I have indicated in parentheses. Saran found that a majority of the immigrants had urban backgrounds, were between thirty and forty years of age (now between twenty-five and sixty-five years in Las Vegas), and had an average family size of four. They were highly educated and concentrated in the professions. While they took an interest in local affairs, their participation was minimal (this has changed nationwide). Leisure activities centered on friends and a growing number of local and regional associations. Close friendships and visiting patterns involved people from the same region, speaking the same language. Immigrants maintained contact with family and friends back home and showed interest in the political affairs of their home countries. On the psychological level, most desired to return to India but lacked concrete plans (most immigrants in the 1980s and 1990s came with the idea of permanently settling in America). Immigrants depended on family and friends for comfort and help in times of need. Husband-wife relationships had not changed much, but parent-child relationships were polemical and strenuous. Raising children in America was a problem and matter of much responsibility. Preference was shown for home-country foods and native languages. Religiosity was about the same as in the home countries, but consciousness of one's religion had become greater.[16]

Saran found that the economic status of most immigrants was quite satisfactory. Many remained savings oriented and made good investments. Employment opportunities were satisfactory and upward occupational mobility was available, although some immigrants experienced discrimination and limited advancement. Immigrants were—and have remained—obsessed with achievement and education. Initially, immigrants reacted favorably to American culture, but some disillusionment and dissatisfaction developed with the passage of time. The immigrants' origin-based sense of identity remained strong, and adaptation to American culture was selective, demonstrating increasing flexibility and tolerance in regard to educational and workplace norms but less inclination to change family life, social networking, marriage practices, and personal behaviors. Most immigrants strove to maintain their cultural traditions.

Nearly two decades have elapsed since Saran offered this profile. Those immigrants who were middle-aged and pursuing their careers are now thinking of retirement. The children have grown, finished their education, and married, and they are established in professions and careers. Something has also happened to the idea of going back home. Those immigrants who arrived during the 1980s and afterward were better prepared for adjustment in America, and dilemmas for them are fewer. For the second generation, America is their home; they have no desire to live permanently in their parents' home countries. Time has eased the discomfort of even the first generation and, having adjusted to American conditions, they, too, are enjoying the benefits of American life and comforts.[17]

Achievements

Most immigrants from the Indian subcontinent hold good professional jobs or own businesses. Though their numbers remain small, their representation as professors, teachers, scientists, engineers, doctors, health and helping professionals, financial experts, managers, businessmen, and consultants is easily visible in cities and towns across America. A large number of them own motels, restaurants, gas stations, grocery and convenience stores, and other businesses. Some work as taxi drivers, store clerks, and in other lower-level jobs, but they are generally recent arrivals, still striving to find a niche in the American economic system.[18]

In Las Vegas, there are an estimated 150 to 180 doctors from the Indian subcontinent, 17 to 19 UNLV faculty members (5 of whom have served as chairs/directors of their departments), 15 to 20 K–12 schoolteachers, and several dentists, architects, chemists, engineers, chartered public accountants, attorneys, social workers, nurses, realtors, financial experts, and other professionals. Between 20 and 25 immigrants own gas stations, 6 own grocery stores, several own minimarkets and convenience stores, some own dry-cleaning businesses, 6 own Indian cuisine restaurants, 2 own travel agencies, 2 own specialty stores, and a number of them own other businesses. Many immigrants work in casinos, as taxi drivers, and in other capacities. In fact, there is hardly an area of the Las Vegas economy in which immigrants from the Indian subcontinent are not presently working and contributing.

Through hard work and diligence, immigrants from India have made a mark on American life. Their professional and economic successes are indeed conspicuous. They have the highest median household income, family income, and per capita income of any foreign-born group in America. A recent (2000) issue of *India News* indicated that Indian immigrants in America had a median family income of $60,093, as compared to the national median family income of $38,885. More than 87 percent of them completed high school, and at least 62 percent had some college education, with 58 percent holding a bachelor's degree or higher. High levels of education have allowed Indian immigrants to become a productive segment of the U.S. population: 43.6 percent worked in managerial and professional specialties; 33.2 percent in technical, sales, and administrative support occupations; and 23.3 percent as operators, fabricators, laborers, and precision production workers. More than 5,000 of them were faculty members in institutions of higher education. The achievements of Pakistani, Bangladeshi, and Sri Lankan immigrants were similar.[19]

Las Vegas shows the same pattern of success on the part of immigrants from the subcontinent, and one easily notices the disproportionate number of businessmen, doctors, professors, teachers, engineers, and other professionals from that region. Not only the immigrants but also their children have done very well. Indeed, most of them have attended prominent schools and colleges and are settled in substantial professional and business careers.

Networking and Organizations

As their numbers grew, immigrants from the Indian subcontinent started networking and established local, regional, and later national organizations to serve their needs and interests. There are currently many such organizations and some transnational organizations as well. Indian immigrants, for example, have four leading organizations at the national level: the Association of Asian Indians in America (AIA), the National Federation of Indian Associations in America (NFIA), the Indian American Forum for Political Education (the Forum), and the National Association of Americans of Asian Indian Descent (NAAAID). The AIA was founded in the mid-1960s, NFIA around 1971, and the other two more recently. The AIA and NFIA undertake political, social, and cultural activities, and the Forum and NAAAID are political organizations. Pakistan, Bangladesh, and Sri Lanka do not have similar organizations at the national level but have regional organizations based on cultural, religious, regional, linguistic, professional, and other interests. There are several Islamic organizations at the national level, such as the Islamic Society of North America and the Islamic Council of North America, in which Indian, Pakistani, Bangladeshi, and Sri Lankan Muslims participate. The transnational organizations focus on cultural, religious, regional, linguistic, professional, and other interests, bringing together people who otherwise would have little in common. For example, the associations for Punjabi language include Sikhs, Hindus, and Muslims from India and Pakistan; the associations for Urdu bring together people from India, Pakistan, and Bangladesh; and the associations for Tamil bring together people of India and Sri Lanka, and the same is true of the religious, professional, and other transnational organizations.[20]

Prior to the establishment of formal organizations in Las Vegas, immigrants from the Indian subcontinent relied on the showing of Indian films for socializing and cultural reinforcement. From the late 1970s a Sindhi businessman, Mannu Punjabi, showed movies at UNLV, in the Clark County Flamingo Library, and in other available places. Movies were shown once every two to three months, costing approximately three dollars per person, and forty to fifty people generally attended. The 16-mm film reels were procured from Los Angeles by air or by Greyhound bus for a night and returned the next day. Food was sold at the intermission. Additionally, the local public-television station, Channel 10, televised Indian movies every Sunday under the multicultural program in the late 1970s and early 1980s.

By the 1980s, as their numbers grew, immigrants began establishing country and cross-country organizations in Las Vegas. Most of these are informally structured, and four are officially registered with the state: Friends of India, the Hindu Society of Nevada, the Islamic Society of Southern Nevada, and the Sri Lanka–America Association of Southern Nevada. The officially registered associations have constitutions, bylaws, and boards of directors. Bangladeshi immigrants tried to establish a formal association in the late 1990s but failed to do so.[21]

Several immigrants formed the Friends of India, an Indian sociocultural organization, in 1983 to bring together Indian families and their American and non-American friends. The main objectives were the celebration of Hindu festivals such as Diwali, Holi, and Dussera; the showing of Indian movies; and other entertainment/cultural activities, including the cultural education and training of children and the observance of India's Independence and Republic Days. The organization's first president was Dr. Raj Chanderraj. Participation in the organization's activities has been cross-country, as members of all nations of the subcontinent have sought one another's company and enjoyed the events. Membership, initially about twenty families, now approaches 550–650 families. The organization has functioned successfully over the years and provides services to members and others. Friends of India also participates in the cross-cultural activities of Las Vegas such as the International Food Festival, which is hosted by different ethnic organizations, and it hosts fund-raising dinners for political candidates at the local, state, and national levels.

The Hindu Society of Nevada, incorporated in 1994, is an Indian religious organization. Its functions are similar to those of the Islamic Society of Southern Nevada, which was established around 1990. The two organizations promote Hindu and Muslim religious ideals and cultural practices within the community as well as the religious education of children. Both have formal boards of directors, with Dr. Ranjit Jain the president of the Hindu Society of Nevada and Khalid Khan leading the Islamic Society of Southern Nevada. The membership in both these organizations is quite large, activities are many, and fund-raising efforts are well planned. The Islamic Society of Southern Nevada has built a new mosque and cultural center in the east side of the city, and the Hindu Society of Nevada has built a new temple and cultural center in the northwest.[22]

Another important organization is Urdu Adab Jamat International, founded by several Pakistani immigrants about fifteen years ago. Each year the organization holds a public recital of Urdu poetry (Mushera) under the leadership of Khalid Khan. The event, featuring esteemed poets from India, Pakistan, California, Arizona, New York, Nevada, and elsewhere, attracts an audience of between 125 and 150 people. This activity is primarily Pakistani, but Indian and Bangladeshi immigrants participate.

Not all organizations have been entirely successful. A local chapter of the

Indian-American Forum for Political Education, whose main objective is political education of local immigrants, was founded in 1984, with Pramod Bhatnagar as its first president. Once very active, this organization has declined. The Pakistan-American Cultural Club and the Islamic Cultural Center were other organizations formed in the late 1970s and early 1980s. The Pakistan-American Cultural Club, established in 1978 by Dr. Nasim Dil and others, sought to educate the local public about Pakistani culture and traditions. This club functioned for two years and became inactive due, its former members say, to excessive demands on the time of the founders and lack of interest on the part of others to come forth and share the leadership. A Middle Eastern businessman established the Islamic Cultural Center in the early 1980s, and as his business suffered the center became inactive.

The Sri Lanka–America Association of Southern Nevada was founded in the late 1990s, with functions parallel to those of Friends of India. Its first president was Sirali Peias, who migrated from California, where he was president of a similar organization. The group organizes functions including Sri Lankan New Year, Hindu New Year, Sri Lanka's Independence Day, Buddha's Birth and Death Days, Id, and Christmas and sponsors Sri Lankan movies, dramas, musical events, and other cultural activities. Famous artists are invited to perform, and donations are collected to meet the expenditures of their visits. The organization also sponsors talks by Sri Lankan political dignitaries.[23]

There is also an inclusive cricket team in Las Vegas, which attracts players from India, Pakistan, Bangladesh, Sri Lanka, and other cricket-playing nations (for example, South Africa, West Indies, and Australia). The cricket team brings a new flavor to Las Vegas culture; it regularly plays against visiting teams in Las Vegas and travels to tournament matches in California.[24]

Religion, Cultural Activities, and Entertainment

Religion is important to the immigrants' way of life; they have built Hindu, Buddhist, and Parsi temples, Sikh *gurudwaras,* and Muslim mosques all over America. With the increase in numbers, subgroups within the main faiths now have their own places of worship.[25] Las Vegas has several places of worship serving the immigrants and others. Presently, there are two Hindu temples, three Muslim mosques, four Buddhist temples, one Sikh gurudawara, and one Muslim academy for the education of children. Hindu immigrants originally performed religious practices at home individually or in small worship groups at the UNLV, the Clark County Flamingo Library, and Paradise Park. The first Hindu temple, devoted to Sai Baba, was built in the early 1980s in the backyard of a Sindhi family's house in southeastern Las

Vegas. This temple was established according to Hindu rites by Narain Baba from Shirdi, near Bombay, in a well-attended ceremony. The second temple, The Hindu Temple of Las Vegas, built in Summerlin by the Hindu Society of Nevada at a cost of $2.4 million, opened to the public on April 29, 2001. This temple was designed by renowned Hindu temple designer Shashi Patel. It has a full-time priest brought from India and is devoted to all major faiths and denominations within Hindu religion. When completed, the temple complex will also house a huge community center. Current activities include daily worship morning and evening and the celebration of Rathyatra Laxmipooja, Janamashtami, and other religious ceremonies. The temple is the site for yoga classes for adults, activities for children, and discourses on religious themes and recital of scriptures by holy people.[26]

Several other Hindu religious groups also exist in Las Vegas, including Radha Swami, Brahmkumari, Bhajan Yogi, Mahesh Yogi, and the International Society for Krishna Consciousness (ISKCON). Each has a committed following in the local area and functions informally. A local chemist, Dr. Bhanu Joshi, organizes monthly worship meetings and celebrations of Hindu festivals and acts as priest for marriages and other ceremonies.[27]

Three mosques and an academy for children's education serve Las Vegas's Muslims. The Masjid As-Sabur mosque has existed in the Downtown area since the early 1980s and is attended mostly by African American Muslims. Former world heavyweight boxing champion Mike Tyson recently donated one million dollars to the mosque, which has been renovated and expanded. In 1993 the Islamic Society of Southern Nevada built another mosque, Jamia Masjid, in the southeastern part of the city. Pakistani, Bangladeshi, Sri Lankan, and Middle Eastern immigrants are the primary users of this facility. A spacious structure, it houses a community center and a weekend school for children. The third mosque, Masjid Haseebullah, serves Muslims in the northwest. Before the availability of these mosques, Muslims used their homes, UNLV facilities, Clark County Flamingo Library, Paradise Park, clubhouses, a duplex bought by Dr. Anjum, and other places for religious practices. The Omar Haikal Islamic Academy for children opened on September 10, 2001, in the Green Valley area of Henderson. The brainchild of Dr. Omar Haikal, this four-million-dollar facility serves children in kindergarten through seventh grade.

Las Vegas also has Thai, Burmese, Laotian, and Sri Lankan Buddhist temples located in the northern, northwestern, and western parts of the city. The Thai temple, founded in the early 1980s, is the oldest. Housed in a rented facility for about ten years, it now has its own building. Rental facilities house the other three temples. The Burmese temple, the second oldest, has been in existence since about 1989. The Laotian temple was opened in 1996, and the Sri Lankan temple in 1998. All the temples' following is primarily by region of origin, but important observances in any temple attract most Buddhists and priests from other temples.

Although only forty to fifty Sikh families reside in Las Vegas, this group of immigrants built its own beautiful *gurudwara* in the northwest in the late 1990s. Previously, the followers of Sikh religion, both Sikhs and Hindus, had been meeting at the house of Manjit Singh, which continues as a gurudwara as well.[28]

Religion, cultural activities, and entertainment often mix in the case of immigrants from the Indian subcontinent. The primary celebrations are Diwali, Ramnaumi, Janamashtmi, Shivratri, Durgapooja, and Laxmipooja for Hindus; Buddhjayanti and other holy celebrations associated with the life of Buddha for Buddhists; Jummah Namaj, Id, and Ramadan for Muslims; and Gurupurabs and other holy days for Sikhs. Gujarati immigrants celebrate Navaratri (a nine-day annual religious festival) during the months of October and November; this event is accompanied by Garbha dance and the sharing of Gujarati food. South Indian immigrants celebrate Onam with dances, cultural activities, and the sharing of food. The celebration is cosponsored by the local Indian Dance Training Academy, which is open from September to June each year and run by a dance instructor from Phoenix. Occasionally, the immigrants also bring in well-known singers, musicians, dancers, poets, *gazal* specialists, entertainers, and other artists from their respective countries.[29]

Services

To facilitate day-to-day living, immigrants from the Indian subcontinent have developed shopping and service facilities all over America. These include grocery stores, restaurants, specialty stores, entertainment centers, and, in bigger cities, newspapers and radio/television stations. By the late 1970s these services had grown to a level allowing even families living in some smaller cities to experience the best of both the worlds—American comforts and conveniences and cultural amenities of the homelands. Earlier, the immigrants visited their home countries to obtain goods and services and to expose the children to family members, relatives, friends, and homeland cultures. Now, most needed goods, services, and cultural exposures are available in the United States and consequently visits to the homelands have become less frequent.[30]

In Las Vegas immigrants from the Indian subcontinent have established four grocery stores to serve the people's needs: India Market, India Bazaar (formerly India Sweets and Spices), India Foods and Spices (formerly India

Spices), and Pak Foods. The first to open, Pak Foods, which was owned by a businessman from Punjab, Pakistan, did business from 1980 to 1984. The current Pak Foods has operated in the southeast under different ownership since the mid-1980s. A Sindhi woman, Rita Vaswani, opened India Sweets and Spices in the Commercial Center on Sahara in the early 1980s. In the mid-1990s a family from Punjab, India, purchased the store and changed its name to India Bazaar. India Foods and Spices, opened by a Gujarati couple in the mid-1980s on Maryland Parkway and Twain, has changed ownership twice. A young Gujarati man has owned India Market, at the corner of Maryland Parkway and Tropicana, for the last twelve years. All these markets stock imported foodstuffs, fresh vegetables, sweets, music CDs and cassettes, and DVD movies for rent, serving immigrants from throughout South Asia.[31]

Six Indian-cuisine restaurants currently operate in Las Vegas. In contrast to the markets, they serve not only immigrants but other residents and visitors as well. The restaurants are Shalimar, near Paradise and Flamingo; Gandhi, also near Paradise and Flamingo; India Palace, near Paradise and Twain; India Oven, on West Sahara; Priya, on South Decatur; and Rasraj, on East Tropicana. Shalimar, the oldest of these, has been in operation since 1982 and is owned by a young businessman from Punjab, Pakistan. Priya restaurant, once a branch of Shalimar, was sold in 1996. Gandhi, owned by a Punjabi Sikh and a Gujarati businessman from India, has been in operation since 1989. India Palace and India Oven, owned by Punjabi businessmen from India, opened in 1998. Rasraj (formerly Bite of India) is the most recent addition. Other Indian-cuisine businesses have come and gone through the years. Two specialty stores in Las Vegas are owned by immigrants from the Indian subcontinent: Signature, in the Galleria Mall in Henderson, and Taj Boutique, on Sunset Road. These stores carry clothes, jewelry, and other imported merchandise.

No local newspapers or radio or television programs specifically serve the informational needs of immigrants from the Indian subcontinent, although some national and regional newspapers and television channels do so. Friends of India, the Hindu Society of Nevada, the Islamic Society of Southern Nevada, and the Sri Lanka–America Association of Southern Nevada have newsletters for their members.

Political Participation

Throughout the United States, immigrants from the Indian subcontinent have increased their political participation in voting, candidate endorsement, issue-directed lobbying, and sponsoring their own candidates at various governmental levels. The first South Asian to serve in the U.S. Congress was Dalip Singh Saund, from Imperial Valley in California, elected in 1956. Other candidates, including Neil Dhillon, Ram Uppuluri, Peter Mathews, Nimi McConigley, Ramakrishnan Nagarajan, and Bill Quraishi, have run unsuccessfully for the U.S. Congress. Some immigrants have been elected to state legislatures, and others have been appointed to prominent political positions.[32]

Indian subcontinent immigrants in Las Vegas have also increased their political involvement in recent years. They have supported candidates running for national, state, and local offices through fund-raising, endorsements, and other efforts and have also engaged in special-interest lobbying across the political spectrum. One immigrant, Rita Vaswani, recently ran unsuccessfully for the state legislature. Politically active local leaders include Dr. R. D. Prabhu, Dr. Raj Chanderraj, Dr. Dipak Desai, Dr. Ranjit Jain, Hira Daulat, Dr. Javed Anwar, Dr. Imran Khan, Khalid Khan, Dr. Golam Choudhry, Dr. Ranjan Sulugalle, and Dr. Naranapiti Karunaratne.

Emotional Challenges

Whether in New York, Silicon Valley, Las Vegas, or other cities and towns across America, immigrants from the Indian subcontinent have faced challenges of adjustment and adaptation. To an outsider it may appear that their educational, professional, and financial successes have come almost effortlessly, but the immigrants are aware of the emotional, social, and cultural costs—costs not easily visible to an outsider.[33] To begin with, the immigrants leave their homelands, family members, friends, relatives, and sometimes well-established living situations. The decision to emigrate is consequently a difficult one and fraught with emotional dilemmas. Upon arrival immigrants find that the game of life is played differently in America, often with different expectations. The cozy and supportive environment of their home countries, where instant help and advice were readily at hand for every hardship, is not available in America, where immigrants make most of their decisions individually, with little or no help from others unless they have family and friends nearby. The immediate questions upon arrival are where to live and how to obtain survival amenities and enroll oneself and one's children for education. Subsequently, immigrants search for needed resources and a job, while trying to make those adjustments that will allow them to achieve a satisfactory standard of living in America. The initial adjustment remains a mammoth task, full of emotional problems and letdowns. Outwardly, the immigrants remain composed in the face of such difficulties, but their personal stress levels are high and take a toll on themselves and their families.

Family life in America presents another challenge. The immigrants readily accept workplace norms but feel that family life is their domain and strive to maintain native lifestyles. Success in maintaining traditional culture is limited to the husband and wife, and even they develop new understandings and make adjustments. Children find the home rules restrictive and incompatible with outside expectations of them. They challenge home rules and demand more freedom, more individual decision making, more space, more privacy, less accountability, and quick gratification of their desires. Parents resist and tensions emerge. Mothers try to mediate. Victory, however, is ultimately on the side of the children. Through these struggles, parents feel a reduced sense of power and control over the family situation. The children suffer the dual pressures of conforming to native customs at home and to American culture outside, where other young people subject them to American ways. Children try to adjust but remain confused, and eventually they start conforming to outside expectations, much to the dismay of parents and elders.

On the positive side, few children from the subcontinent have developed deviant behaviors or problems such as alcohol and drug abuse, teenage pregnancy, gang behavior, or attempted suicide. Much credit for this goes to the watchful eyes of the parents and their unconditional love and care for the children. The children know well that no matter what, the parents will always be on their side and will continue to support them. It is also one of the reasons why these children have performed so well academically and have established themselves in successful careers.

Maintaining native identities remains an important goal for the immigrants, who strive to keep the language, food, dress, behaviors, and living habits of their native lands. Families establish a place of worship at home to orient the children to native religious traditions and use mosques and temples where they are available. Immigrants maintain a circle of family friends and invite others periodically for dinners and other social activities. Events organized by local religious and sociocultural organizations also help support cultural traditions. Success in cultural retention remains limited, as the dominant American culture exercises its powerful influence on immigrants and their families.

Conclusion

Despite the difficulties and challenges, immigrants from the Indian subcontinent are generally happy with their new lives. They have benefited much from this "nation of immigrants" and "land of opportunity." The great hopes and dreams with which they came seem to have been fulfilled in more than one way. Immigrants have certainly suffered from separation from family members, relatives, friends, and the home-country environment and from the prevalent prejudice and discrimination in America, but they also appreciate the many opportunities provided to them and their children. The difficulties and dilemmas they have faced are not unusual for any first-generation immigrants, and these immigrants sense that they have found a new home and a niche in the American way of life. They arrived late on the scene and their numbers remain relatively small, yet their contributions to American development are many. What they brought with them as their cultural heritage has enriched American culture and the American way of life. Oscar Handlin once remarked: "I thought to write a history of the immigrants in America. Then, I discovered that the immigrants were American history." Handlin's statement not only captures the spirit of this chapter but also the mosaic of contemporary Las Vegas.[34]

Notes

1. J. Clifford, "Notes on Theory and Travel," in *Traveling Theory, Traveling Theorists*, ed. James Clifford and Vivek Dhareshwar (Santa Cruz, Calif.: Center for Cultural Studies, 1989), 188. For informational sources on the Indian subcontinent, see K. I. Leonard, *The South Asian Americans* (Westport, Conn.: Greenwood Press, 1997); H. Kulke and D. Rothermund, *A History of India* (New York: Dorset Press, 1986); P. Chatterjee, *The Nation and Its Fragments: Colonial and Post-Colonial Histories* (Princeton: Princeton University Press, 1993); C. Maloney, *Peoples of South Asia* (New York: Holt, Rinehart and Winston, 1974); J. E. Schwartzberg et al., *Historical Atlas of South Asia* (New York: Oxford University Press, 1992); R. Guha, *Subaltern Studies I: Writings on South Asian History and Society* (Delhi: Oxford University Press, 1994).

2. The literature uses the term *Indian* to refer both to people from the Indian subcontinent and people from the Republic of India. Here the term has been used in the former sense, to emphasize the longstanding racial, cultural, historical, economic, and political linkages of the peoples and the nations.

3. Historians date the Indus Valley settlements back to 4000 BC The urban civilization in the valley is dated back to 2800–2600 BC. The Mohenjodaro and Harappa archaeological remains, discovered in 1921, indicated the existence of a highly developed urban culture in the subcontinent between 2300 and 1700 BC. The excavations in Kilibangan in Punjab and Lothal in Gujarat have supported these earlier findings. For further information, see Kulke and Rothermund, *A History of India*.

4. Based on a July 2002 estimate, India's population (in millions) is 1,046. See http://www.cia.gov/publications/factbook/geos/in.html#People. "Joint family system" refers to extended patriarchal family, living in one dwelling and pooling re-

sources for expenditures and meeting the needs of its members. The oldest male is the head of the family and has the power to make major decisions.

5. The Gross Domestic Product is a 2002 estimate. See http://www.cia.gov/ publications/factbook/geos/in.html#Econ. Multiplicity of languages and dialects is one common feature of all nations in the Indian subcontinent. In India alone, more than five hundred languages and thousands of dialects are spoken. The Constitution of India recognizes eighteen official languages: thirteen of Indo-Aryan origin (Assamese, Bengali, Gujarati, Hindi, Kashmiri, Kon Kani, Marathi, Nepali, Oriya, Punjabi, Sanskrit, Sindhi, and Urdu), four of Dravidian origin (Kannada, Malayalam, Tamil, and Telgu), and one of Sino-Tibetan origin (Manipuri). India shares the Urdu language with Pakistan (Hindi is also close to Urdu), the Bengali language with Bangladesh, and the Tamil language with Sri Lanka. For reference sources on India, see A. L. Basham, *The Wonder That Was India* (London: Sidgwick and Jackson, 1963); D. G. Mandelbaum, *Society in India,* vols. 1 and 2 (Berkeley: University of California Press, 1970); D. N. Majumdar, *Races and Cultures of India* (New York: Asia Publishing House, 1973); D. E. Sopher, *An Exploration of India: Geographical Perspectives on Society and Culture* (Ithaca, New York: Cornell University Press, 1980); K. M. Kapadia, *Marriage and Family in India* (Calcutta: Oxford University Press, 1981); A. G. Noble and A. K. Dutt, *India: Cultural Patterns and Processes* (Boulder, Colo.: Westview Press, 1982); Government of India, *The Gazetteer of India,* vol. 1 (New Delhi: Publications Division, Ministry of Information and Broadcasting, 1973); Government of India, *India: 2001* (New Delhi: Publications Division, Ministry of Information and Broadcasting, 2001).

6. For estimates of Gross Domestic Product (2001) and population (July 2002), see http://www.cia.gov/publications/factbook/geos/pk.html#Econ; http://www.cia.gov/ publications/factbook/geos/pk.html#People. See also A. S. Ahmed, *Pakistan, Ethnicity, and Leadership in South Asia* (New York: Oxford University press, 1997); P. R. Blood, *Pakistan: A Country Study* (Washington, D.C.: Federal Research Division, 1995); S. J. Burki, *Pakistan: A Nation in the Making* (Boulder, Colo.: Westview Press, 1986); I. M. Stephens, *Pakistan* (New York: Praeger, 1963); D. N. Wilber et al., *Pakistan: Its People, Its Society, Its Culture* (New Haven: HRAF Press, 1964).

7. For population (2001 estimate) and Gross Domestic Product (July 2002 estimate), see http://www.cia.gov/publications/factbook/geos/bg.html#People; http:// www.cia.gov/publications/factbook/geos/bf.html#Econ. For further information on Bangladesh, see A. Adlakha, *Bangladesh* (Washington, D.C.: U.S. Department of Commerce, Economics, and Statistics, 1993); M. Harris, "Bangladeshis," in *Encyclopedia of American Immigrant Cultures,* ed. David Levinson (New York: Macmillan, 1996).

8. Sri Lanka was formerly known as Ceylon and was called Taprobane by the ancient Greeks and Serendib by Arab traders. The country is richly described in the Buddhist chronicles Mahavamsa and Culavamsa—the "Great Chronicle" and the "Little Chronicle." For further information on Sri Lanka, see K. M. De Silva, *Sri Lanka: A Survey*

(Honolulu: University Press of Hawaii, 1977); R. R. Rossand and A. M. Savada, *Sri Lanka: A Country Study* (Washington, D.C.: Department of the Army, 1990).

9. Important informational sources on Indian subcontinent immigration into the United States include: S. Chandrasekhar, *From India to America: A Brief History of Immigration, Problems of Discrimination, Admission, and Assimilation* (La Jolla, Calif.: Popular Review Publications, 1982); J. M. Jensen, "East Indians," in *Harvard Encyclopedia of American Ethnic Groups,* ed. S. Thernstrom, A. Orlov, and O. Handlin (Cambridge: Harvard University Press, 1980), 296–301; J. M. Jensen, *Passage from India: Asian Indian Immigrants in North America* (New Haven: Yale University Press, 1988); A. W. Helweg and U. M. Helweg, *An Immigrant Success Story* (Philadelphia: University of Pennsylvania Press, 1990); H. Tinker, *The Banyan Tree: Overseas Emigrants from India, Pakistan, and Bangladesh* (London: Oxford University Press, 1977); J. L. Gonzales, "Asian Indian Immigration Patterns: The Origins of the Sikh Community in California," *International Migration Review* 20, no. 1 (1986): 40–54; B. La Brock, "The Reconstitution of Sikh Society in Rural California," in *Overseas Indians: A Study in Adaptation,* ed. G. Kurian and R. P. Srivastava (New Delhi: Vikas, 1983), 215–40; B. Vora, "Sikhs in Yuba City," in *India Abroad* (February 27, 1987): 14–15; *American Demographics* (February 1997).

10. See Helweg and Helweg, *A Migrant Success Story;* S. Sharma, "Indian Migrants in the United States: The Challenges, Adjustments, and Dilemmas," *Guru Nanak Journal of Sociology* 22, no. 1 (2001): 1–15. Chinese, Japanese, and Koreans were the first to arrive in America from Asia. They helped build railroads and worked in gold mines. At the time of the gold rush, one-fifth of the miners were Chinese. For further information, see J. P. Allen and E. J. Turner, *We the People: An Atlas of America's Ethnic Diversity* (New York: Macmillan, 1988); S. Chan, *Asian Americans: An Interpretive History* (Boston: Tawne, 1991); Leonard, *The South Asian Americans.*

11. Helweg and Helweg, *A Migrant Success Story;* Leonard, *The South Asian Americans* (appendix II). For the 2000 figure, see the Lewis Mumford Center for Comparative Urban and Regional Research, State University of New York at Albany, at http://mum fordrdyndns.org/cen2000/AsianPop/AsianSort/ainsort.html.

12. The following provide good information on the push and pull factors relative to immigration from the Indian subcontinent: P. Saran and E. Eames, eds., *The New Ethnics: Asian Indians in the United States* (New York: Praeger, 1980); U. Minocha, "South Asian Immigrants: Trends and Impacts on the Sending and Receiving Societies," in *Pacific Bridges: The New Immigration from Asia and the Pacific Islands,* ed. J. T. Fawcett and B. V. Carino (New York: Center for Migration Studies, 1987), 347–74; M. Hossain, "South Asians in Southern California: A Sociological Study of Immigrants from India, Pakistan, and Bangladesh," in *South Asian Bulletin* 2, no. 1 (1982): 74–82. Nevada and Las Vegas have recently experienced unprecedented growth and are the fastest growing areas in the nation. The cover stories published in *Time, National Geographic,* and *Civilization* indicated that Las Vegas has matured as a city and yet keeps its frontier spirit. For further details, see E. E. Baldwin, "Las Vegas in Popular Culture" (Ph.D. dissertation, University of Nevada, Las Vegas, 1997); R. O.

Davies, *The Maverick Spirit: Building of the New Nevada* (Reno: University of Nevada Press, 1999); M. Gottdiener, C. C. Collins, and D. R. Dickens, *Las Vegas: The Social Production of an All-American City* (Malden, Mass.: Blackwell, 1999); D. Thompson, *In Nevada: The Land, the People, God, and Chance* (New York: Alfred A. Knopf, 1999). Examples of recreational areas include Hoover Dam, Lake Mead, Mount Charleston, Kyle Canyon, Death Valley National Park, and Zion National Park.

13. http://mumford1.dyndns.org/cen2000/BlackWhite/DiversityBWDataPages/ 4120msaBWCT; and http://mumford1dyndns.org/cen2000/AsianPopAsian PopData/ 4120msa.htm. Interestingly, locals have lower estimates than the Lewis Mumford Center. They estimate that there are about 2,350 to 2,585 families from the subcontinent in Las Vegas; 2000–2,100 from India, 200–300 from Pakistan, 50–60 from Bangladesh, and 100–125 from Sri Lanka. This would amount to a total of between 4,400 and 6,000 people.

14. For further details, see Leonard, *The South Asian Americans;* Helweg and Helweg, *An Immigrant Success Story.*

15. India, together with Pakistan, account for almost 90 percent of the immigrants in America from the Indian subcontinent. This high rate of emigration of highly educated people has been labeled a "brain drain" problem for the subcontinent. For further discussion of this topic, see Minocha, "South Asian Immigrants."

16. P. Saran, *The Asian Indian Experience in the United States* (Cambridge, Mass.: Schenkman Publishing, 1985), 113–15.

17. For supporting analyses, see Leonard, *The South Asian Americans;* Helweg and Helweg, *An Immigrant Success Story.*

18. For further details, see Leonard, *The South Asian Americans.*

19. Early indications of the professional and economic successes of the immigrants have been provided in several works, including P. A. Thottathi and P. Saran, "An Economic Profile of Asian Indians," in *The New Ethnics: Asian Indians in the United States,* 233–46; U. Minocha, "South Asian Immigrants," *India News* (March 2000): 7. The article also pointed out that two Indian Americans (the late Har Gobind Khorana and the late Subrahmanyan Chandrasekhar) had won Nobel Prizes in medicine and physics respectively. The NASA's X-ray observatory was named the Chandra X-ray observatory in honor of the late Subrahmanyan Chandrasekhar. Dr. Kalpana Chawla became the first Indian American female to fly in the U.S. space shuttle in 1997. In terms of economic impact, the buying power of Indian Americans in the United States was valued at $30 billion annually.

20. A good discussion of the networking and organizations at the national level is Leonard, *The South Asian Americans.*

21. Information in this and following paragraphs is based on long-term participation in and observation of the South Asian community in Las Vegas and conversations with many of its members.

22. The founding dates of this and other societies, organizations, and business establishments discussed in this chapter are based upon the author's recollection and experiences in Nevada and are, therefore, approximate. The Islamic Society of South-

ern Nevada includes members from Pakistan as well as from other nations, particularly Middle Easterners.

23. The predominant populations in Sri Lanka are Buddhists, Hindus, Muslims, and Christians.

24. Cricket and soccer games are as popular in India, Pakistan, Bangladesh, and Sri Lanka as baseball and football are in America.

25. For further information, see S. Athar, *Reflections of an American Muslim* (Chicago: QAZI, 1994); A. Rajagopal, "Disarticulating Exilic Nationalism: Indian Immigrants in the U.S.," paper presented at the American Ethnological Society Meeting, Austin, Texas, 1995; Leonard, *The South Asian Americans.*

26. Trevor Hayes, "First Phase: Temple Offers Area Hindus Place to Worship," *Las Vegas Review Journal,* April 29, 2001.

27. The author's long-term participation in the South Asian community and conversation with many of its members is the source for the information in this and the following paragraphs.

28. Sikhs and Hindus follow the Sikh religion. Sikhs celebrate several Hindu festivals and go on pilgrimages to many Hindu holy places. Hindus attend and sponsor the recital of "Guru Grantha Sahib," observe Sikh holidays, and visit Sikh temples. *Gazal* is a particular form of Urdu poetry that is sung in a specified style.

29. A number of local professional women have given dance lessons to local children for a small fee. Children are also coached for their dance performances at the annual Diwali function.

30. For further information, see D. S. Saund, *Congressman from India* (New York: E. P. Dutton, 1960); Leonard, *The South Asian Americans.*

31. The information here and in the following paragraphs is based upon the author's personal knowledge of Las Vegas's South Asian community as well as conversations with many of its members.

32. For further information, see Saund, *Congressman from India;* Leonard, *The South Asian Americans.*

33. This section on emotional challenges is based on an earlier article by the author, S. Sharma, "Indian Migrants in the United States: The Challenges, Adjustments, and Dilemmas," *Guru Nanak Journal of Sociology* 22, no. 1 (2001): 1–15. Other significant sources of information are: S. S. Dasgupta, *On the Trail of an Uncertain Dream: Indian Immigrant Experience in America* (New York: AMS Press, 1989); P. G. Min, *Asian Americans: Contemporary Trends and Issues* (Thousand Oaks, Calif.: Sage Publications, 1995); Saran, *Asian Indian Experience;* Helweg and Helweg, *An Immigrant Success Story.*

34. R. H. Baylor, "Series Foreword," in Leonard, *The South Asian Americans,* x.

CHAPTER 15

The Chileans

BERNARDO T. ARRIAZA

Chilean migration to the United States began with the 1849 California Gold Rush. Before reliable overland routes were developed, prospectors preferred the long route around Cape Horn, and the ports serving Chile's agriculturally rich Central Valley provisioned the forty-niners and supplied California with basic foodstuffs for several years. An estimated 30,000 Chileans boarded the forty-niners' ships or migrated to California on merchant ships. Although to the burgeoning population of European Americans the Chileans blended into the broader Mexican population of California, the early California Chileans left their distinctive marks. One of these is the legendary outlaw Joaquín Murieta, who is often considered a Mexican. In 2000 Mayor Willie Brown dedicated a memorial in the Chilecito district of San Francisco to commemorate Chileans' contribution to the city's early history. In Nevada the Chilean presence started as early as 1870 with a few immigrants working as grocers and mule packers in the mining camp of Hamilton.[1]

The Gold Rush did not establish enough Chileans permanently in California to start an immigration stream, and during the subsequent 125 years, there was little Chilean immigration to the United States. Thanks to mining and industrial growth, the Chilean economy was relatively strong by Latin American standards. Chile developed a stable political system and emerged as Latin America's most democratic country. Thus, there were neither economic nor political push factors that might have promoted substantial United States–bound emigration from Chile. Europe and other Latin American countries attracted more Chilean immigrants than did the United States. Those who immigrated did so for personal reasons, such as family reunification, graduate education, university teaching, or greater economic opportunity. While the excellent system of public universities and technical schools produced a highly educated cadre capable of filling well-paying jobs abroad, the location in Chile of numerous agencies of the United Nations and other international organizations, beginning in the 1950s, reduced the pull factor that might otherwise have caused a serious "brain drain."[2]

Chile's relative political stability ended with turmoil and economic crisis between 1970 and 1985, prompting substantial emigration. The election of Socialist president Salvador Allende in 1970, his overthrow by the military in 1973, and the severe political repression and human rights violations instituted by the dictatorship of General Augusto Pinochet (1973–90) propelled some 200,000 Chileans into exile. However, very few Chileans sought asylum in the United States, which supported the Pinochet dictatorship with varying degrees of enthusiasm and barred many Allende supporters from entering the country. Severe economic crises in 1973–77 and 1981–85 swelled the exiles' ranks. Despite the recovery and subsequent rapid development of the Chilean economy and the restoration of democracy in 1990, many exiles have not returned. This is due in large part to the continuing problem of national reconciliation following the dictatorship, whose operatives refuse to collaborate in revealing the facts about the thousands of Chileans killed during the Pinochet regime or the location of the bodies of those who disappeared.[3]

From the second half of the 1980s to the present, the Chilean economy has been dynamic. In the opinion of many, it is the model that Latin America should follow. Often compared with the Asian "tigers," Chile, referred to as the "jaguar," has experienced rapid growth, low inflation, and little corruption.[4] Despite the gleaming macroeconomic statistics, however, unemployment has increased in recent years and health care and education costs have risen, forcing many middle-class families into reduced standards of living. Thus the small but steady stream of immigration to the United States has continued.

According to the 2000 U.S. census, there were over 35,305,818 Hispanics or Latinos living in United States, representing 12.5 percent of the total U.S. population. Of the more than 35 million Hispanics, 68,849 persons were Chilean by birth or descent, representing 0.2 percent of the total U.S. Hispanic population and 0.02 percent of the total U.S. population. Conversely, only 0.46 percent of Chile's population of 15 million reside in the United States, in contrast with an estimated 25 percent of Mexicans, 11 percent of Cubans, over 10 percent of Salvadorans and 3.3 percent of Guatemalans. The Chilean figure is typical of South American countries with the exception of Colombia, which has 1.3 percent of its people residing in the United States. The largest of the small Chilean communities in the United States are in Miami, New York, Los Angeles, and the San Francisco Bay Area.[5]

There is little literature on Chileans in the United States. Unlike most European and several Asian and Latin American immigrant groups, Chileans have no formal nationally elected organization in the United States, hence no national source of data, no national publication, and no nationwide lobby. This lack of a visible national presence is due in part to the small number of Chileans in the United States. A second factor is that in the United States,

Chileans are commonly subsumed with other Latin Americans (and Spanish speakers) under the rubric "Hispanic," not only in most census data but in common practice. Whatever their ancestry (Spanish, Basque, Italian, German, Arab, Croat, native aboriginal, or mixed), when they reach this country Chileans are Hispanics or Latin Americans.[6] However, as is the case in Las Vegas, Chileans do not readily identify themselves as Hispanics or Latin Americans. Historically isolated since the time when their land was Spain's most remote American colony and sealed off by a parched northern desert, the Pacific Ocean, and the formidable barrier of the Andes, Chileans consider themselves a people apart. Only in the age of jet travel and the Internet, and because of political exile, has this sense of separateness begun to break down. It is their strong sense of nationalism and feeling of being different from other Latin Americans that explains why the community of Chileans in Las Vegas is so organized and active.

Chileans Abroad

Chile is divided for administrative purposes into thirteen political regions. It is estimated that about 1 million Chileans live abroad, or in "Region XIV" as it is known, representing 6.7 percent of Chile's total population.[7] In most of the countries where they live, Chileans of Region XIV have created many associations in order to maintain their roots and their socioeconomic and political ties with Chile. In the case of North America the independent organization Centro Cívico of New York, created in 1994, has been extremely active.[8] It has organized three "Encounters of Chileans Abroad": in 1997 in Chicago, in 2000 in New York, and in 2003 in Washington, D.C. I attended the New York meeting, which brought together Chileans from all over the United States and Canada. The opening ceremony at the New York City Hall was an emotional event at which Puerto Rican council member Víctor L. Robles spoke about the hardships of his Latino life and the importance of political participation. He gave a warm welcome, stating: "This is the first time that the Chilean national anthem has been played here in the City Hall of New York. It is a historical moment to have Chilean Americans making a physical presence in the municipality of New York." To commemorate the event Robles presented a proclamation of gratitude to Mario Tapia, president of the Centro Cívico, for his contribution to improving the quality of life for elderly New Yorkers.

Chileans of Region XIV are actively seeking a role in Chile's political economy and lobbying for a just interpretation of their constitution's provisions regarding citizenship. The 1980 constitution, written and adopted during Pinochet's dictatorship, allows the preservation of Chilean nationality even when a second one has been granted by another nation. Yet beginning in 1990, pro-Pinochet elements stripped some 10,000 exiles of their Chilean citizenship in order to prevent their return.[9] Canceling the nationality of many Chileans living abroad has created additional complications for inheritance, property ownership, and pensions, especially for those wanting to return to Chile. At present, children of Chileans born abroad must reside in Chile for one year to be considered Chileans; registration with a consulate is not sufficient. Additionally, Chileans living abroad are not permitted to adopt orphaned Chilean children, nor does the Chilean constitution allow Chileans to vote if they live outside their country. For these reasons Chileans living abroad must fight to obtain equal civil rights. Osvaldo Nuñez, an ex-congressman living in Canada, lamented, "I don't understand why Chile has not made progress in protecting its citizens who live abroad."[10]

Centro Cívico leaders have traveled several times to Chile to urge the Chilean congress to enact a constitutional amendment to help Chileans abroad. In 1993 a bill was sent to the Chilean senate addressing these concerns, but it still has not been passed into law. Since the first day of his presidency in 2000, Ricardo Lagos has supported efforts to integrate all Chileans economically and politically, independently of where they live. Lagos has stated that the knowledge and experience gained by Chileans living abroad can help Chile to speed up its scientific and socioeconomic development. A positive development was the creation in 2000 of the DICOEX (Dirección para las Comunidades de Chilenos en el Exterior), a governmental office designed to attend to the needs of the growing Region XIV and to promote the constitutional amendment granting Chileans abroad equal civil rights.

In fact, Chileans abroad send money to relatives in Chile; they bring relatives to their new country to broaden their economic, academic, and cultural horizons; they often conduct international business and invest in Chile's economy; they engage in research and collaboration with Chilean universities and independently lobby for Chile's economic interests. Moreover, Chileans abroad preserve and transmit their culture wherever they go by publicly exhibiting their traditions and folklore, thus acting as cultural ambassadors for the country.

Chileans of Region XIV have been reconnecting themselves to their Chilean roots thanks to two independent forces. First, they have reached a critical mass. This allows them to have a stronger voice to transcend frontiers and lobby on the problems that affect them directly. Second, easy access to the Internet has created a *ramada,* or point of encounter, particularly on two fronts: within Region XIV and between Region XIV and Chile. There, Chileans can find virtual consulates, news, recipes, songs, sports, and music from their beloved Chile. Reading the Internet newspapers and watching Internet television or satellite TV keep Chileans informed about their native country. One can visit a Chilean home in Las Vegas during a weekend and have the pleasant surprise of watching news or sports from a Chilean TV station.[11]

The Internet allows Chileans a portal into their home country—a way to keep in touch with family and friends and to keep current. A cartoon in http://www.casachile.cl tests how much of a Chilean one is by asking trivial questions.[12] A high score reads, "Aunque se te ha pegado el acento, todavía eres hincha de la roja y de los asados." This means, even though one now has an accent, one still loves the red and barbecue. The *roja,* or red, is a metaphor for the country and represents the national team sport—soccer, of course.

Unfortunately, few formal studies have been done to track down and quantify how, when, and why Chileans chose to leave Chile or what their current socioeconomic status is. Tapia, at the New York "Encounter of Chileans Abroad" meeting, said that the census figure of 68,849 Chileans in the United States is too low. He estimated that in 1990 there were 100,000 Chileans living in the United States and in 2000 there must have been about 140,000. The Lewis Mumford Center at the State University of New York at Albany gives a number of 117,698 Chileans in the United States for 2000 and no data for the previous census. In addition the Chilean authorities (Ambassador Andrés Bianchi, consul in New York Jorge Valenzuela, and DICOEX subdirector Marcel Young), also in attendance at the New York meeting, were shocked to learn that there are hundreds of illegal Chileans living in the United States who are not accounted for.[13]

In 2000, Portal CasaChile.cl (with the support of DICOEX and the Ministry of Education) launched a poll to gather information from Region XIV using the Web and consulates. A total of 3,050 people from eighty countries answered the poll.[14] This information provides a glimpse of the community of Region XIV. The majority of these expatriates are well educated, with 41 percent holding university degrees, 20 percent with postgraduate education, 20 percent with technical degrees, 13 percent with high-school diplomas, and 6 percent with elementary education. Thirty-four percent of Chileans abroad left the country in pursuit of better economic opportunities, and 20 percent left to reconnect with family abroad. Twenty-one percent left for political reasons, 13 percent for academic opportunities, and 12 percent cited other reasons. The exodus of Chileans has been going on for several decades: 4 percent left the country before or during 1970, 17 percent between 1971 and 1975, 17 percent between 1976 and 1980, and 26 percent between 1995 and

2000. A large percentage (55 percent) dream of returning, perhaps echoing the words of Nobel Laureate poet Pablo Neruda when he was living abroad:

Oh Chile, largo pétalo
de mar y vino y nieve,
ay cuándo
ay cuándo y cuándo
ay cuándo
me encontraré contigo . . .

(Oh Chile, long ocean petal, wine and snow, when, when, when I will see you again.)[15]

Chileans living abroad say they feel very in touch and connected with their homeland (51 percent); the majority (73 percent) perceive that Chile is a country making progress, and few (3 percent) think that it is a "backward country."

Chileans abroad regard their folklore groups as essential to the maintenance of their identity. Chilean folklore groups from Sweden (Rucalí Folklore) or Las Vegas (Ecos de Chile) are the center (*la chispa de la identidad*) of their social life, while their social organizations represent the extended families they left behind. Folklore performances project the culture of the country. Songs and the dancing of *cuecas* (the national folkloric dance) strengthen the social bonds among Chileans and friends, bringing out a sense of pride in their national identity. This is particularly true on September 18, Chilean Independence Day, when, for example, in Los Angeles over a thousand Chileans gather to drink Chilean wine, eat *empanadas* (meat turnovers), and celebrate with traditional music and dances. Often Las Vegas's own folklore group, Ecos de Chile, is the guest of honor performing for the Los Angeles Chilean community.

Chileans in Las Vegas

In the year 2000 the total population of Clark County in Nevada, the fastest-growing county in United States, was 1,375,765, reflecting an increase of 85.5 percent in the last ten years. The Chilean-American Association of Las Vegas estimates that there are about 500 Chileans living in Las Vegas. The revised 2000 U.S. census data indicate 906 Chileans, but according to the Lewis Mumford Center this number could be as high as 1,065. Ximena Banks, a Chilean resident of Las Vegas since 1982, agrees with the Mumford estimate. Within the Hispanic community as a whole, Chileans are few compared with the 250,574 Mexicans, 12,006 Cubans, or 12,242 Salvadorans who live in Las Vegas, according to Lewis Mumford Center estimates. However, local

Chileans are in the middle ranks of Las Vegas's South American populations, which range from 2,975 Colombians to 82 Paraguayans.[16]

To get a sense of where the Chilean community stands in this city, with the help of the Chilean-American Association of Las Vegas, we sent a questionnaire to 250 Chileans in 1999. From the 63 replies, statistics were gathered indicating that about 60 percent of Chileans residing in Las Vegas come from Santiago, the capital of Chile, and 13 percent from Viña del Mar, a coastal city near Santiago. The rest (27 percent) come from other parts of the country, but few hail from the south. This is not surprising given that about 40 percent of Chileans live in Santiago and surrounding areas, although as a whole the country boasts a low population density of approximately thirty-four persons per square mile, excluding the Antarctic and Easter Island.[17]

The survey indicates that the educational level of Las Vegas Chileans ranges from elementary education (10 percent) to the doctoral level (3 percent). The greatest number of respondents have college degrees (37 percent). These numbers are consistent with data from Chile, which suggests that a great majority of Chileans seek technical or college degrees but few pursue master's and doctoral degrees. In Chile elementary education is mandatory; illiteracy is practically unknown, and most people obtain a high-school diploma. A few decades ago there were only eight main universities. Today, thanks to the free-market economy, centers for higher education have proliferated. Some have private support, while others receive state financing.[18] Chile's educational system has produced two Nobel Prize laureates, Gabriela Mistral (1945) and Pablo Neruda (1971), as well as contemporary novelist Isabel Allende, the global best-selling author of *The House of the Spirits, Daughter of the Fortune, Portrait in Sepia,* and many other works.

The most common reason for immigration to the United States, including Las Vegas, seems to be economic opportunity. Several respondents added the comment "*No pasa na' en Chile,*" meaning that they were frustrated with the slow rate of Chile's trickle-down economics, the lack of jobs and business opportunities. None of the respondents specifically mentioned being a political refugee.

Marlene Oñate, treasurer of the Chilean-American Association, commented that compared with other Hispanic groups such as Mexicans and Salvadorans, Chileans come to Las Vegas not to get away from basic economic struggles or social instability at home but to improve upon what they already have. You need to have money to get to Las Vegas in the first place, she added.[19]

Samuel Gana, an artist from Viña del Mar in central Chile, came to Los Angeles in 1988 to work for Walt Disney. When things did not work out as planned, he moved to Las Vegas. "Las Vegas has given me a new source of inspiration," he said. "The desert, the casinos, it's a collage of life. I feel rejuvenated here. I am slowly finding my art niche." In Chile art and comics were his work; he drew *Condorito* (Little Condor), a popular and well-known Chilean cartoon. His love, however, is painting. His paintings have been exhibited in Spain, New York, and Las Vegas. "Today, I am becoming myself again, exploring my art, my paintings," he said with a smile. His colorful, figurative impressionistic painting mixes the joy of life with a subtle stroke of mysticism.

According to the 1999 survey results, Chileans residing in Las Vegas had been in the United States an average of seventeen years, but it seems that they have only recently migrated to Las Vegas (mean eight years and median three years). The survey indicates that 36 percent came to the city specifically to take advantage of economic opportunities. Chileans came to Las Vegas alone (46 percent), with their families (46 percent), or with friends (1 percent). They work as hotel employees, musicians, artists, teachers, engineers, real-estate agents, in related occupations, or in the college/university systems. The greatest number work in casinos (27 percent) or as entrepreneurs in business activities (14 percent). Sixteen percent make less than twenty thousand dollars a year, 39 percent make between twenty thousand and forty thousand dollars a year, while 21 percent earn over sixty thousand dollars a year. Many feel they have achieved (72 percent) or surpassed (15 percent) their economic goals. Chilean entrepreneur Ramón Canales is a very successful businessman selling furniture. He encouraged all his relatives to migrate to United States. He said, "It's cheaper for me to bring all my relatives, than for me to continuously go to Chile and help them there. In this way, I can have them all year round."

Although the majority of Las Vegas Chileans are married (67 percent), family size is small, averaging three persons per family. The greatest number are Catholics (26 percent) followed by Mormons (14 percent), Adventists (4 percent), and "other" (39 percent). Following tradition, 44 percent attend church services regularly, while others seek different kinds of social activities, including folklore (19 percent). The data on religious affiliation differs somewhat from that for Chile, where the majority is Catholic (90 percent); other religions include Protestants, Mormons, and a small number of Jewish and Moslem groups.

The 1999 survey indicated that 70 percent of the Las Vegas Chileans belong to the Chilean-American Association, organized in 1991. About 51 percent like to keep in touch with other Chileans in Las Vegas or in the United States, either to maintain their language, enjoy common meals, or watch important soccer matches. The Chilean community is very active in Las Vegas.

Eighty-one percent of Chileans surveyed indicated that, while feeling distinctively Chilean, they also feel well integrated into Las Vegas.

Overall, the results obtained by CasaChile.cl and the survey conducted by the Chilean-American Association of Las Vegas are comparable. An exception was noted in two areas: "level of education" and "the reason to leave Chile." The level of education is higher among Chileans living elsewhere in the world, particularly at the postgraduate level (20 percent versus 5 percent). The "reason to leave" is comparable, except in the subcategory "political reason," which is higher in the Chileans living elsewhere (21 percent versus 2 percent).

The Chilean-American Association of Las Vegas

The Chilean-American Association is a nonprofit organization whose goals are to promote camaraderie among Chileans and maintain cultural roots. Its board consists of Patricio Sarnataro (president), Eugenia Shroeder (vice president), Grace Ryan (secretary), and Marlene Oñate (treasurer). The association provides a monthly printed newsletter, *Chile-Las Vegas.Hoy*, to keep members informed of events and news in Las Vegas and back home in Chile. The association sets specific goals annually. The main goal for the year 2001 was to obtain a consulate for Las Vegas. For the year 2002 the goals were to implement the consulate and to generate scholarships for Chilean students; the goal for 2003 was to create a Chilean sister city with Las Vegas.

Despite its small size, the Chilean community is becoming well known and respected within Las Vegas's larger Hispanic community due largely to the efforts of the Chilean-American Association. In September 2000 the Puerto Rican community honored the Chilean-American Association for its organization and participation within the wider Hispanic community. In October 2000, during the Hispanic Day Parade, Chilean-American Association president Paula Sparkuhl was the grand marshal along with Carmen Mahan of the Colombian-American Association. In November 2000, during the visit of Chilean consul Rodrigo Pérez, Mayor Oscar Goodman and Ronald Remington, president of the Community College of Southern Nevada, honored Consul Pérez by giving him the keys to the city and the college, respectively.

Paulina Bosch, who came to Las Vegas in 1986 to assist her daughter in caring for her new granddaughter, is one of the movers and shakers in the Chilean community. Bosch is the editor of *Chile–Las Vegas.Hoy*. "Our first newsletter, eons ago, was called *Copihue*, named after our national flower, and was edited by Nelson Mackenna," she said. "In August 19, 1992 with Lupe Jimeno we started the *Ultimas Noticias* [The Latest News] and in the year

2000 the Association decided to change the name of the newsletter to *Chile–Las Vegas.Hoy* to reflect the ongoing Internet trends," said Bosch. Paulina loves her volunteer work and does the newsletter not only to inform but more importantly to unite the community.

Bosch also coordinates the Las Vegas Chilean-American Association's local charity work, such as collecting Christmas toys for poor children and visiting older people. Bosch and the association also do charitable work in Chile by sending aid to incarcerated females. Chilean females in Las Vegas are making the greatest effort as leaders of their community. Five of eight presidents of the association have been females.[20]

Paula Sparkuhl, former president of the Chilean-American Association, inherited her love of community service from her mother, Paulina Bosch. Sparkuhl, born in Cauquenes in South-Central Chile, arrived in Las Vegas in 1981. "I came to Las Vegas following in the steps of my husband, Alex Sparkuhl, a physician," said Paula. A business entrepreneur in interior design, she, along with her collaborators, has been very active in bringing the Chilean community together not only at national holidays but also for regular social gatherings. They have lobbied for a consulate to assist the needs of the local Chilean community, and in 2001 Consul General Rodrigo Pérez (stationed in Los Angeles) nominated Paula Sparkuhl as an honorary consul in Las Vegas. "I want the Chilean-American Association to become a social magnet to attract as many Chileans as possible, in order to build an even stronger community," said Paula.

Ecos de Chile Folklore Group

Another social outlet within the Las Vegas community is Ecos de Chile, an amateur folklore group created in 1998 thanks to the enthusiasm of Sonia Yáñez. Ecos de Chile is composed of fourteen to eighteen members— musicians, dancers, and singers. The group varies in size because members' work schedules sometimes conflict with rehearsals and performances. Ecos de Chile has performed in many local events such as the International Food and Folklife Festival and Latin American Heritage Month as well as in other states, (for example, Los Angeles and Rancho San Antonio, California).

Ecos de Chile brings people together. "I am a fan of Ecos de Chile," said retired engineer Leonel Leyton; "every time that I see the group perform it sends shivers down my spine." In November 2001, during a performance to honor Consul Pérez during his first official visit to Las Vegas, Wilson Adaros, a member of Ecos de Chile, commented to the consul, "I learned to dance *cueca* here in the United States and now I feel more Chilean than when I was in Chile."

When Ecos de Chile debuted at the International Food and Folklife Festival of Las Vegas in June 1998, their performance captivated the audience and buoyed the members of the group to continue their work. Ecos de Chile plays music from the different regions of Chile: the north (pan-Andean music), with colorful dancing of *diabladas;* the central region, with the typical Chilean cowboy (*huaso*) and cowgirl outfits; and the south's *chilota* music. The group has several highly talented musicians. Andrés Vargas plays the guitar, flute, accordion, and *charango* (a small guitarlike instrument made from an armadillo shell); Lorena Cottam, a student at the Community College of Southern Nevada, is pursuing a professional career as a singer and guitar player; and Tomás Castillo used to play professionally in Chile. Vargas and Castillo recently released their first compact disc, featuring Christmas songs, with Cottam.[21] Rosa Vargas, Jaime Rodríguez, and Hugo Riquelme are also excellent guitar players. Wilson Adaros plays the drum and dances. Of the eleven dancers, three are particularly talented: Carlos Silva, Miguel Chandía, and Loreto Echague.

Silva has been the artistic director and choreographer of Ecos de Chile since the group's inception. Born in Valparaíso in central Chile, he left with his family when he was fourteen years old. Silva moved to the United States in 1986, after residing in Switzerland for six years. He came to Las Vegas in 1995 to pursue the "American dream." He works as a cook in an elite country club. Despite his many moves, wherever he goes he always finds a way to be connected with folklore. "It runs in the family," Silva says. "My father was a great dancer and my cousins are folklorists too." His passion for folklore and dancing started in the Chilean schools. Now, as a folklorist, he is proud of the accomplishments of the group. All the members of Ecos de Chile have full-time jobs, but they always find a way to practice folklore. Silva remarks, "We love to share our traditions." He feels at home in Las Vegas and says he has never felt discriminated against; sometimes, however, Silva says, he is frustrated because "people don't know enough about Chile and they think we are all Mexicans." Silva does not like politics or sports, preferring music instead. He thinks that through folklore we can teach our children, particularly those born in the United States, not only our language, but also our music and our roots.[22]

Conclusion

Chileans living outside of their homeland have a strong sense of identity. They are deeply interested and remain entrenched in their native country, where they maintain extended families. They still cheer their soccer teams and lament that La Roja did not qualify for the Japan-Korea World Cup

2002. Las Vegas Chileans cope with nostalgia for their homeland by seeking friends in the Chilean community and by engaging in community-related social activities. Thanks to the power of the Internet and satellite TV, they are well informed about their homeland. To help themselves and Chile, residents of Region XIV have created a worldwide coalition and are continuously lobbying to regain two basic social rights: the rights to maintain their nationality and to vote in Chilean elections from abroad. In a global era they feel that whatever happens in Chile still affects them socially, economically, politically, and—above all—emotionally.

In Las Vegas "the children of the jaguar" are doing well financially. They are a small but dynamic group brought together by the Chilean-American Association and the folklore group Ecos de Chile. The various social and cultural gatherings sponsored by these entities play an important role in maintaining and strengthening Chilean identity. Overall, there seems to be a genuine sense of camaraderie and cooperation within the Las Vegas Chilean community.

Notes

I want to thank the Chilean-American Association and Marlene Oñate and Paulina Bosch for sending the questionnaire to the Chilean community to gather background information. Special thanks go to Marta Alfonso, who generously synthesized the data. Lastly, special *gracias* to those people who took the time to reply and answer my inquiries. Personally, as a Chilean, I would like to thank Dr. Tom Wright and Dr. Jerry Simich for inviting me to collaborate in their project. It was a nice opportunity to summarize the sentiments of the Chileans living abroad and to discuss our efforts to create a better Chile that includes us all. Last but not least, my gratitude goes to Dr. Vicki Cassman and Michelle Kaye for their keen editorial eyes in providing constructive criticism.

1. Carlos U. López, *Chilenos in California: A Study of the 1850, 1852, and 1860 Censuses* (San Francisco: R and E Research Associates, 1973); Edwin Beilharz and Carlos U. López, *We Were Forty-Niners* (Pasadena: Ward Ritchie Press, 1976). See also http://www.latercera.cl, December 12, 1998, "Joaquín Murieta se pone de moda," by Leopoldo Pulgar. On memorial, see *Chile–Las Vegas.Hoy* 97 (2001): 7. The 1870 U.S. Census in Hamilton, Nevada, listed the following Chileans: Quinino Guzmán, age forty-six, mule packer; Andrés Sandoval, age forty-five, grocer (his wife, Carmela, was born in Spain, and together they had five children, four born in California and one in Nevada); Laureano Leyvas, age thirty-one, mule packer.

2. The best general history of Chile in English is Brian Loveman, *Chile: The Legacy of Hispanic Capitalism*, 3d ed. (New York: Oxford University Press, 2001).

3. Thomas C. Wright and Rody Oñate, *Flight from Chile: Voices of Exile* (Albuquerque: University of New Mexico Press, 1998); *Informe de la Comisión Nacional de*

Verdad y Reconciliación, March 1991, at http://www.derechoschile.com/espanol/ recursos.htm. This truth commission reported that under the Pinochet regime, 1,322 people were killed and 957 were arrested and missing. Further discoveries have shown the figures to be low; see Chile, Corporación Nacional de Reparación y Reconciliación, *Informe Sobre Calificacion de víctimas de violaciones de derechos humanos y de la violencia politica* (Santiago: Corporación Nacional de Reparación y Reconciliación, 1996). It is estimated that 300,000 Chileans live in Argentina.

4. In 1997 Chile experienced a remarkable 7.1 percent annual expansion of the gross domestic product, but during recent years (1999 to 2002) the growth is around 3 percent, official unemployment rate is high at 9 percent, and inflation is around 3 percent. See *La Tercera,* no. 18473, January 14, 2001, Suplemento de Economía; *Revista Ercilla* 3145, "Economía en ascuas" (September 4–17, 2000): 50–55; http://www.bcentral.cl/esp/politicas/exposiciones/ejecutivos/pdf/2002/gallego_loayza_schmidthebbelagosto192002.pdf; http://www.finanzas.com/id.5179702/noticias/noticia.htm. In recent years (2000 to 2003) corruption made headline news, an unusual development. See *Revista Ercilla* 3147, Editorial, Indemnizaciones indebidas (October 2–15, 2000): 5; Telma Luzzani, *South America,* at http://www.globalcorruptionreport.org/download/rrsamerica.pdf; http://www.estrategia.cl/histo/200303/12/economi/mula.htm (March 2003).

5. U.S. Census 2000, www.census.gov.population/www/socdemo/hispanic.html (La Población Hispana, table 1). The total population in the United States was 281,421,906. Population data taken from UNEP, at http://grid2.cr.usgov/globalpop/lac/appendix.htm. Mexico 95,8M; El Salvador 6,7M; Guatemala 10M; Cuba 11,2 M Argentina 34,3M; Chile 15,1M and Colombia 36,6M. Based on data gathered at informal meetings.

6. Nick Caistor, ed., *Chile. A Guide to the People, Politics and Culture* (Latin America Bureau, 1998).

7. DICOEX, ed., *El Volantín* (Santiago, Chile, September 2001): 14.

8. http://www.siemprechilenos.com.

9. Article 1, section 1, of the Chilean constitution states: "La causal de pérdida de la nacionalidad chilena señalada precedentemente no regirá respecto de los chilenos que, en virtud de disposiciones constitucionales, legales o administrativas del Estado en cuyo territorio residan, adopten la nacionalidad extranjera como condición de su permanencia en él o de igualdad jurídica en el ejercicio de los derechos civiles con los nacionales del respectivo país." (The cause for loss of Chilean nationality, as detailed before, will not occur for those Chileans who, given constitutional, legal or administrative rules of the State where they reside, adopt a foreign nationality as a need to stay in that country or as a need to have equal civil rights or opportunities equivalent to the citizens of such a country.) Exclusivo! Documento demuestra el error oficial, January 20, 2002, at http://www.siemprechilenos.com/somostodos.htm. See also Viernes 11 de Enero 2002 (Friday, January 11, 2002), at http://2002.27.147.27/ciu da dania/consuladovirtual.

10. En foco. Por el honor de ser chileno, 2002, at http://www.CasaChile.cl.

11. See http:/www.casachile.cl and http:www.chilelindo.cl, which are frequent stops for cyber surfers. Newspaper examples include http://www.latercera.cl, http://www.emol.com, and http://www.estrategia.com. See also Internet television, at http://www.tvn.cl; http://www.tele13.cl.

12. Test de Chilenidad, at http://www.casachile.cl.

13. Lewis Mumford Center, State University of New York at Albany, at http://mumford1.dyndns.org/cen2000/HispanicPop/HspReport/page6.html. Oral statement made at the 2000 New York meeting.

14. http://www.casachile.cl/especiales/lraencuesta/.

15. http://www.uchile.cl/neruda/obra/obrauvasyelviento6.html.

16. Lewis Mumford Center, University of New York at Albany, at http:mumford 1dyndns.or/cen2000/HispanicPop/HspPopData/4120msa.htm.

17. Copy in author's possession.

18. Robert Austin, "Armed Forces, Market Forces: Intellectuals and Higher Education in Chile, 1973–1993," in *Latin American Perspectives* 25, no. 5 (September 1997): 25–58.

19. This and other quotations from Las Vegas Chileans were gathered over several years in the author's casual conversations with the individuals quoted.

20. Presidents of the Chilean-American Association, Las Vegas, include: Nelson Mackenna (1991–92), José González (1992–94), María Luisa Nordenflytch (1994–95), Paulina Tilley (1995–96), Olga González (1996–98), Gloria Salvador (1998–2000), Paula Sparkuhl (2000–2002), Patricio Sarnataro (2000–present).

21. lorena@comnett.net.

22. Participants in Ecos de Chile include: Wilson Adaros (musician, dancer), Lorena Cottam (musician, codirector), Tomás Castillo (musician), Hugo Requelme (musician), Jaime Rodríguez (musician), Rosa Vargas (musician), Andrés Vargas (musician, director), Drago Zlatar (musician), Inés Adaros (dancer), Bernardo Arriaza (dancer), Miguel Chandia (dancer), Loreto Echague (dancer), Edmee Marcek (dancer), Héctor Requelme (dancer), Lilian Requelme (dancer), Grace Ryan (dancer), Rosa Ortiz (dancer), Edith Silva (dancer), Carlos Silva (dancer, director).

CONTRIBUTORS

STAVROS ANTHONY earned his M.A. in political science and his Ph.D. in sociology from the University of Nevada, Las Vegas, and is a twenty-four-year veteran of the Las Vegas Metropolitan Police Department. His research and writings have focused on the Greek community in Las Vegas and, most recently, on the structural dimensions of community-oriented police departments.

BERNARDO T. ARRIAZA is a professor of physical anthropology at the University of Nevada, Las Vegas, and a researcher at the Universidad de Tarapacá in Arica, Chile. He is the author of three books, including *Beyond Death: The Chinchorro Mummies of Ancient Chile* (1995), and has contributed to a number of edited volumes and scholarly journals. Arriaza is the recipient of numerous awards, including a medal of honor from the city of Arica for his scientific contributions to Andean prehistory. In 2002 he was nominated for the National Chilean Award in History and Prehistory.

ALAN BALBONI received his Ph.D. from Brown University and is a professor of political science at the Community College of Southern Nevada. He is the author of *Beyond the Mafia: Italian Americans and the Development of Las Vegas* (1996).

EARNEST N. BRACEY teaches American politics and black American history at the Community College of Southern Nevada. A retired army lieutenant colonel, he has received numerous military awards and civilian honors. Bracey is the author of a number of books, including *On Racism: Essays on Black Popular Culture, African American Politics,* and *The New Black Aesthetics* (2003), as well as scholarly articles and two novels. He is the coauthor of *American Politics and Culture Wars* (1998).

SUE FAWN CHUNG received her Ph.D. from the University of California, Berkeley, and has taught history at the University of Nevada, Las Vegas, since 1975. Chung has served as director of international programs and as chair of the History Department. She has published in the fields of Chinese history, Chinese art history, and Chinese American history.

ART D. CLARITO earned a law degree from Ateneo de Davao University in the Philippines. He moved to Las Vegas in 1991 and is a paraprofessional at the Clark

County School District and a contributing editor to the *Asian Reader,* a Las Vegas newspaper focusing on Asian Americans. A native speaker of Tagalog, he has collaborated with coauthor Gary Palmer in research on Philippine language and culture.

MICHAEL GREEN is a professor of history at the Community College of Southern Nevada. He is the author of "Hank Greenspun: Where He Stood" in *The Maverick Spirit: Building the New Nevada* (1999) and a number of articles on Las Vegas history. Green is the editor of the Wilbur S. Shepperson series in Nevada History for the University of Nevada Press.

TED G. JELEN is a professor of political science at the University of Nevada, Las Vegas. His recent works include *To Serve God and Mammon: Church-State Relations in the United States* (2000) and an edited volume, *Religion and Politics in Comparative Perspective: The One, the Few, and the Many* (2002).

E. D. KARAMPETSOS earned his Ph.D. in comparative literature and is a professor in the English Department of the Community College of Southern Nevada. Karampetsos teaches courses in Modern Greek at the University of Nevada, Las Vegas. He has published a book on European drama, *The Theater of Healing* (1995), and numerous scholarly articles on Greek immigrants to Nevada.

MARTHA C. KNACK received her Ph.D. from the University of Michigan, Ann Arbor, and is currently a Distinguished Professor of anthropology at the University of Nevada, Las Vegas. Her ethnographic publications on Southern Paiutes began with *Life is with People: Household Organization of the Contemporary Southern Paiute Indians* (1980); her most recent ethnohistorical book is *Boundaries Between: The Southern Paiutes, 1775–1995* (2001).

HEATHER LAWLER received her B.A. from the University of California, Berkeley, in 1994 and contributed to this volume while pursuing graduate studies in anthropology at the University of Nevada, Las Vegas.

M. L. (TONY) MIRANDA is a professor and served as chair of the Department of Anthropology and Ethnic Studies at the University of Nevada, Las Vegas, from 1993 to 2004. Miranda received his Ph.D. from the University of California, Los Angeles, and is the author of *A History of Hispanics in Southern Nevada* (1997).

EUGENE P. MOEHRING is a professor of history at the University of Nevada, Las Vegas. He is the author of numerous works on urban and Nevada history, including *Resort City in the Sunbelt: Las Vegas 1930–2000* (2d ed., 2000) and *Urbanism and Empire in the Far West, 1840–1890* (2004), both published by the University of Nevada Press.

JESSE DINO MOODY, a graduate of the University of Nevada, Las Vegas, is completing his last year of law school at the Boyd School of Law there. His research interests have focused on American history and on historical and contemporary issues and policy in Las Vegas.

GARY B. PALMER is a professor of anthropology and ethnic studies at the University of Nevada, Las Vegas, where he has taught since 1973. His publications include *Toward a Theory of Cultural Linguistics* (1996) and articles on American Indian, African Bantu, and Philippine languages.

SATISH SHARMA is a professor and former director of the School of Social work at the University of Nevada, Las Vegas. He is the author of four monographs and books, including *Migratory Workers and Their Social Adjustment, Modernization and Planned Social Change* (1982) and *Ghandi, Women, and Social Development* (1982). His research interests focus on third-world nation building, Ghandhian welfare philosophy, and nonviolence and peace studies.

JERRY L. SIMICH is an associate professor of political science at the University of Nevada, Las Vegas. His most recent publication is *General Index to Croatian Pioneers in California, 1849–1999* (2000) with Adam S. Eterovich.

DINA TITUS is a professor of political science at the University of Nevada, Las Vegas, and a Nevada state senator. Her most recent book is *Bombs in the Backyard: Atomic Testing and American Politics* (2d ed., 2001). She also publishes on state politics and atomic culture.

THOMAS C. WRIGHT is a professor of history at the University of Nevada, Las Vegas, specializing in Latin America. His recent books include *Flight from Chile: Voices of Exile* (1998), coauthored with Rody Oñate, and *Latin America in the Era of the Cuban Revolution* (rev. ed., 2001).